Outcomes, Learning and the Curriculum: Implications for NVQs and other qualifications

Jenn Koggen

436-3412

Outcomes, Learning and the Curriculum
Implications for NVQs, GNVQs and other qualifications

Editor

John Burke

 The Falmer Press

(A member of the Taylor & Francis Group)
London • Washington, D.C.

UK   The Falmer Press, 4 John Street, London WC1N 2ET
USA   The Falmer Press, Taylor & Francis Inc., 1900 Frost Road, Suite 101, Bristol, PA 19007

First published in 1995

A catalogue record for this book is available from the British Library

Library of Congress Cataloging-in-Publication Data are available on request

ISBN 0 7507 0288 5 cased
ISBN 0 7507 0289 3 paper

Jacket design by Caroline Archer

Typeset in 9.5/11pt Bembo by
Graphicraft Typesetters Ltd., Hong Kong.

Printed in Great Britain by Burgess Science Press, Basingstoke on paper which has a specified pH value on final paper manufacture of not less than 7.5 and is therefore 'acid free'.

Contents

Contents

Acknowledgments

Acknowledgments are made to *Educational Review* (University of Birmingham)
and Oliver & Boyd (Longmans and The Open University Press) for permission
to reproduce the model on page 73; to London University Press and Oliver &
Boyd (Longmans and The Open University Press) for permission to use the model
on page page 74; to Harper Row, London and New York, for permission to
reproduce the model on page 74.

Abbreviations, Acronyms and Concepts

An unavoidable consequence of rapid developments in Vocational Education and Training (VET) has been the proliferation of widely used abbreviations and acronyms; these can be confusing at times even to people who are professionally involved with the subject — *a fortiori*, they may prove troublesome to the more 'general reader' with an interest in education and training. Although virtually all these terms are explained in the text of each paper when first they appear, it may be helpful to include a list for easy reference.

Where an abbreviation appears elsewhere in this list, it is printed in **bold italics**.

Because some very common abbreviations, such as 'A' levels, which are universally known to British readers may yet be unfamiliar to overseas readers, a very concise explanation is appended in *italics* after some abbreviations. On the other hand, as some of the abbreviations refer to antipodean organizations, British readers may appreciate a similar practice where non-British abbreviations occur.

A second list of terms is appended as a Glossary, in order to explain the technical meaning of many of the concepts which appear in this book. Where a separate explanation of these concept appears in the second list, abbreviations or words treated in this way appear in **bold type**.

The second list of **Concepts** draws heavily on Gilbert Jessup's (1991) book, *Outcomes: NVQs and the Emerging Model of Education and Training*, by kind permission of the author. This is now recognized as a seminal text, and the majority of concepts covered in this second list are very much more fully covered in that book, to which the interested reader is directed.

1. Abbreviations:

ACCA   Chartered Association of Certified Accountants.
ACCFHE   Association of Further and Higher Education Colleges.
AEB   Associated Examining Board, a **GCE** examining body.
AGR   Association of Graduate Recruiters.
'A' level   Advanced level General Certificate in Education (**GCE**) *an 'academic' qualification taken in different subjects, normally at the end of schooling, around 18 years old. The 'A' level is graded, and normal university requirements stipulate three 'A' levels at 'good' grades, normally A, B or C. Entrance requirements for some universities on some courses stipulate very high grades, for example AAA or ABB. Exceptional students sometimes study four subjects,*

	or very occasionally more than four. This examination, which enjoys high prestige, is deemed suitable for only about 30 per cent of the population. **GNVQs**, which are recognized as achieving a similar standard, but which employ an entirely different approach, offer an alternative route to **progression**, and form an important focus for many of the papers in this book.
APA	Assessment of Prior Achievement, *a variant of* **APL**.
APL	**Accreditation of Prior Learning**.
'A/S' levels	Advanced Supplementary **GCEs**, *introduced to broaden the curriculum, are deemed half an 'A' level. However, they have proved unpopular because they are not simply the first half of a two year course, they usually cover aspects of the whole course. As a result, they are considered by many teachers to be more demanding on students, and involve a disproportionate use of staffing resources.*
AEC	Australian Education Council.
ASB	Australian Standards Board.
BTEC	***Business and Technician Education Council***, *one of the most important vocational education and training examination bodies; also used to designate examinations such as the BTEC National Certificate or BTEC Diploma. Along with the **C&G** and **RSA**, BTEC has responsibility for developing **GNVQs** within the **NCVQ** guidelines and criteria . . .*
BP	British Petroleum, *sponsor of education and training.*
CATS	Credit Accumulation and Transfer Scheme. (*See Robinson in this volume*).
CBI	Confederation of British Industry, *the most important employers association, responsible for many influential initiatives on education and training.*
C&G	***City and Guilds of London Institute***, *one of the three major vocational examining bodies, along with **BTEC** and **RSA**.*
CITB	Construction Industry Training Board.
CLO	Common Learning Outcome.
CNAA	Council for National Academic Awards; *before the polytechnics became universities, the CNAA had an important validating role for degrees, certificates and diplomas; now defunct.*
CPVE	Certificate in Pre-Vocational Education.
CSB	Competency Standards Body (*Australia*).
DE	Department of Employment.
DES	Department of Education and Science, *now renamed DEF.*
DEET	Department of Employment, Education and Training (*Australia*).
DFE	Department for Education.
ECCTIS	Educational Counselling and Credit Transfer Information Service.
EITB	Engineering Industry Training Board.
ERA	Education Reform Act.
ET	Employment Training.
FE	Further Education, *post-16 full time or part time education and training; students may progress to other, higher level FE courses, to*

	HE *or into employment. FE colleges are major providers of* **NVQs** *and* **GNVQs***.*
FEFC	Further Education Funding Council.
FESC	Further Education Staff College.
FEU	Further Education Unit, *an important curriculum support body for* **FE***.*
FLI	Flexible Learning Initiative.
GATE	GNVQs And access To higher Education.
GCSE	**General Certificate of Secondary Education***, an examination available in all school subjects, taken separately, normally at age 16.*
HE	Higher Education, *now mostly provided by universities.*
HEQC	Higher Education Quality Council.
HMI	Her Majesty's Inspectorate, *formerly an education inspection service, generally much respected for its high standards and independence.*
IBM	International Business Machines, *the computer company, sponsor of education and training.*
IT	Information Technology.
LEA	Local Education Authority.
LIB	Industry Lead Body, *an industry representative body drawn largely from employers and unions, formed to establish* **standards***. Sometimes a LIB may represent a group of allied industries. The term 'industry' is here used to include professions and any other recognizable, organized avocation.*
MBA	Master's in Business Administration, *postgraduate degree.*
MCI	Management Charter Initiative, *the application of competency-led approaches to management.*
MSC	**Manpower Services Commission***, see* **TA***.*
NC	**National Curriculum**.
NCC	National Curriculum Council, *with responsibility for the* **National Curriculum**.
NCVQ	**National Council for Vocational Qualifications.**
NIACE	National Institute of Adult Continuing Education, *the national organization for adult learning.*
NRA	**National Record of Achievement**.
NTB	National Training Board (*Australia*).
NTI	**New Training Initiative**.
NTTT	National Training Task Force (*UK*).
NROVA	National Record of Vocational Qualifications, now superseded by **NRA**.
NVQ	**National Vocational Qualification**.
NZQA	New Zealand Qualifications Council.
OFSTED	Office for Standards in Education.
'O' level	**GCE** Ordinary level examination, *normally taken at 16 years old, the end of compulsory schooling in the UK; now superseded by* **GCSE***.*
OU	Open University, *the largest university in the U.K. All undergraduates study part-time by distance learning methods, including the use of radio and television broadcasts. The OU has been a major influence on the dissemination of innovative learning methods*

and materials, and has benignly and beneficially influenced the teaching of virtually all subjects not only in **HE** but also in **FE,** as well as the upper forms in schools, especially the **Sixth Form**. *Many of the principles underpinning the OU's approach to learning (for example,* **Open Access***) resonate with the principles informing the approach taken in* **GNVQs** *and, indeed,* **NVQs***.

RS   Royal Society, *the premier learned society in science; Fellowship of the Royal Society, is esteemed as the highest accolade amongst academics in science and the RS enjoys unrivalled academic prestige.*

RSA   **Royal Society of Arts** *Examining Body, one of the three leading vocational examining bodies. There is also an important Learned Society covering 'Arts, Manufacture and Commerce' which is now separate from the examining body.*

SCOTVEC   **Scottish Vocational Education Council***, in many respects, a sister organization to the* **NCVQ***, with which SCOTVEC works very closely to provide* **VET** *in Scotland (the NCVQ's remit covers England, Wales and Northern Ireland only); unlike the* **NCVQ***, Scotvec is not only a validating body, it is also an examining body, providing its own qualifications,* **SVQs***.*

SEAC   Schools Examinations and Assessment Council.

SVQ   **Scottish Vocational Qualifications,** *offered by* **SCOTVEC***.*

TA   **Training Agency***, Department of Employment (previously, TC, the Training Commission, previously,* **Manpower Services Commission***. The TA has had, and continues to have, a major formative influence on* **VET***, especially in respect of the formulation of* **Standards***. It is responsible for a major part of the research effort which informs* **VET***, both in terms of its own personnel, expert consultants and the research it commissions each year in many British universities.*

TEC   Training and Enterprise Council; *there are a network of regional TECs which were put in place to support local VET projects in various ways.*

TUC   Trades Union Congress, the central trade union body.

TVEI   Technical and Vocational Education Initiative, *a major initiative directed towards vocational and mainly pre-vocational initiatives in schools.*

UCLES   University of Cambridge Local Examinations Board, *a* **GCE** *examination body.*

UDACE   Unit for the Development of Adult Continuing Education.

VET   **Vocational Education and Training.**

WBI   Work Based Learning. (*See Levy in this volume.*).

WRNAFE   Work-Related Non Advanced Further Education.

YTS   Youth Training Scheme(s).

2. Concepts

ACHIEVEMENT, the outcome of learning, the acquisition of competence, skill or knowledge.

ACCREDITATION OF PRIOR LEARNING, (also known as Accreditation of Prior Achievement) certificating competence on the basis of evidence from past achievements, often supplemented by current assessments. Sometimes used in a wider sense to include counselling, helping people to recognise the significance of their experience as a prelude to assessment and accreditation, and providing guidance and action planning following such accreditation also referred to as 'accreditation of prior achievement'.

ASSESSMENT (for CERTIFICATION), the process of collecting evidence and making judgements on whether the evidence meets the standards set (by performance criteria) and whether the evidence is sufficient to attest to competence or attainment.

ATTAINMENT TARGETS, the broad objectives specified in a [National Curriculum] subject, setting out the knowledge, skills and understanding pupils are expected to acquire.

BREADTH, a global term which is applied to qualifications, statements of competence, and thereby education and training, to refer to the coverage of competence or attainment, the extent to which it promotes underpinning knowledge and skills and as a result of these and/or by other means, promotes adaptability and transferability.

CERTIFICATE, a document issued to an individual by an awarding body, formally attesting to achievement or attainment (eg of an NVQ, units of competence, other qualifications or achievements).

COMPETENCE, the ability to perform to recognised standards (what this entails is a matter of continuing debate, see Jessup, 1991, Chapter 3)

CORE SKILLS, skills (or facets of skill) which underpin, and are common to, a wide range of competent performance. The acquisition of such skills is believed to facilitate transfer to performance in a wide range of functions and situations.

CURRICULUM See discussion in Chapter 1.

CREDIT, formal recognition of achievement through certification. In particular, the recognition of units or components of qualifications.

CREDIT ACCUMULATION, the general process by which separate components of a qualification system can be separately achieved and certificated, allowing the accumulation of such achievements over time.

CREDIT TRANSFER, the recognition of a credit gained in one qualification, or system of qualifications, as satisfying some or all of the requirements of a different qualification, or system of qualifications. It alleviates the need for repeating assessments (and possibly training) for the award, or that part of the award, for which recognition is given in the second qualification or system.

ELEMENT, the smallest and most precise specification of competence within a statement of competence. A component part of a unit of competence. In GNVQs, the smallest and most precise specification of attainment.

FORMATIVE ASSESSMENT, assessment to facilitate the process of learning; assessment which is fedback to learners including diagnosis of further learning requirements. (May be informal and locally determined.)

FUNCTION, description of an activity by reference to its purpose and outcome.

FUNCTIONAL ANALYSIS, a method of analysing the competence requirements in an area (eg industry, occupation, organisation) according to functions which need to be carried out to fulfil its overall purpose.

GENERAL NATIONAL VOCATIONAL QUALIFICATION (GNVQ), a broad-based vocational qualification, assessed to national standards, which attests attainment, i.e. general skills (including Core Skills) knowledge and understanding which underpin a range of occupations, providing certification of achievement which may act as a springboard to enter employment or pursue further or higher education and training. GNVQs are specified in the form of learning outcomes to be achieved; they are made up of a number of units, and credit may be awarded for each unit separately. Although GNVQs are normally delivered through full time programmes (eg in school or college) access to assessment is open to all and the award of a GNVQ may be made to all who meet the required standards, irrespective of time taken or the mode of learning.

INDUSTRY LEAD BODY (ILB), (or LEAD BODY), an institution or group formally recognised as having responsibility for setting standards (more precisely, determining the statements of competence) within a given area of competence.

INDIVIDUAL ACTION PLAN, a plan which sets out learning targets and learning opportunities to be provided, negotiated between learner and provider, tailored to meet the needs of an individual, taking into account their prior achievements. The targets are stated, where appropriate, as the outcomes specified in units and attainment targets in qualifications.

JOB, the unique work role or group of functions which is/are carried out by an individual in employment.

JOB CATEGORY, a group of jobs encompassing similar functions.

KNOWLEDGE, the 'know-how' or cognitive component which underpins competence or attainment, which may include facts, theories, principles, conceptual frameworks etc. It subsumes 'understanding'. May be elicited through questioning techniques.

LEARNING, the process of acquiring skills, knowledge, and/or competence.

NATIONAL VOCATIONAL QUALIFICATION (or NVQ), a qualification which is accredited by NCVQ and allocated to a place within the NVQ framework. NVQs are required to meet specified criteria for accreditation (see NVQ criteria).

NVQ CRITERIA, the criteria published by NCVQ which NVQs are expected to meet for accreditation. They provide the criteria for the design of NVQs, the primary features of which are a statement of competence and open access to assessment.

NVQ FRAMEWORK, the national system of classifying NVQs according to area of competence and level.

NATIONAL CURRICULUM, the national system of classifying attainment targets and statements of attainment, by subject and levels. The required education provision for school children aged 5 to 16 years in state schools.

NATIONAL RECORD OF ACHIEVEMENT, encompassing a system of prior records, action planning, continuous assessment recording and certificates, deriving from the national system of credit accumulation and transfer.

NATIONAL SYSTEM OF CREDIT ACCUMULATION AND TRANSFER, the system which is being created by a consortium of awarding bodies, co-ordinated by NCVQ, in which vocational qualifications will be offered as a number of units for separate assessment, recording and certification. It includes arrangements for credit accumulation, through the national Record of Vocational Achievement, and the recognition of units awarded by one body by the others.

NCVQ DATABASE, a computerised database of NVQs and other vocational qualifications of the major national awarding bodies, containing detailed information of their units, elements, performance criteria and assessment methods, available for public access.

OCCUPATION, a defined area of competence which is relevant to performance in a range of jobs in different companies and locations, and often different industries.

PERFORMANCE CRITERIA, the criteria which define the standard required in the performance of an element of competence.

PROFESSION, a high level occupation which is characterised by a code of conduct and values, providing identity, normally derived through membership of a professional body.

PROGRESSION, the development or accumulation of competence or attainment by an individual through successive learning opportunities (programmes/courses/ qualifications/experiences) in a systematic manner. Also the related advancement in an individual's career through successive jobs.

RANGE (or RANGE STATEMENT or RANGE OF APPLICATION), an addition to an element which indicates the range of application of the element. Lists primary sources of variation in conditions and contexts in which performance may be required.

RECORD OF ACHIEVEMENT, either a document recording achievement like a certificate or a 'file' for recording and maintaining a variety of achievements and experiences. May also include other features.

SKILLS, the 'performance' component which underpins competence. Distinguished from competence by being more fundamental and frequently common to a variety of different competences. They may also be demonstrated, divorced from context, unlike competence. Skills may be manual or cognitive, or a combination of both.

SKILL TRANSFER, the ability to perform a new function competently, or with a reduction in learning time than would otherwise be required to achieve competence, as a result of the previous acquisition of a skill or skills in a different function or context. Particularly pertinent to core skills which are common and transferable to performance in a wide range of functions. (Can also be used to apply to transfer between contexts, rather than functions.)

STATEMENT OF COMPETENCE, a specification of the competence required in a given area. In NVQs this is set out in a prescribed format of title, units of competence, elements of competence and performance criteria.

STATEMENT OF ATTAINMENTS, the more precise objectives which make up an attainment target, defined at graduated levels of attainment.

STANDARDS, normally a short-hand term referring to statements of competence or components within such statements. A more precise concept of 'standard' is expressed by the performance criteria, within statements of competence (i.e. the standard of performance required by an element of competence).

UNIT, in NVQs a primary sub-division of the statement of competence, representing a discrete aspect of competence. A unit is made up of elements of competence. Units are also offered for independent certification for credit accumulation and transfer. In GNVQs, a sub-division of the outcome statement of a attainment.

UNIT-CREDIT, a credit, formally awarded by the issue of a certificate, based upon a unit of competence, within the national system of credit accumulation and transfer.

VERIFICATION, the process of monitoring carried out by an awarding body, or its representatives, to ensure that assessment is conducted faithfully (i.e. according to specified procedures or within specified criteria), for the purpose of certification.

Preface

In October 1992, Gilbert Jessup, Deputy Chief Executive and Director of Research at the National Council for Vocational Qualifications (NCVQ), commissioned a large number of researchers to write papers for a conference which was held in Croydon in March 1993.

Some of the invitees were NCVQ staff with special research responsibilities but most were independent researchers with a record of publications in the field; from the outset it was recognized that this independence must be preserved in the interests of scholarship, so the views of individual contributors do not necessarily reflect the views of the NCVQ. The first drafts of all the papers were circulated prior to the conference, and each contributor was invited to speak to his/her paper before it was submitted to detailed criticism and examination by fellow contributors. In the event, the concept which caused most critical discussion and dissension was the meaning of curriculum. The concept of learning, likewise, provoked much discussion. The notion of Outcomes proved much less contentious, and there was something approaching unanimity on the value and rich potential which the exploration of this concept offered not only in terms of its application to the school or college curriculum but to applications ranging from the development of professional knowledge to autonomous learning. The three themes on which that conference concentrated, Outcomes, Learning and the Curriculum, became the focus of this book.

In addition to the explicitly eponymous themes mentioned above, a number of other significant threads of meaning have developed to link most chapters in this book at some point: the nature of assessment, the meaning of qualification, the accessibility of provision, the practicalities of implementation. These issues and concerns are expressed in the themes of bringing about coherence and integration; of openness, challenge and opportunity; the desire to extend the debate, to explore, deepen and share understanding; to initiate and further the research effort, to enter into productive partnerships with all concerned. Because, in the final analysis, we *are* all concerned.

While from the nature of this book its primary audience may be the research community, postgraduate students, practitioners in schools, colleges, industry training departments and universities, other fellow professionals such as members of examining bodies, managing agents and policy makers, *our work is ultimately directed towards improving the quality of experience and the level of achievement among our mutual clientele, students and trainees.*

Our aim is not only to help realize the sum of human potential they represent in terms of their own personal development — unquestionably and ineluctably important as we recognize that to be — but to help them realize their aspirations in employment, *and* the needs of their eventual employers. In short, to help bridge the divide between education and training and improve the quality of both, so that both may contribute to the well-being of society, a society which reflects the concerns of a trading nation which must compete in international markets if it is to survive in recognizable form into the twenty-first century.

John Burke
Institute of Continuing and Professional Education
University of Sussex
July 1994.

Note: Most contributors submitted revised drafts of their papers over the months of June, July and August 1993, but some were unavoidably delayed until some time later. A number of authors used the interim period to further revise their drafts to take account of ongoing developments but I have been asked to point out that not all contributors enjoyed this opportunity.

Foreword

When, in 1990, I returned to the United Kingdom after twenty-five years over-seas, I knew I was coming to the most exciting job in higher education. In a generation the Open University had developed from a radical idea, scorned by the educational establishment, into Britain's largest educational and training institu-tion. Hailed as one of the most successful innovations of the century, it was an icon that had already inspired the creation of thirty similar universities in other countries. However, although I had expected the work of vice-chancellor to be rewarding, I did not anticipate the extra satisfaction of being at the helm as the OU sailed into the rapid currents of the most comprehensive reform of post-compulsory education that the UK has ever attempted.

This book addresses key issues at the heart of those reforms. Overt discussion of outcomes, learning and the curriculum is both a key to the success of the trans-formations being undertaken and a cause of the anguish to those who disliked the disruption to the *status quo*.

It is perhaps easier for a returning expatriate, than for people who have spent their working lives in the UK, to assert that the reforms were vital. In *The Audit of War*, a hard-hitting book published in 1986, Correlli Barnett documented the century-long English saga of apathy towards education punctuated by vigorous campaigns to repress or gut the few reforms that were attempted.

The end result of this neglect is that to foreign eyes the ordinary people of Britain are badly educated and its well-educated people are poorly trained. There-fore, individuals at all levels of society are less purposeful, productive and autono-mous than they have the potential to be. Ask British workers why they do things in a particular way. The reply usually begins with the word 'because' and refers back to tradition or to their instructions. Ask the same question to North Amer-ican workers and more often their answer starts with the words 'in order to' and focuses on the desired outcome of the task.

The key objective of the current British reforms is be to empower all mem-bers of an increasingly diverse population to lead fuller lives in a rapidly changing world. That implies a considerable expansion of opportunities for education and training and a sharper focus on the purposes and quality of those opportunities, especially where public funds are involved. Thanks to an enthusiastic response from the public the expansion of post-compulsory education has happened faster than government bargained for. Because habits of public funding designed for an elite system have proved unsustainable with the sudden achievement of mass post-compulsory education there have been predictable squeals from individuals and institutions now receiving less taxpayer support.

However, the more interesting controversies generated by the reforms are the subject of this book. They concern outcomes, learning and the curriculum.

The idea of defining education and training in terms of outcomes is not new. As a visitor to the infant Open University in 1972 I admired the attempt that was being made to agree objectives — sometimes even behavioural objectives — before preparing each course. However, a really thoroughgoing scheme for relating qualifications to practical outcomes had to await the 1980s and the development of the systems of National Vocational Qualifications (NVQs, and in Scotland, Scottish Vocational Qualifications, SVQs) that are the foundation of Britain's current training revolution.

NVQs and SVQs have upset established habits in two ways. First, training qualifications are defined in terms of competencies identified by the industries likely to employ the trainees rather than as a corpus of knowledge determined by the educators who teach the candidates. Second, the assessment of these competencies is unrelated to the process by which they were acquired. As in the national driving test, the focus is on practical performance of the skills, not on how they were learned. More recently General National Vocational Qualifications (GNVQs) have been added to the framework. These focus on the attainment of core skills for employment rather than on the particular competencies of an individual industry.

Like any new paradigm that challenges established malpractice with fresh ideas, the NVQ/SVQ system has suffered attack from polemicists who have been prepared to ignore the conventional canons of academic discourse in order to undermine it. I welcome this book because it gives the contributors, many of whom have been very close to these developments, an opportunity to deploy an impressive intellectual armament against their critics.

As the country's largest university the Open University has alwasys taken seriously its responsibility to become thoroughly involved, both intellectually and practically, in major national initiatives in education and training. The OU has committed itself to promote NVQs/SVQs both as an awarding body and through its Vocational Qualifications Centre. My OU colleagues see in the NVQ/SVQ framework a sign that the UK is finally giving itself an appropriate training system for the contemporary world. They, and the multitude of colleagues in other institutions who also rejoice in these developments, will find this book invaluable.

Sir John Daniel
Vice Chancellor
The Open University

Part One

Introduction

Chapter 1

Introduction and Overview

John Burke

Three cogent organizing concepts inform this book: 'Outcomes', 'Learning' and 'Curriculum'. This collection of papers builds on Jessup (1991) to investigate further the significance of outcomes approaches (and in particular, the Jessup model of Outcomes), to examine more critically the processes of learning, and to relate some of these ideas to the curriculum.

Each of these concepts is briefly discussed (with rather more discussion on the curriculum) before I introduce the substantive focus of each contributor.

Outcomes

The concept of 'Outcomes' is not new to education and training; in common with 'Outputs' or 'Attainments' or 'Products', 'Outcomes' features in many documents and books[1]. Among professional industrial trainers, familiar with Objectives, the term had wide currency[2] but with a few notable exceptions[3] did not figure prominently in academic discourse. What is now ineluctably evident in the perception of many colleagues (but difficult to substantiate or quantify without extensive lexicographical study) is the massively increased salience and prominence of this concept over the past few years in any discussion about further education (FE) and, more recently, higher education (HE). In my view, the single most *efficient cause*[4] contributing to this new emphasis was the publication in 1991 of Jessup's *Outcomes: NVQs and the Emerging Model of Education and Training*. At the time, I noted in the *Preface*:

> This is an important book. (. . .) Although this book is a personal statement . . . its publication marks a subtle but significant shift in emphasis, signalled by the title. The emphasis is on outcomes, the focus on education and training, not, significantly, on vocational education and training. This allows him scope to broach all outcomes (not exclusively 'competency-based') and all education and training. A focus on the outcomes of learning is listed as the second fundamental criterion underlying NVQs but Gilbert Jessup sees it as the key concept in the emerging competency-based model because it confers a vital principle of coherence on all the activities which characterize the NVQ approach. (Burke, 1991b, p. *vii*)

The notion of Outcomes may now be seen as the linchpin of National Vocational Qualifications (NVQs) and General National Vocational Qualifications (GNVQs) and, increasingly, a focus for discussion in HE and the professions.[5]

Learning

All purposive teaching must take place within some kind of curriculum framework, whether this framework is explicit or implicit. However, it is manifest that not all purposive learning takes place within a curriculum. For example, much learning throughout life is serendipitous, based on experience, exploiting learning opportunities when and as they occur. It is a truism that we all know more than we realize. When we organize that learning, it become more purposeful and coherent, it lays bare areas of ignorance which, once recognized, enable us to make-good deficiencies in our understanding, and provides a firmer foundation on which further learning may be built. The value of this sometimes unorganized learning is properly acknowledged within the NVQ approach. The Accreditation of Prior Learning (APL) is an obvious example (Simosko, 1990; Jessup, 1990; Newman and Llewellin, 1990). Taking a broad overview, Jessup (1991) notes:

> The new approach encourages learning in a wide range of locations and by different methods. By recognising the skills and knowledge people already have, it will raise their confidence and give them a flying start in any new programme they embark upon. The targets of learning will be more relevant and relate more to the needs of individuals. Learning will not be equated in the minds of people with 'academic', 'classrooms', 'boredom' and 'failure'. (p. 136)

Curriculum

What is the curriculum? It might be assumed this question could be easily answered by any teacher who is enjoined to teach the curriculum, or indeed, by any undergraduate in any discipline who has recently left school. That assumption is unwarranted; any answer is fraught with difficulties. At the nub of the problem is the elasticity of the concept — it means many different things to different people, and the same person may use the word to encompass many meanings. Sometimes, these meanings may be differentiated by a distinguishing epithet, for example, 'manifest curriculum', 'hidden curriculum', 'expressive curriculum', 'school curriculum' or, more recently, 'national curriculum'. In other cases, the defining characteristics may be unclear even to the user, with the concept deployed to cover a raft of meanings ranging from a synonym for 'syllabus' (cf Richmond, 1971, p. 11)[5] to 'Basically, . . . what happens to children in school as a result of what teachers do' (Kansas, 1958).

Taba (1962) observes:

> When curriculum is defined as 'the total effort of the school to bring about desired outcomes in school and out-of-school situations' (Saylor and Alexander, 1954, p. 3) or 'a sequence of potential experiences set up

in school for the purpose of disciplining children and youth in group ways of thinking and acting' (B.O. Smith, Stanley, and Shores, 1957, p. 3), the very breadth may make the definition nonfunctional. On the other hand, excluding from the definition of curriculum everything except the statement of objectives and content outlines and relegating anything that has to do with learning and learning experiences to 'method' might be too confining to be adequate for a modern curriculum. (p. 9)

Other commentators, for example Lawton *et al* (1978, pp. 2–4) uncover the assumptions on which notions of the curriculum may be constructed; Lawton distinguishes 'the child-centred curriculum', 'the knowledge-centred curriculum' and 'the "needs of society" or "society-centred" kind of curriculum'.

Certainly, before the National Curriculum was devised, for many the notion of curriculum was unproblematic, a happenstance which Goodson (1989) both attests and deplores:

> The school curriculum is a social artefact, conceived of, and made for, deliberate human purposes. It is therefore a supreme paradox that in many accounts of schooling, the written curriculum, this most manifest of social constructions, has been treated as a given.

Goodson, above, is careful to delimit his censures to woolly thinking (or the absence of any thinking) about the *school* curriculum. Many writers make no such distinction; they appear to assume that any mention of 'curriculum' implies locus in a school. Indeed, the early reluctance of the NCVQ to engage in curriculum matters may, in part, be due to a kind of 'halo effect' that the notion of curriculum carries with it; NVQs had nothing to do with schools, and in their early conception, little to do with schooling.[6]

Becher and McClure (1978) deftly identify the underlying importance of our original question; They insist:

> to ask 'what is the curriculum' is not simply to imitate the pedantic judge who displays apparent judicial ignorance in order to force counsel to define something everyone knows. The answer which is given stakes the territory to which the curriculum developer lays claim. (p. 11)

The NCVQ and the Curriculum

From its inception in 1986, the NCVQ distanced itself from any concern with the curriculum. This stance was adopted in response to a very deliberate decision to free up vocational qualifications from the welter of regulations and prescriptions which characterized provision at that time; these prescriptions were perceived as a barrier and disincentive to wider access and participation. The revised *NVQ Criteria and Procedures*, published by the NCVQ in 1989, decreed that National Vocational Qualifications (NVQs) should be independent of:

- the mode of learning. This is made possible by the form of an NVQ, which is independent of any education or training programme which may be provided to develop competence;

- upper and lower age limits, except where legal restraints make this necessary. Assessments for the award of NVQs should be open to people of all
  ages;
- a specified period of time to be spent in education, training or work before
  the award can be made. NVQs should not proscribe the time taken to
  acquire competence. This recognizes the considerable variation in the time
  individuals take to learn, depending on their starting point, learning opportunities, aptitude and motivation.

The focus was very clearly on *learning* rather than *teaching*, the needs of the individual learner rather than a class of trainees or students. Indeed, in the same
document, the NCVQ goes on in further detail positively to encourage diversity
of provision, taking account of individual rates of learning (fast or slow), different
forms of assessment to reflect different forms of learning, and the (previously
often neglected) requirements of those with special learning needs.

NVQs promoted learning and assessment of learning in the workplace. We
have already noticed that the notion of 'curriculum', even among the foremost
proponents of curriculum theory[7], was usually linked to the notion of 'classroom',
'school' or 'college', the traditional sites wherein the curriculum was enacted. In
the brave liberationist attempt to break new ground, it was tacitly assumed that
in a qualification-driven system, with multiple routes to assessment, the imposi-
tion of a curriculum framework would be necessarily constricting, inoperable and
largely redundant. In practice, as the NVQ framework developed, and as more
and more trainees were enrolled, the need for most trainees to locate a significant
part of their training in Further Education (FE) colleges or dedicated training
establishments became apparent. *De facto*, fairly fundamental curriculum decisions
had to be made. These decisions centred on:

(a) the outcomes and objectives to be attained, the aspirations and expecta-
    tions these involved;
(b) the learning *and* teaching to be accomplished, the methods, activities and
    experience to be used, the learning and teaching styles which would be
    appropriate;
(c) the content or subject matter, the skills and knowledge to be acquired,
    how this was to be selected, structured and organized;
(d) the appropriate forms of assessment, the place of tests, assignments, the
    kind of feedback needed and the possible use of profiles and records of
    achievement;
(e) the relationship of each of these concerns to the declared aims and inten-
    tions — the philosophy — underlying the notion of NVQs, so that all
    lecturers or teachers involved, as well as (aspirationally) their students,
    would share a common understanding of intentions in order to bring
    about some notion of consistency and coherence.

Beyond these elements, which, following Eraut (1982) and Taba (1962), may be
said to constitute the bones of a curriculum, there was the need for managers to
obtain resources in the face of legitimate competition from other areas of the
college whole curriculum, and to plan the organization and distribution of these
resources and all the systems necessary to sustain, monitor and build on this
experience.

With the development of General National Vocational Qualifications (GNVQs), the need to explore the implications for the curriculum has become even more pressing. NVQs and GNVQs share many common characteristics[8], but there are some significant differences. The most important difference is that whereas NVQs attest competence in the workplace, the award of a GNVQ implies that the student has achieved a foundation of general skills and the knowledge[9] and understanding which underpin a range of occupations rather than the competence to perform immediately in any particular occupation. The shift to *attainment* rather than competence opens up a completely new constituency[10], *schools and colleges*, which had previously been precluded from teaching NVQs because they lacked the facilities or expertise to offer work-placed experience or assessment.

Although in common with NVQs, GNVQs may be awarded to all who meet the required standards, irrespective of time taken and the mode of learning, in practice the vast majority of GNVQ are institutionally based, in either a school or college. In these circumstances, curricular issues are unavoidably a concern of the NCVQ.

Organization of the Book

Contributions are organized into five further sections:

Part Two:	The Model	Four chapters
Part Three:	Curriculum Consequences	Seven chapters
Part Three	Applications	Five chapters
Part Four	Progression	One chapter
Part Five	International Comparison	One chapter

The chapters here grouped under four distinct organizing concepts all share many common themes, as outlined in the *Preface* (qv) but each group has a different broad focus; taken together they illustrate the multifaceted issues which need to be broached in discussing the notion of Outcomes.

Part Two

This section of the book explores the meaning and implications of the Outcomes approach. The argument of each chapter is briefly discussed under each author.

Gilbert Jessup

Gilbert Jessup sets the scene in Chapter 1 by providing a lucid and authoritative overview of recent and ongoing developments. In the first sentence, he cites the rationale underlying the NCVQ Outcomes approach: (In Jessup, 1991) 'the proposal was made the outcomes model of defining qualifications and learning was applicable to all forms of learning', before going on briefly to establish the context in which developments are being carried forward. The National Curriculum is now being phased into schools, and although the recent review (Dearing, 1993) will result in a welcomed slimming down of the original plans, the shape of the curriculum for children between the ages of 5 and 14 is largely determined. He views the reshaping of Key Stage 4 (14–16-year-olds), with the introduction of a vocational pathway based on GNVQs, as offering interesting new prospects. 'A' and 'AS' GCE qualifications are to remain, but 16–19 educational and training provision for the majority of students is being significantly reshaped by the introduction of NVQs and GNVQs. Higher education is also undergoing change, and Jessup anticipates a more flexible and diverse provision in the future (NIACE, 1994). The trend towards modular degrees is likely to continue and he sees this as offering prospects of aligning degree content with professional requirements. Concomitant developments in NVQs and GNVQs at level 4 and above, he says, will also extend the range of provision at higher levels and further impact on higher education. Having established the context and set one of his most compelling themes of integration and coherence, the rest of the chapter proceeds by concisely describing the emerging framework of qualifications, and examining some of the implications for the nature of curriculum and styles of learning. He warns: 'We shall not be able to achieve a fully integrated system until all forms of learning provision are formulated in a similar manner, namely through the specification of outcomes' and concludes by spelling out the benefits he sees which would accrue from this approach, concluding with conviction: 'Perhaps most importantly, it would encourage people to take responsibility for their own learning, both initially and on a continuing basis through their lives'.

John Burke

John Burke continues the discussion by focusing on a raft of theoretical issues which arise from the Outcomes Model. He stresses the importance of close, continuing scrutiny of theoretical concerns because, as he points out, if the theoretical base is flawed, the whole enterprise is in jeopardy. The Outcomes Model is identified as a species of Objectives theory and this leads to a brief examination of earlier Objectives approaches. He then goes on to analyze six propositions, embodying objections to Objectives or Outcomes. He avoids the accusation of putting up strawmen by consistently citing his sources and giving full rein to criticism with a generous use of quotation. Under each proposition, the focus sharpens to examine the Jessup Outcomes Model in the light of these perceived difficulties by close reference to Jessup's formulation of the model and a wide range of commentators who propound a vigorous and cogent support for Jessup's thesis.

Paul Ellis

Paul Ellis is Head of Research in NVQs at the NCVQ. His chapter focuses on Standards and the Outcomes approach, arguing that if this approach is adopted with sufficient vision and imagination it will have 'an immensely energizing effect' on VET.

He begins his analysis by positing the need to question and be prepared to change if the individual's full potential is to be realized. He points out that that it is of the essence of professional practice to be accountable, and with the explicit statement of intended outcomes, a system of accountability becomes a realistic possibility. He identifies five components which must go to make up such a system: *clarity of intention; flexibility; a broad view of human potential and the range of possible, valued achievement; relevance and the maximization of potential.* These components are subsumed in external and visible standards, realized in the creation of

NVQs and GNVQs, conferring coherence in a national system. An important aspect of coherence, he points out, is a consistent structuring of the format of the qualification. Personally, I think this is an important point because although on first acquaintance, the system may appear forbiddingly complex and unfamiliar, the regular pattern of component parts consistently reappear, and once the investment in time and effort has been made to familiarizing oneself with the necessary, technically precise terminology, the investment is amply rewarded by constant repetition, like the paradigm of regular Latin verbs but without the vowel changes in different conjugations! Ellis provides a very clear presentation of how a unit of assessment is structured, illustrating the detail by providing an example from an Element of competence, its performance criteria and its range. It is clear, he points out, that 'the focus is on what an individual is able to do, rather than what he/she knows', but he is quick to point out that 'demanding competence specifications such as these will require that learning involves a body of knowledge, principles and skills'. Within the NVQ system, he avers, greater numbers of individuals may be motivated to higher levels of achievement while relevance and accountability are enhanced by adherence to explicit standards.

Lindsay Mitchell
Lindsay Mitchell, a Director of Prime Research and Development Ltd, is recognized as one of the leading consultants in VET. Her chapter is based on research she carried out for the DE in connection with the application of NVQ/SVQs to higher levels of the framework.

In her thought provoking chapter, Mitchell explains how occupational standards and functional analysis can be used to develop descriptions of competence for a range of different occupations. Standards are capable of including (a) knowledge and understanding; (b) values and ethics; and (c) aspects often described through the use of personal attribute characteristics. However, the way such aspects are included needs to be carefully considered — it is not just a matter of adding in any suggestions which come the developer's way. Standards, she maintains, must still describe the outcomes of competent performance but competent performance itself is based on knowledge, understanding, skills, values, attitudes etc. Such an analysis and description will not be easy and will involve many diverse groups in exploring and making explicit the assumptions on which practice is based. Such explication allows individuals to evaluate their own practice and seek ways to develop practice and expectations of it.

NVQs and SVQs are almost unique as qualifications in that their focus is the demands of work; this, she explains, is perfectly acceptable as their purpose is to develop a competent workforce. The impact which this focus has on their design has raised many questions and issues for organizations and individuals whose purpose is to facilitate learning. Not least of these are questions relating to the true aim of particular courses or learning inputs and their link to the development of occupational competence.

Finally, she alerts us to the power of the process in developing the standards themselves. In debate about outcomes and the purpose of their work, workers — and amongst them she includes professionals — come to a deeper understanding of what it is they are aiming to achieve and the different ways they have developed of tackling this. The development of outcome statements, she concludes, is a powerful vehicle in itself in developing reflective practitioners.

John Burke

Part Three: Curriculum Consequences

In this section, the focus broadens to examine the curricular consequences which attend the adoption of an Outcomes approach. All the authors in this part of the book display a particular concern for the *workings* of the Outcomes model; two of them, Tom Jackson and Colin Nash, we may notice, have over sixty years' experience between them of teaching at secondary level, while Geoff Stanton has worked for a similar period as each of them, wrestling with the further education curriculum for which, as Chief Officer, he has a particular, professional concern. Dr Michael Young proposes an exciting vision of possible future developments subsumed in his concept of *connectivity*, while Stephen Steadman alerts us to practical problems bound up in assessment encountered by researchers in the Sussex VET research programme. Jane Harrop, principal author, compiler and analyst of the first, massive NCVQ consultation exercise on GNVQs (Harrop, 1992) provides the opening chapter.

Jane Harrop

The new GNVQs were piloted from September 1992 in 108 schools and colleges in England, Wales and Northern Ireland. Jane Harrop reports the great enthusiasm among students and teachers for the style and form of these new qualifications. She comments on the scope which GNVQs provide for centres to design their own courses, which was viewed by teachers in her analysis of the huge returns which resulted from the consultation exercise carried out by NCVQ as the main benefit of GNVQs; they were seen to encourage a range of courses tailored to students' needs, making the best use of local resources. She points out that no two centres are offering the qualifications in quite the same way and a variety of delivery styles is in operation. She agrees that the demands made by GNVQ courses are considerable, and carry many implications for school and college administrators. In addition, teachers and students have found the workload more demanding than they had expected. She points out that the relationship to other qualifications has raised interesting possibilities as centres offer a range of courses with additional studies or other qualifications, although a full discussion about aspects of assessment, both internal and external, are outside the scope of this chapter. (Some of these issues and concerns are picked up by other contributors.) She concludes: 'As some GNVQ centres have said, only a framework of qualifications such as GNVQs could provide them with offer the flexibility and opportunity to take advantage of the system-wide changes now sweeping the 14 to 19 education sectors.'

Tom Jackson

Most of the major curriculum initiatives and projects of the 60s, when curriculum development blossomed as a new and exciting enterprise, failed at the point of implementation. Tom Jackson offers a valuable contribution in providing an informed practitioner's account of piloting the implementation of the first wave of GNVQs. Building on his experience, and the experience of the other hundred-odd institutions which took part in the pilot, many useful lessons have already been learnt and continue to be learnt by the extensive process of consultation and evaluation which is ongoing.

Jackson, the Principal of a thriving sixth form college, offers a fascinating view from the sharp end. His chapter is presented as a case study of a single institution. He takes us through the decision making process which led to the college applying for inclusion in the pilot programme, explained in terms of the needs of prospective students and the national need to improve the quality and availability of provision. He examines the course design, the way in which teachers responded to the challenge and the enthusiasm of students who embraced these new learning opportunities. Nor does he pull his punches. He strictures the BTEC verifier (while acknowledging the outstanding contribution BTEC has made to VET in the recent past) and warns against moves from some quarters to dilute the essential philosophy which underpins both NVQs and GNVQs. He is candid about the problems faced by both students and staff. But he concludes on a decidedly optimistic note, reflecting on three issues: the attraction of GNVQs for his clients, the degree to which GNVQs are meeting their needs, and the influence of GNVQs on the ethos and culture of the college. 'Overall, we feel now that we made the right decision in introducing GNVQ. It was the right decision as regards meeting the educational needs of our students — it was also the right decision in the national context of pressing concerns about post-16 education and training.'

Geoff Stanton
Geoff Stanton is Chief Officer of the Further Education Unit (FEU). The author of numerous reports and publications, he is well known as a witty platform speaker with an understanding of grass root concerns. His chapter is divided into three distinct but related issues. In the first section, he summarizes arguments about the *quality* of qualifications and learning programmes and suggests how these may be linked to give an overall measure of institutional performance. The second part focuses on the problems of mapping units of assessment, taking account of the size of the unit, the level of the unit and the kind of outcome it represents. He proposes three categories of outcome in terms of individual unit: abstract', 'applied' and 'specific techniques'. This leads him to suggest that in terms of the learning acquired, the divide between 'academic' and 'vocational' courses may be more apparent than real; *some* A level GCE programmes (with three subjects) may provide a learning experience very similar in important essentials to the learning outcomes pursued in a vocational programme. He gives as an example, 'A' level Economics, Law and Accountancy, and compares this with 'certain Business Studies programmes'. The overlap in other instances (for example, History, Classics and Literature with Construction) may be very small indeed. The value of this approach, he explains, is that it begins to blur the rigid distinctions between academic and vocational, it provides a better basis for progression and offers the possibility of providing sounder guidance to students. However, Stanton quickly seeks to rebut any charge that he is resurrecting a tripartite categorization reminiscent of the thinking that underlay the Spens Report. In the third and final part, he examines in some detail a series of concerns focused on providing good quality learning programmes.

Colin Nash
As principal co-author of a recent book on Flexible Learning (Eraut, Nash, Fielding and Attard, 1991), and with some thirty years experience in education, mostly as a classroom practitioner, Colin Nash is well qualified to deal with flexible learning.

Nash begins his chapter by indicating the similarities in approach between the outcomes-led model of the curriculum and the approach to flexible learning. He goes on to examine in some detail 'the territory of flexible learning', proposing a conceptual map of the subject. He suggests that the key aspects of Jessup's emerging model can be summarized under five headings which follow logically from each other in the learning cycle and may be superimposed on the corresponding features of flexible learning: 'The common ground for our models is that they both acknowledge that assessment is a process; it is not just something that is done to learning at the end of a course of study. (. . .) It is about progression and progress.' One of the greatest catalysts for change in Flexible Learning Development occurred, he points out, when teachers were able to share their successful experiences, enticing the as yet uninitiated to try the approach for themselves. This is an important point because with so many changes underway, some teachers reeling under the burden of constant innovation may feel understandable reluctance to take on board yet more change. As professionals, they are more likely to respond positively if they can see the benefits for their students, and they know from colleagues the system is workable. He concludes his analysis by focusing on implementation, pointing out that both models are seeking change of considerable magnitude because 'essentially, they challenge many of the ingrained (mis)conceptions about how people learn and how learning should be measured'.

Michael Young

Michael Young secured an enduring pre-eminence in the sociology of education for his brilliant analysis of the social construction of knowledge (Young, 1971). In this book he proposes a new organizing concept: 'connectivity'.

Young addresses the issue of modularization and the outcomes approach, and asks whether this may form the basis of a strategy for moving to a high participation/high achievement system. He sees two goals for this approach (i) overcoming the 'divisions, the fragmentation and the rigidities and the low expectations' of the present situation; and (ii) providing a framework for analyzing new combinations of knowledge and skill, with the incentive to spur on learners towards high attainment levels aided by the concurrent development of new ways of teaching.

Having examined the development of modularization and the outcomes approach in the UK over the past decade, he focuses on some problems associated with the idea of learner centredness, arguing that together they tend to polarize learner-centredness and teacher-centredness. In his analysis, this leads to an examination of a second form of polarization between content and the specification of learning objectives. At this point he proposes the concept of 'connectivity' — connective modularization and connective outcomes, working towards a new paradigm, 'curriculum connectivity'. This notion is analyzed under three headings: purposes, relationships and processes. He concludes that a framework of connective curriculum modularization offers the possibility of students choosing a new combination of study. It implies specific strategies for teaching, modular recording of achievement and the assessment of students. As far as the student is concerned, he avers, 'we stand a better chance of converting the current rhetoric of the need for high achievement into a reality'.

Tim Oates and Joe Harkin

With the exception of Gilbert Jessup, Tim Oates has undoubtedly had the most profound influence on the way in which Core Skills have developed in GNVQs, and is widely recognized as the leading exponent of their use and development.

Immediately after the award of his doctorate in the development of English and Communication in FE, (Harkin, 1991) Joe Harkin was awarded a research contract by the NCVQ to work on core skills in communication, so there has been a close sense of cooperation in the same enterprise and shared expertise between both Oates and Harkin over the last three or four years.

The chapter is divided into two parts, with a different but complementary emphasis. In the first part, Oates concentrates on the technical (and sometimes micropolitical sensitivities) of development before examining some of the implementation issues; in the second part, Harkin continues the discussion and analysis of implementation issues, focusing primarily on the role of teachers, but noting the consequences for learners.

Oates begins by establishing the background to the 1989 initiative, which was inspired by the perceived possibility of enhancing learners' adaptability and flexibility in terms of promoting transfer. Six core skills were eventually divined, he tells us, with four levels of attainment, adopting the unit format which had been successfully developed for NVQs. Core Skills were seen as fulfilling an important role in broadening vocational *and* academic qualifications. He offers a clear but concise analysis of the problems and difficulties which beset development at every stage until it became apparent, he says 'that the NVQ model was beginning to be stretched beyond its original parameters'.

The concept of GNVQs was born of these difficulties, the danger of distorting NVQs and/or distorting school/college programmes. The function of GNVQs was to 'rationalize existing post-16 general education with a vocational focus by introducing a standardized model for all subject areas and levels'. An important part of this design was the inclusion of Core Skills which, in the context of GNVQs, would be free of earlier perceived disadvantages. By making core skills a mandatory requirement, for the first time they secured a firm footing within a qualification system.

The response from the teaching profession was enthusiastic, assigning a key curriculum role to core skills, with experiments not only in GNVQs but also in GCSEs and A/AS programmes. In 1991–2, the Open University devised a personal development course with core skills as an essential component, and developments took place in other OU programmes.

Oates insists that an important aspect of core skill units is their integration. He goes on to present a number of case studies illustrating the different ways in which this may be achieved. He moves on to analyze the major integration issues associated with different delivery patterns.

Harkin continues the discussion, commenting on the implementation of core skills. They are, he says, as much about the process of learning as about content. He proceeds to examine a number of issues including the legitimacy of core skills and the role of the effective teacher, which is analyzed in considerable depth. He maintains there should be a sharing of responsibility with learners, which he sees as vital. He examines the nature of tacit knowledge, which plays such an important part in professional practice, and warns against the temptation to fudge assessment, or collude with students in neglecting aspects of the curriculum. The implementation of core skills, he says, present a challenge to deliver the whole curriculum in ways which enable the learner to be more active in learning and gathering evidence of attainment.

The support of senior managers is a key issue in creating a suitable climate and providing the resources.

He identifies two levels of change required and comments on the flexibility needed by teachers. He concludes: 'in all cases, the best method of learning the skills involved is to experience their use, with time out for reflection and the creation of new professional knowledge'.

Stephen Steadman

Stephen Steadman approaches his subject — the assessment of outcomes — with just a smidgen of levity, signalled in the first subtitle 'a brief and *biased* history'. From my perspective, this approach is very welcome for it must be said that many commentators deal with assessment issues with all the comatose enthusiasm and *bonhomie* of a traffic warden on a wet afternoon. His treatment of the subject is no less rigorous and critical for his lightness of touch.

Having briefly surveyed the history of various attempts to formulate an outcomes approach, Steadman examines the *purpose* of assessment and assessment systems. He notes that most, traditional assessment systems have been designed 'to filter out the — always small — proportion of those who 'pass' and may be allowed to continue to higher education . . .'. This is contrasted with the declared purpose of the NVQ system, leading him to examine the meaning of outcomes and (based on empirical evidence) *what actually happens* in the assessment of outcomes. Not surprisingly, he divines various problems in the practicalities of implementation. From here, he further refines his focus to examine the technical properties of the NVQ system, expressing some anxieties about the vexed question of reliability. opining that the NCVQ position on validity and reliability 'is almost provocative'. Jessup (Jessup, 1991; and Burke and Jessup, 1990) has suggested that the way to ensure rigour in assessments carried out by so many different people in different locations is to concentrate on validity, by strict adherence to standards. Steadman proposes various safeguards which might be instituted but Jessup, in this volume, assures us that these measures are either already in place or in the process of implementation, and this is a concern I return to later in this Introduction. Having touched on further practical difficulties relating to costs and the scale of the overall enterprise, Steadman concludes on an optimistic note, dealing with one of the fundamental objectives underlying the Outcomes Model: 'However, in one important respect, NVQs have already succeeded. They have begun to seep across the academic/vocational divide in the shape of GNVQs and the Enterprise Initiative in HE.'

Part Four: Applications of the Outcomes Approach

In this section, we move out of the conventional curriculum setting associated with 14–19 education and training to consider some of the applications of the Outcomes approach.

One of the most recurrent themes in Jessup (1991) is the autonomy of the learner. Stephen McNair picks up this theme, arguing that an outcomes-led approach gives individuals more opportunity to make informed choices, match their interests, needs and talents to the requirements of 'the real world', contrasting this approach with the traditional 'trust the expert' model. Margaret Levy examines the Work Based Model, which she has been largely responsible for developing, exploring the potential for an outcomes approach in the world of the workplace. With the remaining three contibutors in this section, the focus shifts to higher level competences, and the reader is referred back to Mitchell, (chapter 5) who also strides this terrain. Professor Michael Eraut's contribution links David Mathews' concern with higher level competences in management with Sue Otter's exploration of the learning outcomes of higher education by focusing on the meaning, development and utilization of professional knowledge. The section opens with McNair.

Stephen McNair
As an Associate Director (Higher Education) of the National Organization for Adult Learning, Stephen McNair has long had both a personal and professional interest in issues to do with the autonomous learner. His chapter explores the relationship between the idea of individual autonomy and an outcomes approach to learning. He begins from a belief that an undue concentration on educational processes has led in the past to neglect achievement, and this led to an education and training system which lacked accountability, was inaccessible and inefficient, but where the notion of 'quality' and 'standards' formed a powerful, but fragile, organizing myth.

He argues that the development of a knowledge-based economy, and mass lifelong learning requires that as a community we find better ways of understanding, developing and accrediting achievement of the outcomes of all learning, whether it be institutional, work-based, or voluntary; formal or informal; further, higher or adult; vocational, general or academic. However, he maintains, this does not imply that existing models of outcomes are satisfactory. Rather, he suggests, a better 'lanaguage of outcomes', and better ways of using that language could support the creation of a society where individuals were more autonomous, and that this would benefit both the individual and society.

He points out that the issue of individual autonomy in a post-industrial society is a complex one, and modestly disclaims authority in some of the academic fields it touches on. However, with more than twenty years experience of working with adult learners, and with ten of them at the interface between education and public policy he asserts his claim for a voice. His chapter is presented as an invitation to dialogue, not a summary of conclusions. The more open, democratic learning society, which would be more productive and democratic for its members, will only be achieved through open debate and the genuine *exploration* of ideas.

Margaret Levy
I am sure Margaret Levy will not take offence if I describe her as one of the *gurus* of VET as she has made, and continues to make, such a long-standing contribution to the field. Not least among her abilities has been her *penchant* for spotting talent and subsequently nurturing so many researchers who have thereafterwards come to play such an important rôle in the development of VET, such as Bob Mansfield, David Mathews and Tim Oates.

Her chapter is divided into three sections.

In the first part, Levy comments on developing the good practice model, tools and strategies for implementation, noting curriculum influences on work based learning research and development. She discerns three major aims: (i) to encourage access to learning for all, using an occupational base and real work; (ii) to deliver new standards, new certification, progression and skill transfer; and (iii), to establish a technically competent, versatile, adaptable workforce.

In the second section, she focuses on the operational definition of the good practice model of work-based learning and the need for partnership between production professionals, worker learners and learning professionals, noting that guidance professionals have an important supportive rôle.

In the third part, Levy concentrates on Outcomes and learning issues, explaining the special significance of outcomes in terms of the work-based model and strategies for achieving intended learning outcomes.

Finally, she focuses on the NCVQ emerging outcomes model and issues which need further clarification. She concludes that by introducing appropriate learning strategies which include core analysis and analyses using the job competence model it should be possible to improve the validity of assessment inferences made in respect of statements of competence.

David Mathews

David Mathews is a Director of David Mathews Associates. With Bob Mansfield, he was the co-author of *Job Competence — A Description for Education and Training* (Mansfield and Mathews, 1985), until very recently, probably the most frequently quoted text in British VET. He is widely acknowledged as a leading consultant.

Mathews suggests that the analysis of outcomes provides a novel way of thinking about managers and management. He begins his analysis by briefly reviewing more conventional notions, observing that three factors inform the traditional management curriculum: (i) a concern with organization; (ii) varying degrees of belief that management is learnable or even teachable; and (iii) a focus on the qualities of individual managers or prospective managers. Good managers possess certain 'qualities' and their is a corpus of knowledge which informs the practice of management. He then moves on to consider qualifications and management development, and earlier measures of management competence before arriving at the notion of outcomes; this he conceives has three dimensions: (a) a focus on the results of education, training and development in terms of effective management performance in organizations; (b) a focus on the effects of management action (outcomes in management practice); and (c) a link in identifying the effectiveness of management action, including its ultimate consequences for the organization and its stakeholders.

This leads to a very useful and concise discussion of the technicalities involved in Standards, an area of particular expertise on Mathews' part. He notes the attempt to arrive at National Standards, the work of the Management Charter Initiative (MCI), and briefly but fairly evaluates its successes and shortcomings. He poses a number of questions about the feasibility of a common management curriculum and looks to the possibility of 'a curriculum for the future', touching on one of the most sensitive issues which concerns every occupational group, the extent to which it is possible to devise standards which not only reflect current best practice, but have the capacity to accommodate changing demands.

Outcomes in management, Mathews maintains, are most strongly represented in the management standards so far developed. 'They are imperfect', he admits, 'but powerful and influential.' Most of the work that has gone into the development of standards has been carried forward, (perhaps inevitably, because of its technical nature), in research and development projects rather than in public debate, but as with so many other contributors to this book, Mathews is anxious to involve a wider, informed public in debating the shape of developments. He makes the point in his concluding section: that the development of standards will have considerable implications for the management curriculum. 'This is something in which we are all stakeholders and all liable to have a view.'

Michael Eraut

Michael Eraut is arguably the foremost authority on professional knowledge in the UK. He begins his chapter with an arresting assertion: 'For every incompetent professional, there are probably several who are competently doing the wrong thing'. This apparent contradiction arises from the application of two quite different sets of criteria used in ascertaining professional knowledge; (i) criteria based on performance of the task; (ii) criteria relating to the most beneficial outcomes for the client. This is an extremely potent and important distinction, inherently serious and deserving of sober deliberation, but one is mischievously reminded of a droll anecdote which perfectly illustrates Eraut's point: a doctor displaying what can only be described as 'ambivalent competence' successfully cures a man of a troublesome ailment but kills the patient in the process!

Eraut argues that in all professional education priority should be given to the outcomes of professional action. This not only broadens the range of relevant knowledge, it challenges the validity of that knowledge, which requires to be periodically revised and updated. The outcomes of professional training can only be meaningfully discussed if we know what constitutes professional knowledge and how it is validated. To achieve this, Eraut proposes four requirements: (i) a wider conception of the role of professionals in society and their duties towards clients; (ii) appropriate attitudes towards self-evaluation and accountability; (iii) a wider range of professional knowledge and patterns of thinking; and (iv) a willingness to commit time and resources to improving the quality of professional work. There is a greater likelihood of these becoming outcomes of professional education if a sense of mutually informing partnership between teachers and practitioners can be brought about. This will not easily be achieved unless teachers have a closer appreciation of (a) what Eraut classifies as 'knowledge use' and (b) a closer, reflective appreciation of outcomes for the client; practitioners, on the other hand have an obligation to keep abreast of *continuing* professional education with due evaluation and reflection on actual practice. However, Eraut warns that this partnership requires both a sense of agreed direction and a sense of equilibrium; he concludes: 'They are less likely to become outcomes if either party drifts in the opposite direction, or becomes dominant over the other.'

Sue Otter

For several years, Sue Otter has been involved in research on learning outcomes in HE (cf Otter, 1989 and Otter, 1992). She continues these professional concerns by providing consultancy to a group of different universities in the Midlands, on behalf of the DE.

The early UDACE work began, she explains, from the premise that outcomes were an important means of helping adult learners. By stating the outcomes, APEL, access and the accreditation of work-based learning were greatly facilitated. Outcomes, she says, reflect the fundamental credit in higher education.

In her chapter, Otter acts as an informed and knowledgeable guide to take us through the UDACE Learning Project. The first problem was where to start. Rewriting the aims and objectives of existing courses and modules was inadequate because they tended to leave out outcomes which related to personal skills and competences, and frequently led to problems with assessment.

She delineates the different types of outcomes which were researched, briefly discussing the differences between outcomes and existing objectives, and leads on to a discussion of the problems associated with detailing knowledge requirements, outcome statement levels, unplanned outcomes and the relation of outcomes to National Standards.

In her conclusion, she touches on the content and purpose of the HE curriculum, the relationship between outcomes, and assessment and teaching and learning methods, and the issue of quality and outcomes.

The HE Charter, she says, will place greater emphasis on the student in HE as customer rather than beneficiary. With the ability to 'shop around', students are likely to demand greater openness in assessment, and to seek greater perceived relevance in the content offered.

She concludes that: 'An outcome based curriculum in higher education may provide a better means of integrating NVQ units, and of indicating the achievement of the competences desired by employers of graduates.'

Part Five: Issues In Progression

The issue of Progression is fundamentally important to any system of qualifications. Indeed, one of the reasons that the NCVQ was set up in the first place was to bring about a much needed coherence into a 'system' of competing vocational qualifications which often precluded progression because of the varying standards and levels which did not always 'butt on' to each other and the lack of effective progression pathways this enjoined.

For several years now, Professor David Robertson has played a key role in the debate on access and progression, major concerns in his research on wider policy issues; his treatment of the subject is both authoritative and lucid.

David Robertson
David Robertson begins his analysis by reflecting on the present 'disjointed, and unrewarding jumble of post-compulsory educational provision' which results, he tells us, from an absence of strategic direction. The problem is urgent because we lag so far behind our international competitors.

He sees the new emphasis on the outcomes of post-secondary and higher education as having unparalleled significance. He notes an important trend, a shift from education conceived as principally self-improvement to education as an asset in relevant competition strategy. He goes on to analyze how HE has contributed to the present malaise by an 'unusually distorting influence both upon the curriculum of schools and colleges and upon the chances of gaining access to this secret garden of scholarship'. While the former polytechnics may, in the past, have been more amenable with their historic links with industry and their sometimes overt vocational emphasis, he sees the general character of HE as firmly orientated to the academic reproduction of the next generation of scholars. He divines a danger in some of the 'new' universities seeking status by emulating the style of established universities. The key to changing this situation is much better access and accountability. Essentially, access relates to progression from post-secondary and further education into HE; accountability relates to the extent that the outcomes of post-secondary, and higher education are made available to its stakeholders and consumers. This is not simply a matter of performance indicators: it relates to 'the production of well-qualified graduates capable of using their full potential in gainful employment'.

He sees the NCVQ curriculum model as a fundamental challenge to prevailing orthodoxies, offering a radically different approach to the purpose of learning. Citing Marks (1991), he suggests the NCVQ approach directly challenges the traditional culture and professional values of academic life. His argument proceeds with an analysis of the impact of the NCVQ on HE, suggesting that HE may require significant modification to its current curriculum practice.

The advent of students with GNVQs seeking admission to HE poses a particular challenge, because in contrast to 'A' level GCE students who have pursued traditionally defined subject specialisms (which readily resonate with the HE curriculum) GNVQ students will have a much broader vocational base which cuts across individual subject specialisms. A discussion follows on GNVQs and possible problems of progression. Working towards a creative solution of problems, Robertson proposes a National Framework of Achievement and Progression, leading on to 'An Entitlement Model of Post-Secondary and Higher Education'. He concludes: 'this modernization of the learning relationship cannot be long resisted'.

Part Six: An International Comparison

Peter Raggatt had recently returned from a period of research in Australia during a sabbatical year's leave from the Open University. The first draft of his paper at the conference was, in effect, a different paper. Developments in Australia, as in Britain, are proceeding at a considerable pace. Since completing this chapter, Peter feels that the situation has moved on again, and modestly suggests his account may have the flavour of recent history rather than an up-to-the-minute account. Nonetheless, it provides a valuable comparative dimension with developments in Australia, which has broadly adopted a similar approach to Britain, having cast wide its net in surveying the benefits of different national systems, in particular, the German approach. In Raggatt's account, it is fascinating to notice the re-emergence of so many themes developed by other contributors to this book.

Peter Raggatt
Peter Raggatt establishes at the outset that developments in Australia have a number of features in common with England. Both countries have moved towards an outcomes approach. In Australia this is apparent across the whole of the post-compulsory sector of vocational education and training. It is also clearly evident in the development of competency-based standards in the professions and will, as

a consequence, selectively affect those areas of higher education concerned with professional development.

He points out that the two major reviews of post-compulsory education and training argued strongly that there is a convergence between the concepts of work and education and between working and learning. At the heart of this convergence is the concept of key competencies, which are seen to be as essential for effective participation in work as they are for effective participation in education and in adult life. The further proposals, he suggests, are logical and consistent: the key competencies should be integrated into all school and college learning programmes *and* into occupational standards. In the latter case, the National Training Board (NTB) has encouraged Competency Standards Boards (CSBs) to incorporate key competencies into occupational standards but has stopped short of requiring it. A similar situation, he notes, prevails in England.

Institutionally, the notion of convergence between 'education' and 'training', and 'general' and 'vocational' education is manifested in the development of various initiatives in which schools and colleges, schools and industry, colleges and industry are working collaboratively and in joint ventures. Likewise, he notes, it is apparent in the emphasis on more flexible pathways and progression routes between schools, colleges and industry. The emergence of a system facilitating the kind of flexibility and individual choice evident in the Australian approach will be made easier by the clear specification of the outcomes of learning programmes and the development of credit transfer arrangements.

All this will, Raggatt suggests, call for imaginative approaches to curriculum design and delivery, and new strategies for learning which integrate key competencies in subjects and vocational programmes and provide greater autonomy for learners. It will, he concludes, require a substantial staff development programme to help teachers, tutors and trainers to develop the new skills which they will need.

Envoi

Any new system of qualifications is bound to have teething problems; no matter how well planned and discussed, no matter what process of consultation has been entered into, no matter what lessons may have been learnt from other experiences, the actual process of implementation will reveal deficiencies. The new GNVQ qualification was devised after what is probably the largest consultation exercise ever carried out in the UK (cf Jane Harrop in this volume). Within the first year of implementation, it was massively inspected and evaluated.

Short evaluations were carried out by:

The Employment Department (ED);
The Department for Education (DFE);
The Further Education Unit (FEU);
Her Majesty's Inspectorate (HMI);
The Office for Standards in Education (OFSTED);
The Schools Examination and Assessment Council (SEAC);
The Northern Ireland Inspectorate (NII);
City & Guilds (CGI); and
The National Council for Vocational Qualifications (NCVQ) itself.

At the time of writing, an even more extensive, two-year independent evaluation, building on the experience of all the previous evaluations, is being mounted by the Institute of Education at the University of London in collaboration with the FEU, with major funding provided by the Nuffield Foundation.

Jessup (1994a), writing in the 'Foreword' to a new book (Chorlton, 1994) published by the Careers Research and Advisory Centre, notes:

> This is a very readable account and a fair description of GNVQs. It captures the excitement and enthusiasm that the new courses have generated amongst teachers and students. (. . .) At the same time the book recognises the problems of the early days, many of which, I am pleased to say, have now been sorted out.

In the course of this book, many of these problems are tackled head on by different contributors. In this last section, as editor, I would like to make two general observations.

1   One of the problems which face the National Council for Vocational Qualifications (NCVQ) is prejudice and misunderstanding. But even among otherwise well-informed and open-minded enquirers there may be fundamental misapprehensions built on apparent understanding. Thus, for example, a common reaction from individuals who know little about GNVQs is that they are premised on a narrow behaviourist approach, which *may* be all right when dealing specifically with low level training but is totally unsuited to either education or higher level training. Thereafter, this misunderstanding acts as a filter to colour all further perception or interest, resulting in an inimical or positively hostile attitude.

A spectacular example of misunderstanding and apparent prejudice occurred in December 1993 in the transmission of a television programme *Dispatches*: 'All Our Futures — Britain's Education Revolution'. This was spectacular on two accounts: (i) its provenance: Professor Alan Smithers and his research team at the Centre for Education and Employment Research, University of Manchester; and (ii) the sheer breadth and depth of misinformation it imparted; the NCVQ issued a very detailed rebuttal in a matter of days (NCVQ, 1993), listing no less than thirty-three substantive errors and providing the documentary evidence (both in the text and in seven appendices) to substantiate its assertion. Having made the case for the need for continual improvement and research (cf Jessup, 1989, pp. 75–6; Jessup, 1991, pp. 128–33; Burke, 1992, p. 255) the Statement concluded:

> What NCVQ and its partners in the development of the NVQ and GNVQ systems do not need, however, but received, with damaging effects, in the Dispatches programme and associated report were polemic presented as fact and unrepresentative perceptions presented as if they were widely held. This statement has been prepared to show the extent to which viewers and readers have been given misleading and inaccurate information. (NCVQ, 1993a, ¶36, p. 8)

Important factual errors abounded. For instance, a 'leading academic' (who remained anonymous) commented: 'there has been no proper evaluation of it (GNVQs) whatsoever'. In fact, as we have already noticed above, GNVQs have most probably been more extensively evaluated than any other remotely comparable initiative ever undertaken in the UK; certainly, no other initiative has ever been so diversely evaluated in the same time frame from initial implementation.

The extent of perceived prejudice and misrepresentation may be gauged from a press release from the Electrical Contractors' Association (ECA) issued after the programme. The alleged views of the ECA had been cited to support the thesis that there were inadequate knowledge requirements in NVQs for electricians. The ECA countered:

> The Electrical Contractors' Association is concerned at the misleading comments of Professor Smithers relating to craft training in the UK. It wonders whether the Professor knows the difference between the GNVQ for 13–16-year-old candidates and the NVQ for over 16-year-old candidates? His comments on the Channel 4 Television programme 'Dispatches' were confusing and did no service to training standards in the UK. His starting point seemed to be 'My mind is made up, do not confuse me with the facts'. (. . .) contrary to the views he was propounding the training of electricians is in good hands and the introduction of NVQs will be used to enhance our training, and standards will not be diluted. (. . .) Colleges and training centres will still be required to teach the theory and underpinning knowledge. There will be written examinations and practical skills tests.

2 Most commentators and practitioners examine any new system with the utmost rigour, as indeed they should. But most seem to forget that the existing systems that the new system is seeking to replace are themselves frequently shot through with inconsistencies. Yet the perceived difficulties with the new system are criticized as though the old system were perfect and unproblematic. If we focus on assessment for a moment — and assessment lies at the heart of any system of qualification — my point becomes clear.

The NVQ and GNVQ system of assessment at Advanced Level is proposed as an alternative to the usual system of assessment employed in Advanced Level GCE: timed essays. Stones (1966, pp. 251ff) highlights the difficulties which beset this form of assessment; they include:

> detailed marking schemes set beside analytical and impression marking;
> limited coverage of the syllabus;
> predictability and question spotting;
> cramming;
> model answers for regurgitation;
> variability in different markers' assessments;

variability in the same marker's assessments;
inconsistency;
the deployment of 'examination skills' to camouflage ignorance.

Ingenkamp (1977) notes:

> More attention has been paid to the essay type examination than
> any other form of written examination. It has repeatedly been
> shown that assessment of the same composition can differ to
> such an extent that the entire grading range is covered. (Starch
> and Elliot, 1912; Lammerman, 1927; Hartog *et al*, 1936; Sims,
> 1932)

Against this, Wood, Johnson, Blinkhorn, Anderson and Hall (1988) attest
the basic viability of workplace assessment, while acknowledging the need
for attention and support. So too, Miller, Hoggan, Pringle and West
(1988) who conclude that

> (T)he project reported no significant constraints operating on
> feasibility and widespread acceptance of the desirability of (ob-
> servational assessment in the workplace). (p. 348)

If *in principle* such forms of observational assessment are sound, there is
plenty of scope for improving the process, as Mitchell and Cuthbert (1989)
acknowledge in their excellent report, and Steadman is surely right, in
this volume, when he says:

> Many of these problems will ameliorate as awareness spreads and
> as more assessors are trained and gain experience to pass onto
> colleagues. This will not be an overnight process. It takes time
> to form a community of agreement about acceptable perform-
> ance (. . .) What assessors and verifiers will need is practical and
> experientially based guidance, with examples of recorded per-
> formance on either side of acceptability.

However, Steadman is pushing against an open door. Such materials are
already in preparation, and the first book in a series illustrating good
practice has already been published by the NCVQ (1993b): *Assessing Students' Work — GNVQ in Art & Design*. This series is seen as

> an important means of conveying the standards. (. . .) Addi-
> tional reference points for the coverage and standards in GNVQs
> are contained in text books and other learning materials which
> are rapidly coming on the market. (. . .) NCVQ is working
> with publishers to speed up the process. (Jessup, 1994b)

Further, it will soon be a requirement that all assessors should be trained and
certified to newly published standards, demonstrating that they are able to carry
out assessments to the new standard. Jessup (*ibid*) continues:

Second, there are internal checks on assessment practice by an internal verifier, appointed to each school and college. Third, the quality of assessment must be confirmed by an external verifier who visits centres to check on the assessment practice.

Even with these checks and balances, the assessment regime will not be perfect, for such perfection is a search for 'holy grail', impossible of fulfilment. It should be recognized that *all* assessment is ultimately subjective, a matter of judgment.[11] (Even so called 'objective tests' require a subjective selection, weighting and ordering of material.) While clearly, an assessment should be as reliable as practically possible, there is bound to be a 'trade off' against other practical concerns, such as bureaucracy time and cost, if observational assessment is to operate in real rather than ideal circumstances. If the focus on validity is sharpened, as Jessup suggests (Jessup, 1991; and Burke and Jessup, 1990), the assessment event is more likely to be fair and equitable, but to suggest that Jessup claims *perfect* validity is ever possible is to traduce his position. Nor is a greater reliance on validity unique to the Outcomes approach. The PhD examination, which stands at the apex of prestige in academic respectability, relies very heavily on validity, with only a nodding acknowledgment of the needs of reliability. The major difference, of course, is that it is assumed with something approaching certainty that there is an adequate 'community of understanding' among PhD or DPhil examiners, something that NVQ and GNVQ assessors must work *towards* creating over time even if its full realization is never finally achieved.

In conclusion, I reiterate the principal intended outcomes which have informed this initiative.

Each contributor was invited to write on a particular topic, to draw on his/her own particular expertise, to criticize freely and, where appropriate, to make constructive and creative contributions to the enterprise. The intention of the book is to inform, widen debate and encourage further research; the purpose is to improve education and training for the immediate benefit of students and trainees and the ultimate benefit, no less, of the nation.

Acknowledgments

I am indebted to Gilbert Jessup for reading this Introduction in draft form and for valued suggestions although my observations remain my own responsibility. I am further indebted to Dick Wheeler (of Barnsway Consultants, Kings Langley) for providing the data on developments at Middlesex University and for helpful suggestions; Dick, a former Dean at Hertford, is registered as a DPhil researcher at Sussex in our VET programme. (Draft document quoted, *cum permissu universitatis*.)

Notes

1 First draft of all papers was produced by March 1993. The majority of second draft papers were completed by July. A number of papers were subsequently emended before the book went to press in April 1994 to take account of new developments but not all contributors had this opportunity.

2   Cf First leader in *Times Educational Supplement*, 15 June 1990, p. A19, on the subject of teacher education: 'The industrial trainers (from BP, IBM and Lloyd's Bank) were surprised that objectives in terms of outcomes were not set in advance.'

3   Cf Otter (1989 and 1992) and Open University course texts *passim*.

4   'Efficient cause' in terms of Aristotle's classification of cauality.

5   See Jessup in this volume; also cf Oates (1989), Burke (1991), Raggatt (1991) Otter (1992); since then, the argument has moved on. Middlesex University, for example, issued a draft paper in May 1993, examining the outcomes approach, entitled: *NVQs and GNVQs — What place in Middlesex University?* which posed a number of key questions:

> Faculties and schools should consider whether there are opportunities and advantages in developing NVQ/GNVQ qualifications for their academic areas within a framework either of dual qualifications, or of cross accreditation or of qualifications offered by a lead body. (. . .) The issuer for Middlesex is how far we should incorporate the NVQ style into our practice and how far our qualifications should be expressed in NVQ/GNVQ terms.

An interim report from the Enterprise in Higher Education Project 1992–93 from the University of Sussex goes some way further:

> Recently (. . .) there has been a sense that the programme needs *to shift its focus from inputs to outcomes and learning methods adjusted accordingly.* Course outlines and the Handbook have become clearer about aims and objectives, and about the purpose and criteria of assessment units. This was also a *response to student feedback* where there have been complaints about the more traditional methods, feelings that teaching is not always sufficiently practice-relevant, is patronising to mature students, and is not clearly connected to assessment. Student feedback had stressed that workshop-style teaching was more enjoyable as well as capable of raising more important issues.
>
> *These developments led course tutors to begin to rethink the course in terms of outcomes*: starting with subject content is being replaced by *statements of outcomes and goals and then possible ways of reaching them.* One way of making a broad range of goals attainable is to make the *hidden curriculum more explicit so that certain skills are learnt in the learning process itself.* The EHE project is the first attempt *system-atically and explicitly to influence the learning culture in a way which will involve all tutors* on the programme and which will be transferable to the BA in social policy (Locke, 1993, pp. 4–5, *emphasis added.*)

Interestingly this is a good example of change in HE by osmosis, predicted in Burke 1991.

6   To this day (1971), the common tendency is to equate the curriculum with the 'syllabus', a 'scheme of work', 'a course of study' or quite simply 'subjects' — something whose existence is taken for granted and which can be safely left to look after itself.

7   See also Burke (p. 72 in this volume).

8   Common characteristics shared by NVQs and GNVQs may be briefly noted:

> Both are specified in terms of learning outcomes;
> Both are made up of a number of units;
> Both allow credit to be awarded for each unit;

Both allow the accumulation of credits towards a full qualification;
Both offer access to assessment to all;
Both allow alternative forms of evidence of achievement;
Both are awarded to all who meet the required standards, irrespective of time taken and mode of learning.

9 'Knowledge and understanding' are usually linked together in NCVQ and Department of Employment terminology but Eraut (1994, forthcoming) has pointed out an apparent category mistake involved in separating these concepts:

> Echoes of this narrowest of definitions also appear in the regulations of the National Council for Vocational Qualifications (NCVQ, 1991) which refer to underpinning knowledge and understanding as if it were possible to have underpinning knowledge which one did not understand. (Chapter 1)

Nonetheless, knowledge is not synonymous with understanding, as demonstrated in the cartoon below:

I've been boiling these eggs for half an hour but they are still hard!

Competence assessments may involve more than just a demonstration of skill: an assessment of knowledge and understanding will take place although this will often form part of the same assessment by questioning. In some cases a written test may be required.

Source: John Burke

The (carefully depicted androgynous) trainee chef pursuing his/her NVQ knows that the application of heat may cause at least some apparently solid substances (such as butter) to melt but clearly does not understand the essential principles underlying the boiling of an egg!

One may know that the sun appears to arise in the east without understanding why this is an illusion. The NCVQ requires both knowing and understanding at an appropriate level.

10 It is true that some VI Form Colleges and Schools have successfully introduced NVQs, but the range of NVQs has been necessarily very limited and the organization of these programmes has been fraught with planning difficulties. Where they have been successfully implemented, (for example, Portsmouth College and Castle School, Deal) this is largely a tribute to the determination of some institutions to plug a perceived gap in provision before the introduction of GNVQs.

11 'All generalizations—even *this one*—tend to be inaccurate.' It could be argued that the 'correct answers' which are simply 'right' or 'wrong' *are* 'objective' (e.g. The Battle of Hastings—1066 or 1 + 1 = 2, (NB: the date of the battle is wrong if information is sought about street fighting between Mods and Rockers in the '60s and the arithmetic is wrong if you are using a binary base.)

References

BECHER, T. and MACLURE, S. (1978) *The Politics of Curriculum Change*, London, Hutchinson.

BURKE, J. (1989a) (Ed) *Competency Based Education and Training*, London, Falmer Press.

BURKE, J. (1989b) 'The implementation of NVQs' in BURKE, J. (Ed) *Competency Based Education and Training*, London, Falmer Press.

BURKE, J. (1991a) 'Competence and higher education: Implications for institutions and professional bodies' in RAGGATT, P. and UNWIN, L. (Eds) *Change and Intervention: Vocational Education and Training*, London, Falmer Press.

BURKE, J. (1991b) 'Foreword' in Jessup, G., *Outcomes: The Emerging Model of Education and Training*, London, Falmer Press.

BURKE, J. (1992) 'Exploring a new paradigm: Research degree programme in NVQs', *Education Technology & Training International* **29**, 3. pp. 249–256.

BURKE, J. and JESSUP, G. (1990) 'Assessment in NVQs: Disentangling validity from reliability in the assessment of NVQs', in HORTON, T. (Ed) *Assessment Debates*, London, Hodder and Stoughton, for the Open University.

CHORLTON, W. (1994) *GNVQ: Is It For You? The Guide to General National Vocational Qualifications and General SVQs, the Scottish equivalent*, Student Helpbook Series, London, Hobson Publishing for The Careers Research and Advisory Centre (CRAC).

DEARING, R. (1993) *The National Curriculum and Its Assessment*, Final Report, London, SCAA.

ELECTRICAL CONTRACTORS' ASSOCIATION (1993) Press Release, London, ECA.

ERAUT, M. (1982) *Curriculum Development in Further Education*, Education Area Occasional Paper No 11, Brighton, The University of Sussex.

ERAUT, M. (1994) *Developing Professional Knowledge and Competence*, London, Falmer Press.

ESLAND, G.M. (1971) 'Teaching and learning as the organisation of knowledge' in YOUNG, M.F.D. (Ed) (1971), *Knowledge and Control*, London, Collier Macmillan.

GOODSON, I. (1989) 'Curriculum Reform and Curriculum Theory: A Case of Historical Amnesia, *Cambridge Journal of Education*, 19(2), pp. 131–41. (Reissued in MOON, B. (1990) *New Curriculum — National Curriculum*, London, Hodder and Stoughton.)

HAFFENDEN, I. and BROWN, A. (1989) 'Towards the implementation of competence based curricula in FE' in BURKE, J. (Ed) *Competency Based Education and Training*, London. Falmer Press.

HARKIN, J. (1991) *The Development of English and Communication in Further Education*, unpublished DPhil Thesis, University of Sussex.

HARROP, J. (1992) *Response to the Consultation on General National Qualifications*, NCVQ Report No 15, London, NCVQ.

HARTOG, P., RHODES, E.C. and BURT, C. (1936) *The Marks of Examiners*, London, MacMillan.

INGENKAMP, K. (1977) *Educational Assessment*, Slough, National Foundation for Educational Research.

JESSUP, G. (1989) 'The emerging model of vocational education and training', in BURKE, J. (Ed) *Competency Based Education and Training*, London, Falmer Press.

JESSUP, G. (1990a) *Common Learning Outcomes: Core Skills in A/AS Levels and NVQs* NCVQ Report No 6 with contributions from John Burke, Alison Wolf and Tim Oates, London, NCVQ.

JESSUP, G. (1990b) 'National Vocational Qualifications: Implications for further education', in BEES, M. and SWORDS, M. (Eds) (1990) *National Vocational Qualifications and Further Education*, London, Kogan Page in association with the National Council for Vocational Qualifications.

JESSUP, G. (1991) *Outcomes: NVQs and the Emerging Model of Education and Training.* London, Falmer Press.

JESSUP, G. (1992) 'Developing a coherent national framework of qualifications', in *Educational & Training Technology International* **29**, 3, pp. 189–197.

JESSUP, G. (1994a) 'Foreword' in CHORLTON, W. (1994) *GNVQ: Is It For You? The Guide to General Vocational Qualifications and General SVQs, the Scottish Eqivilent,* Student Helpbook Series, London, Hobson Publishing for the Careers Research and Advisory Centre (CRAC).

JESSUP, G. (*forthcoming*, 1994b) Draft of GNVQ Note *GNVQ Curriculum Model*, London, NCVQ.

LAMMERMAN, H. (1927) 'Vocational education in England', in ROHRS, H. (Ed) *Vocational Education in Western Industrial Societies*, London, Symposium Books.

LAWTON, D. (1973) *Social Change, Educational Theory and Curriculum Planning*, London, Hodder and Stoughton.

LAWTON, D., GORDON, P., INGE, M., GIBBY, B., PRING, R. and MOORE, T. (1978) *Theory and Practice of Curriculum Studies*, London, Routledge and Kegan Paul.

LOCKE, W. (1993) *Social Policy and Social Work Subject Group: Interim Report*, Enterprise in Higher Education Project, Brighton, University of Sussex.

MANSFIELD, B. and MATHEWS, D. (1985) *Job Competence — A Discription for use in Vocational Education and Training* Work Based Learning Project, Blagdon, Further Education Staff College.

MARKS, R. (1991) *Implications of National Vocational Qualifications for the Polytechnic Sector*, Project Report for the Committee of Directors of Polytechnics, London, FEU.

MIDDLESEX University (1993) Draft Paper *NVQs and GNVQs — What Place in Middlesex University?* Middlesex University.

MILLER, C., HOGAN, J., PRINGLE, S. and WEST, G. (1988) *Credit Where Credit is Due*, Glasgow, SCOTVEC.

MITCHELL, L. and CUTHBERT, T. (1989) *Insufficient Evidence, the Final Report of the Competency Testing Project*, Glasgow, SCOTVEC.

NCC (1990) *Core Skills 16–19*, York, National Curriculum Council.

NCVQ (1989) *NVQ Criteria and Procedures*, London, National Council for Vocational Qualifications.

NCVQ and ED (1991) *Guide to National Vocational Qualifications*, London, National Council for Vocational Qualifications and Employment Department.

NCVQ (1993) *A Statement by the National Council for Vocational Qualifications (NCVQ) on 'All Our Futures — Britain's Education Revolution', a Channel 4 Dispatches programme on 15 December 1993 and associated report by the Centre for Education and Employment Research, University of Manchester*, London, NCVQ.

NCVQ (1993) *GNVQ in Art & Design* Assessing Students' Work Series, London, NCVQ.

NEWMAN, J. and LLEWELLIN, N. (1990) 'The accreditation of prior learning (APL) in BEES, M. and SWORDS, M. (Ed) (1989) *National Vocational Qualifications and Further Education*, London, Kogan Page in association with the National Council for Vocational Qualifications.

NIACE (1994) *An Adult Higher Education: A Vision*, a Policy Discussion Paper, Leicester, National Institute of Adult Continuing Education.

OATES, T. (1989) 'Emerging Issues: The response of HE to competency based approaches', in BURKE, J. (Ed) *Competency Based Education and Training*, London, Falmer Press.

OTTER, S. (1989) *Understanding Learning Outcomes*, Leicester, Unit for the Development of Adult Continuing Education, Leicester (*now at FEU, London*).

OTTER, S. (1992) *Learning Outcomes in Higher Education*, London, Unit for the Development of Adult Continuing Education.

RAGGATT, P. (1991) 'Quality assurance and NVQs' in RAGGATT, P. and UNWIN, L. (Eds) *Change and Intervention: Vocational Education and Training*, London, Falmer Press.

RAGGATT, P. and UNWIN, L. (1991) (Eds) *Change and Intervention: Vocational Education and Training*, London, Falmer Press.

RICHMOND, W.K. (1971) *The School Curriculum*, London, Methuen.

SAYLOR, J.G. and ALEXANDER, W.M. (1954) *Curriculum Planning for Better Teaching and Learning*, London, Rinehart.

SIMOSKO, S. (1990) *Accreditation of Prior Learning: A Training Agency Perspective*. Sheffield, The Training Agency.

SIMS, V.M. (1931) 'The objectivity, reliability and validity of an essay examination graded by rating', *Journal of Educational Research*, 24, 216–23.

SMITH, O.B., STANLEY, W.O. and SHORES, J.H. (1957) *Fundamentals of Curriculum Development*, New York, World Book.

STARCH, D. and ELLIOT, E.C. (1912) 'Reliability of the grading of high school work in English', *School Review*, 21, pp. 254–9.

STENHOUSE, L. (1975) *An Introduction to Curriculum Research and Development*, London, Heinemann.

STONES, E. (1966) *An Introduction to Educational Psychology*, London, Methuen.

TABA, H. (1962) *Curriculum Development; Theory and Practice*, New York, Harcourt, Brace and World.

TYLER, R.W. (1949) *Basic Principles of Curriculum and Instruction*, Chicago, University of Chicago Press.

WOOD, R., JOHNSON, C., BLINKHORN, S. and HALL, J. (1988) *Boning, Blanching and Backtacking: Assessing Performance in the Workplace*, St Albans, Psychometric Research and Development Ltd.

YOUNG, M. (1971) (Ed) *Knowledge and Control*, London, Collier Macmillan.

Part Two

The Outcomes Model

Chapter 2

Outcome Based Qualifications and the Implications for Learning

Gilbert Jessup

Introduction

In *Outcomes: NVQs and the Emerging Model of Education and Training* (Jessup, 1991), the proposal was made that the outcomes model of defining qualifications and learning was applicable to all forms of learning. It was argued that if adopted it would open access to learning to far more individuals of all ages, it would lead to more efficient and cost-effective learning. It would further provide a means of relating and aligning academic and vocational education/training.

The announcement by the Government in May 1991 (Department for Education Department of Employment, Welsh Office, 1991) that the NVQ framework was to be extended by the introduction of General National Vocational Qualifications (GNVQs) and the new emphasis placed on achieving parity of esteem between academic and vocational qualifications provided an opportunity to implement the outcomes model in an educational context.

A separate but related initiative, the development of core skills units, defined by outcome statements (Jessup, 1990), has also been taken forward both within GNVQs and other programmes (Oates, 1992). More experience has been gained of expressing degree programmes in the form of outcomes (Otter, 1992), and although assessment has not necessarily followed such outcomes, modularization of degree programmes is rapidly gaining ground.

Since the introduction of National Vocational Qualifications (NVQs) in 1987, with their emphasis on defining outcomes and concentration on assessment, there has been a widespread belief that proponents of this model were not concerned with the process of learning. This is not the case. It is true that the award of an NVQ, quite deliberately, does not specify a particular course or mode of learning. The way in which the outcomes are specified, however, shapes the modes of learning and its content.

The outcome statements in GNVQs are, among other things, a mechanism for encouraging certain forms of learning while not prescribing the learning programme. GNVQ outcomes promote active forms of learning by requiring students to demonstrate a range of cognitive and interpersonal and practical skills, as well as an understanding of the principles which govern them.

The outcomes model is based upon the assumption that learning is a personal and individual experience and that to 'standardize' it by adopting specific modes and time periods is not the most effective means for a group to achieve a set of learning outcomes. Individuals need to manage their own learning experiences in a manner which recognizes where they start from, their preferred styles and modes of learning, and the time and opportunities they have for learning. This is believed to be true for learners of all ages and becomes even more important for mature and adult learners[1], amongst whom individual differences and differences in opportunity are likely to be even greater than amongst the young.

The criteria for National Vocational Qualifications were first published in January 1988 (NCVQ, 1988) although few people in the educational world noticed at the time and those that did thought the new qualifications were only relevant to low level jobs and had no implications for education. At about the same time the National Curriculum was being conceived (TGAT Report, DES, 1988) and although there was no direct contact between the two developments, some common themes were beginning to emerge. It was not, however, until 1990 that the relationship between NVQs and the National Curriculum was articulated (Jessup, 1991).

Although the origins of the two developments were very different, both were seeking to develop methods by which the outcomes of learning could be articulated and serve as the focus for assessment and determining the curriculum/learning provision. The implications for moving towards an outcomes-led curriculum are profound, if followed to their logical conclusion.

This is happening in NVQs and GNVQs, but in the case of the National Curriculum, many compromises have taken place as the new curriculum is being incorporated into a more traditional educational model of classroom practice. In particular the assessment regime has only been partly changed to accommodate the assessment of outcomes in the National Curriculum. Defining the programmes of study as well as the outcomes greatly restricts the flexibility of the curriculum. The different philosophies now sit somewhat uneasily together. This paper will concentrate on NVQs and particularly the new GNVQs, including the core skills initiative which has far-reaching implications for all forms of education and training.[2]

The Post-16 Provision

The central debate in education in the UK today is on the form of the post-16 provision. Post-16 education has been dominated by the influence of 'A' level qualifications and preparation for higher education even though 'A' levels are only considered to be suitable for about a quarter of the 16-year-old cohort of which about one-fifth progress to higher education. By according such status to this minority route the majority of young people have been disadvantaged by comparison. The situation is particularly unhelpful at a time when there is widespread recognition that we need to raise the standards achieved across the whole cohort to prepare young people more effectively for employment in a modern economy.

In line with most industrialized countries, and many emerging economies in the third world, there is a consensus in the UK that we need to increase participation in full-time education within the 16–19 age group. More generally it is felt that all young people in the age group, including those in employment, should pursue some form of education or broad-based training leading to qualifications.

A related Government target is to increase the numbers entering higher education by the end of the century to about a third of the cohort. At the same time there is no expectation that the numbers gaining 'A' level qualifications will increase significantly. The intention is to preserve 'A' levels largely unchanged as the 'gold standard' for 18-year-olds and thus the expansion in higher education will come largely via other routes.

National Vocational Qualifications

A qualification system to meet the future needs of occupational and professional training is being created through National Vocational Qualifications (NVQs). The concept of the NVQ framework is that qualifications will be designed to cover comprehensively all occupations and professions, in fact all occupational functions. NVQs are allocated to one of five levels in the framework with the most basic occupations at level 1 and the senior professions at level 5. Work on the development of NVQs started in 1987 and the framework of qualifications is now largely in place, at levels 1 to 3, while NVQs are available for about half the occupations at level 4. NVQs at level 5 are being developed in some professional areas, and although there is only one NVQ at level 5 (in Management) the numbers are expected to increase gradually throughout the 1990s.

The implications in setting standards and creating qualifications in all areas of employment have probably not been sufficiently appreciated. We now have NVQs, and thus systematic training, in, for example, retail distribution, manufacture and health and social care, covering the functions of shop assistants, care assistants and assembly operatives for the first time. Until recently about half the UK workforce were described as 'unskilled' or 'semi-skilled'; they received no systematic training and certainly no qualifications relevant to the work they performed. Further, the NVQs they now take encompass a far wider range of skills than those of the jobs they have traditionally performed.

This last point needs some explanation in the light of recent criticisms. NVQs, particularly at the lower levels, have been criticized as being too narrow. The problem has arisen when NVQs have been adopted as the basis of a training provision for young people. NVQs have not been designed to provide a learning experience for young people although they can contribute to this objective. NVQs are what they claim to be — a statement of the competence required for an occupation — in some cases a 'narrow' occupation. NCVQ has recommended for some time that programmes for young people should incorporate the development of core skills in addition to NVQs and possibly other studies, if the objective is to provide a broader foundation for future learning and development. It would, however, be inappropriate to build such additional requirements in the NVQs themselves, unless they are requirements of competence in the particular occupational area, as this may debar adults, who were otherwise perfectly competent, from gaining the NVQ. The criteria for the new Modern Apprenticeship programme will include core skills and other broadening studies in addition to an NVQ. By specifying qualifications in terms of outcomes in the forms of separate units, hybrid courses made up of NVQ, GNVQ and core skill units can be created to meet the objectives set for any programme.

Perhaps of even greater significance is the distinctive form of NVQs. NVQs

Figure 2.1: NVQ/GNVQ curriculum model

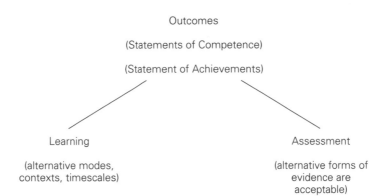

have been deliberately designed to open access to learning for the maximum number of people. This has been achieved by defining the requirement for an award in a 'statement of competence' which is independent of any course or training programme. NVQs thus allow and encourage people to acquire competence through a variety of modes of learning, formal and informal, full-time or part-time and in a variety of locations. It is thus quite legitimate to learn and practise skills in the workplace as well as in schools, colleges and training workshops. In some occupational areas the workplace is the only place where skills can be realistically practised and acquired. Similarly, the knowledge and theory which underpin occupational or professional practice can also be acquired through experience, private study or open learning as well as through more formal programmes.

The assessment criteria for NVQs also promote access to the qualifications by allowing different kinds of evidence to be presented for assessment provided it is relevant to the units being assessed. In particular, NVQs encourage assessment in the workplace in real-life situations where such opportunities exist. The NVQ model is also ideal for the accreditation of prior learning, which is now flourishing. This flexibility in the assessment regime should not be interpreted as a relaxation of standards. The situation is quite the reverse as real demonstrations of competence, in the present or past, are more relevant and valid modes of assessment than simulations and contrived tests.

The curriculum model upon which NVQs and GNVQs are based can be summarized as in figure 2.1 above. The significant features are that learning objectives sought are specified as outcomes independent of learning and assessment processes. This subsequently allows different modes, contexts and timescales of learning to be used to best suit the abilities, preferences and opportunities of the individual learners. Assessment, conceived as the accumulation of the evidence presented, and judged against refined standards, can also take different forms provided they are relevant and valid.

The primary benefits of the outcomes model can thus be summarized as access, flexibility and relevance. A detailed description of the model and the concepts and methodology which underlies the development of NVQs is given in Jessup (1991).

Unit Credits

A further feature which promotes access to NVQs is their unit structure. All NVQs are made up of a number of units, based upon occupational functions, which can be separately assessed and certificated. This provides a considerable degree of flexibility in the way in which NVQs can be built up through credit accumulation over time and in different locations. A national system of credit accumulation and transfer is gradually being established based upon the common currency of units.

The unit structure also provides scope for rationalization within the NVQ framework as many of the same functions are common to many occupations.[3]

Another distinctive feature of NVQs, compared to much of the provision which NVQs are replacing, is that the requirements as presented in the statement of competence are set by employers and employees within industry and not by the educational establishment. This makes NVQs more directly relevant to employment requirements and provides a sense of ownership by employers as well as a benchmark for them as major providers of training. The NVQ framework is the ideal vehicle to promote the mass uptake in training within employment that will be required to meet the highly ambitious National Educational Training Targets that are being supported by all the relevant national agencies and Government (see CBI, 1991).

General NVQs

In May 1991, the White Paper *'Education and Training in the 21st Century'* was published (DES/ED/WO, 1991). In it the Government declared its intention of establishing 'parity of esteem' between academic and vocational education. In particular, the National Council for Vocational Qualifications (NCVQ) was given a remit to extend the NVQ framework to include broad-based vocational qualifications which could be delivered through full-time programmes in schools and colleges. The new qualifications were to be called General National Vocational Qualifications (GNVQs).

The particular target audience for the new qualifications was to be the 16–19 age group although it was envisaged that they would also be relevant to adults and possibly the 14–16 age group (see below). One objective in introducing GNVQs was to encourage a far higher proportion of young people to stay in full-time education beyond the end of compulsory schooling at age 16.

GNVQs will provide a broad-based vocational education. In addition to acquiring the basic skills and an understanding of the underpinning principles in a vocational area, all students awarded a GNVQ will have achieved a range of core skills. The combination of vocational attainment plus core skills will provide a foundation from which students can progress either to further and higher education or into employment and training via NVQs. GNVQs have been designed to link the academic and vocational systems. The standards set are appropriately demanding, and may in no way be construed as a 'soft option'.[4] In particular, the Advanced GNVQ is aligned to GCE 'A' levels as well as NVQs at level 3.

It is the Government's intention that GNVQs, together with NVQs, will replace other vocational qualifications and become the mainstream national provision for vocational education and training. GNVQs and NVQs will provide a progressive framework for vocational education and training similar to, and aligned with, the framework for academic qualifications of GCSEs, 'A' levels, and first and higher degrees.

GNVQs were initially introduced at Intermediate and Advanced level (levels 2 and 3 of the NVQ framework) in five broad vocational areas in September 1993, following piloting in the previous academic year. The first Foundation GNVQs (NVQ level 1) will be introduced in September 1994, again following piloting in the previous year. GNVQs in new vocational areas are being phased in over a period of three years (NCVQ, 1993).

The Advanced GNVQ has been designed to provide access to higher education as well as a foundation for further training and employment.[5] They have been specifically designed to meet a standard comparable to that of 'A' and 'AS' level qualifications. This has been achieved by making each vocational unit comparable in its demands and coverage to one-sixth of an 'A' level qualification or one-third of an 'AS' qualification. This provides a means of comparing achievements in the two systems and offers the potential for credit transfer between GNVQs and modular 'A/AS' qualifications, particularly in programmes which are arranged on the basis of six modules per 'A' level or three per 'AS' qualification.

The Schools Examination and Assessment Council (SEAC) subsequently set criteria for modular 'A' levels which are likely to promote this form of modularization.

Advanced GNVQs are awarded on the achievement of twelve vocational units, the equivalent of two 'A' levels, plus three core skill units in Communication, Application of Number and Information Technology at level 3 (see below for description of core skill units). The twelve GNVQ vocational units consist of eight mandatory units, plus four optional units chosen from a given list. The mandatory units cover the fundamental skills, principles and processes that are common to a wide range of related occupations. The optional units both extend the scope of the mandatory units and cover more specialized applications.

Students may be encouraged to gain units beyond the twelve vocational units, to add to and broaden their range of achievement. Some students may wish to gain units in foreign language competences. Others may need to cover certain additional units in mathematics to gain entry to degree programmes in science or engineering. It is intended that the GNVQ provision will be built up to meet such needs through the creation of additional units. It may also be appropriate for students to take some NVQ units to add to their overall achievement. The flexibility provided by additional units is proving to be a particularly attractive feature of the GNVQ provision in those schools and colleges where they are being introduced. It will be possible for students, if they wish, to combine an Advanced GNVQ with one 'A' level or one or more 'AS' qualifications although the GNVQ provision alone will provide a complete and varied curriculum.

The Intermediate GNVQ (aligned with NVQ level 2 and four to five GCSEs, grades A-C) follows a similar form but is awarded on the basis of six vocational units (four mandatory and two chosen from a list of options) plus three core skills units (Communication, Application of Number and Information Technology) at level 2.

The Foundation GNVQ (aligned with NVQ level 1 and four GCSEs, grades D-F) is also awarded on the achievement of six vocational units (three mandatory and three chosen from a list of options) plus three core skills units (Communication,

Application of Number and Information Technology) at level 1. The Foundation differs in allowing the options to be chosen from different vocational areas, thus providing students with an opportunity to sample different occupational activities.

A target has been set that 25 per cent of the 16-year-old cohort (about 150,000) will be taking GNVQs by 1996. As the uptake in the first year (1993) when only a limited range of GNVQs were available was 82,000, this target should be met comfortably. It has been estimated that by the end of the century as many as half of all 16-year-olds will take GNVQs. The three levels of GNVQ — Foundation, Intermediate and Advanced — together provide suitable courses for about 90 per cent of the cohort.

At the time of going to press, proposals are being formulated for packages of units taken from the Intermediate and Foundation GNVQs to provide a suitable vocational 'pathway' at Key Stage 4 (14–16-year-olds) of the National Curriculum. This follows the National Curriculum review by Sir Ron Dearing.

Establishing access to higher education is crucial to the success of GNVQs. To facilitate this NCVQ is working closely with the Standing Conference on University Entrance (SCUE), BTEC, City & Guilds and RSA to ensure that admissions tutors are fully acquainted with GNVQs.[6] A programme of conferences has already started and will continue to prepare the ground for the first GNVQ-based applications to universities in 1994. In addition NCVQ is in the process of setting up forms of 'compacts' between the schools and colleges offering GNVQs and universities and polytechnics, to ensure that all students who gain an Advanced GNVQ and wish to go on to higher education are interviewed by universities. In so doing NCVQ hopes to ensure that their applications are all seriously considered.

National Record of Achievement

Also relevant to the post-16 strategy is the future development of the National Record of Achievement (NRA). The NRA was introduced early in 1991 by the Secretary of State for Employment as an extension of the Technical and Vocational Educational Initiative (TVEI) for which the Employment Department is responsible. The NRA was made freely available in the first year to all who wished to use it but was targeted mainly at the 16-year-old cohort. In April 1992, NCVQ took over the distribution of the NRA and its future development.

NCVQ is funded to make the NRA available free of charge to school students, in quantities based upon the numbers in their last year pre-16, although we would hope to encourage its adoption from the age of 14 or earlier. It will also be available free of charge to all trainees entering the Youth Training and Employment Training programmes and promoted for sale to other target groups in further and higher education and employment. The plan is to encourage its adoption as the universally recognized record of achievement spanning different forms of education and training.

Within the NRA system the concepts of individual action planning and the continuous recording of achievement will be promoted as well as the curriculum models that these processes assume. The NRA will encourage recording of evidence and achievements within formal qualification systems such as the National Curriculum and NVQs as well as the less formal achievements which have tended to be associated with records of achievements in schools. There is no intention that the various approaches to recording which have been enthusiastically and successfully developed in schools through the 1980s should be discontinued. There is no need for standardization when the primary function of such recording is formative. But when students wish to summarize their achievements for employers or others outside their institution, the adoption of widely accepted conventions is desirable in order to communicate in an intelligible format.

An expanded use of the Record of Achievement was recently advocated by the Royal Society in its report *Higher Education Futures* (1993). It recommended that it should be used in undergraduate courses:

> Innovation in both teaching and assessment will lead to opportunities to change the method of recording a student's achievement. As higher education offers greater variety of course and patterns of study, employers will need more information on the content of study programmes that students have completed, and the range of skills and abilities attained by the student. Current arrangements will do little to satisfy these needs, and a wider range of evidence of achievement must be produced. It will no longer be adequate to record achievement as a single classification, as in the degree system. (3.10, p. 30)

The Report continues, later:

> Adopting The National Records of Achievement system would clearly be in line with certification practices in other sectors of the education system and in many countries. All school-leavers are already issued with a National Record of Achievement. (3.10, p. 30)

In its formal list of recommendations, it concludes:

> Records of Achievement should replace the honours classification system and allow students and their future employers to be more aware of an individual's skills and knowledge. (3.14 Key Points, p. 35)

This recommendation is echoed in the CBI report *Thinking Ahead* (1994):

> The system of classifying degrees needs to be revised so that it strengthens quality. (. . .) Degree courses should ensure individuals take control of their learning, and develop their core skills. A final grade cannot capture this development adequately. It needs to be complemented by a record of achievement and an individual action plan. (Chapter 3, ¶ 70, p. 20)

These developments may be seen to arise logically, and in a sense, naturally, from the principles and assumptions underlying the concept of 'record-of-achievement'. We may recall that the CBI first mooted the idea of an integrated, lifelong, single record of achievement in its seminal and influential report *Towards a Skills Revolution*, published in 1989.[7]

The development and recording of core skills, which has always had an important role in the record of achievement movement, will become more systematic and rigorous with the adoption of the new core skill units.

The NRA has an important role to play, and a symbolic significance, in bringing together achievements at different ages and across different forms of education and training provision.

This chapter proceeds by concentrating on two related concerns: (i) the characteristics of GNVQs and (ii) core skills; it concludes with the presentation of a coherent framework, which draws together all the disparate concerns treated earlier.

Characteristics of GNVQs

GNVQs provide an example of the outcomes model being delivered in an educational context. If the model realizes the aims which have been set for it, and the early feedback suggests that it will do so (cf Harrop, chapter 6 in this volume), it provides a potential model for all education.

As the take-up of GNVQs increases and their use in schools alongside GCSEs and 'A' levels extends, questions are being raised as to how and why GNVQs are different from GCSEs and 'A' levels, particularly in the way in which they are assessed. Yet it is these very distinctions between the qualification systems which make GNVQs popular with both students and teachers, and has extended effective learning to many who have not in the past successfully progressed via traditional routes. It is important that we understand which aspects of GNVQs are fundamental to the curriculum model on which they are based, contribute to their success, and need to be maintained. Other features can be developed, changed or refined over time in response to the needs of students and teachers, and those with whom the credibility of the qualifications need to be established.

GNVQs have been introduced as an alternative to 'A' levels and GCSEs. The differences between the 'academic' pathway and the new vocational pathway, based upon GNVQs, lie in the curriculum models upon which they are based.

Occupational Base

The differences stem partly from the distinction between the subject base of academic qualifications (for example, English, history) and the occupational or employment base of GNVQs (for example, business, manufacturing). However, in areas such as science, art and design and information technology, this distinction cannot be necessarily detected from the title alone. Nevertheless, the orientation of the subject in GNVQs towards practical applications and employment (for example, what scientists do) makes the approach to learning different from that of traditional qualifications.

Generic Skills

More fundamentally, the differences between GNVQs and 'A' levels/GCSEs lie in the priority accorded to both generic and vocational skills, and the kind of knowledge and understanding within the two sets of qualifications. This is most clearly reflected in the differences in the assessment regime. Assessment is at the heart of any qualification; it defines success and failure and sets the goal for students and teachers.

GNVQs have been designed to promote the development of a range of cognitive skills and a body of knowledge and understanding, and some practical skills, in a broad vocational area. The priority given to cognitive skills is signalled in three ways: (i) the core skills of communications, application of number and information technology are mandatory requirements of all GNVQs, and personal skills are promoted as additional units; (ii) the grading criteria place priority on planning, information seeking and handling, and evaluation; (iii) research and investigation themes are embodied in the vocational units. The need to demonstrate these skills for the purposes of assessment promotes active learning through projects, assignments, research and investigative activities. There is also a need to supplement such activity through classroom study and the use of text books or open learning materials to cover the breadth of knowledge dictated by range.

Student Responsibility for Learning

A further important aspect of the GNVQ curriculum, which is a natural consequence of the above approach to learning, is that students take greater responsibility for their own learning.[8] This feature, valued by higher education and employers, allows the use of flexible and efficient learning modes, and makes effective use of teacher time and physical resources. Student responsibility for learning is supported by a period of induction during which they become familiar with the course requirements, action planning, recording and reviewing achievement on a continuous basis.

This approach to learning may be contrasted with traditional approaches. While it is true that in recent years, some of the features described above have been incorporated into academic programmes, such as project and assignments and coursework assessment, in general a much narrower focus on learning has been adopted. Most learning is accomplished through reading and classroom teaching frequently of a didactic nature. There is an emphasis on learning *about* rather than learning *how to*. Often, the most prized skills are developed in assimilating information from the written word and essay writing. Whilst some students may be able to use this learning creatively, all too often the emphasis is on memorizing 'facts' which must be recalled. This further spawns a host of 'examination skills' such as 'question spotting', cramming, learning what may be skipped or left out of revision and other techniques which may well be of value in passing the examination but which have very limited value there afterwards.[9]

Unit Certification

A distinctive characteristic of GNVQs is that they are unit-based qualifications. Every GNVQ, like NVQs, is made up of a number of units, each of which can be separately assessed and certificated. This allows credit accumulation throughout a course, and credit transfer between qualifications with all the attendant advantages. To maintain this fundamental characteristic of GNVQs, assessment is based on the unit rather than the full qualification. Although this tends to lead to modular delivery, this is by no means universal practice. Units can be, and in many current courses are being, integrated in various ways in larger activities extending over several months. This is a perfectly legitimate means of delivering GNVQs. The crucial point to note is that GNVQ (or NVQ) units are **units of assessment**, not units of instruction. The 'content and processes' which are assessed by elements and units to build towards a final qualification may be learnt in any effective way, with as many assessments as necessary; the corollary is, of course, that many different elements may be assessed in a single assessment event. Units may well be achieved in groups rather than singly.

A Basis in Successful Educational Practices

The approaches to learning within the GNVQ curriculum are not new. They have all been well tried and much evidence of their success has been accumulated, particularly over the last decade, from for example, TVEI, BTEC courses, SCOTVEC's experience of the National Certificate and from CPVE, as well as many other initiatives. GNVQs differ in trying to promote a range of good educational practices through the outcomes set and the methods of assessment, rather than from prescriptive courses. Courses are deliberately not prescribed because GNVQs also recognize the need for flexibility to allow schools and colleges to make best use of their local circumstances.

Schools and colleges vary considerably in the nature of their local economy, their contacts and access to companies, their resources, class size, scope for offering joint programmes with other qualifications, and so on.

Establishing National Standards

GNVQs also differ from the previous initiatives described in establishing national standards through the specification of outcomes, partly through approaches derived from NVQs. At the same time many of the quality assurance practices more closely associated with 'A' levels and GCSEs, are being built into GNVQs to ensure rigorous standards are maintained. These practices include publishing examples of students' work to convey standards, agreement trials amongst assessors and scrutiny exercises across subjects and awarding bodies.

Alignment With Other Qualifications

In addition, GNVQs differ in making a very conscious attempt to align standards, wherever possible, against four points of reference: (a) academic standards of 'A' levels and GCSE, at the appropriate levels; (b) NVQ standards in the appropriate areas; (c) the National Curriculum upon which GNVQs build, and; (d) at Advanced level, the requirements for entry to higher education. This process of alignment within an emerging national framework of qualifications is unprecedented in educational history. Such alignments will take time to establish and it is important that GNVQs have a sound curriculum/assessment model otherwise they will lose coherence as they are pulled in one direction or another.

To ensure that students develop the skills, knowledge and understanding outlined above, all these outcomes must be built into the GNVQ assessment regime.

At the same time, assessment must, of course, be technically sound and valid. The credibility of these distinctive approaches to assessment must be established in the minds of a public long nurtured on more traditional examinations.

Comprehensive Assessment

One characteristic of GNVQ assessment, which distinguishes it from assessment in most academic qualifications, is that it covers the curriculum outcomes far more comprehensively. *All* the outcomes, reflected in the units, must be achieved. Students do not, for example, have a choice of questions or sections of the syllabus selected for assessment as in traditional examinations.[10]

There are two components to GNVQ assessment, both of which have to be passed. Doing well in one component cannot compensate for a poor result in the other. The primary component is the continuous internal assessment which runs throughout a GNVQ. The criteria set by each unit must be met. Priority is given to internal assessment because it is the only practical way in which the breadth of cognitive and vocational skills which are built into the curriculum outcomes can be assessed. It is obvious that oral communication skills and teamwork cannot be assessed by traditional methods. But nor can planning, information seeking, information technology applications and a variety of other skills that are built into GNVQs.

Apart from the limitation of the modes of testing and examination traditionally used, time places further constraints on what can be assessed. The advantage of continuous assessment throughout a course means that evidence can be accumulated over weeks or months towards the achievement of an outcome. In the case of core skills and grading criteria, practice and evidence can, if required, build up over a year or two years, depending on the length of a course. Students can demonstrate a range of outcomes, integrated within substantial assignments. Such activities come closer to the requirements of performance in the real world and employment than a series of forty-five minute essays.

Internal assessment

The advantages of such internal assessment methods do not need to be laboured. However, to establish their credibility, various checks need to be put in place.

Conveying Standards

In the context of GNVQs, the starting point is having clear specifications of the outcomes sought, i.e., what must be assessed and to what standards. These are set out in units in some degree of detail but we must recognize that these specifications are not sufficient. Guidance and interpretation are being added on to points which are not entirely clear. This is being further supported by publishing examples of students' work that have been assessed and verified as having been correctly assessed. These are contained in the series *Assessing Students' Work*, published by NCVQ, and are an important means of conveying the standards, including those required for core skills and grading. Other guidance on core skills and grading is also available and more will accumulate as experience grows. Additional reference points for the coverage and standards of GNVQs are contained in text books and other learning materials which are rapidly coming on the market. Text books provide a primary means of conveying content and expected standards for 'A' levels and degrees. Over time, certain texts are regarded as standard works on a subject. NCVQ is working with publishers to speed up the process for GNVQs.

Establishing Quality Assurance Systems

In addition to conveying the standards for assessment, a series of measures has been introduced to ensure they are applied: (a) assessors must be trained — or, more precisely-must demonstrate that they are competent to carry out such assessments which normally requires training.

Standards for such assessment have been set and assessors are expected (it will shortly become a requirement for all assessors) to be certified to those standards; (b) there are internal checks on the assessment practice by an internal verifier, appointed in each school and college; (c) the quality of assessment must be confirmed by an external verifier who visits centres to check on the assessment practice. The award of units, GNVQs and grades is conditional upon the confirmation of the external verifier. External and internal verifiers also need to be trained to ensure they can carry out their functions. Effort is being put into the centralized training for external verifiers from all three GNVQ awarding bodies (BTEC, City & Guilds and RSA Examinations Board) to achieve a consensus on common standards.

Portfolio of Evidence

In order to facilitate assessment and verification, students keep their work — reports accounts, computer print-outs, designs and so on — in what is described as a 'portfolio of evidence'. Although certain skills which need to be observed (for example, oral communication, interaction within groups) cannot be directly stored in a portfolio, a record of such observations should be, and sometimes audio and video tapes are included. This allows assessors to inspect the work, and internal and external verifiers to sample and check the quality of assessments made. It allows others to examine the quality of the work of students, such as school/college inspectors and will assist verifiers or evaluators carrying out scrutiny exercises. Future employers and university admission tutors can, if they wish and have the time, also inspect the quality of a student's work directly, or extracts can be presented by students. Such practices are, of course, well established in art and design. Students must take responsibility for organizing and maintaining their portfolios, which is an aspect of managing their own learning.

The processes described above are operating now, but, given the rapid introduction of GNVQs, they are not fully developed in all respects. As the qualifications are new, both in form and content, it is taking a little more time for teachers and tutors to become fully conversant with them. Because of the rapid take-up and expansion of GNVQs, there is a need to train many new assessors and verifiers. However, considerable effort is being put into establishing the assessment and verification system by schools and colleges, the awarding bodies and NCVQ.

External tests

The second component of assessment is the external tests which are required for each mandatory unit. These tests cover the knowledge and understanding — the concepts, definitions, relationships — which are inferred from the **range** statements linked to each unit. Each unit tested has a test specification which sets out the coverage of knowledge and understanding and the marks allocated to each category. These are available to schools and colleges to clarify what needs to be covered in the courses along with example test items and, of course, past test papers are beginning to accumulate to clarify further what might be expected. The external tests have a pass mark of 70 per cent, which provides a pragmatic interpretation of mastery learning. Tests are set at frequent intervals throughout the year so that schools and colleges can plan courses in a sequence and pace that suits their circumstances, students can take them when they are ready to do so and can retake them if necessary. Because of the high pass mark, and because the tests are of achievement rather than potential, students may retake the tests if they do not pass the first time and no penalty is attached to initial failure.

GNVQ Tests Cannot be Compared with Academic Examinations

Because of the public visibility of the external tests, there is a danger that these will be interpreted as the standard required for GNVQ and compared with GCE 'A' level or GCSE examinations. This would be a mistake. GNVQ external tests serve a very different function from academic examinations. The external tests only attempt to assess one set of the outcomes of GNVQs, and not the most important. The tests check systematic coverage of knowledge over a prescribed area and thus the pass mark is 70 per cent.

To judge the standards required for the award of a GNVQ, it is suggested that one should look at the total volume of work that must be produced by a student to gain an award, including that for merit and distinction grades. The most substantial work will be found in a student's portfolio of evidence, which will contain accounts of projects, how they were planned and evaluated, and much else. The written reports provide perhaps the best basis for comparison with essays and other evidence produced by students for the award, and the grading of 'A' levels. However, such comparisons are difficult, given the different contexts in which the work is produced, and the total amount of evidence necessarily produced for both qualifications must be considered.

Student differentiation — grading

A final distinction between academic qualifications and GNVQs lies in the use of grading. One of the primary functions of assessment at 'A' level and, in particular, GCSE, is to differentiate between students in order to allocate grades. Almost every student who takes a GCSE examination passes. Thus the role of examinations is to determine the award of grades A to G. Examinations are designed accordingly.

This is a quintessential difference in approach from the approach underlying vocational qualifications such as GNVQs and NVQs. It marks a difference in purpose and this purpose has direct consequences for the curriculum.

The purpose of most academic assessments is to differentiate high achievers from the rest of the students for the purposes of selection. GCE 'O' levels, and to a large extent GCSE today, were designed to select those considered capable of benefiting from further study, primarily 'A' levels. 'A' levels are designed to select those considered capable of benefiting from higher education. Because these are the established bench marks, employers also use them to select students. These objectives are not in themselves unworthy, but the implications of designing assessment systems, and thus the consequent courses of study to realise them are profound. The result is that qualifications focus too much on measuring potential rather than achievement and that a large proportion of students, often the majority, are classified as failures.

In marked contrast, vocational qualifications, such as GNVQs or NVQs, aim to attest the actual achievements of all who meet the standards required. Because these standards are vigorously assessed, those who achieve them at the required level demonstrate their potential and capability to benefit from further study or employment where such attainment (or in the case of NVQs, competence) is necessary. This approach is associated with criterion referencing rather than norm-referencing.

In fact, to meet the needs of selectors, GNVQs have introduced a system of differentiation through the application of 'second order' grading criteria, which involves continuously reviewing a student's work against further specified criteria.

Some of the assessment characteristics of GNVQs may be reiterated. The assessment is made to a defined standard, spelt out in the unit specification, particularly the performance criteria. Assessment is not designed to differentiate between students at a point in time, but as a continuous process by which students build up evidence until they have sufficient quantity and quality to meet the required standards. The criteria set for this 'pass' grade are considered to be demanding and to represent a worthwhile level of achievement. It is also assumed that, given time and opportunity, all students accepted on a course can reach the standard and gain the award. Assessment for grades of merit and distinction in GNVQs is made against additional criteria which recognize achievement beyond the criteria set by the units. This characteristic of GNVQs, assessing against a predetermined standard, is fundamental to the GNVQ curriculum model. To place a greater emphasis on grading, while having its attraction to those who wish to use GNVQs to differentiate between students, would lead to redesigning the assessment system with consequent changes in the curriculum priorities. These issues are complex and not well understood.

Core Skills

Another significant new feature in post-16 education is the introduction of units which promote the development of core skills and their assessment and certification.

The origins of the current programme lie in the proposals of Kenneth Baker when Secretary of State for Education and Science (DES, 1989) which were followed up by John McGregor who succeeded him, that a common set of core skills should be developed in all post-16 education and training programmes both because of their inherent value for progression into employment or higher education and as a means of aligning the different forms of provision. Also highly influential was the report of the Confederation of British Industries 'Towards a Skills Revolution' (CBI, 1989), which included similar recommendations.

In education and training, core skills are naturally developed and used. But because they are embedded in an occupation or subject they will tend not to be identified as core skills and their potential for transfer and application to other contexts may be lost or limited. There is much evidence to suggest this is so. If however the core skills are recognised as such by learners their potential ability to use the skills elsewhere is increased. This implies that students would benefit from the opportunity to analyze and label the core skills they are acquiring (cf Burke, 1991, p. 43).

The treatment of core skills within the current initiative goes considerably further than identification. The requirements set in the core skill units are such that the development of the skills is enhanced. The range over which demonstrations are required, or their applications can be inferred, will often stretch learners by requiring application beyond that which would necessarily be required in the immediate pursuit of their occupation or subject.

The initial work following a ministerial remit was carried out by the National Curriculum Council (NCC) and NCVQ, and published in separate but complementary reports in April 1990 (NCC, 1990; and Jessup, 1990). The six core skills identified were:

Problem solving
Communication
Numeracy (now described by NCVQ as 'Application of Number')
Personal skills
Information technology
Competence in modern foreign languages

These were taken forward in the next stage in a joint initiative by NCVQ, SEAC, NCC and FEU in which a four-level framework of core skill definition was agreed. (The framework was subsequently extended to five levels to relate to the NVQ/GNVQ framework.) Building upon this work, NCVQ has formulated the core skill statements as units like other units in the NVQ/GNVQ system.

The units have been subjected to intensive consultation and piloting in a variety of programmes over the last two years (Oates, 1992).

The distinctive features of this development that distinguish it from many initiatives in the 1980s and earlier are that the core skills have been:

- expressed in a manner that makes possible their assessment and certification;
- expressed at five levels, loosely related to the five levels of the NVQ framework, to facilitate and recognize progression in core skill achievement;
- specified to align with the National Curriculum, 'A' levels, NVQs and GNVQs, as far as this is possible;
- expressed independently of any qualification and form of education and training provision but can be built into any academic or vocational programme or qualification.

The core skill units in communication, application of number and information technology were introduced in September 1992 in GNVQs. The foreign language units were introduced at the same time as additional units. The units in personal skills (working with others, improving own learning and performance) were piloted and further refined prior to their introduction as additional units in September 1993. Considerable experience has accumulated in the delivery of the problem solving units and these are now expected to be made nationally available in September 1994 to complete the set as originally conceived by NCC and NCVQ. Development work continues with all the core skills to provide further guidance on assessment and their effective use in different contexts.

The core skill units are also being built into the 14 to 16 curriculum in many schools, into 'A' level courses in a few sixth forms and in the foundation pro-grammes of the Open University. The five-level framework makes the core skills relevant to a very wide range of education provision from lower grades of GCSE to university degrees and professional qualifications.

Coherent Framework

It will be apparent from the above post-16 initiatives that the Government's strat-egy is to enhance the status of vocational education and training in the UK. The implications of this move are profound, not only in preparing young people more effectively for employment — a matter of major concern in the UK currently — but also in its effect on the education system as a whole.

The introduction of GNVQs will have major implications for post-16 edu-cation. GNVQs are seen as the primary route to encourage mass participation in full-time education from 16–19 if 'A'/'AS' levels are to remain relatively un-changed and the preserve of the academic minority. Nevertheless, if GNVQs do become established over the next few years within the post-16 curriculum and the potential benefits of the outcome-unit-based provision are realized, it is difficult to imagine that 'A' levels will remain unchanged in the latter part of the century. GNVQs offer an evolutionary way forward, in which the 'A' level standard can be maintained while a parallel form of provision is tried and established.

Not only are the barriers between academic and vocational qualifications likely to be gradually eroded, but also the artificial barriers which divide pre-16 education, post-16 education and training and higher education. NVQs do not recognize such distinctions, nor will GNVQs after their initial introduction. Their adoption as the vocational pathway from age 14 is imminent. GNVQs at level 4 and above are also on the agenda and can be anticipated within the next few years. The movement towards outcome-based qualifications leads inevitably away from tightly defined institution-based provision, thus opening access to learning to a far larger proportion of the population.[11]

The intention behind the recent initiatives is that the UK should move to-wards a coherent national framework of qualifications embracing all forms of education and training achievement as indicated in figure 2.2. It should be noted that a version of this figure appeared in the recent Government White Paper (DES/ED/WO, 1991).

There are, however, limitations to the coherence that can be achieved given the different curriculum structures and assessment regimes which currently exist in the UK system. We shall not be able to achieve a fully integrated system until all forms of learning provision are formulated in a similar manner, namely through

Figure 2.2: National qualification framework

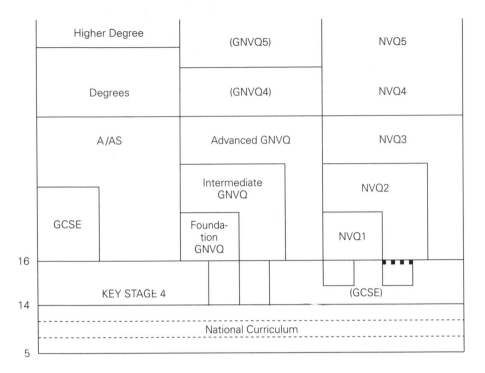

the specification of outcomes. Not only would this provide a coherent system and raise the status of vocational education and training, but many other benefits would accrue.

Such a move would greatly improve access and flexibility to learning programmes. It would expand the range of learning opportunities available and provide scope for individually tailored provision to suit the needs and circumstances of different people. It would result in a more cost-effective system of education and training, focused upon the real objectives that individuals and society seek. Perhaps most importantly, it would encourage people to take responsibility for their own learning, both initially and on a continuing basis throughout their career.

Notes

1   The Enterprise in Higher Education (EHE) initiative has brought about significant changes in the way undergraduate courses are taught. At the University of Sussex, for example, a recent report noted:

> There has been a sense that the programme needs to shift its focus from inputs to outcomes and learning methods adjusted accordingly. (. . .) This was also a response to student feedback where there have been complaints about more traditional methods, feelings that teaching is not

always sufficiently practice relevant, is patronising to mature students and not clearly connected to assessment. (Locke 1993, p. 4)

A further important point, raised in Jessup and Jessup (1975), may be noted in connection with the way many adults naturally tend to expand the boundaries of their autonomy in the workplace, effecting their performance and their enactment of the learning process subsumed in what we normally call 'experience'. Further, the structural demands of work are constantly changing, placing a premium on the ability to respond to changing need:

> It is not only people in senior positions that can shape their job to suit themselves. Most workers do this to some extent and it is entirely reasonable that they should. Effective managers are those who facilitate this process and adapt their organization to meet the needs of their staff and who develop and utilize the skills of their staff to best advantage. (. . .)

> The other reason why jobs might be perceived in this way is that technology is changing so fast that the skills required by employees are likely to change, perhaps several times, during the course of a working life. With the advent of automation certain skills become redundant while the need for new skills is often created.

> If the trends described continue and all the indications suggest they will, jobs in the future will be less structured and individual employees will be required to adapt and learn new skills at various times during their working life. (pp. 128–9)

2 Cf National Commission on Education (1993), pp. 239 ff.
3 It is important to appreciate that the unit structure relates to *Units of Assessment*, **not** Units of Instruction, I return to this point later in the discussion of Unit Certification.
4 Solomon (1994), writing on a GNVQ Evaluation carried out by the Oxford University Department of Educational Studies in *PSSI Forum* offers a robust and informed view of GNVQ Science:

> We couldn't say either that GNVQ science is a doddle, as some of the more enthusiastic authors in the last issue of PSSI seem to suggest, or that it is impossibly hard or pointless, as the notorious and ill-informed TV programme by Alan Smithers asserted. However, it is undoubtedly a new approach to post-16 science education and, in our judgement, a good one. It has different objectives to previous courses and is located in a completely new world order. (p. 4)

The paper concludes:

> And finally a word of warning to one and all — the assignment plays such a key role in GNVQ that the students' commitment to completing their work to high standards and set deadlines, together with the staff's speed of returning work and the thoroughness of marking, becomes the key feature in its success or failure. New institutions take note! The course is enjoyable, can teach valuable leaning skills, will provide new routes to HE, but does require hard work from tutors and students alike. (p. 5)

5   Edwards (1994), of the School of Education at the University of Leeds, focuses
    on the distinctive contribution that GNVQs are designed to make:

> GNVQ has the potential to produce students that are highly motivated,
> with initiative, drive and enthusiasm, as do many A-level programmes.
> However, the approach of GNVQ harnesses this motivation and enthu-
> siasm by developing the abilities to manage their own learning, under-
> stand learning goals and plan courses of action to achieve them, to engage
> in self-assessment and to assess the quality of their achievements; it pro-
> motes independence when learning and the skills of self-presentation and
> of evidencing claims of achievement. In addition, its vocational focus is
> likely to enable students to form clearer, more realistic expectations for
> their careers, be these educational or employment, and therefore, gain
> sense of purpose in applying for, and pursuing, a particular HE course.

He continues:

> Many of these qualities are assessed in the grading criteria, the manda-
> tory core skills and the core skills assessed as additional units and there-
> fore GNVQ (and only GNVQ) is a qualification that gives clear measures
> of these aspects that are so important to success on HE courses. (p. 9,
> emphasis added)

6   The Royal Society report *Higher Education Futures* (1993) comments:

> The challenge for higher education admissions staff lies in the sheer volume
> of the (unfamiliar) evidence presented by GNVQ students, and its dif-
> ferences from the relatively familiar and established A-level. The task is
> compounded by an increase in total entry numbers against a backdrop of
> diminished resources for selection.
>
> Handling such a volume of information, in an unfamiliar language, re-
> quires cooperative action by higher education and Awarding Bodies to-
> gether. The task cannot be addressed satisfactorily by individual
> admissions staff. It will, for example, increasingly be necessary for whole
> disciplines to identify the requirements for entry to their courses, and to
> analyse the GNVQ (and probably A-level) to see where the confirming
> evidence may be found. A similar central exercise may also be necessary
> to approach the matter of the up-to-six additional units in the GNVQ
> from more GNVQ/NVQ units, or from A or AS-levels. (p. 62)

7   In its report, *Towards a Skills Revolution*, the CBI highlighted the following para-
    graph:

> One national system of Records of Achievement and action plans should
> be used both in schools and employment, pre-16 and post-16. This
> would require a coming together of school records with the National
> Record of Vocational Achievement and the embracing of records and
> action plans within one profile. All young people would then be treated
> equally, irrespective of the route of their learning and the profile would
> emphasise that structured learning should take place throughout the 14–
> 18 age range and beyond. (¶39, p. 22)

After a suitable, ruminative period of digestion, some five years later the extension to university courses follows logically and consistently.

8 Cf Hirst (1971) and Illich (1971) discussed in Jessup (1991) p. 145 on the relationship between the concept of teaching and the concept of learning. See also Peters (1967):

> Whereas 'learning' could be characterized without introducing the notion of teaching, 'teaching' could not be characterized without the notion of learning. (. . .) The teacher's success (. . .) can only be defined in terms of that of the learner. *This presumably is the logical truth dormant in the saying that all education is self education.* (p. 3, emphasis added)

Patrick White (1966), a novelist, captures this truth in *The Solid Mandala*, chapter 2:

> 'I dunno', Arthur said. 'I forget what I was taught. I only remember what I've learnt.'

9 See Ingenkamp (1977) and Stones (1966) and Burke (Chapter 3 in this volume). A fuller treatment is provided in Jessup (1991) pp. 46–59 and pp. 152–3.
10 There are also external tests which are discussed later under External Tests.
11 See Cook (1994) for a recent study of GNVQs for adults. The research found that GNVQs can be designed to attract adult uptake, but that this involves significant changes for college organizational structures. Foundation level GNVQs, it is suggested, are likely to be taken up as an entry route to FE, but there are structural barriers at present for progression to HE, where current Access courses provide an easier route for entry. It is hoped that these issues will be resolved in the near to medium future; to this end, NCVQ has recently initiated research in this area.

References

BURKE, J. (1991) 'Competence and higher education: implications for institutions and professional bodies' in RAGGATT, P. and UNWIN, L. (Eds) *Change and Intervention: Vocational Education and Training*, London, Falmer Press.

CBI (1989) *Towards a Skills Revolution*, London, Confederation of British Industries.

CBI (1991) *World Class Targets*, London, Confederation of British Industries.

CBI (1994) *Thinking Ahead*, London, The Confederation of British Industries.

COOK, A. (1994) *GNVQs as a Route for Adult Progression*, a Report for the Employment Department submitted by Transcend Technology Limited in association with Cambridge Training and Development, Rugby, Transcend Technology.

DES (1989a) *Further Education, A New Strategy*, speech by Kenneth Baker, London, Department of Education and Science.

DES (1988b) *National Curriculum Task Group on Assessment and Training: A Report.* Chairman: P. Black; subsequently known as *The Black Report*, London, Department of Education and Science.

DES/ED/WO (1991) *Education and Training for the 21st Century*, Volume 1, London, HMSO.

DEARING, R. (1993) *The National Curriculum and Its Assessment*, Final Report, London, SCAA.

EDWARDS, C. (1994) 'GNVQ science and progression to higher education' in *PSSI Forum* No 13.

HARROP, J. (1992) *Response to the Consultation on General National Vocational Qualifications*, Report No 15, London, NCVQ.

HIRST, P.H. (1971) 'What is teaching?' *Journal of Curriculum Studies*, 3.

ILLICH, I.D. (1971) *Deschooling Society*, New York, Harper and Row.

INGENKAMP, K. (1977), *Educational Assessment*, Slough, National Foundation for Educational Research.

JESSUP, G. (1990a) *Common Learning Outcomes: Core Skills in A/AS Levels and NVQs*, Report No 6, London, NCVQ.

JESSUP, G. (1990b) *Accreditation of Prior Learning in the Context of National Vocational Qualifications*, Report No 7, London, NCVQ.

JESSUP, G. (1991) *Outcomes: NVQs and the Emerging Model of Education and Training*, London, Falmer Press.

JESSUP, G. and JESSUP, H. (1975) *Selection and Assessment at Work*, London, Methuen.

LOCKE, W. (1993) *Social Policy and Social Work Subject Group Interim Report 1992–93*, Enterprise in Higher Education Project, University of Sussex.

NATIONAL COMMISSION ON EDUCATION (1993) *Learning to Succeed: A Radical Look at Education Today and a Strategy for the Future*, London, Heinemann.

NCVQ (1988) *The Criteria for National Vocational Qualifications*, London, National Council for Vocational Qualifications.

NCVQ (1990) *GNVQ Information Note*, London, National Council for Vocational Qualifications.

NCC (1990) *Core Skills 16–19*, York, National Curriculum Council.

NIACE (1994) *An Adult Higher Education: A Vision*, A policy discussion paper, Leicester, National Institute of Adult Continuing Education.

OATES, T. (1991) *Developing and Piloting the NCVQ Core Skills Units*, Report No 16, London, National Council for Vocational Qualifications.

OTTER, S. (1992) *Learning Outcomes in Higher Education*, Leicester, Unit for the Development of Adult Continuing Education (now at London, FEU).

PETERS, R.S. (1967) 'What is an educational process?' in PETERS, R.S. (Ed) *The Concept of Education*, London, Routledge & Kegan Paul.

ROYAL SOCIETY (1993) *Higher Education Futures*, London, The Royal Society.

SOLOMON, S. (1994) 'Getting started on GNVQ Advanced level' in *PSSI Forum* No 13.

STONES, E. (1966) *An Introduction to Educational Psychology*, London, Methuen.

WHITE, P. (1966) *The Solid Mandala*, London, Eyre and Spottiswoode.

Chapter 3

Theoretical Issues in Relation to Jessup's Outcomes Model

John Burke

Introduction

Continuing, close, critical scrutiny of theoretical issues directly affecting the development of National Vocational Qualifications (NVQs) and General National Vocational Qualifications (GNVQs) is clearly very important. On the economic plane, it would surely be a form of madness to commit huge resources to work-based learning, FE, HE and the schools sector to a form of training and education which was fundamentally flawed in its theoretical conception; on the moral and ethical plane it would be indefensible.

Since its inception in 1986, the NCVQ has undertaken or commissioned over 100 research reports, and has been notably assisted in this undertaking by the Department of Employment which has been responsible for the development of standards. In 1989 I regretted (Burke, 1989a) the apparent lack of research interest from HE generally; since then, the situation has been transformed. Last year, for instance, Nicholas (1983) monitored 254 papers in thirty-five research journals dealing broadly with competence issues. The Jessup (1991) Outcomes Model of the Curriculum underpins the development of NVQs and GNVQs and its essential characteristics are advocated for general applicability to all formal learning and much informal learning (Jessup, 1991, pp. 128 and 131)[1]. Yet curriculum issues in relation to NVQs and GNVQs remain an area of neglected interest with few exceptions.[2] For example, among the 254 papers alluded to above, only three touched on the curriculum. With the introduction of General National Vocational Qualifications (GNVQs) and the possible extension of the NVQ model to aspects of higher education, the significance of curricular concerns assumes a new urgency and importance. Hence this book.

A Focus on Curriculum Issues

In this chapter I shall focus on Jessup's (1991) model of the curriculum. Jessup's (1989, 1991 and 1992) formulation of the *Outcomes Model of the Curriculum* is a species of Objectives Theory. Although, as Otter (1992, pp. 5 and 15) points out, a distinction can be made between learning course objectives and outcomes statements, they are not fundamentally different. An 'objective' may be characterized as, essentially, an intention, a learning 'outcome' as the projected realization of that intention. The outcomes model thus shares many of the assumptions and principles of other objectives models and is subject to similar criticisms. However, in certain respects, Jessup's Outcomes Model is clearly different from other emendations of objectives theory; it has a number of unique characteristics which mark it off as different and worthy of study in its own right.

In this chapter, I examine a number of issues which have particular saliency from my experience of talking to different groupings of people about the NCVQ approach to the curriculum. Because this is a technical subject, these groupings have normally ranged among professionals in schools and colleges, postgraduate students and colleagues in universities but have also included professional training officers and managing agents. The development of National Vocational Qualifications (NVQs) and General National Qualifications (GNVQs) is being carried forward under tremendous pressure to make progress, against an extremely ambitious timetable for research, development and implementation, by a very small central staff. In these circumstances, it is possible to understand how issues that concern newcomers to NVQs and GNVQs may be considered as non-problematic by many researchers, if only because they are no longer 'alive' in the perception of those who are preoccupied with more pressing concerns. And yet these issues may present real problems in schools and colleges, for instance, which are only now grappling with the complexities of curriculum planning to accommodate these changes.

Other, more substantive problems arise because the basic paradigm associated with objectives or outcomes approaches is inimical to their conception of the curriculum. They see curriculum as *process* and, following Stenhouse (1975), reject the very notion of objectives or outcomes. Some of the criticisms they raise are very fundamental and must be addressed.

This chapter does not set out to deal with these problems on a comprehensive basis. A whole book on theory would be necessary to attempt to do this adequately. What I do try to do is address six issues (a manageable number) which appear important. These concerns are explored by close reference to the Jessup Model of the Curriculum set against criticisms and commentaries from exponents of differing traditions. Other contributors to this book deal with many other issues in a more detailed and systematic way by focusing on specific curriculum consequences and applications which arise from the outcomes approach. The six issues chosen for discussion may be formulated as propositions. That the Outcomes approach:

    (i)   is inimical to education and the higher forms of training;
    (ii)   is not concerned with the process of learning;
    (iii) is underpinned by Behaviourist theory;
    (iv) inhibits flexibility and spontaneity;
    (v)   limits and deprofessionalizes the role of the teacher;
    (vi) cannot itself justify its choice of subject matter.

Other issues and concerns will be touched upon incidentally as they impinge on these themes. Where possible, I have tended to quote directly from my sources rather than paraphrasing opinions as some views are very robustly held; writing with a tradition of ethnography behind me, I felt there were gains in offering the authentic voice of debate.

Before proceeding any further, we must make two short excursions into other matter. First, I comment on the difference between aims and objectives; these terms are frequently twinned together like Tweedledum and Tweedledee so it may be useful to distinguish them at the outset. Nobody, as far as I am aware, has any problems with the concept of aims, although there is endless, usually philosophical, discussion about what the ends should be; on the other hand, the very concept of objectives is repudiated by some theorists, as we shall see. Secondly, I present a short account of previous attempts to formulate objectives; this is important because it establishes a context and prepares the ground for later discussion.

Aims and Objectives

In curriculum studies literature, there is a generally accepted and useful distinction made between *aims* and *objectives* (Taba, 1962, p. 24; Richmond, 1971, pp. 37 and 185; Lawton, 1973, p. 14; Eraut, 1989b, p. 341). An 'aim' is a more general statement of purpose (sometimes described as a 'goal') or a 'general objective'; an 'objective' is a specific statement, usually expressed in terms of learner behaviour, 'an intended learning outcome' (Eraut, 1989b). Although there is a wide and perennial debate about the aims of education among philosophers, the very *generality* of aims usually means that they are not contentious outside philosophical debate. Thus Jessup (1991, p. 4) lists 'self development', 'cultural development', and 'intellectual development' as worthwhile aims, and presumably nobody would disagree with these, although they might want to list others and/or prioritize them. Marsh (1992, p. 86) comments that because of their open-ended nature, aims will never be completely achieved but provide general guidelines, and Barnes (1982, p. 3), that they do not commit anybody to doing anything in particular. The whole notion of objectives, on the other hand, may be very contentious. Indeed, Stenhouse (1975, p. 72) warns us that 'No issue has been more contentious in curriculum theory than the objectives model'.

Eraut's definition of objectives in terms of *intended* learning outcomes is especially helpful because it short-circuits much of the debate about the feasibility or possibility of identifying or prespecifying *all* or even *the most important* outcomes Lawton (1973) comments:

> Even in teaching areas where an objectives model is not completely offensive to educationalists, there may still be too many objectives for them to be listed and categorized in a simple way; for example, it has been estimated that there are over 3000 generalizations which should be taken into account when drawing up a social studies syllabus. (p. 15)

The sheer complexity of dealing with the number of possible objectives has always been a major problem with the objectives model. (cf Roby, 1990, p. 150, on assessment) The development of a workable methodology is one of the signal achievements of the Jessup model. The notion of units and elements, with associated performance criteria and range requirements enables a large number of objectives to be interrogated; the complexity is still there, but it is manageable. As far as NVQs are concerned, the size or units (i.e., the number or elements) and the number of units required is variable; in GNVQs, the structure is more uniform. If we look at the requirements for an Advanced GNVQ, we see that there are twelve units plus three core skill units required. An average unit has four elements, and an average element has about five performance criteria. Intended outcomes $12 + 3 \times 4 \times 5 = 300$. Note, this does not imply 300 separate assessments as many elements will be assessed in the same performance. What it does imply, however, is that 300 objectives will be encompassed.

Previous Attempts to Devise Objectives

Bobbit (1918) is usually recognized as the first systematic account of Objectives Theory. Bobbit adopted Spencer's utilitarian conception of knowledge selection which proposed that

> the first step must be to classify in order of importance the leading kinds of activity which constitute human life.

Applying time and motion techniques derived from Taylor's (1912) theory of scientific management, he devised his objectives approach to the curriculum.

Charters (1924) advocated a similar approach:

> First, determine the major objectives of education by a study of the life of man in its social setting. Second, analyze these objectives into ideals and activities, and continue the analysis to the level of working units.

Pursuing this approach, Pendleton divined 1581 objectives for English and Billings devised 888 objectives for social studies. Eraut (1989) comments:

> Hence the objectives movement was already collapsing under its own weight when its prevailing utilitarian ideology was eclipsed by the progressivism of the 1930s. (p. 342)

Smith and Tyler (1942) revived interest in objectives, approaching the subject from a quite different angle — diagnostic testing and evaluation. Their approach was underpinned by a different philosophy — individual development rather than utilitarianism. Tyler embarked on an eight-year study of a group of progressive schools, with the intention of formulating educational objectives which would assist pupils in thinking for themselves and applying their knowledge rather than engaging in endless rote learning exercises which then characterized much of the prevailing style of teaching and learning. A former student of Tyler's, Benjamin Bloom, was to carry forward this work with the publication of his taxonomies of objectives (Bloom, 1956).

Tyler (1949) was driven by the need to improve educational programmes; if they were to be effectively evaluated, he maintained, their objectives had to be made explicit. He advocated the use of behavioural objectives which specified both the content and the intended student behaviours. These objectives were formulated at a relatively general level.

Mager (1962) revisited Bobbit for his inspiration, in devising objectives for programmed instruction. Whereas Tyler had worked in schools, both Bobbit and

Mager based their work on military and industrial training. Mager's intention was to improve instructional design rather than facilitate evaluation. He proscribed the use of verbs such as 'know' or 'understand' in describing objectives; these verbs referred to hidden, unobservable processes of the mind; he argued that all intended behaviours should be expressed as *observable behaviours*. Further, he insisted that performance should be specified at mastery or near mastery level and that the conditions of performance should be made explicit. This approach of course, very clearly mirrors the expectations of programmed learning which proceeds by a series of very small tasks.

Gagné (1965), too, was concerned with instructional design. As a behaviourist psychologist, he was interested in determining the *kind* of learning required to accomplish certain tasks, again involving detailed planning and sequencing.

The ideas of Bobbit, Charters, Mager and Gagné have been, and continue to be, very influential in relatively low level training programmes, which easily accord and resonate with many of the industrial concepts which inform some of their work; undoubtedly, Tyler has had a major influence on education and higher level training. His early work on objectives has been taken up and developed by many of the leading curriculum theorists such as Taba (1962), Eisner (1969), Rowntree (1982) and Eraut (1989a and 1994). It is also significant that all the major documents on the curriculum emanating from the Department of Education and Science (DES) and Her Majesty's Inspectorate (HMI) over the past twenty years have all been based on an objectives approach. While that does not, of course, necessarily argue to the unimpeachable soundness of objectives theory, it does attest to both its mainstream respectability and the enduring effect of Tyler's pioneering work.

We turn, now, to consider the propositions mentioned earlier, on page 56.

1   'The Outcomes approach is inimical to education and the higher forms of training'

Stenhouse (1975) repudiated the objectives approach. Because of the enormous respect he justifiably earned for his lasting contribution to curriculum studies this should give us pause for thought.

Stenhouse (*ibid*, p. 79) cites two 'fundamental objections' to the objectives model:

(i)   That it mistakes the nature of knowledge.
(ii)   That it mistakes the nature of the process of improving practice.

The first thing to note is that his focus is limited to education *in schools*; he says education necessarily comprises four different processes: training, instruction, initiation and induction.

He readily concedes that objectives have a place in training (p. 80), may serve initiation, although this is mostly through the hidden curriculum (p. 80), and that the objectives model is appropriate for instruction (p. 81). The problem, in Stenhouse's analysis, lies in 'the area of induction into knowledge.' (p. 81). He quotes Kliebard (1968):

> . . . from a moral point of view, this emphasis on behavioural goals, despite all the protestations to the contrary, still borders on brain-washing

or at least indoctrination rather than education. We begin with some notion of how we want a person to behave and then we try to manipulate him and his environment so as to get him to behave as we want him to. (p. 246)

We saw above (p. 59) that many of the earlier proponents of the objectives model were behaviourist psychologists, and we will observe in a later section how that legacy lives on. Kliebard's criticism can only be reasonably upheld against extreme behaviourist models. Stenhouse goes on to concede that, in fact, our freedom as individuals is extremely limited for men 'are relatively predictable, limited and uncreative' (p. 82). He then asserts it is the business of education to make us freer and more creative. 'This is the nature of knowledge — as distinct from information — that is a structure to sustain creative thought and provide frameworks for judgement.' By prespecifying outcomes, he maintains, there is little opportunity for growing in understanding, and developing serendipitous knowledge.

Education as induction into knowledge is successful to the extent that it makes the behavioural outcomes of the students unpredictable.

He gives examples of essays, in the broadest sense of the word, to include written pieces, oral performances, playing music, designing or making a standard lamp. An essay, he avers, should be individual, creative and not an attempt to meet some prespecification.

Finally he goes on to claim that there is an inherent tendency for the objectives approach to make knowledge instrumental. 'Literary skills are to be justified as helping us to read *Hamlet*. *Hamlet* must not be justified as a training ground for literary skills.'

Stenhouse's second fundamental objection is that 'that there is a good case for claiming that (the objectives approach) it is not the way to improve practice'.

The first objection is addressed in Jessup (1991)

The model recognizes that learning can pursue general objectives of self-development, cultural development and intellectual development, or can pursue more specific objectives and be clearly instrumental in achieving defined goals. The former is associated with education and the latter with training. They are, of course, not mutually exclusive; much of education has been of instrumental value and training certainly contributes to self development. They are closely linked and at best enhance each other. (p. 4)

He says later:

The overall model stands or falls on how effectively we can state competence or attainment. But if we cannot, it raises fundamental issues for education and training, irrespective of the model used. If you cannot say what you require, how are you going to develop it and how do you know when you have achieved it? (p. 134)

Based on my own experience, I find this a cogent argument. When I first began assessing dissertations for Masters degrees some twelve years ago, I felt myself in a considerable ethical quandary. I did not want my students to suffer as a result of my lack of experience and yet there was no readily available guidance, save the badgering of colleagues. Within the university, it was tacitly assumed that all markers shared a 'community of understanding'. In these circumstances I felt obligated to examine critically what my expectations of my students should be. I was forced to devise performance criteria for assessing what was a creative, heuristic exercise. I did this in terms of (a) minimum requirements for a pass; (b) evidence over and above this which I would be pleased to see; and (c) evidence which I might hope to see but could not reasonably expect to find and would therefore denote exceptional work. Having received favourable comments from my colleagues, I published this for my students so that they would know in advance the criteria I was using. (I knew well that this lack of understanding among students, who were mostly fairly senior teachers or lecturers, was a cause of considerable anxiety.)

Rowntree (1982) notes:

> Undoubtedly, most of the agonizing is over affective objectives and the higher level cognitive objectives. (. . .) Yet it would surely be nonsense, and flying in the face of a discipline's critical standards, to assert that there are no ways of stating in advance the kinds of quality one would look for, and the errors one would expect to see avoided, in a student's essay, short story, musical score, research report or whatever. Professionals constantly make such appraisals and judgments about their colleagues' work, and examiners likewise, with even greater show of accuracy, for candidates in the arts. (. . .) If and when they are willing to externalize their criteria for judgment, we shall have our objectives. (p. 55)

Eisner (1969) agrees that such judgments may take place:

> One must judge after the fact whether the product produced or the behaviour displayed belongs to the novel class.

And even Stenhouse seems to admit that objectives may be employed in the guise of criteria:

> One could also sharpen and define the criteria by which students' work might be judged.

Rowntree (1982) adds piquantly:

> To set the student off in pursuit of an unnamed quarry may be merely wasteful, but to punish him for failing to catch it is positively mischievous. Do we sometimes appear to say to the student; 'I can't say precisely what skills or knowledge I want you to acquire from this course. Just do your own thing (guessing what might come into my mind) and I'll give you a grade according to how I feel about it'? (p. 55)

(Some of the problems, and solutions, encountered in HE are discussed more fully in Otter (1992) and chapter 17 in this volume.)

Skilbeck (1984) discerns a further *rapprochement* with Stenhouse:

> A careful reading of Stenhouse's discussion of curriculum planning and his description of the so-called process model suggests that his own position is not so far from some kind of objectives based analysis. The language is different, and that is not without its significance, but the tendency of thought is towards that projective, intentional, action mode where conditions for learning are defined and taken to establish them — in short, towards the same general type enterprise as objectives planning in the curriculum. (p. 229)

Jessup (1991, pp. 150–1) briefly discusses Stenhouse (1975) in a note, pointing out that Stenhouse is concerned only with the curriculum as far as it concerns teachers in schools, whereas his model, as we shall see (p. 64) embraces all learning, wherever it occurs.

Herein, I suspect, lies the kernel of Stenhouse's greatest reservation, his second objection that the objectives approach does not contribute to improving practice. He is surely right to warn against such tendencies as he discerned in 'teacher-proof curriculum packages' which were tried out with dismal results in the sixties. But he is wrong to ascribe similar and necessary tendencies in all objectives approaches. If his criticism is extended to the Jessup outcomes model, it is clearly unwarranted. In fact, I will argue later (p. 74) that the Jessup model enhances teacher involvement where teachers are concerned in delivering the curriculum, which is, of course, in the majority of cases for GNVQs.

Incidentally, I can see no problem in adopting Stenhouse's model of the teacher as researcher; as we shall see, the Jessup model leaves ample scope for developing teacher expertise.

Two other influential critics, Kelly (1982 and 1989) and Holt (1983) have raised similar objections, and their views surface in other parts of this chapter. Kelly, it should be noticed, repeatedly claims he has no major problem in using the objectives approach for training. But as Skilbeck (1984, p. 227) points out, training and instruction have a place in education, including general education and the core curriculum, and there is no inherent reason why training should be narrow, doctrinal, inflexible, propagandist and inimical to student development just because it is precise and highly structured learning. Further (and this objection applies to Holt as well), the fact that training is 'utilitarian' is not a condemnation unless we are disposed to think that there is no place in education and training for useful knowledge and skills. That would be an extraordinary argument recalling a nineteenth century ideology which served to distinguish the 'elite curriculum' of the English public school, which concentrated on classics, from the kind of curriculum advocated for the masses, which was useful for earning a living (cf Ong, 1959; Wilkinson, 1964; Young, 1971). Because training and instruction may sometimes be practised in ways which are inimical to educational ends, this 'does not lead us to the conclusion that there is a fundamental conceptual difference between them and "education"'. Indeed, part of the very *raison d'être* for developing the outcomes model is to bridge the gap between education and training (see Gilbert Jessup and Peter Raggatt in this volume).

What amounts to an oblique rebuttal of both Kelly's and Holt's position was recently published by The Royal Society, the foremost and most prestigious science body in British academia.

Medieval university disputants would frequently invoke authoritative texts to settle arguments. In more modern times we have come to appreciate the primacy of reason over authority. Nonetheless, the power of endorsement is well recognized in the world of advertising, and the view of acknowledged experts in whatever field are worthy of respect. I conclude this section with two short quotations from the Royal Society report, *Higher Education Futures* (1993). This report was prepared by a study group of the Royal Society's Council under the chairmanship of Professor Sir Eric Ash, outlining the measures to be taken in HE to achieve 'a high-quality mass participation system'.

First, I quote a passage expressing their view of GNVQs, the most recent embodiment of the Outcomes approach:

We hope that the GNVQs will earn the approval of the education community and of employers *as a real step towards breaking the academic/vocational dichotomy.* It is particularly critical that the GNVQ in Science commands the respect of both higher education and its customers if it is to be widely accepted as a credible alternative to A and AS examinations. (p. 15, emphasis added)

Without further comment, I turn to their recommendations about assessment on undergraduate science courses:

Assessments must ensure that learning matches the objectives set for the course. It must ensure that *performance, in terms of both skills and knowledge,* has reached an appropriate level, and it will be used to grade that performance. More students will need to be assessed, and *evidence of achievement will need to be sought from a wider range of skills and knowledge* than has been the case previously. (. . .) *Assessment influences learning styles, and the opportunities students have to apply their skills to new problems and in new contexts.* We believe that it is vital that innovation in assessment complements innovation in teaching. (p. 28, emphasis added)

It is clear that the Royal Society, certainly the most academically prestigious scientific body in Britain, endorses the bridging of the vocational/academic divide, endorses an objectives approach, endorses a view that upholds the value of knowledge and skills in higher education. One may reasonably infer, therefore, that it would disparage and reject the view that the objectives approach is inimical to education or the higher forms of training.

2 'The Outcomes approach is not concerned with the process of learning'

The second *Fundamental Criterion* for the accreditation of a qualification as a National Vocational Qualification (NVQ) requires that it should be 'based on assessments of the outcomes of learning, arrived at independently of any particular mode, duration or location of learning' (NCVQ and ED, 1991, p. 5). The intention here was to free up access to assessment from the log-jam of restrictions and regulations which previously impeded progress towards qualification. This appeared to distance the interest of the NCVQ from curriculum matters. Jessup (1991) comments:

An assumption is often made that because NVQs, and the broader models described here, are defined only by their outcomes that the proponents of such approaches to education and training are not concerned with the process of learning. In one sense this is true, in so far as competence and training is recognised irrespective of the process by which it is acquired. In another sense it is far from true.

The overall model is designed to promote learning. It incorporates many features which make learning more attractive and easier to access. The emphasis on performance and attainment encourages more active and participative learning. (pp. 137–8)

He goes on to add in a note:

In so far as the process of learning is related to curriculum theory, it is important to appreciate that the outcomes model does not neglect the other essential constituents of a curriculum, which may be listed as teaching and learning, subject matter, and assessment, linked together by aims. The 'outcomes' model is outcome-led — not outcome dominated to the exclusion of everything else. Because all the constituents in a curriculum are essentially related, if one is affected, all are affected. The outcomes model seeks to bring about change by focusing on outcomes referenced against requirements outside education. This external reference provides an anchor point around which the other variables may swing. (p. 157)

At the outset, then, it is important to establish that the Jessup Outcomes Model of the Curriculum has one major difference from most other models of the curriculum. It is at the same time more ambitious and more modest.

It is more ambitious in that it is directed to encompassing all learning pursued purposively towards intended outcomes; this learning may take place in the classroom, as in most curriculum models, but it is by no means limited to that arena (see Stephen McNair in this volume). Thus learning may be accomplished by 'distant learning', on an individual basis or any 'flexible arrangements', in the workplace, in schools or colleges or any other means (see, Colin Nash in this volume).

It is more modest in that the model tells us little about how the programme of learning should be specified. The anchor point is the outcomes; any (presumably, efficacious) programme of learning directed towards achieving these outcomes may be pursued; any appropriate form of assessment may be used. The important point is that the programme of learning does not dictate the assessment regime, and, more importantly, the assessment regime does not prescribe the programme of learning.

This lack of prescription confers many potential benefits on the learner, and as we shall see later, the teacher, if the logic of the model is followed through. We saw earlier that all models involve simplification, and that there is a trade-off between complicating a model so that it does not distort but becomes confusing, and simplifying so that it is more easily understood but runs the risk of distorting. The visual representation of the unit (figure 3.1 below) may be criticized for appearing to isolate each component, and thereby disguise the essential interaction which is designed to occur. A common misunderstanding, for example, is that

Figure 3.1   Structure of an NVQ

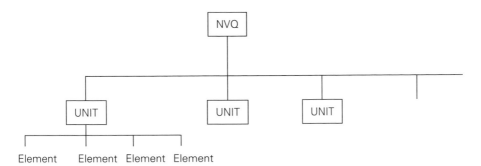

each element requires a separate assessment. The interrelationship, and the benefits they confer, need to be stressed, and may be stated briefly:

> attainable targets are clearly defined as outcomes to be achieved;
> assessment is based directly on these outcomes;
> both formative and summative assessment may be integrated with learning.

Additionally, we may notice:

> motivation is enhanced because relevance (which resides in the perception of the learner, not in content) is clear;

> alternative modes of learning are encouraged as learning styles are not prescribed.

> The 'breakdown' of the unit is explained in detail in the next chapter.

> What the model does not do is assume there is only one way to learn *or even that there is a best way*. It recognizes individual differences and individual preferences and opportunities. *Above all it does not prescribe the form of learning*. (Jessup, 1991, p. 138) (emphasis added)

3 'The Outcomes approach is based on assumptions and theories from Behaviourist Psychology'

We must establish at the outset that objectives models, which rely on behavioural evidence in making assessments, are not dependent on the *Behaviourist Psychology* associated with Skinner (1959) and Holland and Skinner (1968), a fallacy common among postgraduate students new to the outcomes approach. Certainly, Charters, the earliest applicant of objectives theory to the curriculum was a behaviourist, as was Bobbit (1918). Both Mager (1962) and Gagné (1965) were behaviourists although Gagné eventually modified his position, moving from strictly observable behaviours to the concept of 'learned capability' (cf Gagné and Briggs 1974) and both were interested in programme learning. Rowntree (1981) comments on the importance and necessity of drawing inferences from observable behaviour without being hamstrung by some doctrinaire imperative not to go beyond the strictly observable:

> The fact is, people's behaviour — what they say and do — is our only way of getting to know their beliefs and capabilities and understandings. We have no direct access to anyone's state of mind, except our own . . . Hence the power of educational technology's suggestion that learning objectives are expressed in behavioural terms. (. . .) Of course, we must not be naïve about this. We must always ask what lies behind the behaviour. (. . .) We seek behavioural changes in our students, we can help towards behavioural objectives, *without using any teaching strategies derived from or reminiscent of behaviourist psychology.* (. . .) We are ultimately concerned not with the *process* of behaviour (the physical events) but with its *praxis* — what it means to the learner. (p. 16)

Behaviourism focuses on the study and experimentation of behaviour under laboratory conditions, where the 'subject' has a passive role with limited freedom of choice and is associated with conditioned response techniques and operant conditioning. The approach is criticized, in Hunter's (1977) delightfully apophthegmatic summary, as 'an elegant but superficial pursuit of trivial problems couched in arid language and too artificial to have relevance for "real life problems"' (p. 57). Skinner (1968) argued by analogy from the training of pigeons and rats that the human learner could be worked upon to change or shape his/her behaviour. Am I alone in reading a similar (oblique or subliminal) understanding of objectives in Grundy (1987)?

> This means that implicit with objectives models of the curriculum, such as Tyler's (1949), is an interest in controlling pupil learning so that, at the end of the teaching process, the product will conform to the *eidos* (that is the intentions or ideas) expressed in the original objectives. (p. 1)

Kelly (1989) appears to leave no doubt: he assumes that the objectives model is necessarily linked to behaviourist principles:

> The important point to note is that this [objectives] approach to curriculum planning assumes that education must be planned in a step-by-step linear manner. It is in fact an attempt to translate into classroom terms that linear step-by-step process which behavioural (*sic*) psychologists have discovered to be the most effective way of conditioning animals — dogs, cats, rats, pigeons and so on. (pp. 53–4)

Kelly's (1987) unequivocal alignment of the objectives model of the curriculum with Skinnerism issues in certain consequences:

> We noted in chapter 1 the view that education must be concerned to promote understanding in the individual pupil and, ultimately, some form of intellectual autonomy, the ability to think critically for oneself. . . . It [objectives model] must regard the pupil essentially as the passive recipient of the curriculum that is offered, rather than as an active participant in his or her own education. It adopts what has been called a 'passive

model of man', a view of the human being as a creature upon whom external forces work . . . (p. 88)

It should be noted that the second part of this statement is antithetical to practically everything that Jessup has ever written while he fully endorses the first. (cf Stephen McNair in Chapter 13). We shall note some of these antitheses in more detail later; at this point it is sufficient to focus on one section in *Outcomes* (pp. 136–7):

> The model is designed to promote learning and maximize efficiency in the process of learning. . . . (Features of the model which promote this) include:
>
> - the effective provision of information and guidance . . . ;
> - recognition of prior achievements . . . ;
> - the development of individual action plans, which allows considerably more choice and participation by the learner in the targets they choose to pursue in any course or programme. Flexibility and choice is considerably enhanced by unit-based qualifications and modular delivery. There will also be choice in the modes and timing of learning, and the duration of programmes . . . These features will perhaps be more evident in the post-school provision, where adults will tailor their action plans to fit in with the rest of their lives. Within schools pre-16, the National Curriculum will largely dictate the targets of learning, but there will be increasing choice through individualized learning with projects and assignments and progress at different speeds through the provision;
> - clear understanding by learners of what they are expected to learn (as set out in statements of attainment or competence) and the performance levels by which they will be assessed, will give them a degree of control over the process which has not been a feature of traditional programmes;
> - the above allows self-assessment and participation in summative assessment through a dialogue with the assessor on what the learner has demonstrated they know and can do.

Jessup adds a little later:

> What the model does not do is assume there is only one way to learn or even there is necessarily a best way. It recognises individual differences and individual preferences and opportunities. Above all it does not prescribe the form of learning. (p. 138)

That does not look much like Watson or Skinner! If anything, it is more like Maslow[3]. As Rowntree points out, some adherents to the objectives model may be Behaviourists but there is no justification for rejecting the model on that score; Jessup's (1991) model of outcomes is clearly not behaviourist either in intention or formulation; his *Outcomes* model is directed to liberating and empowering the individual rather than controlling or merely modifying behaviour.

This assertion of liberation and empowerment, and the inherent *suitability* of the outcomes approach to education, is powerfully attested by recent commentators on GNVQ.

GNVQ is the embodiment of the outcomes approach applied to the curriculum. I conclude this section by citing (i) a key recommendation from Education Quality Council's Report (1994a and 1994b), and (ii) a recent commentary on GNVQ science by Chris Edwards of the School of Education, University of Leeds.

(i)   The Higher Education Quality Council's CAT Development Project makes eight 'Key recommendations'; the third recommendation comprises:

An Associate Degree, coupled with a GNVQ4, as a new interim qualification in higher education. (1994b, p. 8)

The pellucid inference we may draw from this requires no comment. In like manner, Edwards is unequivocally clear in his trenchant appraisal:

(ii) GNVQ has the potential to produce students that are highly motivated, with initiative, drive and enthusiasm, as do many A-level programmes. However, the approach of GNVQ harnesses this motivation and enthusiasm by developing the abilities to manage their own learning, understand learning goals and plan courses of action to achieve them, to engage in self-assessment and to assess the quality of their achievements; it promotes independence when learning and the skills of self-presentation and of evidencing claims of achievement. In addition, its vocational focus is likely to enable students to form clearer, more realistic expectations for their careers, be these educational or employment, and therefore, gain sense of purpose in applying for, and pursuing, a particular HE course.

Many of these qualities are assessed in the grading criteria, the mandatory core skills and the core skills assessed as additional units and therefore GNVQ (and only GNVQ) is a qualification that gives clear measures of these aspects that are so important to success on HE courses.

Edwards concludes:

This seems the strongest argument of all for GNVQ. With the changing nature of HE, modularisation, semesterisation, pressure towards more open and flexible delivery styles, the decline of traditional examinations and much more, *there seems to exist an opportunity to bring forward students with the very skills and qualities needed to cope with the new 'scene'.* (Edwards, 1994, p. 9, emphasis added)

4   *'By prespecifying outcomes, the Outcomes model inhibits flexibility and spontaneity, and leads to a narrow, impoverished curriculum'*

There are two separate but connected ideas here. The first is seen as a threat to the autonomy of both teacher and learner; the second, that learners may be confined to tramlines in their learning and all unintended outcomes — and all the many other possible objectives — will be neglected or relegated to the unimportant. A third idea, which is often linked to both of these, is that only easily assessable outcomes will be targeted.

At this point it is necessary to notice one major difference in the Jessup model of Outcomes from more general Objectives theory. While objectives may be expressed as intended learning outcomes in all models associated with outcomes, in the Jessup model, the outcomes are expressed as units and elements of *assessment*, not as *instructional* objectives. (cf Jessup in this volume, and note 3 at the end of his chapter.) Thus vociferous condemnation of the perceived straightjacket which critics see Objectives Models as imposing on the curriculum (cf Jackson, 1968 and Sockett, 1976) are wide of the mark if applied to the Jessup Outcomes Model. In any case, most proponents of the objectives model would claim that these strictures only apply to extreme behaviourist models.

Kelly (1987), who is obviously thinking of extreme behaviouralist formulations of the model, *and in that context* is entirely justified, warns:

> (S)uch forms of planning must lead to serious restrictions on the autonomy of both teachers and pupils in the educational process, and thus, indeed, to constraints on the development of the curriculum. (. . .) (Objectives take us) away from the ideas of education as negotiation and transaction. (. . .) A good teacher will be prepared to make adjustments to what he or she has planned while actually in the process of implementing it. (pp. 87–8)

So far in the discussion, I have kept to fairly generalized points; it is time to look at an actual example of a learning outcome, and briefly examine the kind of learning involved (and the consequences for any teaching) so that the reader may make up his or her own mind empirically by studying the evidence at first hand.

The example I have selected, almost at random, is an Intermediate GNVQ in Leisure and Tourism.[4] Note, the primary purpose here is to illustrate the working of the model, not GNVQs, but for those as yet unfamiliar with GNVQs this example may prove doubly useful and instructive (cf Ellis in this volume for an explanation of the way that an NVQ or a GNVQ is constituted in terms of Statement of Competence/Attainment (respectively), Units, Elements, Performance Criteria and Range requirements).

Element 1.1: Investigate the local leisure and tourism industry.

Performance criteria:
1   the different contexts which make up the local leisure and tourism industry are correctly described.
2   examples of leisure and tourism products and services in each context are identified.
3   the significance of each context is accurately explained.
4   examples of facilities operating in each context and sector are identified.

The performance criteria act as statements of outcomes.

These outcomes are further defined by Range.

> local: single travel to work area
> significance: local; economic (for example, numbers employed, turnover, etc., relative to other industries in the area); social; environmental
> sectors; public; private; voluntary
> contexts: accommodation, catering and hospitality; entertainment and education; travel and tourism; sports and recreation

Finally, advice is given in terms of the kind of evidence required: 'Evidence Indicators':

> A report, describing the structure and scale of the local leisure and tourism industry. The sources should be identified.
>
> The use of examples will demonstrate the candidate's awareness of the diversity of L&T products and services, the facilities which provide them, and their key impacts on the local area.

The outcomes are clearly stated and easily understood by the student. It could be argued that in this example there are unintended ambiguities in the Range: eg, how wide is the 'single travel to work', and what does it mean precisely. Nowadays, people commute long journeys daily, and in the context of outer London, for example, 'local' may involve several boroughs. But these criticisms aside (or with the help of a teacher) the instruction is reasonably clear. The evidence indicators are a model of clarity: students do know what is required of them.

We might reasonably say, then, that the outcomes are quite closely prespecified. On the other hand, we could equally argue that there is enormous variation possible and acceptable within that specification. These are not tightly defined, 'straightjacket' outcomes. Unless two or more students have closely collaborated (and that is acceptable as long as the assessor, through questioning, for example, can identify the individual contribution) it would be extremely unlikely that any two students would come up with closely similar outcomes in the way that they frequently do when coached towards an essay in history or any other subject in the traditional examination format. Far from limiting autonomy or creativity, both are encouraged and given ample scope for expression. Quality is further assessed by the grading system, which is accessible and open so that students know in advance that there is no artificial ceiling on achievement, although the minimum requirements are plainly stated.

Jessup (1991) comments:

> Whether pursuing general or specific objectives individuals will learn more effectively if they are clear about the targets or outcomes they are trying to achieve. Learning is a purposeful activity and should be targeted on explicit outcomes. This should not discourage unplanned, additional learning taking place en route, nor should it stop people following tangential lines of enquiry out of curiosity. In fact, such additional learning is more likely to be stimulated within the context of a learning plan. (p. 5)

Richmond's (1971) strictures lose their force when set along side the GNVQ outcomes illustrated above:

> . . . what (could be) more arid than an educational practice which found no place for inspired guess work, for unexpected flair or for acts of faith. Like it or lump it, education is an activity which people engage in without being absolutely sure what they are trying to do. It is, therefore, a disservice to planning to pretend that routes leading to desired outcomes can be laid down in advance. It is an even greater disservice to pupils to disguise the fact that the learning process is hedged about with uncertainties, since learning to live with uncertainty may well be reckoned the ultimate aim of education, 'that for the sake of which everything else is done'. (p. 185)

Students attempting Element 1 are quickly introduced to uncertainties. This is clearly not a form of indoctrination, as Kelly (1987, p. 88) describes the objectives approach. They have to think for themselves, to plan and prioritize activities, make decisions about where to find information or informants, what to concentrate on, what to leave out, how to write it up.

We may note in passing that the type of teaching required to support this kind of learning in no way infringes the teacher's professionalism or autonomy.[5]

An objection which has more substance, but is often lumped in with the charge above, is that by prespecifying outcomes, unintended outcomes may be ignored, unrecognized or relegated in value to the unimportant or peripheral. This is a serious charge because it is clearly impossible to prespecify all the important learning outcomes, or even, some would argue, an adequate, representative cluster. And by definition, unintended learning cannot be prespecified.

This concern, and the concern about the fracturing or atomizing of knowledge, is again more easily addressed by looking at the example quoted above.

In order to arrive at the intended learning outcomes, many enabling objectives have to be set and attained. These form part of the action plan which every student has to complete. Portsmouth College (cf Tom Jackson in this volume) has prepared a planning guide, from which I quote:

Drawing up your action plan

1 Decide how you are going to proceed.
2 Think about how you can include evidence of your core skills in what you do.
3 Decide if your evidence will be part of a wider project covering other elements as well.
4 Write up your action plan. Your plan should include each of the following steps and the date each step will be completed.

a Gaining knowledge
   How you will gain the knowledge and understanding needed for an element, eg, taught by teacher, individual research from text books, library or elsewhere; shared research with colleagues; a combination of these.
b Collecting evidence
   What steps you take to collect the evidence required.

    c   Checking the evidence
       How you check the accuracy (validity) of information that you collect.
    d   Presenting evidence
       How you will present your evidence: eg, written report; observed performance; oral presentation; tape recording; video.

There follows further advice on 'recording your progress', 'monitoring your progress' and evaluation.

Without going into any further detail, it is obvious that students are encouraged to pursue their targets purposively, developing their interests and building on these multiple 'stepping stone' attainments en route to their eventual goal, the complete unit with its various elements sub-divided into individual performance statements.

5 *'The Outcomes approach limits and deprofessionalizes the role of the teacher'*

A common assumption in books on the curriculum is that the curriculum necessarily involves an institutional setting (for example, a school) and therefore the conduct and control of the curriculum is (or post National Curriculum, *should be*) in the hands of the professionals (i.e., the teachers). Thus, for example, Holmes and McLean (1989), *The Curriculum: A Comparative Perspective:*

> This book is for readers who want to know *what should be taught in schools*. (Preface, p. vi) (*emphasis added*)

Beauchamp (1961, p. 1):

> (The curriculum is) a design of a social group for the educational experiences of *children in school*. (*emphasis added*)

Lofthouse (1990, p. 1):

> The curriculum is the medium through which education is conducted *in schools*. (*Emphasis added*)

Jessup (1991) emphasizes that his model is designed to encompass not only the school but also any site where learning may be accomplished:

> If learning is perceived from the viewpoint of the learner rather than that of the teacher or trainer, and more particularly those who manage the education and training industry, one has to change the conventional model and the concepts used. If one accepts that the central process with which we are concerned is learning[6], and that learning can take many forms, education and training can be seen to take many forms, and education and training may be seen as helping to make that possible. The focus on learning would also help to eradicate the distinction between education and training, and the establishments and agencies which divide learning into two camps. As a learner I do not make this distinction. My head does not have separate compartments to receive education and training. (p. 4)

He says later:

Many previous initiatives have been limited to the conceptual model of learning upon which they are based. Stenhouse (1970, pp. 70–83) only addressed the issue in relation to its implications for curriculum development, which was conceived as teaching in a classroom:

'In short, curriculum study should be grounded in the study of classrooms.' (*ibid*, p. 75)

'Rational curriculum planning must take account of the realities of classroom situations. It is not enough to be logical.' (Stenhouse, 1970, p. 78, reproduced in Stenhouse, 1975, p. 75)

The model presented here is based upon a more fundamental conception of learning, wherever it takes place. It sees the classroom as just one context. It also makes a very clear distinction between learning and teaching. (pp. 150–1)

There is a most significant difference between this model of the curriculum and every other model with which I am familiar. In many models, it is assumed — or explicitly stated — that the *teacher* lies at the heart of the model. See, for example, Lamm (1966) in figure 3.2 below:

Figure 3.2: Lamm: Model of the curriculum

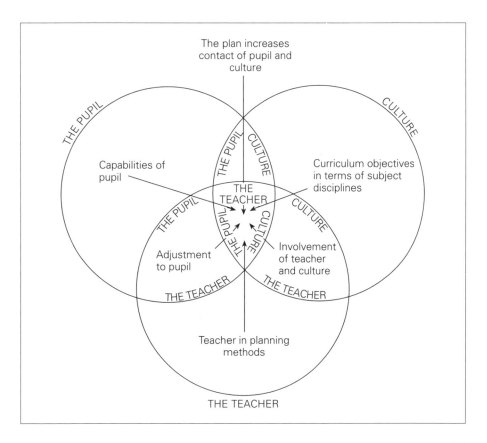

Other models (cf Eraut 1982) have suggested a more balanced approach which reflects both teaching and learning. Kerr (1968) proposed a model which is close to Jessup (1991), especially as he speaks of 'evaluation' where we would now use the term 'assessment'.

Figure 3.3: Kerr's model of the curriculum

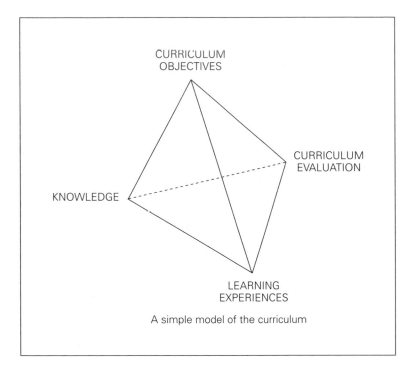

A simple model of the curriculum

It is easy to see why the teacher-centric view to persuasive. If teaching is an essential component, it is the teacher who makes all or most of the significant decisions to mediate learning. As Stenhouse (1975, p. 24) asserts: 'Teaching is not merely instruction, but the systematic promotion of learning by whatever means' in the Jessup model, it is the *learner* who is central. Indeed, in this model, the *teacher* is another (if important) *resource*, where available. This is not an argument that the teacher is 'an optional extra' but that the model embraces modes of learning, and instances of curriculum, where the teacher is absent from the process of learning. The effect of this very different emphasis is not to marginalize the role of the teacher in the sense of deprofessionalizing the role (cf Bowles and Gintis, 1976; Apple, 1981; and Lawn and Ozga, 1981) but to promote and celebrate the professionalism of the teacher. For although the teacher may be absent from the working of the model in some circumstances (for example, in self-learning mode) in the majority of applications (most obviously in GNVQs, for example) the teacher crucially plays a very important function in facilitating the learning of the learner.[7] In McCutcheon's (1986) terms, the teacher is 'the filter through which the mandated curriculum passes'. The choice of teaching style, the methods used, the time spent, the other resources employed are all the preserve of the professional teacher who is empowered and enjoined to make these professional choices within the constraints only of the operating environment. One, not insignificant reason, why teachers in the GNVQ pilot responded with such enthusiasm to GNVQs was precisely because the working of the model, with its emphasis on guidance and counselling (and paradoxically, both *because of* and *in spite of* its demands on teachers to make the crucial assessments) fully recognizes and celebrates the professionalism of teachers. Stenhouse (1975) says roundly:

> It is the thesis of this book that curriculum development must rest on teacher development and that it should promote it and hence the professionalism of the teacher. Curriculum development translates ideas into classroom practicalities and thereby helps the teacher to strengthen his practice by systematically and thoroughly testing ideas. (pp. 24–5)

That thesis sits comfortably alongside the Outcomes approach, which fully recognizes the professionalism of the teacher, with its lack of prescription about *how* the teaching is to be accomplished. In the implementation of the first wave of GNVQs, Jane Harrop (in this volume) reports the wide diversity of strategies and approaches adopted by different teachers in different institutions. For example, although NVQs and GNVQs are assessed in elements which, taken together, form units, these are 'units of assessment', and *not* 'units of instruction'; teachers are encouraged to explore the most efficacious methods of facilitating learning. Clearly, as Michael Young reports in this volume, there are distinct pedagogic advantages in adopting a modular approach to teaching, but he identifies the ways in which this can create unintended polarities. His concept of *connectivity* further emphasizes the way in which teachers, with a professional concern for the enactment of the curriculum can extend the effectiveness of the outcomes approach.

It is worth noting that in some schools during the pilot year of GNVQ implementation, teachers took advantage of the freedom which modules of assessment allowed, to defer the completion of some units until the end of the year because, in their judgment, this enhanced the learning process in an holistic way, avoiding the danger which some critics discerned that the learning *process* would necessarily be fragmented. The possible fragmentation of learning involved in units or modules of *instruction* (rather than *assessment*) was earlier recognized by Mansell *et al* (1976).

Although the model is not prescriptive, there *are* implications which need to be explored.

The *role* of the teacher in teaching NVQs and GNVQs, for example, is distinctly different from the traditional 'chalk and talk' approach which still obtains in some institutions. If teachers are to create learning opportunities and support learning in a flexible manner, they may well find they cannot sustain their performance as 'experts' in content as discovery approaches may lead their students into many areas where they cannot reasonably claim expertise. This places different demands on their pedagogic skills and understanding. Their guidance and counselling skills will come to the fore when advising on action plans and the feasibility of projects. They will need to develop new skills in many different forms of assessment. They will have to think carefully and very critically about the organisation of teaching time in view of the different pace at which individual students progress. In short, they will need to adopt a stance not dissimilar from what Stenhouse advocates.

If we return for one moment to consider the example of an element from a

GNVQ (cf pp. 69–70) and reflect on the different teaching skills and strategies that it requires, we can see that the teacher has a supportive, facilitating, counselling, assessing role as well as an instructional one, where such direct interventions are deemed appropriate by the teacher.

The *curriculum implications* for teaching in FE are explored by Haffenden and Brown (1989), Burke (1989c), Shackleton (1989 and 1990), Jessup (1990), Millington (1990), Pettit, Crook and Silver (1990) and numerous publications from the Further Education Unit (FEU), for example: FEU, 1989; FEU 1992; Wolf *for the FEU*, 1993; FEU, 1994a and FEU 1994b. Eraut (1989) addresses implications for the initial education for teachers. Otter (1992 and this volume), Burke (1991) and Eraut (in this volume) deal with HE and the professions. As already mentioned, the NCVQ is in the course of publishing a new series on different GNVQs, the first one (GNVQ, 1993) dealing with the assessment of Art and Design (itself lavishly illustrated with full colour reproductions of students' work) and the regular *GNVQ Newsletter* first issued in October 1993. As far as NVQs are concerned, the NCVQ has already published an extensive series of *NVQ Notes*, dealing with a range of occupations and avocations (for example, *Assessing Competence in Unpaid Work*, 1993) and a series of research reports dealing with issues such as Core Skills (Jessup, 1993 and Oates, 1991). *Competence and Assessment* is issued quarterly by the DE, covering a large number of research concerns in a very accessible and informative way.

6 'The objectives approach cannot itself justify its choice of subject matter'

Before I address the substantive issues in this section, a prefatory note is indicated. To touch on this subject is to open a Pandora's box of discrete but related topics largely concerned with issues about control of the curriculum, government intervention and teacher autonomy. In the interests of brevity, I intend to prescind from these subjects; my intention is to examine briefly a very important criticism of all Objectives theory and assess the consequences.

A fundamental criticism of objectives approaches, recognized by all commentators, is that the model cannot say anything definitive about the basic *selection* of content beyond an appeal to utilitarianism or political intervention. Objectives models say nothing directly about the values which must be established in determining choice of content (from a possible universe of many differing contents with competing claims for inclusion). Eraut (1989c, p. 348), with a commitment to objectives, is very clear on this point:

> What the objectives model cannot do is resolve disputes over what should be taught, though sometimes they may help to map out the issues.

Kelly (1987, pp. 88–9) highlights this lacuna with trenchant effect:

> (The objectives approach) cannot answer any questions directed to exploring *why* we should teach certain things . . . (. . .) in the sphere of education, it can tell us *how* we might most effectively teach (NOTE an interesting admission in view of his total opposition to the model) Latin or science or the art of torturing; it cannot tell us *whether* we ought to be teaching any or all of these things . . . That is why its adoption, especially in those current official documents in the UK . . . must lead to . . . a very limited form of curriculum planning. (pp. 88–9)

The question of what should be included is clearly very important, as Jessup (1991) acknowledges:

> Few people have asked why History is included at all in the National Curriculum. (I am not suggesting it should not be included *but I think the question should be asked and answered.*)

If an Objectives Approach cannot of itself say what ought to be taught, where else can we seek this information?

An obvious first place to look might be our Aims, but several critics of the objectives approach point to the difficulty or impossibility of deriving objectives from aims. The attempts of Kratwohl (1965) and Wheeler (1967) ('ultimate', 'mediate' and 'proximate' in Wheeler's terms) to distinguish three levels of specificity have been criticized by Kelly (1989, pp. 53–54) as leading to a linear, step-by-step process associated with behaviourist psychology in conditioning animals.

Eraut (1989b, p. 338ff) argues that it would be naïve to expect a totally consistent relationship between aims (in the technical sense) and objectives since statements about aims and statements about objectives are formulated for different purposes and different audiences. Nor are aims the only (or, indeed, usual) source for objectives:

> In theory there are no limit to the number of places where people may find ideas for objectives. In practice, existing curriculum traditions probably serve as the major source. Second, there are no generally agreed or universally applicable procedures for deducing objectives from aims. (Hirst 1973)

Citing Bloom *et al* (1981), he gives two kinds of arguments for the justification of objectives: feasibility and desirability. Clearly, objectives should be do-able but they ought also be desirable. Desirability arguments, he suggests, are of two kinds: evidence of expressed preferences and arguments from basic values.

Eraut discerns four main category of argument:

- occupational practice;
- roles in society;
- cultural and academic knowledge
- the interests of the learner.

> Objects relating to occupational practice can be justified in terms of national manpower needs, in terms of local needs for particular kinds of knowledge and skills, or for an individual's need to be able to work with application. (. . .) Roles in society include citizenship, membership of the local community, family life so on. (. . .) Much that is found in the role of society.

> 'role of society' category can also be subsumed under the heading of 'cultural knowledge', a term to which curriculum thinkers are often attracted to but whose implications have not yet been worked out. Thus it has been used both in the context of justifying attention to the arts and humanities and in the context of preparing students to live in a multicultural society. (. . .) Arguments based on the learners' interest

are of two main types. The motivational argument (. . .) (and) the needs argument. (p. 135)

Rowntree (1982, p. 63) has a similar conception. Objectives, he says, arise in the perception of all who have a stake in education. They come from the views we hold about the future needs of people in society, insights expressed in various arts, crafts and sciences, and the present needs and interests of students. This conception is illustrated in a model, shown in Figure 3.4 (*op.cit.* p. 63):

Figure 3.4: Source of Objectives

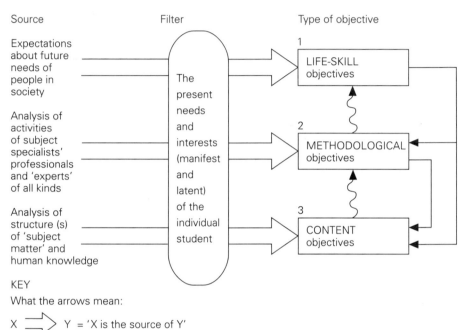

KEY

What the arrows mean:

X ⇒ Y = 'X is the source of Y'

X ⤳ Y = 'The attainment of X may help in the attainment of Y'

X ⟶ Y = 'Views about X may influence the strategies used in teaching Y'

There are, then, well established and legitimate ways of deriving Objectives or Outcomes which, while not arising out of Objectives theory itself, may be deployed successfully. This perceived deficiency may dent theoretical elegance after which so many social scientists strive in formulating theoretical models, but as Blumer (1969) reminds us, the touch-stone of all social science should be 'obdurate reality'. Obdurate reality may be, and often is, untidy. Attempts to encapsulate that untidiness within a single theory at every point are bound *not* to succeed. It is important to remember that *all* theory is based on assumptions, which are usually unstated. Different theories have different utility in illuminating different aspects of reality. While care must be exercised in combining different theories (their assumptions must not be antithetical or mutually incompatible) there is, *a priori*, no reason why compatible theories should not be used together. There is no metaphysical reason why Objectives Theory should provide all the answers. If education is concerned with the intrinsically-worthwhile, (Peters, 1967, pp. 3–4) what is intrinsically worthwhile may be determined by other means. It may be said that the Objectives, determined (for instance in the ways discussed by Eraut, above) are assumed to be worthwhile at the point at which Objectives Theory comes into play. While education (intrinsically worthwhile) and training (utilitarian) may be conceptually distinct, and while there may be good reasons for maintaining that distinction in certain contexts, in other contexts there may be (indeed, I would contend, *there are*) good reasons for bridging the gap. This is most obvious at higher professional levels (for example, postgraduate medicine or law) but this 'bridge' is surely important at much lower levels where young people are being prepared to assume the mutifaceted responsibilities of adulthood, which include both self-development and earning a living.

Notes

1 See Mathews, Eraut, McNair and Raggatt in this volume.
2 The FEU has consistently published support material for lecturers and tutors in FE. Recent publications on GNVQs and the curriculum include FEU (1994a) and FEU (1994b). FEU (1989) is one of many publications dealing with the competency-based curriculum. These publications were outside the scope of Nicholas who concentrated on journals and papers.
3 Maslow is a very Influential Humanistic Psychologist; Humanistic Psychology and Behaviourist Psychology may be viewed as occupying opposite ends of a continuum.
4 See Mitchell in this volume for an example of a more sophisticated Unit, taken from an NVQ at post qualifying level for the Chartered Association of Certified Accountants; similar principles apply.
5 Cf Harrop in this volume on the flexibility there is in deciding how to deliver the curriculum with GNVQs.
6 Cf note 4 in Jessup's chapter in this volume.
7 Cf Young p. 175, and Oates and Harkin, p. 194 in the volume.

References

APPLE, M. (1981) 'Social structure, ideology and curriculum' in LAWN, M. and BARTON, L. (Eds) *Rethinking Curriculum Studies*, London, Croom Helm.
BEAUCHAMP, G.A. (1968) (2nd edition) *Curriculum Theory*, Albuquerque, Kagg Press.
BEES, M. and SWORDS, M. (1990) *National Vocational Qualifications*. London, Kogan Page.
BLOOM, B.S. (1956) (Ed) *Taxonomy of Educational Objectives*, New York, McKay.
BLUMER, H. (1969) 'The methodological position of Symbolic Interactionism' in HAMMERSLEY, M. and WOODS, P. (Eds) *The Process of Schooling*, London, Routledge & Kegan Paul in association with the Open University.
BOBBIT, F. (1918) *The Curriculum*, BOSTON, M., Houghton Mifflin.
BOWLES, S. and GINTIS, H. (1976) *Schooling in Capitalist America*, New York, Basic Books.
BURKE, J. (1989a) 'Research in NVQs' in *Competence and Assessment,* 8, pp. 12–18.
BURKE, J. (1989b) (Ed) *Competency Based Education and Training*, London, Falmer Press.
BURKE, J. (1989c) 'The implementation of NVQs' in BURKE, J. (Ed) *Competency Based Education and Training*, London, Falmer Press.

BURKE, J. (1991) 'Competence and higher education: Implications for institutions and professional bodies' in RAGGATT, P. and UNWIN, L. (Eds) *Change and Intervention: Vocational Education and Training*, London, Falmer Press.

BURKE, J. (1992) 'Exploring a new paradigm: Research degree programme in NVQs' in *Education Technology & Training International* **29**, 3.

CHARTERS, W.W. (1924) *Curriculum Construction*, New York, Macmillan.

ED (current) *Competence and Assessment*, Quarterly Journal from Employment Department, Moorfoot, Sheffield.

EDWARDS, C. (1994) 'GNVQ science and progression to higher education' in *PSSI Forum* No 13.

EISNER, E.W. (1969) 'Instructive and expressive educational objectives: Their formulation and use in curriculum', in POPHAM, W.J. *et al* (Eds) *Instructional Objectives* (AERA Curriculum Evaluation Monograph 3) Chicago, I., Rand McNally.

ERAUT, M. (1989) 'Initial Teacher Training and the NCVQ Model', in BURKE, J. (Ed) *Competency Based Education and Training*, London, Falmer Press.

ERAUT, M. (1989a) (Ed) *The International Encyclopedia of Educational Technology*, Oxford, Pergamon Press.

ERAUT, M. (1989b) 'Selecting and Justifying Objectives' in ERAUT, M. (Ed) *The International Encyclopedia of Educational Technology*, Oxford, Pergamon Press.

ERAUT, M. (1989c) 'Specifying and Using Objectives' in ERAUT, M. (Ed) *The International Encyclopedia of Educational Technology*, Oxford, Pergamon Press.

ERAUT, M. (*forthcoming*, 1994) *Developing Professional Knowledge and Competence*, London, Falmer Press.

FEU (1989) *Implications of Competence Based Curricula*, London, Further Education Unit.

FEU (1992a) *NVQs in the Construction Craft Industry*, London, FEU.

FEU (1992b) *The Assessment of Work Based Learning*, London, FEU.

FEU (1994a) *Introducing GNVQs: Staff Development*, London, FEU.

FEU (1994b) *Introducing GNVQs: Planning, Coordination and Management of the GNVQ Curriculum*, London, FEU.

GAGNÉ, R.M. (1965) 'The analysis of instructional objectives for the design of instructions' in GLASER, R. (1965) (Ed) *Teaching Machines and Programmed Learning Vol 2, Data and Directions* Department of Audio-visual Instruction, National Education Association (NEA), Washington DC, pp. 21–65.

GAGNÉ, R.M. and BRIGGS, L.J. (1974) *Principles of Instructional Design*, New York, Rinehart and Winston.

GRUNDY, S. (1987) *Curriculum: Product or Praxis?* London, Falmer Press.

HAFFENDEN, I. and BROWN, A. (1989) 'Towards the Implementation of Competence Based Curricula in FE' in BURKE, J. (Ed) *Competrency Based Education and Training*, London, Falmer Press.

HARROP, J. (1992) *Response to Consultation on General National Vocational Qualifications*, London, NCVQ.

HIGHER Education Quality Council (1994a) *Choosing to Change: Extending Access, Choice and Mobility in Higher Education*, the Report of the HEQC CAT Development Council, London, HEQC.

HIGHER Education Quality Council (1994b) *Change*, an executive summary of the Report of the HEQC CAT Development Council, London, HEQC.

HIRST, P.H. (1974) *Knowledge and the Curriculum; A Collection of Philosophical Papers*, London, Routledge & Kegan Paul.

HOLMES, B. and MCLEAN, M. (1989) *The Curriculum: A Comparative Perspective*, London, Unwin Hyman.

HOOPER, R. (1971) (Ed) *The Curriculum: Context, Design and Development*, Edinburgh, Oliver and Boyd, in association with the Open University Press.

HOLT, M. (1983) *Curriculum Workshop: An Introduction to Whole Curriculum Planning*. Routledge & Kegan Paul, London.

HUNTER, I.M.L. (1970) 'Behaviourism' in BULLOCK, A. and STALLYBRASS, O. (1977) (Eds) *The Fontana Dictionary of Modern Thought*, London, Collins.

JACKSON, P.W. (1968) *Life in Classrooms*. New York, Holt, Rinehart and Winston.

JESSUP, G. (1989) 'The Emerging Model of Vocational Education and Training', in BURKE, J. (Ed) *Competency Based Education and Training*, London, Falmer Press.

JESSUP, G. (1990) 'National Vocational Qualifications: implications for further education', in BEES, M. and SWORDS, M. (Eds) (1990). *National Vocational Qualifications and Further Education*, London, Kogan Page.

JESSUP, G. (1990a) *Accreditation of Prior Learning in the Context of National Vocational Qualifications* Report No 7, London, NCVQ.

JESSUP, G. (1991) *Outcomes: NVQs and the Emerging Model of Education and Training*, London, Falmer Press.

JESSUP, G. (1992) 'Developing a coherent national framework of qualifications', in *Educational & Training Technology International*, 3, 29.

KELLY, A.V. (1987) *Education*, London, Heinemann.

KELLY, A.V. (1989) 3rd ed. *The Curriculum; Theory and Practice*, London, Paul Chapman.

KERR, J.F. (1968) (Ed) *Changing the Curriculum*, London, University of London Press, and reissued in HOOPER. R. (1971).

KLEIN, M.F. (1989) 'Curriculum design' in ERAUT, M. (Ed) (1989a) *The International Encyclopedia of Educational Technology*, Oxford, Pergamon Press.

KRATWOHL, D.R. (1965) 'Stating objectives appropriately for program, for curriculum, and for instructional materials development', *Journal of Teacher Education* Vol 16, pp. 83–92.

LAMM, Z. (1966) *Curriculum Planning Models* (unpublished) cited and illustrated in TAYLOR, H. (1967) 'Purpose and structure in the curriculum' in HOOPER, R. (Ed) (1971) *The Curriculum: Context, Design & Development*, Edinburgh, Oliver & Boyd, Edinburgh, in association with The Open University Press.

LAWN, M. and OZGA, J. (1981) 'The educational worker? A reassessment of teachers', in BARTON, L. and WALKER, S. (Eds) *Schools, Teachers and Teaching*, London, Falmer Press.

LAWTON, D. (1973) *Social Change, Educational Theory and Curriculum Planning*, London, Hodder and Stoughton.

LAWTON, D., GORDON, P., INGE, M., GIBBY, B., PRING, R. and MOORE, T. (1978) *Theory and Practice of Curriculum Studies*, London, Routledge & Kegan Paul.

LOFTHOUSE, B. (1990) (2nd ed), (Compiler) *The Study of Primary Education: A Source Book. Vol 2, The Curriculum*, London, Falmer Press.

MAGER, R.F. (1962) *Preparing Instructional Objectives*, Palo Alto, CA., Fearon.

MANSELL, T., BECHER, T., PARLETT, M., SIMONS, H. and SQUIRES, G. (1976) *The Container Revolution: A Study of Unit and Modular Schemes*, Group for Research and Innovation in Higher Education, London, Nuffield Foundation.

MARSH, C.J. (1992) *Key Concepts for Understanding Curriculum*, London, Falmer Press.

MACKENZIE, N., ERAUT, M. and JONES, H.C. (1970) *Teaching and Learning: An Introduction to New Methods and Resources in Higher Education*, Paris, UNESCO and The International Association of Universities.

MILLINGTON, J. (1990) 'Engineering training and further education: a changing relationship', in BEES, M. and SWORDS, M. (Eds) *National Vocational Qualifications and Further Education*, London, Kogan Page in association with the National Council for Vocational Qualifications.

NCVQ and ED (1991) *Guide to National Vocational Qualifications*, London, National Council for Vocational Qualifications and Employment Department.

NCVQ (1993) *A Statement by the National Council for Vocational Qualifications (NCVQ) on 'All Our Futures — Britain's Education Revolution'*, a Channel 4 Dispatches programme on 15 December 1993 and associated report by the Centre for Education and Employment Research, University of Manchester, London, NCVQ.

NCVQ (1993) *Assessing Competence in Unpaid Work*, London, NCVQ.

NCVQ (1993) *GNVQ in Art and Design*, Assessing Students' Work Series, London, NCVQ.

OATES, T. (1989) 'Emerging Issues: the response of HE to competency based approaches', in BURKE, J. (Ed) *Competency Based Education and Training*, London, Falmer Press.

OATES, T. (1992) *Developing and Piloting the NCVQ Core Skills*, Report No 16, London, NCVQ.

ONG, W.J. (1959) 'Latin language study as a Renaissance puberty rite' in *Studies in Philology* LVI, 2, pp. 103–24.

OTTER, S. (1992) *Learning Outcomes in Higher Education*, London, Unit for the Development of Adult Continuing Education.

PETTIT, A., COOK, G. and SILVER, R. 'NVQs and the role of guidance in competence-led curricula', in BEES, M. and SWORDS, M. (Eds) *National Vocational Qualifications and Further Education*, London, Kogan Page in association with the National Council for Vocational Qualifications.

POPHAM W.J., EISNER, E.W., SULLIVAN, H. and TYLER, L.L. (1969) (Eds) *Instructional Objectives*. (AERA Curriculum Evaluation Monograph 3) Chicago, Rand McNally.

RICHMOND, W.K. (1971) *The School Curriculum*, London, Methuen.

RIDING, R. and BUTTERFIELD, S. (1990) (Eds) *Assessment and Examination in the Secondary School*, London, Routledge.

ROBY, B. (1990) 'Assessment and the Curriculum' in RIDING, R. and BUTTERFIELD, S. (Eds) (1990). *Assessment and Examination in the Secondary School*, London, Routledge.

ROWNTREE, D. (1982) (2nd ed) *Educational Technology in Curriculum Development*, London, Harper & Row.

ROYAL SOCIETY (1993) *Higher Education Futures*, a report by a study group of the Royal Society, Council under the Chairmanship of Sir Eric Ash, London, Royal Society.

SAYLOR, J.G. and ALEXANDER, W.M. (1954) *Curriculum Planning for Better Teaching and Learning*, London, Rinehart.

SHACKLETON, J. (1989) 'An achievement-led college', in BURKE, J. (1989) *Competency Based Education and Training*, London, Falmer Press.

SHACKLETON, J. (1990) 'NVQs: a whole college approach' in BEES, M. and SWORDS, M. (Eds) *National Vocational Qualifications and Further Education*, London, Kogan Page, in association with the National Council for Vocational Qualifications.

SKILBECK, M. (1984) *School-based Curriculum Development*, London, Harper & Row.

SMITH, E.R. and TYLER, R.W. (1942) *Appraising and Recording Student Progress*, New York, Harper.

SMITH, O.B. STANLEY, W.O. and SHORES, J.H. (1957) *Fundamentals of Curriculum Development*, New York, World Book.

STENHOUSE, L. (1970) 'Some limitations of the use of objectives in curriculum research and planning' *Paedagogica Europaea*, 6, pp. 73–83.

STENHOUSE, L. (1975) *An Introduction to Curriculum Research and Development*, London, Heinemann.

SOCKETT, H. (1976) *Designing the Curriculum*, London, Open Books.

TABA, H. (1962) *Curriculum Development; Theory and Practice*, New York, Harcourt, Brace and World.

TAYLOR, F.W. (1912) *Scientific Management*, New York, Harper.

TYLER, R.W. (1949) *Basic Principles of Curriculum and Instruction*, Chicago, University of Chicago Press.

WHEELER, D.K. (1967) *Curriculum Process*, London, University of London Press.

WILKINSON, R. (1964) *The Prefects*, Oxford, Oxford University Press.

WOLF, A. (1993) *Assessment Issues and Problems in a Criterion Based System*, London, FEU.

YOUNG, M. (1971) *Knowledge and Control*, London, Collier Macmillan.

Chapter 4

Standards and the Outcomes Approach

Paul Ellis

Introduction

Very few of those who have made their careers in helping others to learn, or studying how this can best be achieved, would question the importance of having effective education and training arrangements in place. Increasingly these views on the central role of education and training are being widely shared by others who start from a range of differing perspectives.

This growing recognition of the importance of education and training is accompanied by a better understanding of the economic consequences of investing in human potential, demands for greater accountability in return for the resources that are made available and a questioning of existing arrangements and willingness to change. The essence of the emerging consensus is captured by Sir Christopher Ball writing in the Royal Society of Arts publication *Profitable Learning* in 1992 where he argues 'Those nations that invest in learning gain economic, social and personal benefit for their citizens. Those that fail to do so suffer economic decline . . . But existing systems produce existing results. If we want something different we must change the system'.

The Need to Question and Change

This willingness to question and change is crucial to bringing about improvement. All too often recognition of shortcomings in the effects of education and training is accompanied by a form of fatalism and shifting of blame from education professionals to others, frequently the students. However, to quote Sir Christopher Ball again, this time from 1991 'It needs to be considered whether problems of the UK education and training systems are not created more by the culture and attitudes of those responsible for their supply than by the poverty of the aspirations of our people'.

The need to attend to low levels of aspiration and achievement which can be engendered in individuals by their experiences, combined with a willingness to explore possible changes and a drive towards accountability, are emerging themes in diverse parts of the education and training system. In a press report on primary school arrangements in 1991 Professor Robin Alexander described some provision as 'Strong on values and assertion, weak on substance and justification . . . A tendency to acquiesce in low expectations . . . more attention to teachers and class-rooms than children's learning'. Peter Morgan, Director General of the Institute of Directors is reported in HRD News (1990) as saying that Britain's academic establishment has created a system that has 'incredible disregard for human poten-tial'. Major changes in the education system are called for to break the academic mould and discard the idea that 'the function of education is not to help us earn a living but to humanise our inner nature'. There is, of course, a place for 'human-ising' and other important aims *alongside* preparation for employment.

The disregard for human potential which can result from certain arrange-ments is an increasing cause for concern. Talking about 'A' levels, Professor Roger Blin-Stoyle in his Presidential Address to the Institute of Physics in 1991 commented on what he saw as

> A set of rigid tramlines on which there are no intermediate stops or changes and culminating, for many, in disaster at the end of the track (leading to the) . . . ridiculous situation that last year 25.2 per cent of those on the physics tramline failed the examination and had nothing to show at the end of their journey.

The Audit Commission OFSTED report published in 1993 concludes starkly that the cost of the courses taken by students who do not achieve their intended qualification aim is £500 million each year.

A Restricted View of Human Potential

There is also a strengthening acknowledgement that we have been hampered by a restricted view of human potential and achievements. The monoculture of aca-demic measurement of achievement neglects the strengths of the greater portion of our population. Professor Sternberg of Yale University has suggested that the talents of thousands of young people are being wasted because educational sys-tems measure only academic success and not practical creative or interpersonal skills. He argues that 'practical' intelligence is of more use than academic intelli-gence; tacit knowledge — the ability to succeed at work — would bring higher success. This tacit knowledge is not correlated with IQ, academic tests do not predict it. We therefore need to change measures to look for practical intelligence not just academic abilities. He concludes that the mediocre pupil who assimilates on the job experience after starting work is more likely to excel than the school swot who scores 'A' grades in every subject.

Accountability

Accountability is an increasingly dominant component in any area of public de-bate, but this is not just a fad or fashion; there are good reasons why this should be so. It is of the essence of professional practice to be accountable; to be open to question and to be required to justify what you do as a professional. This in turn may dictate change. Change may be uncomfortable, evaluation and self-criticism may be very demanding disciplines. It is more comfortable, warmer and cuddlier to have an unquestioning set of beliefs on which you act, and to continue with inherited practices without evaluation, but this is hardly sound ethical professional practice.

More specifically in terms of the focus of this discussion, there are powerful reasons for requiring that education and training arrangements should be transparent and accountable. They consume economic resources and also the time and commitment of those who participate in the arrangements, the clients of the system. Accountability is thus dictated by arguments relating to both efficiency and fairness. The activities of those who have responsibility for education and training cannot be determined solely by their own boundaries of comfort. Bob Spooner, in the August 1992 issue of *Education*, describes bad teachers as those who 'make the demands that they believe that children of a particular age should be able to meet without ever modifying them to suit the individual's need. They do what a computer programme could do, but with more malice and less patience'. The implication is not, of course, that 'bad teachers' abound, but neither are they unknown. A professionally critical approach and a willingness to reappraise and where necessary change is thus a necessary characteristic at the level of both the individual and the overall system. Clearly complacency has no part to play in our approach to education and training, but what sort of progress should we be looking for, what sort of changes are likely to be for the better? I want to suggest a number of steps which while described separately, do in fact strongly interrelate.

As a first step I would wish to suggest that in creating education and training systems we need to be explicit as to their intentions; what it is we will strive to achieve as a result of them. This approach promotes clarity and openness thereby contributing to informed debate and rational decision-making, involving a wide community of stakeholders in the education and training process.

By stating the intended outcomes of the system accountability becomes a realistic possibility by opening up arrangements to measurement. There is also protection against unintentional drift, which must be a real danger over a period of time if the objectives of a particular system are only vaguely documented. The result of such drift can be that an originally well intentioned curriculum intervention can lose relevance and coherence over time, especially as its application is widened beyond tightly knit inner design groups.

When made available to learners, explicit statements of intended outcomes encourage clarity and ownership. Learners are able to take charge of their own learning to a much greater extent, and indeed to take part in the discussions as to what they should be expected to achieve. The real intention of learning ceases to be a mystical and largely inaccessible secret in the hands of a few. There is growing evidence that this open approach has extremely positive effects on learner autonomy, motivation, levels of achievement, and on the utility and transferability of these achievements to new situations.

There are of course, strongly held views in opposition to outcomes approaches; these views stress the primacy of processes. It is remarkable though how frequently a circularity occurs in the position which is taken. The case for defining process is usually ultimately made in terms of the effects (outcomes) it is assumed to promote! (cf Buke, Chapter 3 in this volume).

Flexibility and Intended Outcomes

The second major step which I wish to suggest is to allow flexibility and the possibility of innovation into the system. This is closely linked to the first step of being explicit regarding intended outcomes. By stating what is to be achieved it is possible to establish accountability without the rigidity which is introduced by limiting *how* this is to be brought about.

A common misunderstanding of outcomes approaches it that, because they start with a definition of what is to be achieved rather than how the learning is to take place, they have no concern for, or interest in, the efficiency of learning. In fact quite the opposite is true. It is part of what I call the outcomes anomaly. Simply put, outcomes approaches do not specify in advance the learning process, but allow maximum discretion and innovation to maximize the effectiveness of that process. It is rather like giving someone you love the space to grow and develop rather than smothering them. Outcomes approaches do not outlaw considerations of the curriculum; they bring them to the forefront and need to be allied with them. Assumptions about how learning can be best achieved and rigid prescriptions are thus avoided.

Broad View of Human Potential

The third component of my suggestion is that we need to take a broad view of human potential and the range of achievements that we value. The case has already been made that an academic monoculture has done a disservice to our populace and the economy. This is not to argue that there should not be a specification of academic achievements, only that there are additional domains of achievement.

Even within a domain, however, a narrow vision can dominate when specifying what lies within its boundaries. If we are going to be explicit about intended outcomes we need to include *all* the intended outcomes. This will involve taking on board a number of different perspectives and seeking to incorporate all the nuances and complexities which are an essential part of the richness of human ability and performance. The complex, judgmental, and interdependent aspects of what people do need to be incorporated as well as the simple and obvious. Core skills, which are the topic of a later chapter of this book, are an instance.

This position will be welcomed by many who are concerned with the breadth of vision that we should espouse. There will undoubtedly, though, be some objections along the lines that it is unethical to attempt to influence the attitudes and behaviour of individuals through education. It needs to be asked whether all those who promote this argument act on their own professional practice as though they have no interest in the effect that their actions have on students.

Relevance

The fourth step I would propose is that the specification of intended outcomes should be audited for relevance. The case for this is perhaps most pointed in vocational education. Raizen (1989), for instance, notes a move towards more academic courses in search of rigour leading to a mismatch between the culture of the school and the culture of the workplace. The effects are to devalue the ability to solve real problems which present themselves in complex and contextualised forms. Raizen quotes the USA Committee for Economic Development which in 1985 declared:

> Many 'vocational education' programs are almost worthless. They are a cruel hoax on young people looking to acquire marketable skills. So many different, and in many cases, unproductive programs in our public schools have been called vocational education that most existing programs need to be disbanded or reshaped.

Moonie (1993) has a related concern that there can be emphasis on surface decontextualized knowledge for its own sake rather than recognition of the need for individuals to construct and design their own interpretative structure to cope with the demands of employment. This is not intended to imply that academic outcomes are inappropriate in all contexts. The essential point is that all specifications should be validated for fitness for purpose. This purpose will itself exhibit differentiation between domains and thus so too will the outcomes which are judged to be fit.

Maximizing Achievement

The fifth and final step that I propose is that we should consider how we can maximize achievement from our pool of human potential, rather than simply select out the most able according to one conception of achievement. In part this involves recognizing the different domains of achievement as described earlier. It also involves including everyone in on the opportunities to achieve rather than selecting out a small minority.

It is a simple statistical fact of life that outstanding individuals are few and far between. Professor John Kay of London Business School argues strongly 'I can't repeat often enough that running businesses in the long term is not about individuals of great genius, but turning people of ordinary ability into an efficient structure'. Moonie (1993) believes that 'The outcomes model offers several major benefits compared to normative systems. Normative assessment provided for the selection of a sample of high achievers from a pool of talent. The system implied the necessity of winners and losers in competitive assessment for qualifications. The outcomes model provides the possibility of maximizing the "pool" of talent by providing opportunities for all to reach the specified standards. Outcomes hold out the possibility of enlarging the pool of human resources available to the country'. The best match for our requirements thus lies in criterion referenced rather than primarily competitive educational paradigms.

The Need for Clarity of Intended Outcomes

It is evident that explicitness and clarity of intended outcomes is not a current characteristic of major parts of the education and training system, as is evidenced by stories which abound on such issues as disappointing training courses and bad luck in examination question spotting. Otter (1993) reports on a study in higher education: 'The debate . . . posed some interesting questions about the extent to which students understood the implicit cognitive skills they were expected to develop. It was not clear from the consultative exercises with students that these were the skills which students themselves expected to develop as a result of a degree course. It was equally not clear that all courses were designed to develop, or give students opportunities to practice these skills. This became even more apparent when methods of assessing outcomes were considered'.

The Need for Standards

What we need are external and visible achievement standards, open to both teachers and learners, as a basis for assessment. Authors such as Sadler (1987) propose the use of natural language descriptions used in conjunction with exemplars as the solution. Sadler's achievement standards utilize multiple criteria to enable statements to be made about a student's quality of performance or degree of achievement without reference to other students.

NVQs and GNVQs as a Solution to the Problem

This solution is very similar to that being pursued in Britain with the development of National Vocational Qualifications (NVQs) and more recently General National Qualifications (GNVQs). Qualifications are a powerful medium for carrying messages about the nature and intent of the education system and are particularly suited as the focus of an outcomes approach. In 1986 a government sponsored review of qualifications in Britain identified concerns very similar to those documented by Raizen. The review concluded that there were several weaknesses in the qualifications arrangements which existed at the time. These weaknesses included:

— Limited take-up of vocational qualifications.
— Insufficient recognition of learning gained outside of education and training.
— Assessment methods biased towards the testing of knowledge rather than skill or competence.
— Barriers to access to qualifications and inadequate arrangements for progression and transfer of credit.
— Considerable overlaps and gaps with no readily understandable pattern of provision.

Action was proposed to rectify these weaknesses. This involved creating a system of qualifications which would benefit individuals, employers and the economy by clearly incorporating outcomes reflecting the standards required in employment. A new National Council for Vocational Qualifications was set up to introduce these NVQs. The remainder of this chapter focuses on the standards which are the central component of these NVQs. A later chapter explores the closely aligned characteristics of GNVQs. (Cf. Harrop, Chapter 6)

NVQs are an extensively developed instance of what Jessup (1991) has termed an outcomes approach. They allow industry to specify its performance requirements, documenting these within qualifications as the targets or intention of the vocational education and training system. They bring into effect all the benefits previously outlined including, crucially, allowing the creation of new routes to achievement. At the same time coherence is preserved by certificating a shared set of end achievements.

Coherence

A consistent structuring contributes to coherence across the NVQ framework. Each NVQ is composed of units of competence (figure 4.1). The unit of competence is a relatively self-contained achievement and should insofar as possible be complete. It has a title (for example, 'establishing ornamental borders') which indicates the area of competence covered.

Figure 4.1   Structure of an NVQ

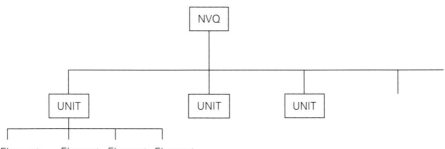

The competence is further detailed in elements of competence. An element of competence is a description of something which a person working in an occupational area should be able to do. In other words it is an action or behaviour that the individual should be able to demonstrate. It will consist of a short sentence including a verb specifying an activity and the object of the activity. It is constructed in such a way that it can be prefaced by the words 'the candidate should be able to'.

Within this basic structure a great deal of methodological work has been undertaken to ensure that the specifications developed are complete and accurate. Occupational competence is rich and complex and must be fully captured if the power and quality of the outcomes approach is to be realized.

This methodological development is evident when the format of the NVQ Statement of Competence is explored within an element. Each element has several performance criteria associated with it (figure 4.2). The element indicates what someone should be able to do, the performance criteria describe how well it needs to be done. Each performance criterion includes a critical outcome and an evaluative statement. The performance criteria are, in effect, the quality statements

Figure 4.2   An element of competence from unit 'assess candidate using diverse evidence'

COLLATE AND EVALUATE EVIDENCE

Performance Criteria

*   candidate is encouraged to identify and
     present relevant evidence

*   evidence is accurately judged against
     elements and performance criteria

*   only the specified performance criteria
     are used in forming judgments

*   the evidence can be reliably attributed to
     the candidate

*   inconsistencies in the evidence available
     are clarified and resolved

*   adequate safeguards are operated to
     ensure authenticity of evidence and
     currency of competence

Range

Source of Evidence:
Natural performance; simulations; projects
and assignments; questioning

Direct assessment; judgment of other
assessors; candidate and peer reports;
candidate prior experience

attached to the function detailed in the element 'stem'. By attaching several criteria
to each function, each criterion representing a distinctive necessary quality, the
true complexity of occupational competence is acknowledged.

There is a further component to the specification which makes up an element
in the NVQ statement of competence; the range statement. Range statements are
used to identify the contexts in which the element with its performance criteria
applies. The range statement is crucial in representing the full occupational expectations of a NVQ including the fact that the competent individual should be able
to adapt to a variety of differing circumstances and both present and future demands.
Through range statements this requirement is made explicit and is given precise
boundaries allowing the design of both learning and assessment arrangements to
be accurately targeted.

A Focus on What the Individual Can Do

From this description of the format of the statement of competence it is evident
that the focus is on what the individual is able to do, rather than on what he/she
knows. It is also clear that demanding competence specifications such as these will

require that learning involves approaching a body of knowledge, principles and skills. The evidence that is considered in judging an individual's claim to competence will also usually be a mixture of evidence from practice and evidence of knowledge. The focus on performance in the statement of competence is however conceptually critical within the approach, making it clear that recourse to knowledge is a means, not an end in itself.

The format of the NVQ statement of competence is sufficiently sophisticated to represent the richness of occupational competence. To complement it analytical strategies have had to be developed which allow powerful and insightful exploration of the nature of the competences to be represented. A weakness of many of the previously available analytical approaches is that they produce detailed but superficial and atomized descriptions.

The analysis process for NVQs starts with identifying the key purpose for the whole occupational sector viewed in very broad terms. This is described by Mansfield (1991) as comparable to the idea of a 'mission statement'. Some key purposes might be:

- *STEEL MANUFACTURE*: Manufacture and supply a range of iron and steel goods by processing raw materials to meet anticipated and actual market requirements.
- *BUILDING SOCIETIES*: Provide financial advisory and investment services to individual and group (non-corporate) customers.
- *TRAINING AND DEVELOPMENT*: Develop human potential to assist organizations and individuals to achieve their objectives.

The key purpose is the reference point from which all further stages in the analysis are developed.

Progressive desegregation is then applied to break down the key purpose into smaller components, without losing sight of this key purpose. The basis of this further breakdown might be:

- stages in a process or system
- different products which require different standards
- different methods which require different standards
- different applications (for example, processes applied to people; processes applied to organizations)

and so on. There are many such possible 'desegregation rules' and the appropriate ones for the occupational sector being studied will need to be explored. Mansfield graphically illustrates this process of desegregation for the steel manufacture key purpose by showing the analysis in figure 4.3.

The focus provided by the key purpose is one safeguard against trivializing the specification which emerges through analysis. A second safeguard is repeated reference to a conceptualization of competence which sees four distinctive but interrelated aspects to all work roles. These are:

- *TECHNICAL SKILL*: Normally the most immediately apparent aspect of performance involving the ability to perform component tasks.
- *CONTINGENCY MANAGEMENT SKILL*: The ability to deal with non-routine and unexpected occurrences and variances in procedures.

Figure 4.3: Progressive desegregation of a key purpose

KEY PURPOSE: Supply a range of iron and steel products by processing raw materials, to meet anticipated and actual market requirements

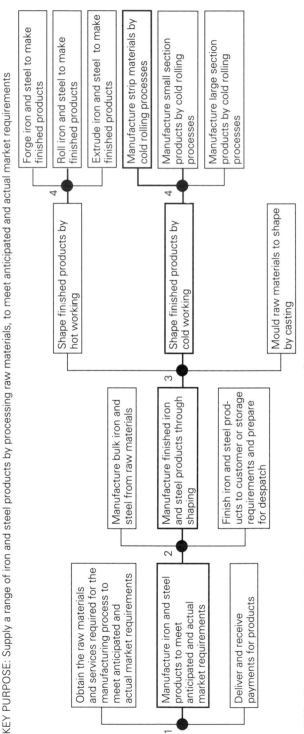

NOTE: Bold boxes show the detailed route taken to develop the Units and Elements structure

● = point at which a 'rule' is applied

1. System — input (obtain supplies), process (make products), output (deliver)
2. Process — making bulk steel, shaping, finishing
3. Method of changing shape — hot working, cold working, casting
4. At point four two rules are applied — method and product

- *TASK MANAGEMENT SKILL*: Managing the individual task components, and competing demands, in realising the overall organizational objective.
- *JOB ROLE ENVIRONMENT SKILL*: Interpreting the job demands, dealing with colleagues and clients and, in effect, adapting the performance to the often complex demands which shape real activities.

It is considered that each of these four aspects should be fully evident in each stage of the descriptive desegregation process. Checks that this is indeed the case keep the analysis on course.

There are some similarities in the methodology described to the approaches adopted in the existing technique of hierarchical task analysis. However, in analyzing occupational competence the various components of what has come to be called in the British system 'Functional Analysis' combine into a formidably powerful and sophisticated approach.

Potential for Encompassing Complex Professional Activities

It is not unusual to encounter the view that all that has been described may be well and good for routine or lower level competence, but that it could not be used to capture the essence of complex professional activities. There are, it is argued, less tangible features of performance at these levels that are not amenable to this approach.

These issues were extensively explored at a recent seminar which Gealy (1993) reports as concluding:

> Breaking down competence by functional analysis into units which can be used as building blocks of vocational qualifications was universally acknowledged as useful. The breakdown of units into elements each of which has a set of performance criteria was also endorsed.

Eraut following a study of assessment in the professions expresses the following view:

> We are convinced that all professions should have public statements about what their qualified members are competent to do and what people can reasonably expect of them.

Undoubtedly the extension of the outcomes approach into higher levels will bring new challenges into focus. Despite this the fundamental principles are sufficiently robust to be equally applicable.

The most frequent concern is that personal qualities such as creativity, flair or probity, or values, such as concern for the environment, might be neglected. There is no reason why they should be, but they need to be transformed from highly interpretative terms referring to some assumed internal state of the individual into something more concrete. This transformation involves asking what is the *consequence* of having the assumed quality.

If we ask what is the desired effect of an architect processing creativity we might conclude that amongst other things it results in a unique use of space and form in meeting a client's brief. Concern for the environment is converted into designs which conserve energy and minimize environmental input. At the end of the day justification for taking an interest in these internal states is that they have a discernible, indeed a crucial, effect on the quality of performance.

Edmonds and Teh (1990) explored how this applies to management competence. In the management area it is common to identify personal qualities which are seen as central to effective performance by the individual manager. Instances might be 'showing sensitivity to the needs of others' or 'showing concern for excellence'. Edmonds and Teh point out that the outcomes approach, by defining what has to be achieved, allows individuals considerable freedom to develop their own personal style of responding to the work role.

The objective is not to produce a cohort of management clones with identical characteristics and attributes. What is important is that an individual is aware of his or her own unique pattern of strengths and weaknesses and can optimize the way these are applied to meet differing circumstances. Thus while personal attributes do not appear within outcomes, a study of these attributes may assist in the design of effective programmes of personal development which help an individual in achieving the specified competences.

An interesting line of development is opened up by Fleming (1991) who argues that many higher level competences are in the nature of meta-competence, acting on more specific competences to produce change and flexibility, allowing the individual to utilize the particular competences in completely new situations. If so it is important to describe them explicitly so that they can be accurately targeted. Slipping into delivering knowledge for its own sake, or as an ill thought out proxy for meta-competence, is a poor substitute.

The principle of some competences organizing or working through other competences has found another outlet in core skills specifications which are described in Chapter 11. The idea that education and training should develop basic skills that underpin performance in a wide variety of situations is, of course, not new. What is new is the existence of an agreed national specification, shared by education and training using a sophisticated outcomes based format to allow core skills to be assessed and certificated. Competence in core skills is acquired in context, and assessment also occurs in context; separate certification ensures that they are given importance and promotes transfer of the core skills to new contexts.

I have argued in this chapter that adopting an outcomes approach, if done with vision and imagination, can have an immensely energizing effect on vocational education and training. Greater numbers of individuals can be motivated to higher levels of achievement while improving relevance and accountability within the system. Clearly the realization of these benefits will pose many challenges along the way. Later chapters will explore some of these challenges in depth and show how the outcomes approach has been extended to a new form of qualification known as GNVQs and to the specification and assessment of core skills.

References

AUDIT COMMISSION/OFSTED (1993) *Unfinished Business*, London, HMSO.
BALL, SIR CHRISTOPHER (1991) *Learning Pays — The Role of Post Compulsory Education and Training*, London, RSA.

BALL, SIR CHRISTOPHER (1992) *Profitable Learning*, London, RSA.

EDMONDS, T. and TEH, M. (1990) 'Personal competence: Where does it fit in?' *Competence and Assessment*, 13, pp. 6–8.

ERAUT, M. and COLE, G. (1993) 'Assessing Competence in the Professions', R&D Report 14, Sheffield, Methods and Standards Unit, Employment Department.

FLEMING, D. (1991) 'The concept of meta-competence', *Competence and Assessment*, 16, pp. 9–12.

GEALY, N. (1993) 'Development of NVQs and SVQs at Higher Levels', *Competence and Assessment*, 21, pp. 4–10.

JESSUP, G. (1991) *Outcomes: NVQs and the Emerging Model of Education and Training*, London, Falmer Press.

MANSFIELD, B. (1991) 'Deriving Standards of Competence', in Fennell, E. (Ed) *Development of Assessable Standards for National Certification*.

MOONIE, N.P. (1993) 'Outcomes and autonomy', paper presented to the Educational and Training Technology International Conference at Glasgow and to appear in *Aspects of Educational Technology*, 27, Kogan Page.

MSC/DES (1986) *Review of Vocational Qualifications in England and Wales*, London, HMSO.

OTTER, S. (1993) 'Learning outcomes in higher education', *Competence and Assessment*, 20, pp. 18–22.

RAIZEN, S.A. (1989) *Reforming Education for Work: A Cognitive Science Perspective*, Berkeley, CA, National Centre for Research in Vocational Education.

SADLER, R.D. (1987) 'Specifying and Promulgating Achievement Standards', *Oxford Review of Education*, 13, 2, pp. 191–209.

Chapter 5

Outcomes and National (Scottish) Vocational Qualifications

Lindsay Mitchell

Introduction[1]

National (Scottish) Vocational Qualifications (NVQs/SVQs) are outcome-based — formed from groupings of occupational standards. The outcomes in NVQs/ SVQs are derived from, and defined in respect of, the requirements of employment. As such, NVQs and SVQs have an external reference point — a consensus about the expectations of employment in a particular occupational sector or area of work.

NVQs and SVQs attest to the occupational competence of an individual against nationally-recognised occupational standards. The reason for the development of NVQs and SVQs is somewhat wider than this, based on the Government's commitment to improving the occupational competence of the UK workforce. NVQs and SVQs are a central plank in Government policy and their purpose is linked to this aim — the improvement of occupational competence across the UK workforce and hence, so the argument goes, to enhance the UK's ability to compete in world markets.

The essential focus of NVQs and SVQs is work and demonstrated evidence from an individual that s/he can meet the standards required in employment.

This chapter concentrates on:

- occupational standards as outcome statements;
- the incorporation of standards into NVQs and SVQs;
- the impact of NVQs and SVQs on learning;
- the use of occupational standards in describing occupational competence, particularly for those aspects which are seen to be 'beyond description, formalization or outcomes'.

Occupational Standards and Outcomes

The purpose of occupational standards is to make a clear link between the requirements of the economy and the competence of the workforce. Occupational standards do this by focusing on the expectations of people at work — the functions which need to be performed and the outcomes which indicate successful performance. Occupational standards are made up of three aspects:

- elements of competence which state the functions which are needed in particular occupational areas;
- performance criteria, which are attached to each element, describe the quality of the outcomes of successful performance;
- the indicators of range describe the potential dimensions or parameters of the function — what is included in the coverage of the element and performance criteria and what is not.

Occupational standards are descriptions of performance which establish benchmarks against which an individual's performance can be judged. They are derived using a process known as functional analysis which focuses on the roles which are performed in an occupational area and the expectations (in terms of the outcomes) of any individual performing that role[2]. Functional analysis is an iterative process which seeks to establish a consensus of views about best practice in an occupational area including the inherent tensions with which practitioners have to cope. During the analysis process, developers not only have to take account of the technical requirements of the specification but also the economic contexts and value systems within which that specification may be applied.

The result of a functional analysis is a functional map which describes the key purpose of the occupational area broken down into a number of functional groupings based on homogenous sets of functions. Occupational standards are level free — the functional map describes all of the functions across an occupational area: it does not place them in any form of hierarchy or level them in any way. All of the functions are important in their own right and play a part in achieving the key purpose of the occupation.

When standards are grouped and incorporated into NVQs and SVQs, a level is assigned to the particular grouping of units which makes up a qualification and it is the qualification which is given a level relating to the vertical axis of the NVQ/SVQ framework.

The Use of Standards in NVQs and SVQs

Occupational standards as descriptions of the expectations of successful performance have a variety of applications. The major application in terms of Government initiatives and investment is the development of NVQs/SVQs. However this is not their only use, they may be used as the basis for job descriptions, for job profiling and skill mix, appraisal systems and so on.

An NVQ/SVQ is a selection of units drawn from a functional map of the occupational area with the addition of precise range statements and evidence requirements. A functional map is likely to offer a number of different qualifications because there are many potential ways in which units can be put together into qualifications. The particular grouping of units in a qualification is given a name or title so that users are able to identify exactly what it is the qualification contains. The qualification title together with the detail in the units of competence, elements of competence, performance criteria and range statements are jointly known as 'a statement of competence' i.e. the NVQ/SVQ makes a statement about the competence of any individual who possesses the qualification.

As qualifications are developed from standards, certain changes may take place to the structure of the standards. For example, units developed in the functional map may be further disaggregated to facilitate access to certification and/or create units which are seen to be of 'more equal size' for accreditation purposes. Units may also be adjusted to reflect the different levels of qualification. The guiding principle, however, is that the units of competence used within qualifications remain true to the functional statements within the analysis of work roles.

Uses of Standards and Their Effect on Learning

When standards are used within NVQs and SVQs, they form the basis against which an individual's achievement is judged — they are also, therefore, targets for learning and consequently have an impact on the content of learning. However, occupational standards are independent of the process of learning, the approach to learning or any teaching or development processes adopted. The act of describing and specifying the bench marks against which an individual's occupational competence is to be judged, does not dictate the learning approach. What it does, however, is clarify and make explicit the standards expected and which have been achieved when a qualification is awarded.

Learning facilitators are constrained by the standards within the qualifications in only one way — by the clear specification of outcomes. The challenge they face is to find the most effective way(s) of enabling individuals to achieve the outcomes specified. Many facilitators are likely to find it extremely challenging to have the outcomes not only specified, but also open and accessible to those who wish to learn and develop. Consequently, learners are able to challenge the learning methods and processes adopted for the extent to which they help them meet the standards specified. Learning facilitators are likely to be held more accountable for what they offer and deliver.

NVQs and SVQs are often seen as problematic for education and training deliverers because their design is not based on the needs of the organization. As occupational standards are derived solely from work expectations, they do not take into account the nature of particular learning environments or the learning stages through which individuals may need to go before they are able to consistently demonstrate the outcomes specified.

For teachers and trainers who are constrained by a particular location or institution, the emphasis on choice of location and its appropriateness for learning can be very problematic — what it is possible and practicable for an individual organization to offer may not be sufficient or appropriate to help individuals meet the standards. Organisations are placed in the position of considering how their particular environment can be adapted or arrangements made to provide a sufficient range of learning opportunities and environments.

However, this design feature, which is not organization or location-based, is also one of the key strengths of NVQs and SVQs — it allows learning to be recognized and encouraged wherever it takes place. Methods of learning and locations for it are broadened and extended. For example, mentoring and coaching can be used to develop occupational competence and the contribution of the workplace to learning is recognized. Learning is also freed from its institutional focus and greater stress can be placed on learning for life: learning organizations and continually developing individuals may thus become a reality.

NVQs and SVQs, and the occupational standards on which they are based, are not designed around learning states — they describe the expectations of employment. In this sense, they are the outcomes of effective learning but not in the way that many are used to seeing 'learning outcomes' in education (or in GNVQs). Learning outcomes describe the expected achievements of individuals which occur at the end of a course, learning module or even a lesson — a specification of what an individual should have learnt as a result of that particular learning input. The outcomes in occupational standards, and hence in NVQs and SVQs, will be achieved by individuals as a result of learning but they are not linked directly to learning programmes. Their reference point is not a learning programme or stage but employment requirements.

Consequently learning facilitators often need to work back from the standards to develop different learning points on the way to achieving the standards. For the outcomes in NVQs and SVQs at levels 1 and 2, the linkage may be quite direct — the employment outcomes can (almost) serve as the learning outcomes. For the occupational standards incorporated into NVQs and SVQs at the higher levels, the links are more complex and it may be necessary to develop several staged learning outcomes through which individuals progress before they are able to achieve the outcomes in the occupational standards. This picture is further complicated by the fact that the knowledge, understanding and skills necessary to achieve the standards are usually not in a one-to-one relationship with them. Learning facilitators often find that effective learning programmes initially bring together knowledge, understanding and skills from across a number of units of competence before individuals are helped to apply their learning to achieve the occupational standards concerned.

Increasingly lead bodies, who are responsible for the development of occupational standards in a sector, or other organizations are undertaking some of this background development work centrally so that individual teachers, trainers or organizations do not each have to develop their own programmes. Whilst this is of short-term benefit to education and training establishments, they may find that it does not offer the flexibility of provision which they would like to offer and which is the hallmark of NVQs and SVQs.

The Effectiveness of Occupational Standards as Outcome Statements

Occupational standards describe the outcome expectations of a particular work role. The extent to which standards sufficiently describe all of the outcomes required for competent performance, and hence influence an individual's development towards those standards, is a key issue for learning, development and accreditation — if the standards are deficient, then learning towards achievement of the standards will be partial; individuals will be accredited as competent but fail to meet the requirements of employment.

There appear to be three key areas of concern related to the effectiveness of occupational standards for describing performance, particularly at 'professional' levels of practice. These are:

- knowledge and understanding — how can standards cover the scope of knowledge content required by professionals and the ways in which knowledge and understanding is applied in action?
- values and ethics — how can standards reflect the type of moral judgments which workers and professionals have to make?
- personal attributes — how can standards capture the qualities and personal attributes which are assumed to be an essential part of professional practice?

Competence Statements — the Requirements of ED, NCVQ and SCOTVEC

Looking at the requirements placed upon developers by ED, NCVQ and SCOTVEC, the following statement is made:

The NVQ statement of competence should be derived from an analysis of functions within the area of competence to which it relates. It must reflect:
— competence relating to task management, health and safety and the ability to deal with organizational environments, relationships with other people and unexpected events;
— the ability to transfer the competence from place to place and context to context;
— the ability to respond positively to foreseeable changes in technology, working methods, markets and employment patterns and practices;
— the underpinning skill, knowledge and understanding which is required for effective performance in employment. (*Guide to National Vocational Qualifications*, NCVQ, 1991)

The NVQ criteria and guidance in relation to the design and incorporation of occupational standards into NVQs and SVQs require the very things about which many express concerns. The criteria emphasize the need for standards to take a broad rather than narrow (task) view of competence (as detailed in the Job Competence Model, Mansfield and Mathews, 1985), stress the need for occupational competence in contrast to job competence[3], emphasize the demands of the future are key factors in the setting of standards and underline the role of knowledge, understanding and skill in effective performance.

Simple statements that such aspects are included in the criteria are not sufficient however. They do nothing to convince the already unconvinced that occupational standards are sufficient and effective for describing the whole range of work roles which exist in the economy. Not only is it necessary to have criteria — they need to be applied, and be seen to be applied, across all of the qualifications accredited in the NVQ/SVQ framework — if the descriptions of outcome in the occupational standards are weak, partial or procedural, how can they truly describe the requirements of practice, particularly at 'professional levels'.

The draft functional framework produced by the Construction Industry Standing Conference provides perhaps one of the best examples to date of how professional, technical and managerial roles can be described. It is designed to cover such professions as architects, quantity surveyors, construction engineers etc. (see appendix). In general the draft framework has been well-received within the industry and it has already been used to inform the design of one or more higher education courses.

At a broad level of description then it is possible for professional and management level activity to be described using standards. Much of the concern regarding the effectiveness of standards occurs at a more detailed level, however, affecting the descriptions of elements, performance criteria and range. The remainder of this section looks at how the three main areas of concern expressed above (knowledge and understanding, values and ethics, and personal attributes) can in fact be captured in standards.

Knowledge, Understanding and Skills and Standards

There is a requirement that knowledge and understanding related to standards and NVQs and SVQs be specified, both for the design of effective assessment processes and to inform learning activities and processes.

Standards describe the outcome expectations of a particular work role and act as a benchmark against which individual performance is judged. Individuals achieve the outcomes by applying their knowledge, understanding and skills. Knowledge, understanding and skills enable individuals to achieve the standards as thinking is inseparable from action. There is an ongoing interaction between thinking and action; individuals construct models to guide their actions and continually evaluate their actions to adjust and refine those models. Individuals usually do not make a distinction between knowledge and their actions but use the one to inform and develop the other.

Knowledge, understanding and skills are implied by standards and can be seen to be embedded within them — they do not directly specify knowledge, understanding and skill in a way which people are used to seeing. The term 'performance criteria' does not negate the role of knowledge, understanding and skills in performance, it simply focuses on the concept of 'performance outcomes' rather than on that of 'inputs' required to produce the performance. Standards include the results and consequences of performance even when the outcomes are heavily dependent on a large and complex knowledge base, such as that of a professional discipline, or the application of understanding.

An example from the standards for registered auditors will illustrate how a great deal of information about knowledge and understanding can inhere in the standards[4].

Unit: Evaluate the truth and fairness of an organization's financial statements
Element: Determine, record and test the organization's accounting system and the information which it produces
- details of system design and operation are accurately and clearly recorded in a manner which facilitates the understanding of the system and the operation of the audit;
- the adequacy of the accounting system as a basis for the preparation of financial statements is assessed prior to determining the appropriate nature of detailed audit tests;

- where the external auditor intends to place reliance on the work of an internal auditor with a view to reducing the level of her/his own detailed work, the internal auditor's independence, integrity and quality of work is reviewed and evaluated prior to use;
- the nature, timing and scope of audit tests are sufficient to obtain relevant and reliable evidence on the financial accounting systems and the information contained within them;
- results obtained from the different tests are evaluated against each other and the materiality threshold decisions;

etc.

An auditor's work is based on a considerable range and depth of knowledge and understanding which is likely to take several years to acquire. The concept of materiality referred to in the last performance criterion given runs through much of the auditor's work. S/he is constantly reviewing evidence and information for its materiality level — is there any discrepancy in the information, any procedure which has been used which could lead there to be a significant fault in the information put forward? Are any discrepancies in the information sufficiently material to lead to further investigation or even a complete review of the financial statements which have been produced?

The concepts used in accountancy (as in any other profession) are there to guide and inform action. It is likely then that they will appear in the standards, not as something separate but as something inherent in performance: and will do so because competent performance depends on them.

Examples from the construction industry provide further illustration. For the element:

Evaluate the socioeconomic impact of development options

Some of the performance criteria are:

- all significant areas of potential socioeconomic impact arising from development options are clearly and separately identified and prioritized for further investigation;
- a feasible investigation brief and schedule indicating priorities for investigation, mode of investigation and accurate estimated time and costs is agreed with the client;
- work is carried out and/or commissioned in accordance with the brief and schedule using methodologies which are sufficiently valid and reliable to identify the socio-economic impact of development options.

The contexts of the performance criteria are given in the range indicators and show the detailed level of knowledge and understanding which is being proposed. For example some of the range covers:

Mode of investigation: standard investigation procedure, reference to relevant principles and research findings, investigative research requiring knowledge and understanding of theory and practice of social and economic research.

Areas of socioeconomic impact: population movement and removal, changes in demand for labour skills, travel to work areas, population catchment, market catchment areas, disposable income, demands for goods and services, import/export of labour, tourism.

The complexity of the performance criteria and the dimensions of the range indicate the scope both of the knowledge content and the application of knowledge and understanding to meet the outcomes of performance.

Standards (when they conform to available guidance) therefore imply knowledge content, the understanding of that content and the ability to apply knowledge and understanding in particular situations. This implied relationship helps define the knowledge and understanding necessary to achieve the outcomes in the standards and can consequently lead into the design of effective learning and assessment processes. Standards can be written to include the knowledge and understanding implicit in competent performance without resorting to lists of syllabus topics or undermining the basis of the standards.

A particular benefit of occupational standards is that they emphasize the use and application of knowledge, understanding and skills — the context of their application and the reasons for their use. Learners and those who facilitate learning are able to see from the standards why such knowledge, understanding and skills are necessary and how they are to be applied. There is a drawback — those who have traditionally run courses and programmes are being asked to explain the relevance of the course content and its relationship to occupational competence. For example, 'why do auditors need to know the history of the audit?'; 'why is it necessary to know the difference between overt and covert forms of discrimination?', 'why are the principles of thermodynamics included for individuals in this course?'. Sometimes the answers are straightforward, but often they are not. Is it so wrong that learning facilitators should be challenged about the content and structure of their course? Whose interests should predominate in programmes whose primary aim is the development of occupational/professional competence — learners or teachers/trainers?

Values and Ethics

Professional level work is often characterized as involving moral and ethical decisions as well as an extensive knowledge base. This debate around values and ethics is also taken to imply that the individuals who work in these occupations have to possess certain personal characteristics or attributes in order to demonstrate these values and ethics. Leaving the second point aside for the moment, this section will consider whether and how values and ethics can be described in standards. The next section will look at descriptions which imply certain personal attributes.

Richard Winter in his 'Outline of a general theory of professional competences', which considers the social work domain in particular, provides a useful summary of the debate surrounding values and ethics in professional practice. Winter and colleagues in their work on the Asset Programme drew on methods for developing occupational standards but adapted them to inform the training and assessment for professional levels of responsibility. Whilst there are similarities in approach between the outcomes developed for the Asset Programme and occupational standards, there are differences in the ways in which the outcomes are expressed. Essentially this can be summed up as the use of outcome statements for learning and development — the Asset Programme — and outcome statements to describe employment requirements — occupational standards. Notwithstanding the differences in the expression of outcomes, the background analysis by Winter into professional practice is extremely useful in detailing the different factors which need to be taken into account.

Drawing from Carr (1989), the distinction is made between intrinsic criteria and extrinsic criteria for judging practice. The argument is that each profession is intrinsically concerned with a particular practical aspect of a good quality existence. For example, teachers with the realization of capacity to understand, lawyers with the realisation of justice, doctors with health and presumably standards developers and trainers with the realization of competent performance!

Professional practice requires the exercise of usually complex and difficult 'moral' decisions which might be in conflict with each other against guiding principles. The guiding principles are (or should be) to do with ethics of the profession rather than from any self-interest. The complexity of these decisions is seen in the daily press in debates about how the limited resources of the health and social services should best be spent and the commitment which professional carers (such as nurses) should have to their organizations in contrast to the needs of their patients. For example, should they inform the press about insufficient resources or not?

Winter also stresses the obligation within professional practice to avoid 'oppressive judgments' (those which make non-justifiable discrimination on the basis of gender, age, sexuality etc.) as professional workers have an inherent responsibility to all members of society. The extent to which such an obligation is solely the responsibility of professionals is debatable. One would hope that it is expected of all workers although it is perhaps more explicit or obvious in some professions or occupational groups than others (for example, those who work in the caring professions).

Into this equation, Winter brings the emotional dimension of professional work. He characterizes the reason for this as:

(i)   professional practice being essentially about problem solving — problems bring anxieties;
(ii)   professionals need to empathize with the client's problem and its associated anxieties and yet preserve emotional distance from the client;
(iii)   by the nature of the professional being an 'expert' there is a power dimension; the professional becomes an authority figure whom the client can blame if necessary and therefore relieve anxiety.

Winter sees that emotions can be a resource as much as a hindrance and recognizes that 'irrational emotions are not an avoidable and regrettable indication of professional failure but an inherent aspect of the professional situation, which (like its other aspects) needs to be understood and effectively managed'. If we take the view that individuals develop personal knowledge from their own experience — how they do things, the situations which they are placed in and through reflecting on what has happened to them, leading to their own individualized way of perceiving and knowing — emotions can readily be seen to form a part of this. Learning is not just with the head but with the heart and feet. A competent individual draws from a variety of influences and ways of perceiving to perform competently in any situation.

If Winter's evaluation of professional practice is valid, then there are implications for standards describing professional performance. Some individuals of course will argue that this is not correct and that standards are 'objective' descriptions of practice obtained from observing individuals at work. Such a viewpoint ignores the moral and ethical dimension of human action and assumes that occupational competence is an objective truth. Any reader of social science texts will know that each puts forward systems which are based on differing views of human behaviour. Standards are the same, they reflect the 'moral and ethical' views of their developers, lead bodies and evaluators. Whilst some 'ethical' decisions regarding an individual's right to gain admission to the profession or to continue practising within it may well be professional membership issues, there is no ignoring the fact that values are embedded within standards.

Values and ethics are also an issue at all levels of the NVQ/SVQ framework — they are not the sole domain of professionals. All workers are likely to face ethical and moral dilemmas at some point in their working life even if these arise as much in their relationships with other workers (for example, should they join in the racist taunts made by their work team to another worker?) as they do in their relationships to clients or members of the public.

The three main aspects detailed above regarding values and ethics are:

- intrinsic criteria of professional practice related to the nature of the profession rather than the organization for whom the professional works;
- the duty of the professional to the public at large and all members of the public rather than to a select group or individual her/himself;
- the emotions which arise in professional practice and the ways in which these can be handled constructively and be used to improve performance.

In terms of *intrinsic criteria*, these are usually reflected in the nature and purpose of the profession itself and the tensions and conflicts which the professional has to balance throughout her/his work. Within the standards, intrinsic criteria will arise in two major ways. Firstly in the key purpose statement and secondly within individual performance criteria. Some examples are given below.

In the work which Winter has carried out in social work, the key purpose developed for social workers working with young children and their families is:

> To protect and promote the welfare and development of children and young persons in partnership with their families but ensuring that the welfare of the child/person is paramount.

The tension here is between the needs and wishes of the children and those of their families — they may not always be in line.

For construction the key purpose is:

> Establish, maintain and modify the built environment balancing the requirements of clients, users and the community.

Here the 'balancing act' is explicit — the implication is that these requirements are not likely to be the same.

What one would expect of the standards which derive from these key purposes is that these tensions are embedded throughout the analysis at more detailed levels. So, for example, within the social work analysis, there are the following statements which reflect similar tensions:

- work with children / young persons and their families to provide the optimum environment for the child / young person and for other family members;
- maintain interpersonal relationships and self-presentation while working within painful and dangerous situations.

For the construction industry, there is the following:

- evaluate the environmental and ecological impact of development options.

Standards are therefore able to reflect and describe clearly the intrinsic criteria by which professional action is judged. In fact, one of their strengths is that they make these tensions explicit, open to debate and more capable of informing and evaluating professional action.

The *duty of the professional to the public at large and to the individual client* are covered in a number of ways but largely at performance criteria level except where such monitoring and evaluation is a function of the work role. An example of the latter is included in the construction industry standards:

- Monitor the environmental effects of built environment policies and operations.

And also in the standards for auditors:

- Evaluate the truth and fairness of an organization's financial statements.

In the draft standards for quality management, the values which are being promoted can be seen within some of the element titles. For example,

- support and empower individuals and teams to take action in line with quality strategies and policies;
- promote quality as a central force in the organisation's strategies for success.

Such duty is expressed in more detail at the performance criteria level by such criteria as:

- where a client misleads or misinforms in order to obtain a tax advantage, permission is sought to inform the tax authority and where this is not forthcoming, the contract is terminated;[5]

- information obtained from and/or about a potential client is disclosed only to individuals who are entitled to receive it;[6]
- information obtained from a client is sufficient to confirm that the services can be carried out without prejudicing the firm's independence and/or objectivity;[7]
- the worker's practice in the work setting is promoted in ways which are consistent with the worker's role and legislation and charters concerning individual rights;[8]
- where an individual communicates information to the worker which indicates that the individual or others may be put at risk, a clear explanation that the information may need to be shared with others is given in a manner appropriate to the individual;[9]
- the manner, level and pace of communication is appropriate to the individual's abilities and personal beliefs and preferences;[10]
- the working environment is suitable for the activities undertaken within it and meets and/or exceeds the needs of those who have to use it;[11]
- a design programme is prepared that meets the requirements of the brief, the constraints on the design team and meets the expectations of the client in respect of quality, consultation, timetable and phasing of design development;[12]
- policies are regularly revised against emerging trends in social policy and legislation and recommendations are made which improve the welfare policy response of the organization.[13]

Elements and performance criteria are therefore capable of addressing areas in which values and ethics are important criteria for professional groups and other workers. Not only are they capable of doing so, they implicitly do so as the terminology used implies certain values. Some lead bodies[14] have carried this further and made the values, on which the standards are based explicit at the start of their documentation relating to standards and qualifications. This allows users to evaluate whether the values are those to which they wish to subscribe.

Such explication of values and ethics in occupational standards has a knock-on effect to learning towards those standards and assessment of an individual against them. Learning content and approaches will need to include such process outcomes as how to handle 'dodgy clients', complex issues around the confidentiality of information and access rights, the active promotion and support of anti-discriminatory practice, communication in difficult and life threatening situations as well as routine ones, the impact of personal beliefs and preferences on communication, and so on.

The third area identified by Winter is the *emotions aroused by professional practice*. These are perhaps not so well described especially in the area of the monitoring of emotional response to improve professional performance, as one might expect of the reflective practitioner. Within the Care Awards there are explicit criteria related to the way in which the worker is expected to handle their emotions recognizing that this is often a difficult area. For example, for the element:

Comfort and support the partner, relatives and friends of those who have died or suffered loss.

there is the performance criterion:

- the worker's own feelings aroused by a client's loss are managed in a way which is likely to be supportive of her/himself and minimizes the effect on the care setting.

This is supported in the knowledge and understanding specifications by such areas of knowledge as:

— the grieving process in relation to anyone involved in, or associated with, death or loss;
— the possible emotional conditions of the partner, relatives and friends and how this may affect their behaviour, etc.

The relationship of emotions to competence warrants further investigation but there is no reason to believe that the arousal of emotions and the ways in which these are handled cannot be described in standards providing that the worker has it in their power to do so. For example, it is not always possible to require the worker to share their emotions with another because there may not be someone suitable with whom to do this or the organization may not encourage it. However, if as Winter suggests 'professional work has an emotional dimension in the same way as it has cognitive and ethical dimensions: emotions (their own as well as the clients) are a topic, an obstacle as well as a resource', then the effect of emotions is worthy of considerable further investigation and incorporation into occupational standards and learning towards those standards.

The inclusion of values and ethics in standards is likely to extend and enrich learning rather than restrict and constrain it, not least in the necessary discussions which will need to take place around the many grey areas and difficult decisions. In developing clear standards of performance for what was known as 'the value base' in health and social care for support staff, the concern which was most commonly expressed was that professionals would have trouble meeting such standards of good practice — it was felt that current professional practice failed to meet the standards being set for support staff — a real challenge for development and learning. Since the NVQs and SVQs have been implemented in organizations, there have been reports that having thought about the standards and discussed their meaning, support staff are challenging their managers about practice within their organization and making suggestions for improvement — learning individuals developing a learning organization. Standards can therefore lead to both the challenge of practice and improvements in it, even in an area as 'soft' as values and ethics.

Personal Attributes

Personal attributes are not directly described in standards nor should they be accredited. I believe it is, for example, morally dubious to accredit an individual's honesty or integrity for life[15]. When individuals or groups make claims about the need for workers in an occupation to possess certain personal characteristics, they may well be indicating that the standards are perceived to be deficient in some way.

Mansfield, in an article on Components of Creativity for the CISC[16], distinguishes between two distinct groupings of concept when considering personal attributes:

- performance characteristics (such as judgment and quality);
- personal characteristics (such as flair and creativity).

He states that:

> the performance characteristics require further expansion to identify what is meant — is 'judgment' the ability to make realistic and valid judgments, if so about what and in what circumstances? Is 'quality' the ability to produce work consistently to recognized standards of quality? If this is the case in both instances then these performance characteristics are perfectly capable of being incorporated into the standards since they are performance criteria.

Personal characteristics are seen as different in kind:

> They are assumed mental or cognitive states and are unlikely to exhaust the concepts which people use to describe a number of diverse capabilities within the various professions which are concerned about them. (Bob Mansfield, 'Components of Creativity')

Whilst they are not within the direct remit of the NVQ/SVQ design criteria, outcomes and performance characteristics can be developed which result from the application of these assumed states.

The first major step is to gain agreement within the occupational area on the meaning of the concept(s). Then a series of descriptions which will fit standards methodology can be developed.

Mansfield notes that whilst personal attributes can be described in the standards at element level, they are more likely to appear as performance criteria. Taking some examples from his paper, he gives the following as examples of elements[17]:

- Monitor and maintain the quality of work in progress (concern for quality).
- Contribute to the improvement of product quality and customer satisfaction (innovation).
- Instigate and recommend new . . . (innovation, flair, creativity).

For performance criteria, some of the examples are:

- customers and clients are treated politely and in a manner which promotes goodwill and trust (personal effectiveness, caring attitude);
- work is completed to schedule (reliability);
- significant factors which may have environmental implications are identified and clear recommendations made to reduce negative environmental impact (concern for the environment);

- form and colour styles are adopted which improve and enhance the appearance of the design (creativity, artistry).

In terms of personal attributes, it is therefore necessary to consider first whether the characteristics concerned should feature in a public accreditation system. Secondly, it is necessary to look behind any suggestions for additions to the standards or criticisms of the standards for the added value which they might bring. This does not mean that it is necessary to start adding personal attributes to the standards, drop standards for personal attribute models or use personal competence models as well as standards. Rather developers need to explore with evaluators of the standards the focus of their arguments to determine whether their comments can be used to improve the specification.

Where items which have been identified as personal attributes can be included in the standards (as in the examples above), this can contribute to learning by clarifying for the learner exactly what the requirements are. For example, if they are criticized for being 'unreliable' this is linked back to the fact that they do not complete work to schedule. Learning becomes more focused and centred around outcomes and hence prevents the 'labelling' of individuals from an early part in a programme.

NVQs/SVQs and 'Higher Level Roles'

Higher level roles (or those likely to occur at level 4 or 5 of the NVQ/SVQ framework) can be characterized as those where:

- action is based on considerable bodies of underpinning knowledge — facts, views, theories, concepts etc.;
- much action can be viewed as 'knowledge in action' — an individual's performance within an occupation often revolves around rapid cognitive processing — the outcomes of action are the results of this cognitive processing;
- initiation and the origination of work for others are likely to be key competences at this level and will involve individuals in synthesizing information in new ways to offer one or more solutions to problems;
- action takes place over a wide range of contexts which are subject to wide variation and uncertainty and are often complex in nature;
- the results or outcomes of action are likely to be long-term or have long-term consequences with actions tending to be future focused rather than concerned with the immediate here and now;
- the results or outcomes involve high degrees of criticality either in terms of value or for their personal and/or social consequences;
- process outcomes tend to be more predominant than product outcomes;
- the work tends to involve interactions with environments and systems outside of the employing organization;
- individuals have a high degree of autonomy and usually take final responsibility for the consequences of their actions.

Whilst such facets may be seen to characterize higher level roles, they are not restricted to them. Each of the characteristics may be found in occupations which have been accredited at other levels of the NVQ/SVQ framework. Higher level roles are distinguished by the greater incidence of these characteristics and their occurrence in combination.

At the time of writing, there is considerable discussion about whether NVQs and SVQs can effectively cover higher levels and if they do so, will and should they 'look' the same as at the other levels of the framework. There is considerable evidence of elitism operating in discussions relating to the 'higher levels' of competence or 'level 5' of the NVQ/SVQ framework with assumptions that what works at the 'lower' levels cannot possibly work for 'professionals' or for those who have graduated from higher education because 'they are by their nature different'. Comments can include: 'this method of analysis cannot possibly work because it was first tried on occupations related to the Youth Training Scheme'; 'this cannot be appropriate to senior managers, because what they need is personal competence not statements of outcomes' and so on. Such elitism must be challenged if we are to develop individuals who can fulfil their true potential, whether that is in relation to the workforce or outside of it.

In common parlance, level 5 in the NVQ/SVQ framework is taken to mean those areas of occupational practice which include the professions and most levels of management. In practice, the actual concept or coverage of level 5 is unclear, with professional groups claiming that their qualifications will be located at level 5 even when no such decision has been made, while others talk bravely about 'above level 5' not readily accepting that it will be, or might be, possible for all 'professional qualifications' to be included at the one level. The 'battle' as to who and what will actually be at level 5 is still to be faced and it is likely that at least some of the qualifications currently gained by professionals, particularly at the start of their professional lives, will be accredited at levels 3 or 4 of the NVQ/SVQ framework.

The position regarding level 5 was clarified by John Hillier, the Chief Executive of NCVQ, at a conference in 1992. He stated:

Two key things about level 5 in the framework. First of all there will only be a level 5, there will not be levels 5, 6, 7, 8, 9 and 10. The arguments that would develop about who would be in 5 or 6 or 8 would be endless and all over what is ultimately a very small proportion of the total workforce anyway. Something like 85 per cent of the adult workforce is going to be contained in levels 1–4 anyway.

The second thing about level 5 is that of course it does not mean that because a person is in an area that is described as 'professional', it is automatically a level 5 qualification. The decision as to what level a qualification is in the framework relates to the descriptions of levels in the NVQ criteria. . . . There are professional bodies who are offering qualifications at level 3 of our framework, so it is by no means a foregone conclusion that a body that describes itself as professional is automatically at level 5 of the framework. It could in fact be put the other way around. What we are concerned about is that all levels of the framework should be professional, that is they should all reflect what is best in the concept of a professional qualification; what is needed to perform across a range of circumstances, what is needed both now and in the future; that they should reflect not just those things which directly characterize performance but also the underlying knowledge and understanding and underlying values and ethics which form part of the best professional qualifications. There is no reason why these characteristics should be limited to only one level of the framework. (Hillier, 1992)

In addition, I would argue that if ED, NCVQ and SCOTVEC are serious about the development of the methodology to higher levels of the framework, it is imperative that the eventual philosophy and methods are good for all levels. If issues and developments at 'higher levels' lead to changes and developments in methodology and philosophy, then these changes must apply across the NVQ/ SVQ framework. If changes in method or criteria are applied to level 5 alone, then there is no NVQ/SVQ framework since there is a break in the route of progression, and access through the framework is effectively limited. Progression and access are fundamental criteria.

This is not to say that NVQs and SVQs should serve as the main or sole focus of education or training. NVQs and SVQs have the primary purpose of improving the occupational competence of the UK workforce and a focus on work and the ability of an individual to perform at work. This is different from education as a whole which has a number of purposes. Higher education is not solely concerned with the development of occupational competence but can be characterized as the development of individuals' capability to pursue a number of different activities. Professional bodies are concerned with the achievement of competence, the recognition of entitlement and continued professional competence and conduct. Whilst they are interested in occupational competence, this is not focused on the point of qualification but extends throughout a member's life. Membership can be rescinded, qualifications cannot. Whilst NCVQ, SCOTVEC, higher education and professional bodies therefore have a number of interests in common, they also have fundamental differences — we ignore those differences at our peril.

Notes

1   A major part of this chapter is drawn from a paper commissioned by the Employment Department — Methods Strategy Unit — to stimulate debate regarding the application of National Vocational Qualifications and Scottish Vocational Qualifications to higher levels of the NVQ/SVQ framework — see Mitchell, L. (1993) *NVQs and SVQs at Higher Levels: A Discussion Paper to the 'Higher Levels Seminar, October 1992'*, March, Methods Strategy Unit Briefing Series no: 8, Employment Department, Sheffield.
    I would like to thank the Employment Department for permission to use the original paper as the basis of this chapter.
2   See Mansfield, B. (1991) 'Deriving standards of competence' in Fennell, E. (Ed) *Development of Standards for National Certification*, Employment Department.
3   The term 'job competence' as it is used here is different from its use in the title of the Job Competence model. Job competence here is designed to refer to the requirements placed on an individual within her/his current job, whereas occupational competence refers to the expectations of an individual performing a function(s) at any point within the occupation. The Job Competence model details the different components which make up competence whether this is within a

single job or within an occupation. Because of the inherent breadth of the Job Competence model, it can more readily be related to occupational competence rather than job competence in spite of its name!

4   Chartered Association of Certified Accountants, (1991); ACCA. Not to be reproduced without permission of ACCA. Registered auditing is a post-qualifying award i.e. after an accountant has qualified s/he may undertake further training to register as an auditor.

5   Taken from the Chartered Association of Certified Accountants (1991).

6   *Ibid.*

7   *Ibid.*

8   Taken from the Value Base Unit, Care Awards, Level 2 and 3. The Value Base unit is specifically designed to detail the principles of good practice on which all interactions with individuals are based. Although all other units have the principles of good practice embedded in them, the Value Base unit gives a more precise interpretation of these principles and values.

9   *Ibid.*

10   *Ibid.*

11   Quality Management standards (draft), MCI (1992).

12   Construction Industry Standing Conference (draft standards) (1992).

13   *Ibid.*

14   For example, the Care Sector Consortium in the Care Awards, the Child Care Awards and the Criminal Justice Awards. The Training and Development Lead Body in its Code of Good Practice.

15   A key reason for this is that the methods and techniques used to directly assess personal qualities are not designed for public accreditation purposes.

16   Mansfield, B. (1991) 'Components of creativity', paper for the Construction Industry Standing Conference, November.

17   Personal attributes to which these might relate have been added in brackets by the author.

References

CARR, W. (Ed) (1989) *Quality in Teaching*, Lewes, Falmer Press.

HILLIER, J. (1992) *The First Natural Conference on Education and Training*, CISC, April.

WINTER, R. (1992) 'Outline of a general theory of professional competences' in ANGLIA POLYTECHNIC and ESSEX COUNTY COUNCIL SOCIAL SERVICES (Eds) *The Asset Programme Volume II: The Development and Assessment of Professional Competences*, Chelmsford, Anglia Polytechnic and Essex County Council.

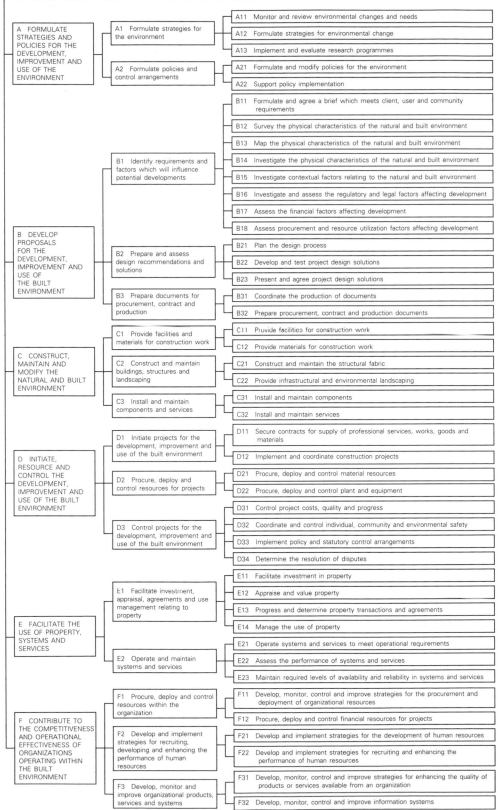

KEY PURPOSE: ESTABLISH, MAINTAIN AND MODIFY THE USE OF THE NATURAL AND BUILT
ENVIRONMENT, BALANCING THE REQUIREMENTS OF CLIENTS, USERS AND THE COMMUNITY

CISC Functional Map

A FORMULATE STRATEGIES AND POLICIES FOR THE DEVELOPMENT, IMPROVEMENT AND USE OF THE ENVIRONMENT

A1 Formulate strategies for the environment
- A11 Monitor and review environmental changes and needs
- A12 Formulate strategies for environmental change
- A13 Implement and evaluate research programmes

A2 Formulate policies and control arrangements
- A21 Formulate and modify policies for the environment
- A22 Support policy implementation

B DEVELOP PROPOSALS FOR THE DEVELOPMENT, IMPROVEMENT AND USE OF THE BUILT ENVIRONMENT

B1 Identify requirements and factors which will influence potential developments
- B11 Formulate and agree a brief which meets client, user and community requirements
- B12 Survey the physical characteristics of the natural and built environment
- B13 Map the physical characteristics of the natural and built environment
- B14 Investigate the physical characteristics of the natural and built environment
- B15 Investigate contextual factors relating to the natural and built environment
- B16 Investigate and assess the regulatory and legal factors affecting development
- B17 Assess the financial factors affecting development
- B18 Assess procurement and resource utilization factors affecting development

B2 Prepare and assess design recommendations and solutions
- B21 Plan the design process
- B22 Develop and test project design solutions
- B23 Present and agree project design solutions

B3 Prepare documents for procurement, contract and production
- B31 Coordinate the production of documents
- B32 Prepare procurement, contract and production documents

C CONSTRUCT, MAINTAIN AND MODIFY THE NATURAL AND BUILT ENVIRONMENT

C1 Provide facilities and materials for construction work
- C11 Provide facilities for construction work
- C12 Provide materials for construction work

C2 Construct and maintain buildings, structures and landscaping
- C21 Construct and maintain the structural fabric
- C22 Provide infrastructural and environmental landscaping

C3 Install and maintain components and services
- C31 Install and maintain components
- C32 Install and maintain services

D INITIATE, RESOURCE AND CONTROL THE DEVELOPMENT, IMPROVEMENT AND USE OF THE BUILT ENVIRONMENT

D1 Initiate projects for the development, improvement and use of the built environment
- D11 Secure contracts for supply of professional services, works, goods and materials
- D12 Implement and coordinate construction projects

D2 Procure, deploy and control resources for projects
- D21 Procure, deploy and control material resources
- D22 Procure, deploy and control plant and equipment

D3 Control projects for the development, improvement and use of the built environment
- D31 Control project costs, quality and progress
- D32 Coordinate and control individual, community and environmental safety
- D33 Implement policy and statutory control arrangements
- D34 Determine the resolution of disputes

E FACILITATE THE USE OF PROPERTY, SYSTEMS AND SERVICES

E1 Facilitate investment, appraisal, agreements and use management relating to property
- E11 Facilitate investment in property
- E12 Appraise and value property
- E13 Progress and determine property transactions and agreements
- E14 Manage the use of property

E2 Operate and maintain systems and services
- E21 Operate systems and services to meet operational requirements
- E22 Assess the performance of systems and services
- E23 Maintain required levels of availability and reliability in systems and services

F CONTRIBUTE TO THE COMPETITIVENESS AND OPERATIONAL EFFECTIVENESS OF ORGANIZATIONS OPERATING WITHIN THE BUILT ENVIRONMENT

F1 Procure, deploy and control resources within the organization
- F11 Develop, monitor, control and improve strategies for the procurement and deployment of organizational resources
- F12 Procure, deploy and control financial resources for projects

F2 Develop and implement strategies for recruiting, developing and enhancing the performance of human resources
- F21 Develop and implement strategies for the development of human resources
- F22 Develop and implement strategies for recruiting and enhancing the performance of human resources

F3 Develop, monitor and improve organizational products, services and systems
- F31 Develop, monitor, control and improve strategies for enhancing the quality of products or services available from an organization
- F32 Develop, monitor, control and improve information systems

Part Three

Curriculum Consequences

Chapter 6

The Introduction of General National Vocational Qualifications: The First Year — September 1992 to June 1993

Jane Harrop

Introduction

The creation and development of GNVQs described by Jessup in an earlier chapter resulted in the first GNVQs being piloted from September 1992. The findings of the autumn 1991 consultation on GNVQs (Harrop, 1992) confirmed the main features of the qualifications while indicating that some aspects would need to be reviewed during piloting. It was clear that while unit delivery and outcomes assessment could offer students real advantages in motivation and achievement, the differing views expressed on assessment, including grading, indicated that these would need further development and clarification. In addition teachers would need training and support in new approaches to learning and assessment. This has proved to be the case and has been taken up by NCVQ and the awarding bodies as a priority. However, many other factors have to be taken into account as important influences on the 'success' of GNVQs. The following pages show how many of these factors affect each other.

The Role of GNVQs

GNVQs have an important function for students in providing choices within the full-time and part-time education system for the type of course they want to take and for progression beyond the course they choose. The choices of academic or vocational, and academic plus vocational, are more widely discussed in this country than ever before. Colleges and schools not yet doing GNVQ courses are discussing why and how they should offer these choices to students. There are many reasons schools and colleges give for providing GNVQ courses. There are views that current academically-based examinations are not suitable for many students; that many students wish to take a mix of academic and vocational courses; that a wider range of students should have access to higher education; that flexible learning courses which can make best use of institutional and local resources will deliver a better learning experience for students; that students are better motivated to achieve if they can relate their learning experiences to the real world; and so on. These views are likely to continue to be debated. The advent of GNVQs has added to choice and its intent is to clarify the routes which will lead to success for those with a wide range of talents and interests. The framework of GNVQs is not yet complete and needs to become widespread over a longer period in order to consolidate its effectiveness.

The implementation of GNVQs has provided opportunities to address the issues raised above, but can only do so in the context of the existing educational system. There is no blank sheet to start with. All GNVQ centres are building upon, complementing, or adding to their existing course provision. Changes of funding and management structures, and increasing emphasis on market competition in the last eighteen months have encouraged schools and colleges to take advantage of GNVQ possibilities in order to meet educational needs. In consequence, the choices offered by GNVQs are part of the melting pot of educational provision. Potential changes to the National Curriculum, if not also to 'A' levels, add to the impression of uncertainty and opportunity.

The colleges and schools who chose to join phase one of the GNVQ implementation were pilot centres, both for the individual qualifications, and for the function, structure and framework of the GNVQ itself. They explored the choices for their students, and came up with many different models for implementation. This paper describes some of that diversity.

Setting Up Phase One

GNVQ courses began in September 1992 as the first phase of the introduction of GNVQs in post-16 schools and colleges. Five qualifications were available for piloting at both intermediate and advanced levels. (In 1992/93 these were known as levels 2 and 3.) NCVQ asked the three designated GNVQ awarding bodies, BTEC, City and Guilds and the RSA Examinations Board, to select approximately thirty centres according to the following criteria.

- All centres were expected to have previous experience of vocational education and have existing connections with that awarding body.
- The awarding bodies would aim to achieve both a geographic spread across England and Wales, and a selection including schools, sixth form colleges and further education (FE) colleges.
- Awarding bodies were asked to encourage centres to provide at least two of the five vocational areas and at both intermediate and advanced.
- All centres volunteered to participate in the pilot.

NCVQ aimed to have approximately 5000 students undertaking GNVQs in 1992/93, and, in the event, exceeded this by enrolling 8800 students. The selection criteria were given to encourage centres to build on sound prior experience of vocational education, and to indicate to their students that a variety of vocational areas was available as well as progression from intermediate to advanced. There was no attempt to achieve a representative sample of schools and colleges across the country but it was hoped that a wide variety of volunteer institutions would provide valuable experience of different approaches to GNVQs in a range of contexts. Awarding bodies were also asked to recruit full-time students. It was feared that part-time students taking longer to complete courses would be subjected to many changes of programme as revisions were made following the initial year's experience.

The awarding bodies were encouraged to build on their strengths and to encourage centres to do the same. For instance, City and Guilds selected centres which already had strong courses in the Diploma of Vocational Education which meant that the majority of their centres were schools. BTEC recruited centres delivering the BTEC National or First qualification across a range of vocational areas, and these centres tended to be in the further education sector. RSA and BTEC had a number of centres which were consortia of schools and colleges or linked centres with some formal and informal support networks, and these consortia increased the number and range of institutions offering GNVQs.

There was no attempt to try to equalize numbers across the vocational subject areas. However, as business education has traditionally the highest recruitment, centres were encouraged to offer a minimum of two subject areas so that at least one other area was offered in addition to business. The five new subject areas were markedly different from each other in that business replaced existing qualifications whereas others were new combinations of existing vocational subject areas, such as health with social care, leisure with tourism, and art with design. The GNVQ in manufacturing was a new name and a new subject area to most centres and NCVQ anticipated that there would be small numbers of centres and students who would experiment with it.

The awarding bodies mounted extensive information briefings on the structure and implementation of the qualifications for centres during 1992 and these became more frequent during the summer as centres carried out rapid recruiting drives to students and parents. Development of the qualifications had begun only in the summer of 1991 so important details of the qualification were still being developed through the summer months of 1992 up to the time the courses started. Information was fed to centres as quickly as possible before term started. Centres carried out their planning based on quite limited information and staff continued to develop their courses as the picture became clearer through the autumn of 1992.

At the beginning of the autumn term many centres were waiting for student decisions based on GCSE examination results and were still uncertain of their recruitment, and consequently which qualifications they would deliver. Courses started with teachers and students exploring the details of the qualifications in operation for the first time. Many decisions regarding which students would take what qualifications were made during September to November. It emerged that some centres had been unable to fulfil the criterion to offer a range of GNVQs, but that others were delivering a full range with large recruitments.

Distribution of Centres

Nearly two-thirds of centres (65 per cent) were colleges (further education and sixth form colleges) and they were mostly registered with BTEC and RSA. Colleges provided the largest number of students per institution, on average 108 students per college, the highest enrolment was 521 and the lowest seven.

Schools made up over one-third of centres and over half were registered with City and Guilds. Nearly 1500 students were enrolled in schools with an average of thirty-seven per school, the highest enrolment was ninety-two and the lowest seven.

Geographical distribution gave some clustering of institutions around major metropolitan areas in the Midlands, the North-east, the North-west and London, as well as some clustering through consortia or local networks such as South Devon and East Dorset. A consortia in Wales provided centres from north and south, and two consortia in Northern Ireland focused on two FE colleges and some local schools.

Enrolment of Students

Intermediate enrolment was 56 per cent of the total, with many schools only offering intermediate GNVQs, while colleges enrolled larger numbers of students for the advanced GNVQs. Both colleges and schools indicated that they would build on their intermediate cohort by starting their advanced courses the following year.

The percentage of students for each subject area in 1992 showed the anticipated interest in business with 38.4 per cent and low recognition of manufacturing with 4.7 per cent. The three other subject areas enrolled numbers similar to each other: leisure and tourism: 19.4 per cent; art and design: 19.2 per cent, and health and social care: 18.3 per cent.

Recruitment and Entry Criteria

All centres had some prior experience of vocational education, either through other vocational qualifications or through business links such as the Technical and Vocational Education Initiative (TVEI) or work experience schemes. To some extent students were recruited on the basis of existing vocational courses as well as directly to the new GNVQ courses. The majority of BTEC centres made decisions late in the summer of 1992 and therefore had already recruited a cohort to run BTEC Firsts and Nationals. This cohort was mostly converted into a GNVQ cohort with little difficulty. In some cases students were given a choice of either a BTEC First or National award or a GNVQ and both courses were running separately. The Diploma of Vocational Education from City and Guilds gave similar possibilities and in some cases two qualifications were run together so that students might achieve either or both. After the first few months this was found difficult to achieve because of the different demands of the qualifications and most centres eventually determined to run each qualification separately.

The expected cohort for these qualifications was the 16–19 age group. In September 1992 enrolment was highest at 16 with 37 per cent; 18 per cent were aged 17 and 23 per cent were 18. The remainder were aged 19 plus with 3 per cent aged over 25. The prior achievement of GCSEs by these students ranged from four or five passes at grades A-C for advanced GNVQ and the grades of C-F across four or five subjects for intermediate students. Although no-one anticipated that 'A' level students would at this introductory phase, flock to GNVQ courses, mixed programmes of GNVQ and 'A' levels were popular in some centres (cf Jackson, this volume). The two levels of GNVQs offered a choice for those already looking for an acceptable alternative. Many centres expected that in the following year, high achieving students would find GNVQs an attractive option.

Administrative Decisions and Support

The role that GNVQs were given in the overall context of centre programming appeared to have a considerable impact on many aspects of GNVQ planning and delivery. When GNVQs formed an integral part of the overall programme and curriculum offerings they appeared to be more immediately successful in terms of what teachers and students felt they were able to achieve. Institutional provision which focused on other types of qualifications, especially traditional academic qualifications, appeared to have some difficulties in the status, marketing, staffing, resourcing and timetabling of GNVQs. Indications so far show that GNVQs which were placed in the mainstream of institutional programming were beginning to demonstrate their full potential.

Teachers commented that senior management needed to show that they considered GNVQs to be a highly esteemed part of their institution and to give clear support for their introduction. Several teachers reported that the status of vocational qualifications had risen as a result of introducing GNVQs and students felt they were getting more respect from 'A' level peers. This was partly due to students comparing the type and quantity of work required for both qualifications.

One of the main advantages of GNVQs which institutions appreciated and used for marketing purposes was the flexibility which the structure allowed. This flexibility applied particularly to curriculum planning and timetabling. Activities were planned by teachers to cover small or large parts of the course, as units do not have to be taken in a particular order, nor as a single entity. For instance some teachers took a unit by unit approach while others took a thematic approach across units, drawing together aspects from several units which fitted into a particular activity or project.

The type of work carried out by students was frequently planned and supervised over a period of time which varied according to the scale of the activity and to a student's individual progress. Students in the same course might have individualized learning plans which allow different activities and units to proceed at the same time. At other times, all students were addressing the same unit and the same activity. Flexible blocks of time were needed, for instance a half-day for a group project, or a whole day for a work-site or exhibition visit, or a series of individual tutorials. Students who had to fit these activities into a standard academic timetable with shorter fixed periods of tuition found they were unable to do both adequately. The qualification content encouraged activities which needed diverse resources, such as increased access to information technology, and opportunities for work-related activities. This often required timetabling in relation to the world outside the school or college.

Staff resourcing tended to follow existing patterns but centres began to review this in the light of their experience. As GNVQs include a significant amount of general education, for instance the core skills of communication, application of number and information technology, as well as planning and evaluation skills, staff needed appropriate experience of both the vocational areas and the academic subjects associated with each qualification. They also needed to be able to integrate the core skills when planning students' work. In centres where a team of staff was able to contribute to each qualification, these demands were usually met by a cooperative approach. This had additional benefits for the assessment process where staff could consult each other for expert advice.

Making best use of staff frequently depended on the flexibility of the timetabling. Staff in GNVQ courses are needed to fulfil several roles; instructor, individual tutor for planning and reviewing work, assessor, team member — whether for core skills or a vocational subject area, and so on. As the GNVQ portfolio of evidence is central to the assessment process, teachers found that their role in evaluating evidence produced by students was continuous and demanding. However, this role was integral to the learning and review process for each student. As feedback on an activity was given, this generated plans for the next activity.

Teachers were concerned to demonstrate their professional competence and credibility in carrying out such feedback and assessment. A large number began working towards certification in the *Assessor and Internal Verifier Units*. These units were frequently referred to when staff discussed assessment. Many noted that working towards these units was a valuable experience as staff themselves went through the same process they were taking their students through, and for some it was a very helpful introduction to a completely different style of learning and assessment.

The physical resources for each qualification varied considerably from institution to institution, but the specifications of the qualifications often indicate the need for a wide range of equipment and materials, and opportunities to observe or to be involved in work activities. Some centres already had links with business, industry and public services to provide appropriate contexts for activities and evidence collection. Although some centres recorded difficulties with work placements, as these were not a requirement of the qualification, they were often able to organise sufficient external support. A few staff indicated that during this first year they felt they had an advantage before large numbers of schools and colleges began requiring workplace experience. A task for many centres was to coordinate their business links and plan activities to make best use of time for the employers, students and teachers themselves.

Types of Courses

In March 1993 it became clear that one of the most controversial aspects of GNVQs was the array of different courses offered by the centres. The type of course and its resources have an impact on the quality of the GNVQ itself. All reports indicated that no two institutions were offering GNVQs in exactly the same way (Employment Department, 1992; OFSTED, 1993; WJEC, 1993). Certain patterns were more prevalent in colleges which tended to concentrate on vocational studies with the GNVQ forming the basis of study with additional units or modules in the vocational subject area being added alongside. The emerging pattern in schools was to offer academic qualifications alongside GNVQs, usually GCSE with intermediate and 'A' level with advanced. A few 'A' level students were also taking the intermediate GNVQ.

There are two fundamental aspects of the GNVQ which promote flexibility in programming — the outcomes model and the GNVQ structure. In the outcomes model there are no constraints on how a student achieves each unit. Any course leading to any qualification might potentially provide opportunities to achieve GNVQ units. This allows teachers, and senior management in particular, to decide that some learning courses could perform dual or triple functions preparing for several qualifications simultaneously. A common example is the 'Y model' in which students begin a joint 'A' level and BTEC National programme for several months and decide later which qualification they will select. However, in general, they would not complete both courses. The GNVQ flexibility of delivery suggested to some centres that students might achieve two qualifications, such as advanced business GNVQ with Business Studies 'A' level, or advanced art and Design GNVQ with art 'A' level. There is debate as to the educational value of this duplication. However, in this early stage of the GNVQ it is clear that many in the educational world are also seeking insurance that student achievement will be recognized by people unfamiliar with GNVQs.

The development of courses, including different subject areas, either academic or vocational, has been welcomed by many centres. The impetus for this has come from the GNVQ structure. The design of GNVQ has aimed at equivalence with academic qualifications; Advanced GNVQ was given equivalence of two 'A' levels (grades A-E) and intermediate GNVQ four to five GCSEs (grades A-C) with respect to the content and standard set for the vocational units. The GNVQ course also requires the completion of three core skills units, which can add substantially to the workload, and contributes to the breadth of the GNVQ. Many schools and colleges regard both qualifications as full-time courses without any additional studies and consider that the Advanced GNVQ is as demanding as three 'A' levels, and the intermediate as five GCSEs. The advanced GNVQ structure has offered scope for some students to add a contrasting 'A' level alongside, or other specialized GNVQ units. This type of programme has been commented on by all evaluators as having mixed results so far. It is reasonable to expect that students likely to achieve three good 'A' levels could also achieve a good GNVQ plus one 'A' level result. Where students are not expected to achieve three 'A' levels, it seems less likely that they will be successful at adding one 'A' level to an advanced GNVQ course. There were a few reports of students who embarked on an ambitious programme including an advanced GNVQ and more than one 'A' level but have since reconsidered and dropped at least one course. On the other hand, some encouraging aspects of a mixed programme reported by a few teachers so far indicate that the enthusiasm for the GNVQ self-directed style of learning has carried over positively in students' approaches to 'A' level work. Teachers have also been heard to comment on rethinking their 'A' level teaching styles.

Course Time

The question of how much time is needed for any one course is significant because of the flexibility of the GNVQ structure. Timing has proved a considerable challenge to centres who had to make decisions for resourcing. The range of time allowed varied from eight hours a week to twenty-six hours for an advanced GNVQ. Some reports (OFSTED, 1993) showed that those allowing less than ten-twelve hours a week were limiting opportunities for their students who were under pressure to produce appropriate evidence in the time. Some students had plenty of time with twenty-six hours a week, and teachers were investigating additional studies of different kinds. There is ongoing debate as to what hours per week include, particularly when 'class contact hours' is not an appropriate measure because of the need for individual and group support, work-related activities, and so on. Some students were encouraged to do far more self-directed study which was not necessarily accounted for in the timetable. With dual studies there was overlap with other qualifications that contributed to the students' achievement.

Clearly a significant part of teachers' time had to be spent with individual students or small groups, particularly in the early stages of a course. The integration of planning, feedback and assessment in this tutoring process was important in focusing students on achieving each step of the course. Time for guidance and assessment was allowed for by most colleges and schools with vocational experience, but less so amongst those with more rigid timetabling. Reports showed this time was crucial for staff and students. Without it staff were not able to carry out important initial assessment and continue to guide students through many decisions. Examples of this were how much time the student might need for any single activity, where students could go for appropriate information and research, what other qualifications might be taken alongside, what additional work might be needed to catch up on core skills, and how students might integrate activities with other studies or extra-mural experience, or what potential there might be for demonstrating higher achievement through the higher levels of core skills and the merit and distinction grades. These needed regular review and teachers were beginning to recognize that this was as important to the course as teaching. In a few centres the balance of teacher input had changed to a completely non-instructional role which left students to sink or swim. This clearly had significant disadvantages for the student and led to poor achievement and disillusionment.

Teacher Approaches to Delivery

The change to a new qualification presented teachers with the problem of determining exactly what was required of them in devising detailed learning courses. With no past lesson plans or assessment exemplars, such as previous exam papers, teachers looked for standards extrinsic to the GNVQ specifications themselves.

The first reports from evaluators indicated that many teachers were basing their delivery on previous experience with similar qualifications. The benefits of this were in providing indications of level of demand on students, both in quantity and difficulty, relative to qualifications offered to a similar cohort. For instance, experience with GCSEs, the BTEC First or the Intermediate Diploma of Vocational Education was drawn on to give some comparison with the scope of the Intermediate qualification.

In some cases teachers used assignments or lesson plans they had developed for other qualifications, either modified to meet the new specifications or unchanged from previous courses. The advantages were that this provided a basis for teaching where teachers felt secure and did not need much preparation time during a very demanding period of change. The disadvantages were that teachers did not necessarily look closely at the specifications in order to plan assignments which fulfilled the scope of the units. In some cases realization of this came late, at the stage when teachers were assessing students' completed work against the required standard. The work might have considerable merit in its own terms, but was not necessarily relevant to a unit, so the student might be unable to achieve all the unit criteria.

Meetings with centre representatives during February-March give encouraging indications that teachers were reviewing their teaching/learning activities in order to meet the performance criteria for assessment. A widespread comment from teachers was that next year they would be able to plan assignments far better in order to meet the demands of the qualifications.

The Student Cohort and Access

The decisions taken with regard to access and threshold requirements had considerable implications for teachers. Some GNVQ courses had recruited more widely than for previous qualifications leading to a greater range of prior achievement and experience among students. Some teachers said how this presented a new or exacerbated problem of approaching 'mixed ability' teaching. This was particularly obvious where teachers took a more traditional classroom approach to teaching in which all students were expected to proceed at the same pace on the same assignments.

After one term's experience, teachers were beginning to recognize what might be useful, or indeed necessary, preparation for each student starting a qualification. This was important experience as the specifications identified the final outcome but teachers had to determine *how* to get there. Time, prior learning (not necessarily identical to examination results), learning resources and opportunities influenced whether a course could cope with a wide variety of students or not.

An intermediate manufacturing teacher commented that lack of drawing experience (to the extent of not knowing which end to sharpen a pencil) meant that the starting place for teaching a unit on product design was extremely elementary and that additional teaching time was needed. An advanced health and social care teacher was deciding that since a number of written reports were necessary, some competence in extended writing could be required and a reasonable threshold for next year would be GCSE English at grade C or above. These comments indicate a tension for teachers between expanding the accessibility of qualifications through more flexible and individualized learning styles and the constraints of the teaching environment where time and achievement rates are the reality.

However, there are examples of courses where an extended initial assessment period allowed teachers and students to make realistic judgments about the potential match of student with the qualification. In particular, where several weeks of induction courses were run, or intermediate and advanced qualifications were run parallel for the first two or three months, students were guided to the appropriate course to take. Matching the demands of the course with the potential and prior achievement of the student continued to be critical questions for teachers and administrators.

For some teachers it was almost a surprise that students not only have to be assessed for the core skills, but they actually need them in order to achieve the units. This is most relevant to the core skill of communication as discussion, record keeping, presentation and report writing form the basis of a large number of units across all the qualifications. During the first term, many teachers ignored the core skills completely, concentrating on the vocational units. Review meetings in November and December 1992 showed that perhaps half the teachers had planned to develop the core skills alongside certain vocational units and were preparing to incorporate, if not already incorporating, many of these skills into various activities. Others were delaying this, partly through lack of time to plan, and partly through the idea of assessing them late in the course and catching up on deficiencies then.

However, the problem of access also related to the core skills. Teachers did not expect vocational experience from students but did expect to rely on basic skills for students to fulfil assignments. Teachers could either set threshold requirements to exclude those with poor core skills, or determine the extent to which core skills development was needed by each student and implement various ways of addressing this need through the overall learning programme. Some centres chose to use an initial assessment of core skills achievement as a method of determining which level of a GNVQ the student was ready for. When core skills were part of an initial assessment and immediate steps were taken to develop these core skills, students were also developing a range or skills useful for preparing their assignments.

Internal and External Assessment

Internal assessment required a focused interpretation of the specifications of the GNVQ. Initially, many teachers found the format of the GNVQ units difficult to interpret. Some who had NVQ experience were at ease with the format but others found the first impact of the terminology created barriers. During the first term this was a common criticism, but there was also a growing number of favourable comments from teachers who had taken the opportunity to reconsider exactly what they were requiring their students to do and why. By the second term teachers were reconsidering some of their assignments and planning to approach new units differently. Some were surprised at the manner in which students had grappled with the specifications and had themselves created opportunities for achieving different parts of units. The age range of students in some courses gave opportunities for mature students with some professional experience to help inexperienced students create opportunities for producing evidence.

A serious issue, in terms of the validity of the qualification is the uncertainty teachers had about whether they were assessing to the correct standard. This was partially being addressed by the awarding bodies as verifiers made visits to centres and as assessors attended meetings to discuss evidence. It is inevitably a major problem for any new qualification, but one which needs addressing seriously, particularly through staff development, guidance and support materials. There were other problems which teachers had not encountered before such as finding space to store evidence. This could be partly related to the first issue as staff and students collected any and all available evidence rather than selecting evidence sufficient and necessary to meet the requirements.

The recording of evidence raised problems for teachers. A range of approaches was offered by different awarding bodies, and many teachers developed their own recording systems with varying success. Some found the documentation from awarding bodies too prescriptive and complicated, others found it too simple and lacking in sufficient detail. The process of assessment was often confused with the recording of assessment which threatened to become an end in itself. As verifiers, evaluators and inspectors made frequent visits to the pilot centres, the pressure to record everything for inspection purposes was intense. The new qualifications attracted a high level of scrutiny and many people involved in the assessment chain felt they had to confirm their position with more detailed paperwork.

External assessment caused anxiety and frustration during the autumn term as centres waited for information on the format and content of tests. In the minds of the public, the teachers and the students, the traditional importance of examinations far outweighed the substantial demands of the portfolio. The principle of external testing, especially in a vocational context, continued to be rejected by some GNVQ teachers although others considered there were benefits, especially related to external credibility, but also in relation to motivation. When actual results of external tests proved that some groups of students had achieved far lower than expected, there were deeply felt anxieties. The quality of external tests attracted considerable negative criticism and a detailed programme to improve the tests was begun by the awarding bodies and NCVQ. By the summer students began to collect passes on their units, and many felt they had tangible success and a bench mark for continuing the qualification.

The assessment debate continues as both the principles and practices of external testing are modified in the light of experience. The weight and balance of internal and external assessment are under review, and the particular forms of assessment will need experience and evaluation to provide answers to some of the more difficult tensions.

Grading Criteria

The concept of uniform grading criteria applied across all GNVQs was new to many teachers. The majority were used to grading students in relation to the subject material they taught. The GNVQ grading criteria relate to studying and thinking skills, skills which are in demand from both higher education and employers. These criteria are then contextualized by the student and the assessor in relation to the portfolio of evidence for each qualification. By demonstrating these criteria it is proposed that students achieve both high quality work and show potential for improving their work.

There was some confusion as to how to use the grading criteria. The application of grading criteria to a completed portfolio of evidence gave some teachers the impression that these criteria need not be considered until the final stages of the qualification. Some teachers applied interim and formative marks which bore no relation to the grading criteria but were based on teacher assessment of a good piece of work. Discussion of grading criteria in March 1993 indicated that although most teachers were willing to apply the grading criteria and considered the criteria to be appropriate, they wished in addition to apply criteria related to the content of the vocational subject area. These content-related criteria were those they had been accustomed to using as they marked or graded other qualifications. A few felt that regular classroom testing was the most appropriate method of grading and marking achievement. Many were comfortable with norm-referenced models of assessment, and wished to be able to differentiate between students on that basis.

The grading criteria presented some clear cases of delayed implementation which limited students' potential. At meetings in March some teachers explained how the themes of planning and evaluating could have been developed to assist students in learning to work independently. However, as some teachers concentrated on the unit specifications and unit tests, they left grading till last. Intermediate courses tended to be delivered in a more directed form which left little scope for students to achieve the merit or distinction grades such as planning their own work. At the same time, some evidence produced by advanced students included examples where students' initiative showed planning and evaluation strengths. An example of this in art and design showed some advanced students working independently on their portfolios; each produced a variety of products in different media developed from a wide range of external sources they discovered for themselves. In the business context aspects of mini-enterprises run by the students themselves provided ideal opportunities for recognising these initiatives through a higher grade. Students who were able and encouraged to direct their own learning were well on their way to merit or distinction grades and the self-confidence to achieve again.

Conclusion

GNVQs offer a new character and dimension to the national educational system. Vocational qualifications have been available for a century or more but have never been part of a single national system. This raises a paradox in many educationalists' minds. GNVQs are introducing new national standards, but paradoxically their very flexible structure allows for considerable variety of delivery.

The students taking GNVQs have a wide ability range, and diversity in age and background as well as more varied aspirations. Coping with the needs of students has led schools and colleges to provide variation in length of course and the time devoted to it, as well as the contexts in which students can achieve units. This reflects the demands of the student population and the ways in which schools and colleges must respond to this market. Student-centred learning has helped to support this process and staff and students are recognizing and responding to the opportunities this offers them. This diversity makes it much less easy to determine which factors contribute to the success of meeting such varied demands.

So far, the increased enrolment for the second year and upcoming third year of GNVQs indicate considerable recognition of its strengths and a growing commitment to its potential. Estimates of student persistence on courses are high and indicate that GNVQs are providing a way of meeting the growth in staying-on rates. Many students have been expected to accomplish more than ever before, and have risen to the demands of the courses. Many have not completed all they set out to achieve, but are continuing because they are stimulated by the course and their teachers.

Schools and colleges are promoting the advantages of diversity they can offer and take pride in meeting the varied needs of their students. This demanding task is compounded by current significant changes in the management of the education system itself. As some GNVQ centres have said, only a framework of qualifications such as GNVQs could provide them with the flexibility and opportunity to take advantage of the system-wide changes now sweeping the 14–19 education sectors.

References

EMPLOYMENT DEPARTMENT (1992) *Introducing GNVQs into Schools and Colleges*, Quality Assurance Division, Study 10, Sheffield.

HARROP, J. (1992) *Response to the Consultation on General National Vocational Qualifications, NCVQ Report No 15*, London, NCVQ.

OFSTED (1993) *GNVQs in Schools: The Introduction of General National Vocational Qualifications 1992, A Report from the Office of Her Majesty's Chief Inspector of Schools*, London, HMSO.

WELSH JOINT EDUCATION COMMITTEE (1993) *Learning from the GNVQ Pilot Experience in Wales*, Cardiff, WJEC.

Chapter 7

Piloting GNVQ

Tom Jackson

In the history of English further education — if such a thing exists — the academic year 1992–93 will be noteworthy for two major changes, the incorporation of FE and sixth form colleges and the introduction of General National Vocational Qualifications to the post-16 curriculum. Colleges had no choice about their incorporation, but no college was forced to become a first phase or pilot institution for the introduction of GNVQ.

Why Become a Pilot?

A dispassionate observer might well ask why, when faced with the turmoil and extra burdens on all staff imposed by incorporation, a college would not merely choose, but beg to be allowed to take on the further work and uncertainty of introducing GNVQ, then barely more than a curricular glimmer in the collective eye of NCVQ and the nominated examination boards, BTEC, City and Guilds and the RSA.

The simple answer to this question, 'To prepare for incorporation', may seem facile. It is nonetheless true. At Portsmouth College we saw the curricular philosophy of NVQ and of GNVQ as being in tune with the primary implications of incorporation. If accessibility, involvement, relevance and responsiveness are at the core of the GNVQ approach, then these were, and are, entirely complementary to the themes of growth, diversity of provision and responsiveness to the market which are essential to the success of the incorporated college. Does this mean then that the high-minded aims of GNVQ expounded elsewhere in this collection, have been cynically subverted or exploited by practitioners? Far from it.

The National Context

In the broadest context we saw ourselves as responding to challenges thrown down by the Government. The first of these came in the White Paper of 1991 in which the following issues were put in sharp focus:

1   To bring some coherence to the post-16 qualifications and to bridge the academic-vocational divide.

2   To encourage parity of esteem between academic and vocational qualifications.

3   To stimulate significant and rapid growth in the rate of participation in 16+ education and training.

Simultaneously, two other related issues were part of the national debate:

(i)   The development of systematic approaches to progression which allowed flexible accumulation and transfer of credit between different types of qualification.

(ii)   The National Education and Training Targets, since adopted by the Department of Employment, but originally evolving from debate within and between a number of industry-led organizations, such as the CBI. The current form of these targets is:

(a)   80 per cent of young people to reach NVQ Level 2 by 1997;

(b)   NVQ Level 3 available to all who can benefit by 1997;

(c)   50 per cent of young people to NVQ Level 3 by 2000;

(d)   education and training to develop self-reliance, flexibility and breadth.

The College and Its Students

Quite apart from the wider national context which helped to provide these answers for the question, 'Why GNVQ', for us there were also answers related to the needs of the college and its students which bulked large in our decision.

(i)   We wanted to continue to adapt the culture of our institution to accommodate change.

(ii)   We wanted to improve breadth and balance for individual students and encourage the bridging of the 'divide' between the academic and the vocational.

(iii)   As a sixth-form college offering predominantly 'A' levels and GCSEs we were concerned about the lack of suitability and relevance of our curriculum for many of our existing students, one-third of whom were on one-year courses.

(iv)   The likelihood of short-term, significant growth in numbers of students on purely 'A' Level courses was small. If the College was to grow in a highly competitive local context, we would have to broaden our client base to attract students who would not otherwise have considered the curriculum on offer at any local college.

(v)   We had been offering courses leading to NVQs at levels 1, 2 and 3 for two years and were very pleased with their success, but we felt there was an increasingly strong message that for a college like ours, without extensive capital plant to simulate closely workplace conditions, this curricular route was closing.

(vi)   The proposed structure of GNVQ was likely to be far more compatible with our subject-based curricular structure than courses such as BTEC diplomas, which were in any case likely to be subsumed into the new structure.

(vii) We were lucky to have the staff and resources in place which would allow us to deliver GNVQ with a minimum of new appointments or virement of resources.

(viii) We were committed to progressive development of a College culture in which students were more self-reliant and responsible for the structure and progress of their own learning.

(ix) We had become tired of hearing the fatalistic excuses that until something revolutionary happened at national level to reform 16+ qualifications, there was no point in trying to do anything with the tools to hand at college level. Now that something was happening, we wanted to move quickly to develop a new programme type for our students which would allow a true mix of the academic and the vocational.

(x) Related to this, we wanted to have more control over the direction of our own curriculum. It seemed to us that a primary means to accomplish this was through involvement in a pilot project which might give directly influence on curriculum development at national level which would benefit and be more suitable for our students. More selfishly, we also wanted a focus for collaborative, College-based development.

Of course all this careful analysis in retrospect of our reasons for wanting to become a first phase institution could be summarized at the emotional level at that time by the statement, 'We thought it would be good for our students and we wanted to get on with it.'

There would undoubtedly have been some advantages for the College in reducing pressures had we taken an incremental approach to the introduction of GNVQ, offering perhaps only one or two areas. In the final analysis it was felt, however, that we had already tested the water with NVQ. What is more, there were also seen to be advantages in having a broadly-based team drawn from across the curriculum for the developmental stages.

Preparing the Way

The GNVQ courses we had opted to introduce were art and design, business, health and social care, leisure and tourism, all at both Levels 2 and 3, and manufacturing only at Level 2, because we were not well enough equipped in this area for Level 3 and were frankly sceptical that a sufficient market existed. Many of the tasks of implementing these courses were no different from any other course introduction; choosing the key programme and team leaders, marketing to potential students and choosing an examination board. At the time the latter decision was an easy one, because the Royal Society of Arts (RSA) had chosen us, but the attraction was mutual and based on a long-standing and fruitful relationship. This relationship has continued to develop, based both on the contribution of the College to the Society's development of its GNVQ courses and on the RSA's ability to balance responsiveness to individual centres with the maintenance of high, credible standards.

Some areas of implementation proved surprisingly easy. Remarkably, finance did not prove to be a significant issue. The GNVQ courses proved no more expensive to launch than any others. It has to be admitted that because there was no injection of financial support for pilot institutions, there was still a significant extra burden on the College's staffing budget, which we would not otherwise have chosen in the run-up to incorporation. The similarity of GNVQs in some areas such as art and design, business, health and social care and manufacturing to existing or preceding courses meant that large investments in other resources were not necessary. Only in leisure and tourism was a significant injection of funds needed.

Despite the availability of considerable staff experience and expertise, there was a significant need for staff development. Much of this was of a collaborative, sharing nature, both within the college and with staff in other colleges. However, given the dearth of central funding to support the introduction of GNVQ, we were very grateful for allocations from Hampshire's GEST funding for staff development and the support from Hampshire TEC for general staff development work and specifically to train staff as assessor trainers, giving us the ability subsequently to train the rest of our team as assessors. In addition, one member of staff undertook training in Assessment of Prior Achievement (APA) in order to add this string to our collective bow. Despite the extra demands which this training threw onto the particular members of staff involved, there is no doubt that the availability of the resulting expertise on a daily basis in-house did a great deal to build confidence among all the staff in the GNVQ team.

What has also been interesting is how many very experienced teachers have commented on the new light which assessor training has thrown on their own teaching and assessment methodologies. Most comment that such training has made them much more conscious of the need for precision both in setting aims and in the detached but sympathetic observation of their achievement by students; they also comment that this consciousness has helped them tighten up their own teaching processes.

With little experience in the introduction of vocational programmes, a major priority and task for us was ensuring that there were clear lines of progression from the new courses, not only into employment but also higher education. Our Vocational Education Coordinator was nominated for the NCVQ's Committee on Progression to HE and we secured a compact with the University of Portsmouth for favourable consideration for GNVQ students. Since then large numbers of universities have made similar undertakings. From the other direction we were particularly pleased to receive a number of applications from students just completing BTEC First diplomas at a local FE college who wished to move on to GNVQ Level 3 courses, usually combining them with an 'A' level of particular relevance or interest to them. We have also held seminars for officers of the Hampshire Careers and Guidance Service, representatives of higher education institutions along the south coast and for local employers.

Planning for quality assurance and systematic evaluation were also clearly essential. Regular team meetings, senior staff involvement, monitoring by external agencies including LEA and HMI, student evaluation and statistical monitoring were all built into the programme. Naturally staff have also been trained as internal verifiers as part of the in-built internal and external verification procedures of GNVQ. Most importantly the normal processes of quality assurance in the curriculum have also been applied including departmental supervision and, in our case, regular audits by senior staff of the curricular provision in specific areas.

Programme Structure

There was a key assumption which underlay all of the planning work undertaken by staff in preparing GNVQ courses for delivery at the College. This was that all students on GNVQ courses would also be following other courses, both examination and non-examination, as part of their programmes at the College.

When the draft structure of GNVQ was first indicated at a regional meeting in the early summer of 1991, I made representations to NCVQ that the GNVQ should be seen as equivalent to two 'A' Levels rather than three. At that time we already had a small number of students following courses leading to NVQ Level 3, who were also studying for an 'A' Level. It seemed to us that this kind of genuinely mixed programme was an ideal vehicle for the bridging of the 'divide', yet the original proposal for an 18 Unit GNVQ Level 3 would have precluded such a combination. What we were looking for was the maximum flexibility particularly for students but also for providers.

Though we understood the fundamental differences between GNVQs and the rest of our subject-based curriculum, we saw GNVQ as being compatible with, and adding significantly to, the variety which already existed among our seventy-eighty examination subjects and eighty-100 non-examination courses and activities.

We were entirely happy that other colleges would wish to offer GNVQs basically following a similar pattern to the successful and popular BTEC National Diploma and therefore full-time courses of up to eighteen units all held together by a single vocational theme. Our own approach, which is we believe shared by quite a number of the pilot institutions, was designed to cater for those whose initial commitment to a single vocational goal was not perhaps as high or who might actively wish to keep open several options. Though we were obviously concerned that our students should emerge from their courses with credible qualifications,.our purpose in encouraging mixed programmes was not, as it was for a few providers, to take out an insurance policy against the failure of GNVQ.

Of increasing concern to us recently has been the pressure which is being brought to bear on NCVQ to abandon the fundamental principle of NVQs that they assess competence — or in the case of GNVQ, achievement — and that it is this which is fundamental, *not* the nature of duration of the experience which leads to that competence or achievement. We were frankly alarmed by one external verifier who appeared to have had his original training as a BTEC moderator and could not shake off that different brief. The focus of BTEC on the implementation of an educational philosophy seems to be at the heart of the problem. BTEC moderators appear to have a brief to ensure that students have an experience of a particular type and of a certain duration; this would seem to be their primary concern. Of secondary interest to them is the quality, validity and comparability of assessment. The assumption is that the aims of the course will be fulfilled if students receive the type and quality of experience which was approved in the original submission.

The determination of BTEC to impose its philosophy on providers is understandable in the context of the excellent, early, curriculum development undertaken by BTEC to introduce more liberal broadly-based education to the vocational sector. However, there is a growing feeling among providers who are not used to this BTEC approach that it is inappropriate to the contemporary context. For us certainly, it was precisely to escape this kind of centralized, monolithic orthodoxy and its associated bureaucracy that the College embraced both NVQ philosophy and the GNVQs offered through the RSA. It seemed to us that the needs of students, and therefore the style of programme which they follow, are best assessed as close to the student as possible, ideally in a dialogue between the student and those who actually design and deliver the course. Obviously if a qualification is to have national validity and credibility there must be carefully structured, precisely defined controls. This is exactly what GNVQ does, and because it does so there should be no need of further definition of the nature or length of the learning experience.

In saying this we are aware that some of those who conceived GNVQ and NVQ would prefer not to see GNVQs drawn into cohabitation with 'A' Levels and other general academic qualifications in a single programme. They see GNVQ as being entirely viable as a coherent qualification in itself. We would not disagree. However, there is no doubt in our minds that the mixed programme also serves the needs of a range of students who are not served by a purely vocationally orientated programme — no matter how 'general'. So long as these students have learning experiences which enable them to produce evidence which satisfies the performance criteria it should make no difference whether or not they have completed the same number of hours as a student in another college. Certainly it should be possible through the mechanisms of APA and the drawing of evidence from a variety of sources outside the limits of a 'course', for the part-time mature student to complete units or even the whole course in significantly fewer hours than a full-time student.

At present, for sixth-form colleges and schools with larger sixth-forms, GNVQ is opening up a door to introduce both vocational and mixed programmes, while still each maintaining a distinctive ethos. If this door to wider choice is closed and we return to a pattern of binary choice — vocational or academic — post-16 education will be the poorer and colleges like ours will have a stark choice either to regress to be specialist general academic providers or to become the poor relations of our larger FE neighbours.

If the lobby to turn GNVQ into a mere reflection of BTEC diplomas prevails, GNVQ will be a significantly weaker, less flexible instrument for the development of a broadly based, coherent system of post-16 qualification and assessment. We consider that one of the primary strengths and goals of the introduction of GNVQ is the increased accessibility to further education which it will bring. If the introduction of GNVQ is perceived as a mere revamping of existing vocational qualifications, this increased access will not take place.

Students!

Having made a considerable effort to prepare for the introduction of the new GNVQ courses we awaited with some eagerness student enrolment in September. Our marketing revealed that there was considerable interest in GNVQ both from students coming to us from our partner schools and from our own students who were intending to progress from one-year courses to more advanced courses. Our predictions in July suggested that we would recruit viable numbers for each of the GNVQ courses we were offering.

Enrolment of students is done by personal tutors, who in most cases are not course tutors and will not teach the students they enrol. It was therefore particularly important to establish guidelines and criteria for the enrolment of students onto the new GNVQ courses. Quite apart from wishing to ensure that students did not enrol on inappropriate programmes, we were also concerned to establish the credibility of GNVQ courses generally and particularly the parity of esteem sought between GNVQ Level 3 and 'A' levels.

For Level 2 courses, students would preferably have a minimum of grade E or above in four GCSE subjects. For Level 3 courses, students would preferably have a minimum of four GCSEs at grade C or above and have achieved a minimum of grade D in English language and mathematics. The Level 2 guidelines are significant in that they reflected our belief that although Level 2 GNVQ courses would be suitable for most of our one-year students they would be too demanding for those with the lowest GCSE grades. This assumption has subsequently proved correct. The Level 3 guidelines were the same as those for enrolment onto any of our 'A' level courses and reflected our belief that GNVQ Level 3 courses would be as demanding and difficult as 'A' levels and were intended for 'A' level calibre students, though not necessarily students who would happily or willingly enrol for 'A' Levels alone.

Having set out these guidelines, there was also some flexibility, so that students who could demonstrate an appropriate background of study or experience were accepted onto courses though they might lack the formal qualifications given above. We felt that it would be a mockery of the NVQ structure if entry were not possible in this way. Had we expected sufficient numbers of students we might have adopted the approach of some other colleges where students were enrolled into programme areas and only allocated to a course level after the first six weeks during which thorough diagnosis and some APA were possible. Though we did not use this approach this year, it is likely that it will be used with Level 1 and 2 students next year.

Enrolment onto the GNVQ courses turned out as follows:

Table 7.1   *Student enrolment*

	Level 2	Level 3
Art and Design	15	7
Business	14	9
Health and social care	22	15
Leisure and tourism	15	13
Manufacturing	7	–
Total	73	44
Grand Total		= 117

All the students enrolled onto GNVQ courses were also taking other College courses as part of a mixed programme of academic and vocational study appropriate to their needs, interests and career or higher education aspirations. The following examples of students' programmes illustrate the degree to which students have chosen to complement or supplement their GNVQ courses:

Table 7.2 Examples of student programmes

With GNVQ Level 3

Matthew:	GNVQ Leisure and Tourism Level 3 'A' Level Sociology
Jayda:	GNVQ Business Level 3 'A' Level Art and Design GCSE English Language
Zoe:	GNVQ Health and Social Care Level 3 'A' Level Biology
Steven:	GNVQ Art and Design Level 3 'A' Level Sociology
Michelle:	GNVQ Leisure and Tourism Level 3 'A' Level Business Studies GCSE Mathematics
Douglas:	GNVQ Business Level 3 'A' Level Mathematics GCSE Sociology

Course Design

What kind of courses are these GNVQ students experiencing? From what we were given in terms of units, elements, performance criteria and knowledge specifications we had decisions to make about the design and delivery of each GNVQ course.

The six-month lead time from notification of pilot status to the enrolment of students was a considerable constraint on preparation, especially since most aspects of the courses were at best in outline form and, in some cases, not even that. In many ways, however, this was an advantage to us. A cross-curricular team was formed almost immediately and set its basic timetable and targets for the design of the nine courses across the five vocational areas. Having done so and got over the shock of realization of the task before them, the members of the team adopted a dynamic, proactive approach. As a result, they not only completed their own course maps, but in several cases were instrumental in moulding the shape of units and assessment criteria at national level.

The teachers involved soon realized in designing their courses that though the definition of units and assessment criteria in GNVQ are precise, there is very considerable latitude in the way in which these may be approached. The cross-curricular nature of the team also had two complementary effects. On the one hand, the similarities in some of the courses encouraged cooperative approaches, which were reflected later in joint timetabling, team teaching and joint approaches to projects, investigations and themes. On the other hand, quite different approaches were developed between some subject areas in the way that the performance criteria were mapped onto the course in delivery.

The unit structure of the GNVQ model suggests the possibility of modular course design, with each unit being a module of the course. Taking the units as course modules was an approach favoured by one of the areas — health and social care. On the health and social care courses the sequence of the modules is determined by the course staff and the pace of the course is determined by the need to complete the units according to specified end of module deadlines. Perhaps the fact that the health and social care team leader had been involved in the writing of the assessment criteria may have influenced her view of the coherence of the units.

Staff designing the other GNVQ courses have adopted a different approach. They have favoured designing sequences or programmes of work which may involve the completion of elements from different units. On the art and design course, for example, instead of completing each unit in turn, students may undertake a task or project which involves completing say, two or three elements from two or three different units. On the Level 3 course, for example, a student may gradually complete the elements of a unit over the two years of the course and only complete the unit at the end of the course.

The reasoning behind this approach was the perception that many of the skills and much of the knowledge required to complete the elements of particular units needed to evolve and mature over a longer period of time than course modules based on one unit would allow.

Certainly there are clear advantages in paralleling modules of delivery with the assessment structure of the units and disadvantages in mapping assessment criteria across more 'natural' modules of work. Quite apart from the added complexities and end-loading of assessment in the latter approach, it is also far less likely that students will be able to achieve significant partial credit accumulation if they leave the course at the half-way stage. In addition, the motivation of many students is supported more consistently by the regular feedback of assessment in a unit/module approach and, of course the end-loading of assessment makes it much more difficult for students to retake tests or improve the quality of the evidence in their portfolios.

Nevertheless, there is a clear message here for those reviewing the unit structure that it is important to consult actively with practitioners to ensure that courses can readily be designed to follow the unit structure, which will then allow both students and teachers to accrue the full benefits of this approach. We believe that a fundamental design criterion for those developing the units of GNVQ courses should be the susceptibility of those units to inclusion in a programme of flexible accumulation of credit.

Another aspect of course design and delivery was our perception that the GNVQ courses had certain features in common. Obviously, each of the courses required the development and assessment of the same core skills. Although the core skills needed to be as fully integrated as possible, there would be advantage in being able to provide additional support sessions for core skills development which could be attended by students from the different GNVQ courses (for example, IT support). There remains concern in our minds that some of the core skills elements, while laudable in themselves are not easily integrated with the vocational elements of the courses. Where there is excessive artificiality or incongruence in the relationship between core skills and vocational elements, it is the perceived relevance of core skills generally, not merely the single core skills element, which suffers. We feel that further careful thought should be given to this relationship.

Several of the courses also contained related units and elements: Health and Safety at Work and aspects of marketing crop up, for example, in several of the courses. We also saw that there were possibilities of cross curricular activity with students on one GNVQ course (for example, Business Level 3) working with students on another course (for example, Leisure and Tourism Level 3) on, for example, a marketing project.

There seemed to be opportunities here for staff with particular expertise to contribute across the courses, and for students on different GNVQ courses to work together. For these reasons, in order to ease crossover between courses of staff and students, we decided that the GNVQ courses should be timetabled in parallel for at least half of the weekly course time.

Another important aspect of course design and delivery is the emphasis the GNVQ model places upon students developing the abilities required to manage their own learning and to move from dependency to increasing self-reliance. Students need to develop skills of research, investigation, analysis, decision-making, and planning which are reflected in the various kinds of projects and assignments produced for assessment.

We predicted, and our predictions have since been proved correct, that the teaching and learning styles required would not necessarily be familiar to our students, and that some of them might experience a form of culture shock. In an attempt to overcome this we built into each of the courses an induction phase, focusing particularly on the development of enabling core skills, which would lead students gently into the different culture, expectations and work patterns of GNVQ. Though this approach has generally borne fruit, some staff feel that this induction may have been too gentle, not preparing students adequately for the very rigorous demands of the later parts of the courses. On the other hand, some staff feel that they threw students in at the deep end of the GNVQ approach, heightening the degree of culture shock, and that on reflection they would be more supportive and directive in the initial phases. Clearly a balance must be struck.

We felt that the culture of GNVQ demanded flexibility of both staff and students since we did not want the courses to be off the shelf packages delivered to passive learners. There had to be room for individual action planning and opportunities for students to set targets and determine directions.

The active role of the students is reflected in the processes of evaluating and recording achievement. We spent a great deal of time devising record-keeping systems which would enable staff and students to jointly monitor, evaluate and record progress, using log books, work diaries and systematic course-mapping. On GNVQ courses assessment is definitely not something which only the teachers do and which only the teachers understand: it is characteristic of GNVQ that the students require a high degree of awareness of what they need to do to satisfy the assessment criteria. It is worth saying that in this respect we found it a distinct advantage that the institutional culture and organization of the College generally aims to involve students in the processes of evaluation and assessment through for example, individual action planning with personal tutors and the preparation of records of achievement for all students. There is no doubt that GNVQ courses can take root more easily in compatible soil. In fact one of the most impressive aspects of the involvement of students in their courses has been their ability not only to cope with the initiative and self-reliance required, but even to help to develop and improve the systems of recording assessment.

Proof of the Pudding

On the evidence we have so far we have every reason to be pleased with our introduction of the GNVQ courses. However, it would be misleading to give the impression that there are no problems to be resolved or difficult issues still to confront.

In the first stages of the course there was considerable uncertainty concerning the nature of the externally set tests which are linked to each mandatory unit.

Even now that the excellent results for the first sets of tests have arrived, we are not convinced that the requirement for these tests and the kind of preparation needed fits comfortably with the overall framework of GNVQ assessment and the teaching and learning methods appropriate to vocational education. We are also concerned that the constraints imposed by the timings of the testing process may have an excessive influence on the structure of GNVQ programmes.

The other concern about assessment in GNVQ which is reflected among our own staff, but was expressed most strongly by visiting HMI is that the structure of the assessment process and its importance in the process of delivery may over-awe other potentially more important aspects of the learning process for students and of teaching and enabling methodology for staff. The assessment processes are certainly very time-consuming and some would say cumbersome. In the context of the efficiency gains demanded of colleges by the Further Education Funding Council (FEFC) this approach to assessment may require refining and streamlining while retaining the essential qualities of thoroughness, precision and ownership.

We are still thinking hard about how we may best deliver the optional and additional units for GNVQ Level 3. In order to meet the interests and needs of individual students we feel we will need to make a considerable investment in developing opportunities for supported individual and resource-based learning. We are looking at the development of optional and additional language units for which unit credit might also be gained by students not on GNVQ courses. It has to be admitted that our primary approach to additionality at present is through the other courses studied by our students.

Progression remains a key area of concern. Though the GATE Committee nationally and the pilots locally have done a great deal toward establishing the routes for progression from GNVQ Level 3 to degree courses, there is still work to be done in reassuring higher education concerning the standards of GNVQ Level 3 and its parity with 'A' level. This is especially true in respect of the knowledge content of science-based courses. Despite these concerns, we have received very positive feedback from higher education and employers and there has been considerable interest in what we are doing from other post-16 providers. What we find most worrying with respect to progression is the surprising lack of clarity which still exists concerning progression routes from GNVQ courses to NVQ qualification routes.

Our experience so far has sharpened our awareness of the urgent need for the introduction GNVQ Level 1, which we will be piloting next academic year. We are hopeful that this will help to fill the gap in provision for those students in the post-16 age group who are not yet ready for GNVQ Level 2 but for whom a further experience of GCSE courses is inappropriate. Our only major concern is that there will not be a sufficient orientation toward skills in Level 1. This reflects our general concern that in some ways the search for conceptual rigour in developing GNVQs may have placed too much emphasis initially on the conceptual at the expense of skills. Certainly staff in more than one area feel that the conceptual demands of GNVQ Level 3 are in some ways greater than 'A' level, while Level 2 is not only more demanding in many ways conceptually than GCSE, but has also made excessive demands in terms of the sheer quantity of evidence expected.

It will be clear by now that we embraced GNVQ with high hopes. I would like to conclude by reflecting upon the extent to which we now feel these hopes have been fulfilled.

We hoped that the courses would prove attractive to our clients and we have found that they are indeed popular and that the level of student satisfaction is high.

We hoped that the courses would meet the needs of students and we do have evidence to suggest that we are now able to cater for students for whom wholly academic courses of GCSEs or 'A' levels would not have been suitable.

The introduction of GNVQ has, as we had hoped, contributed to the achievement of College-wide curriculum goals. There has been an increase in the impetus towards cross-curricular projects, the integration of core skills, modularization of courses, experiments with teaching and learning styles and resource-based learning. GNVQ has without doubt contributed to, and accelerated, the changing culture of the College both for staff and students.

Overall, we feel now that we did make the right decision in introducing GNVQ. It was the right decision as regards meeting the educational needs of our students — it was also the right decision in the national context of pressing concerns about post-16 education and training.

Acknowledgments

This article was written with cooperation and support of Richard Westbury, Vice Principal (Curriculum) and Ellen Pinnington, Vocational Education Coordinator. The views expressed have been prompted by the particular experience of the College in piloting GNVQ courses. Inevitably this experience is anecdotal and may not be subject to generalization. Where possible, however, the views and experiences of other pilot institutions are reflected.

Chapter 8

Quality in Qualifications and Learning Programmes

Geoff Stanton

Preamble

Section 1 of this chapter summarizes the argument about the quality of qualifications and the quality of the learning programmes, and indicates how these may be linked to give an overall measure of institutional performance.

Section 2 expands on issues relating to qualifications, and *section 3* on issues relating to learning programmes.

Introduction

Adopting one definition for the quality of qualifications, and another for the quality of learning programmes, enables us to design stable and well-recognized qualifications, whilst having learning programmes which could vary widely in their structure and approach.

To make best use of this flexibility, whilst maintaining cost-effectiveness for both provider and learner, we would need to introduce a common means of recording achievement, which would help with route planning, the documentation of outcomes achieved, and the accumulation of these into qualifications when appropriate. The implications of this are not addressed in this paper, but are in a recent FEU publication *Managing Learning*.

The key to good quality qualifications is their ability to be clear about what someone knows, understands and can do. The key to good quality learning programmes is an understanding of the different kinds of routes and learning environments learners may need to be able to choose between.

There is no consistency about the way in which the five types of qualification available in further education define their levels, the amount of learning in their constituent parts, and the outcomes of that learning.

This inconsistency has serious practical implications. It diminishes the possibility of:

— providing effective and understandable guidance;
— establishing parity of esteem between the different routes;
— encouraging credit accumulation;

— allowing credit transfer;
— avoiding duplication or voids when moving from one programme to another;
— permitting systematic measurement of added value.

There are technical problems associated with adopting a common convention for analyzing all qualifications into units of achievement. However, the debates and development work which will be necessary to resolve these issues are worthwhile activities in any case.

Quality of Qualifications and Learning Programmes

A commonly accepted definition of 'quality' in the industrial and commercial world is 'that which fits the purpose of the customer'.

The 'customer' of a qualification is usually some kind of 'gatekeeper'. They use it to assure themselves that the individual concerned can cope with a further course, is competent to undertake a particular occupation, and so on.

The customer for the learning programme or curriculum, on the other hand, is the individual learner. Learners need to have a programme designed to suit their background, previous attainments and learning styles, and which provides them with the most efficient and attractive route to the qualification for which they are aiming.

It therefore follows that the criteria to be met by a good quality qualification are *not* the same as those that need to be met by a good quality learning programme. Attempts to control the quality of learning programmes by adapting the criteria which qualifications have to meet are unrealistic and cause distortion. Nor can achievement of the qualifications themselves be used to indicate that the learning programme has been good.

At present, teachers, learners, employers and parents have to understand four languages in order to discuss the choices available to them post-16. (The languages in which the National Curriculum, 'A' levels, GNVQs and NVQs are described.) The National Curriculum has 'statements of attainment' and 'programmes of study'. 'A' level syllabuses are a list of topics. GNVQs have 'statements of achievement' and are composed of units, all of which are of the same size, and which have levels. NVQs are described in terms of 'statements of competence', and are composed of units, which are not all of the same size and do not have levels. The National Curriculum has levels (1–10). GNVQs and NVQs also have levels (1–5, but on a different scale). 'A' levels have grades indicated by letters.

We need a common language. This does not mean that each qualification should have a common purpose.

One of the criteria which good quality qualifications should meet is that they should be clear about what the candidate has to demonstrate they 'know, understand and can do' if they are to acquire the qualification, or gain a particular grade. Failure to be clear about this is unfair, inhibits effective feedback and therefore learning, and tends to mean that the qualification has to be gained by a fixed route. Lack of clarity can also mean that standards may slip, or be thought to slip, over time. This may be described as expressing the qualification in terms of 'outcomes'.

Since the rest of this chapter depends on the feasibility of defining qualifications in terms of outcomes, I need to spend some time dealing with possible objections to this.

Are Outcomes Appropriate?

Some would argue that this outcomes-based approach is not appropriate for 'A' levels. I do not find this persuasive, since it has been applied to the National Curriculum, some degrees, and GNVQs in subject areas which overlap with some 'A' levels. What may be meant is that the method of specifying outcomes adopted by NCVQ is not applicable. This is more likely.

Some who have doubts about what they would refer to as 'competence-based approaches' are, in fact, pointing out that the *source* of the outcomes which are embodied in academic qualifications is different from that which is embodied in vocational ones. This is, of course, the case. In fact, another advantage of thinking in outcomes-terms is the need to be clear about who has the authority to specify the outcomes concerned, and upon what basis. Potential sources include the requirements of an occupational role, the need to be able to undertake defined tasks, traditions of scholarships of various kinds, and the requirements of citizenship in adult life in general. Some qualifications clearly relate to one of these sources (NVQs, for instance), others may need to draw upon more than one source (the National Curriculum, for instance). Even when the source is clear and agreed, there always remains the question of which individual or group has the right to speak on its behalf.

Even when *this* is clear and accepted, there can remain the debate about how far the qualification in question should be wholly *determined* by the requirements of a particular source (to the extent of requiring neither more nor less than the source requires). This raises questions about the politics of education and training, which I do not plan to go into further in this chapter.

Some outcomes-based qualifications are designed on the basis that there can be no 'graded' achievement, since an outcome is either achieved or it is not. This is sometimes mistakenly represented as a debate between criterion and norm referencing. In fact, of course, it is perfectly possible to have criteria for the awarding of grades. The real debate seems to be about:

(i) the requirements of the users of the qualification;
(ii) the nature of achievement.

Some 'gatekeepers' or other users of a qualification *are* only interested in whether an individual can perform a role, or a task, to (say) industrial standards. In this case, an 'on/off' award is appropriate. Others, particularly those recruiting to an industry or to a course, need to be able to rank candidates (for short-listing purposes, for instance). It is arguable, using the 'fitness for purpose' definition, that a qualification that fails to fit this purpose is not good enough quality as far as they are concerned. In any case, it is noticeable that if the qualification fails to allow users to rank candidates, when they need to do so, then they find alternative and less systematic means of doing this.

The question about the nature of achievement is more fundamental. My own view is that a reporting system which makes it possible to distinguish between the quality of various examples of performance — all of which are at least satisfactory — is both more in accordance with experience of the real world, and more rigorous. I would argue that, in the world of experience, we do in fact come across some job-holders who fully deserve their pay, and others who not only do this but are exceptional at what they do — without it being the case that they are competent at the next higher level within the occupational structure. Not to be able to report on these distinctions means that performances which everyone agrees are in fact different one from another are forced into the same category, and it also means that appropriate feedback cannot be given to the individual concerned.

Are Outcomes Enough?

Some people object to outcomes-based qualifications because they feel it diminishes the importance of the *process* by which learning is acquired. Many outcomes-based approaches are deliberately agnostic about process, on the very good grounds that unnecessary specification of process bars access to the qualification for many learners and citizens.

On the other hand, many of us are unconvinced by the suggestion that someone's overall competence can be adequately reflected by the acquisition of a large number of separate units, by whatever means. I think there may be two kinds of worry here, which can be addressed in different ways.

The first is concerned with whether, despite the acquisition of a large variety of areas of skill and understanding, an individual may nevertheless fail to deploy them effectively, in a manner which is timely and appropriately synthesized. Those that advocate the outcomes-based approach would say here, I think, that this simply reveals that we have a missing 'unit'. In other words, we need to add a set of outcomes which are concerned with someone's ability to deploy the other outcomes appropriately. (This may have, of course, significant implications for methods of assessment, and its timing.)

This leads me on to my second point. One advantage of the outcomes-based approach is that it becomes possible to offer alternative sources of evidence for the same set of outcomes. However, at the present state of our knowledge and understanding it may well be that the *only* evidence which we can find for certain outcomes is that someone has been through a certain process of learning, or has been engaged in a given activity for a given length of time. If this is the case, then it becomes possible to 'write in' these processes as the necessary evidence for a given set of outcomes.

Sometimes the worry about the outcomes-based approach is its assumption that only one defined set of units can make up a certain qualification. I have some sympathy with this objection. It seems to me that it would be fairly simple to overcome it, however, as long as we do agree to describe units in terms of levels and types of attainment. It then becomes possible to say that whilst a certain group of units may be essential for a qualification, there may be some choice about the additional kinds of achievement which go to make up the rest. This 'core plus options' approach also enables local flexibility to allow for the differences in perception and requirement which will doubtless continue as between different 'gatekeepers'.

The Position with Regard to Existing Qualifications

It would improve the accessibility of 'A' levels, as well as defending the standards they represent, if we could develop clearer definitions of what one has to 'know, understand and be able to do' in order to gain different grades. However, the way in which the necessary outcomes are specified has to be sufficiently flexible so as not to inhibit or discourage some of the best curriculum practice which currently takes place.

The National Curriculum is defined in terms of attainment targets with a number of statements of attainment at each of ten levels. Programmes of study are also specified.

NVQs and GNVQs, on the other hand, are specified only in terms of outcomes. NVQs have one 'Statement of Competence' for each qualification, comprising units, elements, assessment criteria and range statements. GNVQs adopt a similar approach, with the differences that a 'Statement of Achievement' is referred to, and the units are all of the same size, they have levels, and a fixed number go to make up the qualification.

Some outcome-definitions are not sufficiently succinct at present, possibly because it is believed that extending the description can reduce any remaining ambiguity. I think it has to be accepted that this is chasing a mirage: eventually the extended length itself becomes a barrier to understanding. Reliable interpretation of standards can best be obtained by *combining* the clear statement of outcomes aimed for by NVQs, with the development of a common understanding amongst assessors which occurs in 'A' levels through examiners meetings and discussion of exemplars.

If different but complementary forms of development could be promoted with regard to academic and vocational qualifications, this would increase the likelihood of being able to describe them in terms which would allow proper comparisons to be made between them, existing overlaps and comparabilities to be identified, and the true nature of the academic/vocational 'divide' to be seen.

The first stage of these developments would be to:

(i)   identify the units of learning which exist within existing 'A' levels, and the outcomes to be achieved for given grades;

(ii)   simplify the way in which NVQs and GNVQs are defined, but supplement these descriptions by mechanisms through which assessors could develop a common interpretation of them;

(iii)   allocate levels to NVQ units;

(iv)   devise a mechanism by which *sizes* of units which occur in NVQs, GNVQs and within 'A' levels can be measured on a common scale (a way of doing this is proposed in the FEU discussion document *A Basis for Credit?*);

(v)   devise a common scale of *levels* to which units could be allocated.

(vi)   investigate the possibility of categorizing units, so that differences in kind can be distinguished from differences in level.

All this would be well worth doing in any case, and would be to the benefit of all the existing qualifications looked at independently. In addition, however, it would lay the ground for the creation of a common 'framework' within which all the units of which existing qualifications are currently composed could be located.

This could lead, in the medium term, to a situation in which a school or college, or training organization, catering for learners in the post-compulsory sector, would offer an 'array' of such units. If necessary, they could simply be reassembled to form existing qualifications (as happened to a large extent, when the Scottish 'Action Plan' was first introduced). However, displaying the offer on this framework would not only make it much easier for learners to compare, contrast, and be clear what was expected of them, it would also make future developments much more straightforward and cost-effective.

It would, for instance, allow us to develop rules governing the way in which units could be combined, in order to deliver principles such as coherence, breadth, and balance which most people would wish to have applied to the post-16 curriculum.

It would also permit the school or college to identify the 'distance travelled' by a learner during their time at the institution. This distance might be up or across the framework. This approach to reporting the results of an institution could be a more accurate representation of its performance, and would also encourage it to remain accessible to learners of all types and levels of attainment.

If Key Stage 4 of the National Curriculum was part of this framework, then the school-leaving record at 16 would form the baseline from which progress would be measured. However, there could be problems about:

(i) learners moving on to some vocational programmes;
(ii) adults returning to learn.

The recent Audit Commission OFSTED report *Unfinished Business* indicated little correlation between GCSE scores and performance in some vocational qualifications. Many adults will have no recent formal qualifications. For both groups diagnostic assessment periods may be required at the start of programmes in order to provide both guidance and a base-line.

This all sounds very complicated. In fact, it would provide a much simpler and easy to manage system than currently exists. It would also allow us to evolve from our present situation, in a way which preserves current good practice, and is sensitive to public and political opinion. It does require an effective *system for recording achievement*. Used on an ongoing basis, this replaces the timetable as the primary mechanism for curriculum management.

FEU's work has also given us views on the criteria which should apply to Quality Learning Programmes post-16. These might include the availability of impartial guidance and various learning support services, plus the ability to have some degree of choice with regard to learning style, mode of study and location.

Some colleges have encapsulated these 'service entitlements' into learner contracts, and the Government has now proposed a Learner Charter for FE. Perhaps a key element in any charter should be that a written contract *should* be issued. It would be for individual colleges to decide its precise terms, but if they were publicly available there would be protection for those who wished to maintain good standards of service.

All this may be summarized in the suggestion that schools and colleges (and the local system of which they are a part) could measure quality in terms of a *combination* of

— qualifications achieved;
— distance travelled;
— services offered to specified standards.

Section 2 of this chapter says more about the way in which all qualifications would have to be specified if it is to be possible to measure distance travelled. Section 3 expands on the issue of services to learners, in general, and the alternative learning programmes they need to have available, in particular.

Issues Relating to Qualifications

This section expands on some of the technical questions which have to be addressed in order to provide a framework onto which all 'units of assessment' could be mapped.

In order to 'map' a unit of assessment, it is necessary to be able to identify:

— the size of the unit (how much learning it contains);
— the level of the unit;
— the type of outcome it represents.

We also need to define what combinations of units are acceptable for gaining a given qualification. (By comparison with other questions, this is a fairly simple issue.)

Size

The issue of 'size' is also fairly simple. A crude but workable solution is to relate the unit to the number of learning hours an average learner in the presence of an average teacher in an averagely equipped institution would take to achieve the outcomes described. This is by no means the perfect method, but it does seem to be the least bad and most workable. Crucially, it does get over the need artificially to require all units to be of the same 'size'.

Levels

The issue of allocating levels is likely to be far more contentious. I am sure that the attempt to do this will flush out fundamentally different value judgments about what learning matters, and why. Various approaches to this are being explored. Some refer in a somewhat circular manner to the level of prerequisite qualifications. Others assume that certain topics are intrinsically more difficult than others. Others take this a bit further, by attempting to define 'difficulty'. Sometimes this might be done in terms of the degree of learner autonomy implied or required. It may also be a matter of the extent to which certain 'core skills' of analysis, problem solving, synthesis, task management, and so on, are demonstrated in the course of tackling a given topic, issue or role.

None of this is new, of course. For instance, if we attempted to reinvent the whole system of higher education at this point, we would have similar debates and difficulties when it came to deciding what a degree of a given class in history had in common with one in economics or another in physics. However, we will have to accept that in the creation of a new system all this will be ignored, and we may have to accept that when these difficulties eventually emerge, there will be the normal risk of the messenger being shot.

Types

The next step would be to allocate units (of a given size and level) to certain categories. The need for categories at all may be less obvious than the need for levels and sizes. However, I want to propose three simple ones for the sake of the argument in this chapter, and use them to explain the need for them and their purpose.

The three categories I wish to use have the working titles of:

* Abstract
* Applied
* Specific techniques

The 'applied' category can be used to explain the other two. Units in this category would test whether those who had a theoretical understanding in a given area could act on that understanding in a timely and appropriate manner. It would also be possible to test whether those who had acquired certain techniques (sometimes to a very sophisticated level) understood the principles upon which they were based.

It is important to emphasize that these categories apply to individual units, rather than to qualifications as a whole. A given qualification will almost certainly include a combination of all three types of unit. However, different qualifications will show different proportions of these units.

Let me apply this to the further education phase. For someone who is continuing after the end of compulsory schooling with academic subjects, it is likely that — when these subjects are broken down into units of outcomes — a large proportion of the units will appear in the 'abstract' category. The shape of a typical 'A' level programme might be as shown in figure 8 (a).

An occupationally-specific vocational qualification (NVQ) will, typically, have a higher proportion of job specific and applied units, as illustrated by figure 8 (c).

A general, more broadly based, vocational qualification (a GNVQ) will probably have the majority of its units in the 'applied' category, but will also include abstract and job-specific units. A typical 'shape' for this is shown by figure 8 (b).

However, whilst these are typical shapes and proportions, particular programmes or qualifications may vary considerably from the norm for their category. In England students who go on to what we call an advanced level programme

Geoff Stanton

Figure 8

| **'ABSTRACT'** | **'APPLIED'** | **'SPECIFIC TECHNIQUES'** |

(a)

N. V. Q.

~ ~

G. N. V. Q

(b)

~ ~

(c)

'A' Level Programme

(In practice, each kind of qualification would overlap at each level.)

between 16 and 19 years of age usually only take three subjects for two years. If these three subjects were, for instance, history, classics and English literature, then a very high proportion of the units concerned might fall into the abstract category. However, a fellow student might be taking 'A' levels in applied physics, craft design and technology, and geology. In this case, although there would still be a significant number of abstract units, an equally significant number might fall into the 'applied' category, and it is also likely that a number of specific techniques will be acquired which have direct relevance to certain kinds of employment.

The 'shape' of the overall qualification being gained by a student studying these three subjects might, in fact, be almost identical to that being achieved by another student on what we might call a 'vocational' programme. For instance, and to switch my examples, analyzing into outcomes what a student on certain business studies programmes is learning to know, understand and do might reveal that it is very similar indeed to what a fellow student studying the three 'A' level subjects of economics, law and accountancy might be acquiring. We can immediately see, therefore, that these two qualifications, although presently categorized differently as 'vocational' and 'academic' are in fact almost identical. However, that is not to say that *all* vocational and all academic programmes of the same level are equivalent in this way. The degree of overlap between a qualification in construction and one of a similar level in history, classics or literature might be very small indeed.

You might be able to discern from this why I anticipate that the issue of defining levels might be very problematic. On what basis will we say that a qualification in construction and one in classics is the same 'level'?

However, the value and purpose of categorizing units into types can, perhaps, now be also seen.

The Reasons for Categorizing Outcomes

First of all, it begins to dissolve the so-called academic/vocational divide.

Secondly, it enables us to plan progression on a far more rational basis. If the higher level course on to which a learner wishes to progress requires high level performance on abstract units, then either an academic or a vocational programme which provided this might be appropriate. In some cases, of course, it will be necessary to have some content knowledge as well, but whether this is the case often depends upon whether the subject being offered at university level is also on offer within the school curriculum. As far as employers are concerned, it would enable them to distinguish (say) those applicants whose English qualification contains applied units, from those with a qualification in the same subject where the units were more 'abstract': the latter might be less well equipped to do such things as minute meetings, analyze reports or conduct interviews.

Thirdly, it gives us a much better basis upon which to offer students guidance about which subjects or courses they would wish to enrol for in the first place. At the moment, in our country, although you may get information about prerequisite qualifications and about the topics covered by the course you are considering entering, you rarely get an analysis of the types of learning required. This leads to, for instance, learners applying to study psychology because they have an interest in people, but without realizing that there may be a requirement for the understanding of statistics. It also leads to learners enrolling on vocational courses in (for example) child care, with an overly romantic notion of what would be required of them.

The Risk of Categorizing Outcomes

Finally, in this section, I perhaps ought to recognize that this division of units into these three types would be dangerously reminiscent, for some, of the division of schooling into grammar, secondary technical and secondary modern, which was proposed by our 1944 Education Act in the UK. The crucial difference is, of course, that by accepting that such differences exist, but *within* each qualification, we avoid the damaging assumption that there are three types of people who have to be selected for three quite different types of schooling, with very little possibility of transferring between them once the selection has been made.

Issues Relating to Learning Programmes

This section expands on what may be involved in producing good quality learning programmes.

I want to consider the range of choices which learners might legitimately wish to have available to them if they are going to be in a position to find a learning programme fit for their particular purpose. I will explore this by discussing five kinds of choice which may need to be made available.

(i) *Location*

Some learners may wish to continue their personal and career development in a place of employment, with the status of worker. They would wish their work to be designed (within the constraints of the nature of production) to give them as many learning opportunities as possible. Other learners are much more attracted to being a member of a student body, being based therefore in a school or college. All too many, however, are not given these choices. We therefore have a situation which, in a time of recession, some people who would wish to continue their learning in the workplace are forced to stay on as full-time students, whilst others, because perhaps of difficult domestic financial circumstances, are forced to go out to work when they would rather continue the life of a student. However, the framework I was attempting to describe earlier should mean that even when these choices are 'forced', the location of learning should not determine the nature of the qualification they obtain.

(ii) *Subject-based or integrated*

Some learners find the variation provided by a subject-based curriculum to be stimulating and enjoyable. They like the fact that different teachers have different approaches, and can tolerate the fact that little attempt is or can be made to relate what they are learning in one subject to that of another. Others find this destructive and disorientating. They would prefer to have their work on communications, numeracy and science units (for instance) linked by a common thread, such as a vocation like motor vehicle engineering.

(iii) *Vehicle for learning*

Some learners would prefer to continue their personal and career development through the study of a traditional academic subject, such as history or literature, whereas others might wish to achieve very similar objectives through following up an interest in a vocational sector such as nursing or business administration. In some cases identical outcomes might be achieved on any of these routes.

If I now link these last two choices together, it enables me to point out that in England, at any rate, it is not possible to follow a programme based upon academic subjects which is also integrated. We have no equivalent of the French Baccalaureate. On the other hand, many vocational schemes are becoming increasingly integrated, making access to them somewhat difficult for those who can only acquire units one at a time.

All of this also raises the question of what exactly is meant by the 'academic/vocational divide'. I would wish to maintain that it means two distinct things. On the one hand, it can refer to the nature of the outcomes being worked towards, and who or what defines them. In the case of 'academic' qualifications some of these outcomes derive from the tradition of scholarship and research within a given academic subject area. In the case of vocational qualifications, outcomes are derived from the requirements of certain occupational roles. On the other hand, there is also a very important second meaning of 'vocational' as opposed to 'academic': namely, whether someone wishes to use an academic subject or a vocational sector as a vehicle for their personal learning and development, of whatever kind. (The outcomes achieved could be very similar, whichever 'vehicle for learning' was chosen.)

(iv) *Learning style*

Another choice that can be very important to learners is that of 'style'. For instance, some need to be active learners, participating in practical and group work. Others find this much more threatening, and are content to be a relatively passive spectator in the presence of a teacher performing with skill and wit. In some cases, of course, the style needs to be dictated by the nature of the outcome being worked towards. In many cases, however, it is determined rather more by the preferences of the teacher, ignoring the variation of preferred style which may exist amongst the student body.

(v) *Sequence*

Finally, learners vary in the order in which they wish to acquire their learning. It is a conventional wisdom to suppose that we all wish to lay a broad foundation, before specializing. Unfortunately, I do not think this corresponds with everyday experience. Many of us enjoy and even need the motivation of the reward and status which come from a high degree of specialization. This may particularly apply to school leavers at 16. In their case, an insistence upon laying a broad foundation, the relevance of which may not be immediately apparent to them, may result in them refusing to participate at all. However, I have the faith that most of them will, within a comparatively short time, come to realize that without broadening out their motor vehicle studies (say) to include an understanding of finance, employment law and interpersonal skills (for instance) not only will some of their larger vocational ambitions not be achieved, but they will fail to make the best use of their own abilities and potential.

To summarize then, I am suggesting that learners may benefit from a choice of:

— *location* and status (employment-based/worker, versus education-based/student);
— *mode* of learning (discrete subjects versus integrated programmes, full-time versus part-time, and so on);
— *vehicle* for learning (academic subjects as opposed to an interest in a vocational sector);
— *style* of learning (for instance, formal as opposed to informal);
— *sequence* of learning. (A broad base leading to a narrower specialisation, or vice versa.)

All this variety, and all this choice, can be provided cost-effectively within a comparatively simple qualifications framework as outlined earlier, as long as the distinction between

(i)   the specification of qualifications (plus the evidence necessary for awarding them); and
(ii) the design of learning programmes is understood and made the best use of.

Colleges which are attempting to make full use of this potential flexibility will have found that they need to review their structure, the roles of staff and the way resources are deployed. However, staff in some areas and in most colleges have always handled groups within which individuals are working towards different outcomes (in art and design studios, for instance) or have used well-designed learning materials to free them to tutor individuals (the Open University, for instance). The requirements for a 'flexible college' are explored in a recent FEU publication of the same name.

Chapter 9

Flexible Learning and Outcomes

Colin Nash

The outcome-led model of the curriculum and the flexible learning approach to its delivery have much in common. Not least in the perception of many educationalists that they represent nothing 'new'. Jessup (1991) readily recognizes that 'the outcome-led model . . . is of course built upon a lot of good practice in education and training' but declares that

> It attempts to bring together most of the progressive developments in education and training which have developed over recent decades, particularly during the 1980s, and weld them into *a coherent national system*. (my emphasis) (pp. 12–13)

Similarly in the research into the effective management of flexible learning in schools at the University of Sussex it was understood from the outset that no claims were being made that 'flexible learning' was an amazing new discovery. What was asserted was that

> Flexible learning is a fresh approach to the problems of teaching and learning and that there is *an identifiable structure or framework* (my emphasis) which can enable teachers to effect long term change. (Eraut, Nash, *et al*, 1991, p. 11)

It is the attempt to bring coherence and structure to disparate developments which is common. But there are other significant factors which bring the outcomes-led model and flexible learning together. Firstly it is necessary to define the territory of flexible learning; secondly, to consider the relevance of outcomes to flexible learning; and finally, to see how flexible learning may assist in the implementation of an outcomes model.

The Territory of Flexible Learning

The term 'flexible learning' is used here primarily in the context of TVEI's Flexible Learning Development[1] and the research carried out in secondary schools and post-16 institutions. In the early stages of the development 'flexible learning' was treated as an umbrella term subsuming a wide range of innovations in the management of teaching and learning. The common ground was a twin focus on meeting individual learning needs and giving learners responsibility for their own learning. Important contributory innovations include resource-based learning, supported self-study, records of achievement and TVEI itself. Mayne (1992) argues that TVEI's emphasis on student entitlement has 'had a powerful influence on change in approaches to teaching and learning in the classroom' and has been 'instrumental in challenging teachers . . . to review their classroom practice' (p. 70). What may have been an unintended consequence of the initiative was its impact on the practice of teachers. The recognition that 'active learning' required radical rethinking about pedagogy was part of the motivation for flexible learning being established as a substantive development within the whole Initiative.

In the early stages of the project many teachers naturally asked 'what is flexible learning?' or 'will I be able to recognize it when I see it?'. As with the term 'good teaching' it is easier to point to examples of good practice than to produce a comprehensive definition. Trayers (1989) has pointed out 'it is difficult and probably undesirable to produce rigid definitions of something which is in itself (and by definition) flexible'. However it was essential to get some purchase on the concept by describing its features. The touchstone for identification was the key objectives defined by Trayers (1989):

1 To meet the learning needs of students as individuals and in groups through the flexible management and use of a range of learning activities, environments and resources.
2 To give the student increasing responsibility for his or her own learning within a framework of appropriate support (p. 2).

A profile of the most common features was drawn up from the research fieldwork and from this a conceptual map was constructed to give some coherence to the thinking about the nature of flexible learning. (see figure 9.1). The main elements were:

Teaching and learning styles (flexible, proactive, student-centred)
Tutoring (teacher's role involving direct interaction with individuals or small groups)
Recording achievement (assessment, profiling and the processes involved)
Resources (all aspects of resourcing for students and teachers to work more flexibly)
Environment (flexible working conditions for students and teachers)
External relations (two-way support process — parents, community, industry).

In most schools visited some degree of change was observed in these areas. But the institutions which could be said to have adopted flexible learning were those that had moved beyond small-scale innovations to a holistic approach which was informing and driving their strategic planning and staff development. Most significant of all, however, was what we called the 'student-centred ethos'. It was a view of the centrality of the learner, which had become part of the fabric of the institution. This philosophy was underpinning the action as well as the thinking and was frequently articulated in both formal and informal meetings and discussions. But it was not just an idealistic notion of student autonomy. It rapidly became clear that 'the learner-centred approach is one that requires planned support and development' (Eraut, Nash *et al*, 1991, p. 13).

Figure 9.1: *Flexible learning in practice*

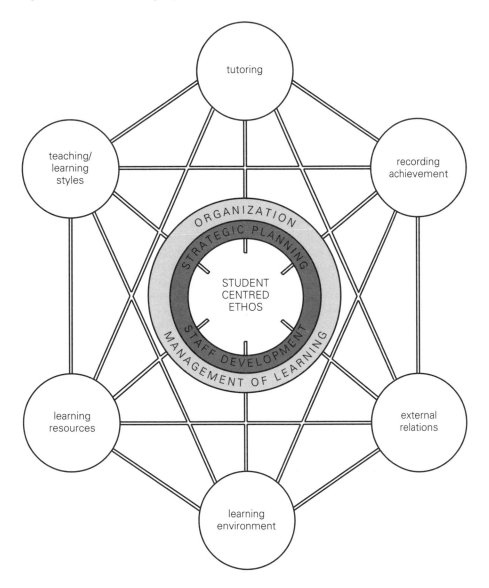

Source: Erant, Nash, Fielding and Attard (1991).

The emphasis on planned support and development was taken further by TVEI in its 'Flexible Learning Framework' (1991) which was presented as a means for schools and colleges to 'move in a systematic and managed way to a learner-centred approach with the emphasis on achievement by the individual student and to help them monitor and evaluate its effects'. There are three components to the 'Framework':

Managing student-teacher partnerships
Managing student use of resources
Managing student learning pathways

Each component is elaborated in terms of teacher aims and student outcomes. It will be seen from the diagram of the 'framework' (figure 9.2) that the outcomes listed for the students are generalized ones focusing on the processes and skills of learning, for example:

* negotiating and reviewing learning targets, making Individual Action Plans;
* identifying and using relevant learning resources (including IT), managing information: analyzing, presenting and reporting;
* working in teams, small groups or individually to achieve action plans; able to access appropriate support, to manage their learning targets and to collect, present and record outcomes in a portfolio of work.

This 'Framework' is advocating flexibility on three fronts. It presents a model of the teacher-student relationship as one which has as its goal the autonomy of the learner and which aims to achieve this by enabling the learner to understand long-term objectives, set appropriate targets and measure their own progress. Secondly, it looks to help the learner to develop a repertoire of core skills that give ownership of the learning process. This includes self-management, information management and interpersonal skills as well as those of literacy, numeracy and communication. Thirdly, it aims to open up the pathways of learning through flexibility of access, assessment and accreditation as well as finding appropriate tasks and pace of working.

With a national launch of the 'Flexible Learning Framework' in January 1991, the Employment Department promoted flexible learning as an important feature of its TVEI strategy with the ambitious aim of 'embedding' it into the curriculum of all 14–19-year-olds. By this time the Sussex-based project was beginning to investigate flexible learning in the post-16 sector: particularly in further education and sixth-form colleges. The situation was more diffuse than in the schools (particularly in the larger colleges) which made it more difficult to arrive at a prevailing understanding of flexible learning in this sector. However, the varied expression of aims in respect of flexible learning yielded three broad categories:

(i) Learner-centred — those aims that are closest to what is conveyed in the Flexible Learning Framework (for example, individual entitlement, achievement-led client-centred model).

(ii) Pragmatic — those aims that focus on the practical aspects of flexibility in teaching and learning (for example, quality goals, support in literacy and numeracy).

(iii) Instrumental — those aims that imply that flexible learning is a means of coping with problems of staffing and resourcing (for example, more cost effective, attract more customers).

While the instrumental considerations were not seen as unimportant, the experiences of the schools' project indicated that the development of flexible learning needs to be rooted in an educational view of the primacy of the learner. Other aspects of the development in schools were found to hold good in post-16 institutions.

Figure 9.2 *The flexible learning framework*

A strategy to help teachers manage effective learning

MANAGING STUDENT/ TEACHER PARTNERSHIPS

Aims of the Teacher:
To enable students to
♦ discuss and understand the objectives of the programme of study
♦ identify short-term and longer-term targets which are relevant both to the achievement of the programme objectives and their own development needs
♦ negotiate learning activities which contain relevant targets
♦ identify and gain access to appropriate support
♦ review and assess target attainments

Outcomes for the Student:
Students are able to
♦ negotiate own learning targets
♦ construct and agree an Individual Action Plan with specific tasks, outcomes and timescales
♦ reflect on progress
♦ gain constructive feedback on progress
♦ review and negotiate record of what has been achieved
♦ identify further learning needs
♦ set further learning targets and agree action
♦ make further progress on their individual action planning

MANAGING STUDENT USE OF RESOURCES

Aims of the Teacher:
To enable students to
♦ access sources of learning without going through the teacher
♦ gain topicality and breadth through using a variety of resources
♦ plan how to use resources and with what purpose
♦ develop core skills, eg self and information management competencies, literacy, numeracy, communications and interpersonal skills develop competence in using sources of learning, eg a resource centre, a library, a town hall, a local firm

Outcomes for the Student:
Students are able to
♦ identify, plan access to and use relevant resources
♦ manage information and other outcomes of use
♦ select, analyse, present and report
♦ use databases including electronic
♦ use IT for above and other purposes
♦ develop 'ownership' of learning and of competencies which accrue from direct interaction with resources

MANAGING STUDENT LEARNING PATHWAYS

Aims of the Teacher:
To enable students to
♦ reach high levels of achievement in relation to their capabilities
♦ suit learning tasks and activities to their needs
♦ proceed at their optimum pace
♦ be involved in planning and organizing their learning
♦ have a Record of Achievement which is progressively updated as a result of formative assessment and self-appraisal

Outcomes for the Student:
Students are able to
♦ work in teams, small groups or as individuals in carrying out their action plans
♦ access appropriate support, eg careers officer, database, at relevant times in order to carry out their plan
♦ manage the achievement of learning targets; collect, present and record outcomes thus developing a portfolio of work
♦ have their achievements accredited when they decide they are ready

There were common concerns about resources and environments for learning, different styles of teaching and learning, and the assessment and recording of achievement. Underlying everything else was the need for a whole-institution approach to change through strategic planning and staff development based on a learner-focused policy.

Because the prior learning and experience of each potential student is so varied, there is inevitably a greater emphasis on the needs of the individual learner in this sector. To meet such diversity requires not only the appropriate range of courses and levels but the flexibility and responsiveness to tailor the provision to meet the need. Three main areas have been identified in the management of flexible learning in the post-16 sector (they correspond broadly to the three components of the Flexible Learning Framework): learner support, learning resources and learning systems.

Learner Support

What happens to the potential learner prior to embarking on a course of study is crucial to ensuring that previous achievement is taken into account, specific needs are properly identified and an appropriate learning route is planned. Three strands are identified in the process of learner support: access, induction and progression.

Access

* open criteria: the notions of 'learning for all' and 'lifelong learning' are translated into real possibilities by the development of nurseries and crèches, outreach centres, student shops, drop-in counselling facilities, specific targeting of those who would be reluctant to make the first move towards further education.
* prior learning/achievement: for every learner it is important to recognize the level of experience and/or previous training and education and to build on that in order to give confidence, to avoid unnecessary repetition and to give appropriate credit for achievement.
* appropriate entry point: course arrangements need to be flexible enough to allow learners to take-up a course at the most appropriate point or level and not be required to spend time on skills or knowledge already obtained.

Induction

* impartial guidance: trained, skilled counsellors who specialize in guiding the learner to find the most appropriate pathways are essential if the very best deal is to be obtained. Decisions about course choices should not be constrained by the needs of the institution (for example, minimum numbers to make a course 'financially viable'). Flexible provision can both meet individual learner needs and cope with the wider management issue.
* needs identification and analysis: the induction process must involve a thorough investigation of the learner's needs and potential and a careful analysis that will lead to the most appropriate learning route. It is important that the pathway is as flexible as possible so that a change of track (for example, to a different level of achievement) is not prevented.

Progression

* personal tutoring: however flexible the arrangements for learning, the interaction between learner and tutor is vital to ensure that there is progression in the learning.

* action plans and targets: the formalizing of the process helps to ensure that learning goals can be identified, specific tasks negotiated and planned, and progress recorded.
* assessment and accreditation: the charting of progress is enabled by a variety of means of assessment and evaluation which involve both learner and tutor. The accreditation of achievement (from the institution and from external validating bodies) should be related to the formative and summative assessments made throughout the learning period.

Learning Resources

The development of resource-based learning has been one of the important precursors of the Flexible Learning Initiative. Particularly in FE colleges, the setting up of resource bases, IT centres, learning workshops and the writing of open learning materials have in most institutions become normal features. The importance of establishing the appropriate learning resources cannot be underestimated. But resources alone will not achieve an improvement in the effectiveness of learning. It is the *use* to which resources are put that matters. The two other corners of the triangle — learner support and learning systems — provide the means of enabling appropriate use.

Learning Systems

The term 'system' is used here in a broad sense to describe a wide range of organizational arrangements which are put into operation to assist more effective learning. The key feature of such arrangements for the purposes of this chapter is that they create flexibility so that the overall system or framework will be better able to respond to the needs of the individual learner. Such systems will support and enhance the concept of 'ownership' whereby the learner is at least a partner in controlling her/his own learning.

The figure 'Key Features' (figure 9.3) is a visualization of the main points discussed above. It is a sketch rather than a precise map. The three elements — learner support, learning resources and learning systems — have a symbiotic relationship which is focused on the learner. It can also be viewed that the resources and the systems form the tangible bedrock on which a flexible learning framework can be built. But the apex of learner support is about the interrelationship between learner and teacher which is essential to nurture long term progress in learning.

The theory of flexible learning outlined in the models 'Flexible Learning in Practice' (figure 9.1) and 'Key Features of Flexible Learning Post 16' (figure 9.3) has been developed from observed and recorded practice in schools and colleges. In terms of Glaser and Strauss (1967) the theory is 'grounded' in the 'situational facts'. It is conceded that as a totality, each of the models represents an idealized situation in that it is unlikely that any institution is developing on all fronts. They do indicate, however, the need for a holistic approach to the management of learning both for the 'classroom' and for the whole 'learning institution'.

Figure 9.3: *Key features of flexible learning in post-16 institutions*

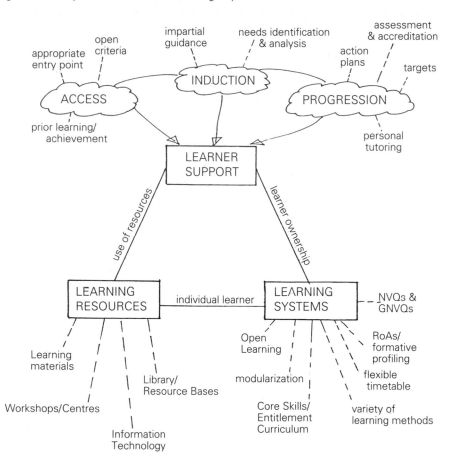

The Relevance of an Outcomes Model to Flexible Learning

If 'flexible learning' is to serve any purpose it will more than anything else enable the learner to have a sense of direction through planned and well-defined learning targets which in turn are based on defined criteria in terms of knowledge, skills and understanding. The attainment of these criteria is likely to lead to a recognition (formal or informal) of 'competence' in a particular field. It is the notion of 'competence'[2] which underlies an outcomes model of the curriculum. Unfortunately 'competence' is a word that has been debased in some common usage and it is therefore necessary to re-define it for our purposes.

Jessup (1991) dismisses the use of the term to indicate 'a lowish or minimum level of performance' and interprets competence as referring to 'the standard required successfully to perform an activity or function'. This moves the definition away from a narrow focus to the wider one of 'quality' which is more familiar to industry than education. Jessup (*ibid*) goes on to assert that being competent means performing to professional or occupational standards. In most professional and occupational areas there is no scope for 'second best' standards. (p. 25)

There are several issues arising out of this view of competence which have implications for flexible learning in terms of its underlying philosophy and its practice as a broad approach to the organization of learning.

The need for 'breadth' was widely advocated both from an employment perspective (CBI, 1989) and from an educational one (DES, 1985) and found expression in the structures of NVQs and the National Curriculum. This need for breadth shifted the emphasis from the analysis of competence by task to a functional analysis which focuses on the purpose and outcome of the activity. Competence in the workplace is thus recognized as involving more than the ability to carry out tasks particular to a specific occupation. There is a range of skills common (to a greater or lesser degree) to most fields of employment which fit into the CBI's eight Common Learning Outcomes which, because they are not so tangible (for example, problem-solving, positive attitudes to change), are not always recognized as important. Evidence of these areas of competence need, however, to be gathered. Ideally this should be done in the workplace and this highlights the need within training programmes for appropriate work experience or, at the least, simulations and practical activities which replicate the experience. The effective delivery of such training would only be possible through a flexible approach both to the learner and to the organization of the learning experience. A false dichotomy has been made in some educational circles between competence on the one hand and knowledge and understanding on the other. But Alison Wolf (1989, p. 41) has shown that all three terms are constructs and that knowledge and understanding contribute to competence. Similarly sterile arguments surround the notion of learning as being divisible into 'academic' or 'vocational' categories. An outcomes model focuses on evidence of competence. Flexible learning, as a means of enabling the achievement of competence, supports the contention that learning occurs essentially through use.

> Skills and concepts do not become part of a learner's 'action knowledge' or repertoire, until they have been used in a range of contexts. Indeed, most of the learning of concepts and skills occurs not at preliminary acquaintance but during subsequent use. This is where we so often get our priorities wrong. We put most of our teaching efforts into communicating new ideas to students, and very little towards helping them put those ideas into use. (Eraut, Nash *et al*, 1991, p. 25)

Jessup (1991) asks the question:

> How can we not only train people for the jobs they have to do now, but also give them a basis of competence to cope with, or acquire quickly, the skills they will need for work they might be performing in two years or five years from now? (*ibid*, p. 28)

He sees the specifying of competence on the basis of outcomes as a more appropriate basis for enabling people to be able to cope with changes in the kinds of work they may do in the future. It is important too that people should not only be able to adapt to changing circumstances of work but also to make progress across boundaries that may be drawn by occupation specific requirements. An important part of the agenda of flexible learning is that the individual will develop a repertoire of learning skills that will enable her/him to operate autonomously and to progress to new levels of achievement. Clearly the individual who has established ownership of her/his own learning is more likely to be in control of the ways in which the learning path can be adapted to suit particular needs in terms of employment or, indeed, any other goals. A closer look at the emerging outcomes model defined by Jessup (1991, chapter 12) will open up a number of important questions for the delivery of education and training. His essential thesis is that

> . . . if education or training is defined by outcomes, it opens access to learning and assessment in ways which are not possible in traditional syllabus or programme based systems. Once learning is targeted on outcomes, the other features of the model follow as a natural consequence. Many of the problems we face in education and training could be solved by this model. (*ibid*, p. 89)

These may seem bold claims but it is significant that the essential features that Jessup goes on to describe relate very closely to many of the features of the flexible learning frameworks or models described in the earlier part of this chapter. The significance lies (for this writer at least) in the fact that similar conclusions are being reached from different starting points. The outcomes model has developed from a need to find an effective way to assess performance in vocational training. Flexible learning is an 'educational model' (i.e., it was developed within the school/ college context) which has developed from a need to find more effective strategies for learning and teaching. The common ground, however, is that both models have emerged from an employment focus on education and training. While this could leave both open to the charge of utilitarianism, a closer look in both cases should reveal that they address the much wider issues of motivation for learning, the nature of knowledge and how learning occurs. It is not within the scope of this chapter to pursue these global issues but for a further consideration of aspects of this debate, the reader is referred to Alison Wolf's discussion 'Can competence and knowledge mix?' in Burke (1989).

The key aspects of Jessup's emerging model can be summed up under five headings which follow logically from each other in the learning cycle. Alongside each of these are the matching features from figure 9.3 (Key Features of Flexible Learning in Post-16 Institutions).

1   Initial assessment/accreditation of prior learning   *ACCESS*
Starting with what the individual learner already knows and has experience of is important (especially with adults or those who have previously not been successful in academic terms) in order to establish confidence and to avoid pointless repetition and time wasting on skills that are part of that learner's repertoire. To achieve this may require someone skilled in guidance to elicit the facts since learners who have not followed a traditional educational route are not always aware of what they have actually achieved. With such help a profile of previous learning

and experience can be built up and appropriately accredited. Many young people moving from the compulsory phase of schooling into further education or work training will nowadays have experience of records of achievement. Increasingly students are being involved in the process of keeping records of what they have achieved: this will include personal and social achievements as well as the more obvious evidence of examination results, and coursework (including examples in some cases).

2   Information and guidance   *INDUCTION*
Once a clear picture has been established of the learner's achievements at this stage, it is then necessary to relate these to her/his needs and work out the appropriate learning pathway towards the particular levels of competence that are required. This is a crucial stage where the learner needs suitable resources both in terms of adequate and relevant information and skilled personnel to guide her/him through the process.

3   Action planning   *PROGRESSION*
Action planning is much more common in further education colleges and vocational training in general than in the school sector. This is beginning to change, largely through the impact of TVEI and the Flexible Learning Initiative. The logic for it is inescapable; once again it is about the process ensuring that the learner knows where she/he is going, has the targets mapped out and understands what has to be undertaken.

4   Programmes of learning   *LEARNING SYSTEMS*
The keynote here is 'flexibility'. Programmes of learning are understood in this context as the practical working out of the action plan; to achieve this so that the individual's requirements are unequivocally met means flexibility in terms of time, place and resources. The outcomes model is a blueprint for a national approach to education and training. Rightly it is not concerned to prescribe how this may be worked out in institutions. Although flexible learning is also a national development it has been grounded in the issues of managing learning within institutions and is therefore more concerned with 'learner systems'. Fixed notions about timetables, length of teaching periods, size of teaching groups, etc. are all challenged if the initial proposition is to meet the learning needs of individuals. The scope of resources (equipment, materials, personnel) and their deployment is a major issue for all providers whether from education establishments or from industry. There are obvious concerns where a small business, for example, does not have the resources to meet the needs of its trainees. This highlights how necessary it is to have a coherent national approach so that all learners, of whatever age, status or background, have equal opportunity to access the learning resources they need to progress.

5   Continuous assessment   *PROGRESSION*
At the time of writing this chapter there is a great deal in the news about testing and assessment in schools with a vociferous lobby calling for a return to 'pencil and paper' tests. There is a dilemma here for teachers: on the one hand they feel themselves being swamped by bureaucratic mechanisms whereby it seems that more time is spent on recording assessment than engaging in teaching and learning;

on the other hand, there is an unwillingness to lose the ground that has been hard won in making systems of assessment fairer, more broadly-based in terms of methodology and more comprehensive. Within industrial training the move has for a long time been towards a variety of assessment methods and for assessment in the workplace. In higher education there is a growing awareness of the need to review approaches to assessment and learning. It is difficult to see how this tide of change is likely to be turned back.

The common ground for our models is that they both acknowledge that assessment is a process; it is not just something that is done to learners at the end of a course of study (although end-testing may be a *part* of that process). The emphasis is on *continuous* assessment because assessment is seen as part of the learning process as well as a means of evaluating what has been learned. It is about progression and progress.

In concluding this section it is useful to restate that the outcomes model was designed to

(i)   promote learning;
(ii)   emphasize performance and attainment;
(iii) encourage active and participative learning.

As to the way in which the learner should learn, the model is neutral and is intended to be applicable whatever the differences and preferences of the learner. 'Above all', says Jessup (1991, p. 138), 'it does not prescribe the form of learning'. It might be conceded however that some forms of learning can be more easily categorized as 'active and participative' and are therefore much more likely to be operable in relation to this model.

Flexible learning is less neutral on this issue. While practitioners have always been at pains to point out that so-called 'didactic' methods are a valid part of the teaching repertoire, the reality is that the emphasis is on activity and participation. The problem is not with the use of didactic method where direct instruction is necessary and appropriate but with teachers who tend to rely almost exclusively on this method and allow very little room for the active participation of the learner in terms of questioning, challenging, thinking and finding solutions to problems.

Flexible Learning and Achieving Outcomes

While the outcomes model is primarily concerned with the recognition of competence and attainment and is therefore not directly involved with how this is achieved, it would not be true to suggest that it is in no way concerned with the process of learning. This model is in fact designed to *enable* the learner. This learner-centred focus is one of the main reasons that so much common ground can be found with flexible learning. On the one hand flexible learning requires defined outcomes to give a focus to learning, and on the other, the outcomes model needs flexible learning (and similar approaches) to enable the delivery of its objectives. Criticisms of student-centred learning tend to home in on a belief that it is synonymous with a lack of purpose and direction. If that is the case then such an approach is as unsatisfactory as a didactic approach that appears to believe learning occurs by osmosis. The reality is rather different. Flexible learning eschews six-ties' flabbiness and requires considerable rigour from both teachers and learners. Everything is now in the open for them both. The teacher can no longer hide behind spurious authority or professionalism and the student can no longer expect to be a passive recipient. There are different motivational factors for the youngster at school and the mature adult worker seeking employment. While the drive for the adult to get work may be much stronger than the youngster's commitment to learning, at the end of the day both will vote with their feet. The adult may survive a little longer but ultimately they will both reject any process of education that fails to be relevant to their needs.

Models are frequently idealized expressions of what planners hope to achieve. Problems arise when those with executive power seek to implement the model in the cheapest way possible. Whiteside (1992) warns that

> The danger is that flexible learning which could offer significant oppor-tunities will be viewed in a narrow managerial way as a mechanism for expanding participation in the system without increasing resources. If this is the case there is a considerable danger that while participation is increased, a marked improvement in attainment will prove more elusive. (p. 18)

This does not mean that flexible learning or NVQs are inherently more expensive than other systems of delivery or assessment. But in the early stages of any ini-tiative, adequate and appropriate resources are essential to enable development and implementation.

Resistance to change is always to be found when existing structures and methods are challenged. Burke (1989), in looking at implementing NVQs in colleges, observed that 'the change from lecturing a whole class, to a more student-centred approach caused practical difficulties and was far more demanding' (p. 124). But managers and planners have to be convinced as well as the grassroots practitioners. There is still a potential conflict between the kind of practice devel-oping in post-16 education and the tendency to regress to 'traditional methods' which is being advocated for schools. Whiteside (1992) expresses concern at pos-sible resistance to the agendas for change in education.

> Flexible learning, student-centred learning, accreditation of prior learn-ing, modular routes, credit accumulation and transfer . . . seem to be directly in conflict with the views of Conservative educationalists who have already opposed moves to child-centred teaching and have argued forcefully for the virtues of didactic teaching. (p. 23)

While it is right to be concerned about inconsistencies between governmental educational policies, it also seems that many of the developments discussed in this chapter have a momentum of their own. The development of flexible learning, as described at the beginning of this chapter, was not externally imposed but has grown out of the practice and convictions of teachers engaged in seeking the best for their students. Likewise the development of NVQs was not just inspired by concerns about poor training standards but from concerns within vocational train-ing circles about the quality of learning.

Both models under consideration here are looking to change of considerable magnitude because essentially they challenge many of the ingrained (mis)conceptions about how people learn and how learning should be measured. To support this process of change there is a need for carefully gathered evidence to evaluate what is actually happening so that we can have some sense of the success of these models. At the local level of 'learning institutions' the need, as Burke (1989) describes (p. 12), is for them to become proactive rather than reactive in responding to change. From the experience of the Flexible Learning Development it was surmised that one of the greatest catalysts for change occurred when teachers successfully operating a system were able to share and communicate that experience with other practitioners and so enable them to try that system for themselves. There is a sense in which this brings us full circle. This catalytic effect is a clear example of active and participative learning in action.

Notes

1 The TVEI Flexible Learning Development had two main strands: regional projects involved in actively promoting and developing flexible learning strategies; and national projects, such as the one carried out at the University of Sussex from 1989 to 1992, which fulfilled a supportive role through research and development.
2 It is important to recognize that in the context of National Vocational Qualifications, competence has acquired a specialized meaning. 'Competence' is usually used as a short hand term for 'occupational competence.' Thus, in the context of GNVQs, 'attainment' is used rather than competence because there is no suggestion that students will have acquired occupational competence. Nash here refers to the general notion of competence. (*Ed*)

References

BURKE, J.W. (1989) 'The Implementation of NVQs' in BURKE, J. (Ed) *Competency Based Education and Training*, London, Falmer Press.
CONFEDERATION OF BRITISH INDUSTRY (1989) *Towards a Skills Revolution*, Report of the Vocational Education and Training Task Force, London, CBI.
DEPARTMENT OF EDUCATION AND SCIENCE (1985) *Better Schools*, London, HMSO.
EMPLOYMENT DEPARTMENT (1991) *Flexible Learning: A Framework for Education and Training in the Skills Decade*, Sheffield, Employment Department.
ERAUT, M., NASH, C., FIELDING, M. and ATTARD, P. (1991) *Flexible Learning in Schools*, London, Employment Department.
GLASER, B. and STRAUSS, A. (1967) *The Discovery of Grounded Theory*, London, Wiedenfeld and Nicolson.
JESSUP, G. (1991) *Outcomes: NVQs and the Emerging Model of Education and Training*, London, Falmer Press.
MAYNE, M. (1992) 'Teaching and learning styles' in WHITESIDE, T., SUTTON, A. and EVERTON, T. (Eds) *16–19 Changes in Education and Training*, London, David Fulton.
TRAYERS, M. (1989) 'The TVEI flexible learning development and the extension', TVEI *Developments 10 — Flexible Learning*, Sheffield, Training Agency.
WHITESIDE, T. (1992) 'The "alliance" and the shaping of the agenda' in WHITESIDE, T., SUTTON, A., and EVERTON, T. *16–19 Changes in Education and Training*, London, David Fulton.
WOLF, A. (1989) 'Can competence and knowledge mix?' in BURKE, J. (Ed) *Competency Based Education and Training*, London, Falmer Press.

Chapter 10

Modularization and the Outcomes Approach: Towards a Strategy for a Curriculum of the Future

Michael Young

Introduction

In this chapter I want to link consideration of the outcomes approach to defining curriculum content to an assessment of the potential of modularization as the basis for the structure of the post-compulsory curriculum. The criteria that I bring to the analysis arise from the argument first developed by Finegold and Soskice (1988) that the education and training system in this country is related to the economy through what they described as a *low skill equilibrium*? It is the educational implications of their analysis that are of concern to me in this chapter and these were taken further by Finegold *et al* (1990) in developing the concept of an early selection-low participation system[1]. Both these analyses start from the assumption that it is only high skill economies that will stand a chance of being competitive, and therefore of being the basis for stable democracies, in the next decades. The question that I seek to address therefore is the extent to which modularization when linked to an outcomes approach can be the basis of a strategy for moving to a high participation/high achievement system. Such a strategy would have two goals. Firstly, it would need to point to ways of overcoming the divisions, the fragmentation, the rigidities and the low expectations of the current system. Secondly, it would need to provide a framework for developing new combinations of knowledge and skill, and the incentives for learners to reach high attainment levels as well as for teachers to develop the new pedagogies that would characterize a high achievement system.

Educational innovations are developed in specific contexts which shape their implementation (Raffe, 1984; Young, 1993); modularization and the outcomes approach are no exception. In this country, modularization developed as a result of localized teacher initiatives in the early 1980s (Wilmott, 1983). In contrast, the outcomes approach arose from Department of Employment policy arising from the launching of YTS (Jessup, 1991). In examining these different *contexts* and how they shaped the *content* of the two developments, I shall argue that it is useful to separate their *intrinsic logics* as educational reforms (what they were intended to do) from the *institutional logics* involved in their implementation (Raffe, 1992). In terms of *institutional logic* modularization, in that it developed as a local initiative with little national support, can be seen as an example of the fragmentation and voluntarism that have been features of education and training in this country. The outcomes approach, with its initial association with low level qualifications for YTS trainees, was the victim of another feature of the UK system, the low status of vocational education and work-based training in particular. Both therefore can be seen as part of a *low skill equilibrium* rather than as ways of moving out of it. Locating these developments within their *institutional logics* does not contradict their *intrinsic logics* of increased flexibility, access and the empowerment of learners through which they could (at least in theory) be part of a high skill-high achievement system. The distinction between *intrinsic* and *institutional logics* is useful in explaining why the aims of modularization and outcomes approaches have not been realised in practice. It does not, however, suggest how the constraints of institutional logic may be overcome. This question will be returned to in the last section of the chapter.

The chapter has four parts. The first three are concerned with how implementing both modularization and outcomes approaches have been shaped both by their own limitations and by the wider social and political context. Part 2 analyzes how a divided system of qualifications and a low achievement/low status vocational training system influenced the way in which modularization and the outcomes approach were initially developed. In this analysis I go beyond the broad categories of modularization and outcomes and suggest that it may be useful to see them as generic strategies that, depending on the context, can take a number of forms. Part 3 begins by identifying learner-centredness as a key feature of both modularization and outcomes approaches. It then goes on to examine the problems associated with learner-centredness in a political era dominated by what might be called an anti-provider culture. Part 4 takes the issues of access and participation that have been associated with both modularization and the outcomes approach and considers how they have been undermined by the dominance of a highly selective subject-based curriculum. In the final part of the chapter, I draw out from the previous analysis the principle of connectivity as the key distinguishing feature of a *Curriculum of the Future* (Young and Spours, 1992) which would involve both modularization and an outcomes approach. I point out that though implementing a *Curriculum of the Future* would need to be part of a much wider political, industrial and economic strategy, elements of connectivity can be found in the links between a number of current local and national developments.

Modularization and the Outcomes Approach in the UK Since the Beginning of the 1980s

The different origins and aims of the two developments, which in many ways are closely related, is itself a reflection on the fragmented nature of education and training in this country. As stated earlier, modularization started as a series of *local* initiatives (though sometimes supported by national funding) of groups of teachers, usually to improve access to the pre-16 academic curriculum. The outcomes approach, on the other hand, had its origins in the *national* training policies (Jessup, 1991), launched by the Department of Employment (and later NCVQ) in the early 1980s. The adoption of an outcomes approach to assessment for YTS, and later for NVQs, was an example of the Government's determination to move away from a 'provider-led' (or teacher-dominated) curriculum for vocational education to one which was 'learner-led' and in which consumer interests were given priority. This focus on consumers meant that a policy designed to raise standards all too easily became part of the 'low skill equilibrium', as employers wanted to keep training costs down and young people wanted work not training. From the point of view of teachers, the close connections of the outcomes approach with NCVQ, together with the narrowness of the competences of the early NVQ 1s and 2s, meant that an outcomes approach could be seen as anti-educational, or at best representing a very limited view of vocational education.

The separate origins of modularization and the outcomes approach are not only an expression of the academic/vocational divide but also of the tensions between local attempts to increase curricular flexibility and Government attempts at rationalization and greater regulation at the national level. Two recent developments, though limited by the Government's obsession with external assessment and their distrust of teachers, are at least indications of the way the two strategies might be brought closer together. I am referring to the National Curriculum which is subject-based and non-modular but defined in terms of learning outcomes, and to GNVQs which are unitized and defined in terms of learning outcomes, but not competence-based. These developments, despite criticisms that can be made of them, point to the possibility that an outcomes approach could incorporate the education and training system as a whole. In the remainder of this section, I shall consider modularization and outcomes approaches separately as generic curricular strategies which, in the UK context, have taken particular forms.

Modularization

As a generic strategy, I shall define *modularization* as the breaking up of the curriculum into discrete and relatively short learning experiences. These may or may not have separate learning objectives and assessment requirements. I shall trace the development of modularization in this country and then discuss the relationship between modularization and a curriculum strategy designed to reach the achievement levels of other European countries. In order to do this I will distinguish three forms that modularization can take, *internal*, *external*, and *connective*, all of which can be illustrated in recent developments.

If we exclude higher education, modular curricula first developed in the UK in the secondary schools in the 1980s and primarily around the new GCSEs emerging with the support of TVEI (Wilmott, 1993). These developments had two aims; firstly, they were designed to provide the curricula and accreditation for the new kinds of learning that was being encouraged by TVEI but was not deliverable within the conventional subject divisions, and secondly they enabled assessment to be more directly related to the learning experiences of students. This link between modularity and the accreditation of new kinds of learning was also a feature of the pre-vocational courses that were developed at the time by BTEC and City and Guilds. Spours (1989) suggests that these initiatives can be described as *modular developments* rather than *modularization* as they were only modular *within* particular qualifications. For the purposes of this chapter, I shall refer to modular developments within qualifications as *internal modularization*. Using different terminology, Raffe (1992) describes any use of modules that does not change the relationship *between* qualifications as an *integrative strategy* in which modules are regarded as a convenient unit within which to develop alternative pedagogic approaches. For example, a module might be based on a specific activity or project designed to develop specific skills or capabilities.

The way modular GCSEs of the 1980s took on certain features of mode 3 (teacher-assessed) 'O' levels of the 1970s is illustrative of how *internal modularization* of qualifications is likely to be shaped by a divided qualifications *system*. In becoming associated with providing access to those excluded by more conventional routes, modularization came to be seen as only appropriate for lower level courses, and therefore to be associated more generally with low standards. It was this equation of *context* (low status students and low level courses) with *content* (modularization itself) in a political climate in which maintaining standards was seen as liked to externally marked examinations that led, in the 1990s, to the demise of pre-16 modularization.

As TVEI began, in the late 1980s, to have an impact on the curriculum after 16, schools and colleges became increasingly aware of the problems of progression and the confused 'jungle' of duplicating and non-comparable qualifications. Not surprisingly, *internal modularization* provided no solution to this problem and schools and colleges began to develop what Raffe (1992) describes as an *aggregative* modularization strategy. I shall refer the design of modules to be part of more than one qualification and to the possibility of students combining the modules from different qualifications as *external modularization*. The best examples were the so-called Y-models in which BTEC Nationals were developed with 'A' levels in association with the Associated Examination Board (AEB) and the University of Cambridge Local Examinations Board (UCLES). In each case, credit transfer was possible as the modules completed by a student could be credited towards either qualification. There is little research on the success of these developments, though evidence from the case of GLOSCAT (Gloucestershire College of Arts and Technology), which indicated that in practice there was very little transfer between qualifications, would again point to the power of the divided qualifications system.

There are important differences between the schemes associated with the two examination boards which have implications for any future curriculum strategies. Whereas UCLES modular 'A' levels were devised by an examination board and offered to all schools and colleges, the AEB/Wessex scheme was a three way collaboration (between schools/colleges, a group of LEAs and the Examination Board). The Wessex Scheme was not just involved in modularizing the curriculum; it expressed a whole approach to the curriculum which influenced the role of guidance, the preparation of materials and the availability of learner support that students would need if they were to benefit from the opportunities of choice within modular systems. In linking module design both to guidance and supported self-study and to an overall view of the purpose of the curriculum expressed in the appointment of a coordinator, the Wessex Scheme demonstrates many of the features of what I will refer to as *connective modularization*. The idea of connectivity will also be applied to outcomes approaches in the next section. Its relevance to the curriculum as a whole will be developed further in the last section of the chapter.

Initiatives such as the Wessex scheme created a great deal of interest among teachers and provided curriculum models for two of the most influential reports on post compulsory education and training — the IPPR *A British Baccalaureate*, referred to earlier, and the Royal Society's *Beyond GCSE* (1991). However, attempts to work with examination boards across the academic/vocational divide came up against almost insuperable difficulties of their totally different approaches to assessment. This difficulty could well be exaggerated by the recent encouragement given by the Government to examination boards to become more competitive, and therefore to emphasize the distinctiveness of their awards. A further constraint on the development of *external* let alone *connective modularization* has been the Government's insistence on terminal, externally set and marked examinations for 'A' levels. In their recent pronouncement on modular 'A' levels, SEAC/SCAA (1993) state that external assessment will be necessary at the end of the course and at the end of each module. This is not only likely to make modular 'A' levels prohibitively expensive, but by linking them to a highly selective assessment system, most of their pedagogic advantages will be lost. Again we have an example of *institutional logic* (maintaining standards by selection) shaping *intrinsic logic* (encouraging choice and flexibility).

The Outcomes Approach

The outcomes approach can also be seen as a generic strategy which, like modularization can take a number of forms. I shall define an *outcomes approach* as one which asserts that the curriculum can (and should) be expressed in terms of measurable learning outcomes. It contrasts sharply with traditional curricula which are frequently expressed in terms of inputs (for example class contact hours). An outcomes approach can, in principle, refer to any kind of educational outcome, not just the units of competence with which it has been associated through NVQs.

Following the analysis of three possible types of modularization, I will distinguish three kinds of outcome approaches — unitized, integrated and connective.

- *Unitized Outcome Approaches*: These refer to approaches such as that adopted in NVQs, and the original Scottish National Certificate modules. Both maximize choice and flexibility, but provide no mechanisms for encouraging coherence or progression on the part of learners.
- *Integrated Outcome Approaches*: These refer to approaches such as those exemplified in GNVQs and in the National Curriculum subjects (and later developments within the Scottish National Certificate), when outcomes are grouped together to form the basis for a qualification. An integrated outcomes approach could also be the basis for modular 'A' levels.
- *Connective Outcome Approaches*: These refer to when outcomes are grouped together not only in relation to specific qualifications but in relation to how learners are able to incorporate their purposes into the curriculum as a whole.

As in the case of modularization, the form that an outcomes approach takes (and therefore its specific content and consequence) depends on the context. For example, *integrated* or even *connective* outcomes of adult training are much more likely when employers have a strategic approach to training and investment and trade unions view training as key elements in their negotiations. In the examples already discussed of NVQs and the National Curriculum, the way context has shaped the form that outcomes have taken is clear. The official aims of the National Curriculum are to achieve higher standards in the core and foundation subjects. However, a policy of over-specification of outcomes and little consultation with teachers (and parents) was designed to monitor school achievements rather than to provide incentives for teachers to take more responsibility for raising the achievements of their schools. In the case of NVQs, the separation of outcomes from processes encourages colleges to concentrate on assessment and leaves it up to them whether to invest time in devising new learning strategies.

Any form of outcomes approach to the curriculum is radical when contrasted with typical input approaches and to the extent that it challenges conventional assumptions that link teaching and learning. This challenge can be seen from the point of view of the student, the teacher and the institution. From the point of view of the student, outcomes provide criteria for allowing them to demonstrate that they are qualified without necessarily attending a course of study. Furthermore, if the student does decide to join a course he/she has criteria by which to judge the teaching. From the point of view of teachers, an outcomes approach requires them to examine their practices in relation to what they expect students to achieve. It also provides them with criteria with which to question the administrative arrangements within which they work. From the institution's point of view, an outcomes approach specifically does not prescribe either time or method of study. Whether this becomes an incentive for institutions to take greater responsibility for achieving outcomes depends on both its overall curriculum strategy and the incentives for developing such a strategy from the system of funding.

In its separation of outcomes from processes, and the opportunity that it provides for the recognition of prior learning, an outcomes approach is likely to appear more relevant to adults than young people. Nevertheless, the two broad principles that follow from an outcomes approach, that the curriculum should be expressed in terms of what a school or college expects a student to achieve, and that it defines the responsibilities of the school or college, remains important for any age of learner in a high achievement system. The limitations of an outcomes approach are that it is only about outcomes and therefore can never be a complete curriculum strategy. Institutions also have to make decisions about input priorities, whether they are in terms of credits or notional learning time.

In this section, I have argued that the form that modularization has taken and the kind of approaches to outcomes that have been developed reflect the *context* of their implementation rather than their *content* as innovations. There appears to be nothing *intrinsic* to either modularization or outcomes approaches that links them to low level programmes or a low skill equilibrium. However there are two features of the context in which they have been developed that make it likely that this is how they will be experienced in practice — a neglect of the learning process and a tendency to devalue the professional expertise of teachers. In the next sections, therefore, I deal first with a key aspect of the content of both innovations — their learner-centredness and how the wider context has exposed its limitations in the form it has been developed.

Some Problems with the Idea of Learner-centredness

Both modularization and outcomes approaches can claim to be learner-centred approaches to the curriculum, though from rather different points of view. Whereas an outcomes approach starts by asking what a learner can expect to achieve (or how it is possible to recognize learning that has already been achieved), modularization focuses on the learner as a decision-maker and chooser.

The idea of the active learner who takes responsibility for her/his own learning is an attractive one and is a recognition of something which content-dominated models of education have all too easily forgotten. However, in practice, there are a number of fundamental problems with the concept of learner-centredness which are magnified when it arises in a wider political context in which government distrusts teachers as a professional group.

A more learner-centred curriculum implies that students should be given more opportunities to make their own learning decisions. However the capacity to make learning decisions cannot be separated from the level of learning reached; it is itself something which it cannot be assumed will be learnt (something at least recognized in the popularity of the idea of *learning to learn*). Raising levels of overall achievement involves increasing the capacities of those groups of students and trainees who have in the past shown they lack either the motivation or the capacity to learn. It follows that a learner-centred approach cannot be just about access and choice; it must be about new pedagogies, new relationships between teachers and learners and the development of new learning strategies. In other words, a learner-centred approach, even if it begins by separating outcomes from processes, has to be complemented by a focus on support for learners by teachers. This may, of course, involve a number of activities such as guidance and diagnostic assessment which have not in the past been the work of teachers (Shackleton, 1988).

Moving to a high-participation/high achievement system will undoubtedly mean that teachers will have to give up many of their current practices. However, it will mean placing more, not less responsibility on them (cf Burke p. 75 in this volume). Counterposing teacher-centredness with learner-centredness, particularly within the context of an outcomes approach which gives so much attention to assessment, can all too easily distract attention from the development of a learner-centred pedagogy. There are interesting parallels with the new management theory. Zuboff (1989) and others have found that not only is the traditional knowledge basis of a command approach to management disappearing, but that such an approach is no longer effective as company organization becomes less hierarchical. Management, in other words, becomes more like teaching, or at least, the encouragement of learning.

This critique of learner-centredness has focused on the limitations of approaches emphasizing the active role of learners that, in doing so, neglect the new roles for teachers (and trainers) that would be involved. In suggesting that students or trainees will learn by themselves if certain barriers, such as college-attendance at particular times, are removed, the proponents of learner-centredness may be searching for a new version of the old apprenticeship model of learning by doing. The only difference would be between the old restrictions of time serving and the new restrictions of over-specified national standards. Such a notion may be attractive, if the objective is to reduce the role (and the cost) of teachers in the process of improving the qualifications of the workforce. However, the question remains as to what value would be attached to qualifications that depended less and less on teaching. It is difficult to see how such learner-centred learning on its own could get beyond trial and error form of pragmatism.

This would not seem to be a basis for a high achievement system when more and more jobs are requiring conceptual knowledge and skills that cannot be learnt on the job alone.

This section has focused on one of the main features of a modular curriculum and outcomes approaches, their shift from the teacher-centredness which dominates traditional curriculum to learner-centredness. The limitation of learner-centred approaches is that in the context of wider efforts to reduce the influence of teachers and professional educators, it leads to the neglect of the need for new pedagogies, and more broadly, of a new professionalism among teachers. The next section turns to another aspect of the curriculum which learner-centred innovation neglects — its content.

Modules and Outcomes and the Organization of Educational Knowledge

I argued in the previous section that modularization and outcomes approaches tend to polarize learner-centredness and teacher-centredness. In this section, I want to turn to another polarization, that between content (in the sense of syllabuses, textbooks and bodies of knowledge) and the specification of learning objectives (which may be attainments or competences). Just as in polarizing learner and teacher-centredness the issue of pedagogy remains, so when outcome-led curricula are presented as alternatives to those that are content-led, we are left with the question as to what organization of knowledge will replace the traditional school subjects. This section examines some aspects of this question and argues that it cannot be resolved by modularization and an outcomes approach on their own but only if they form part of a broader and connective strategy for a curriculum of the future.

School subjects have been associated with low participation, narrow forms of specialization, a neglect of generic knowledge and skills, and the failure to provide any overall coherence for learners. However despite these weaknesses, and partly in the absence of any alternatives, subjects persist as the dominant organizing form of the post-16 curriculum. In the remainder of this section, I want therefore to consider how a modular curriculum based on learning outcomes might address these issues.

Incentives for Learning and Improving Participation

The IPPR report *A British Baccalaureate* (Finegold *et al*, 1990) argued that what distinguishes the English system of post-compulsory education from those of other comparable countries is its lack of incentives for learning for the majority. Selective 'A' levels, low status vocational alternatives and, at least until the recession, relatively attractive labour market opportunities for 16-year-old school leavers, all contribute to keeping down participation and achievement. The issue here is the extent to which incentives might be different within a modular system. The evidence provided by Raffe (1992) from a survey of students on the Scottish National Certificate (a modular and outcomes-based qualification), is that while its greater flexibility was welcomed by students, this did not lead to increases in participation or achievement. The reason, Raffe suggests, is that, although modularization does remove constraints by increasing choice and being more flexible, it does not (and on its own cannot) create incentives for higher perform-ance. Incentives are located in the institutional context. In the case of the Scottish National Certificate, this context was one in which vocational qualifications were still seen as signs of failure rather than achievement. It follows that either modularization needs to be part of a move towards a less divided system or that specific strategies for the recognition of vocational qualifications (by HE and employers) need to be put in place.

Breadth

The over-specialized nature of the English post compulsory curriculum has been widely recognized (CBI, 1993; Young, 1993), though breadth has often been expressed in a rather limited way (HMSO, 1988). By breaking up one and two year long courses into units of thirty or forty hours (Rainbow in Tait, 1993) modularization offers the flexibility needed for greater breadth of study. Breadth needs to be specified in terms of rules of combination of modules and criteria for balancing between specialized and broadening studies. Without such specification, student choices, as well as the modules offered by institutions, will be shaped by the pressures for over specialization expressed through the demands of HE admis-sion tutors.

Generic Knowledge and Skills

The problem of over-specialization concerns not only the limited range of studies of most post-16 students in England. The insulated form of subject specialization limits their access to any new forms of knowledge and skills that are not subject-specific. A variety of attempts have been used to describe these new kinds of *generic* knowledge — overarching capabilities (Prospect Centre, 1991), connective knowledge and skills (Young and Spours, 1992), and symbolic analysis (Reich, 1991). All are trying to address the same issue — that the process of applying knowledge is as important as the knowledge itself. A modular curriculum can offer such possibilities and they can be defined in outcome terms. However, the development of generic knowledge and skills requires the specification of proc-esses (for example, industrial experience, group work etc.) and therefore would require a curriculum that went beyond learning outcome criteria.

Coherence

Coherence in the present post-16 curriculum is limited in two senses. Firstly, it only applies to a small minority — those doing BTEC (National) and the 'A' level students whose subject choices relate clearly to their future. Secondly, in a subject-based curriculum, the possibilities for links between subjects are very limited. Again modular curricula create a whole new set of possibilities, at least in principle. However without a common system of credit, identifiable routes and integrated systems of guidance (Young, 1992) modularization can easily lead to fragmentation.

Each of these examples illustrates one of the main themes of this chapter. Modularization and learning outcomes approaches to curriculum content are not an adequate basis, on their own, for an alternative to the existing organization of educational knowledge. Crucial decisions about content and process remain. In so far as such decisions are not made explicit in a new curriculum strategy, the old tendencies to selection and division of the subject-based curriculum will remain dominant. The final section, therefore, considers the elements of a broader curriculum strategy within which modularization and an outcomes approach would be a part and which could lead to a high participation/high achievement system.

Curriculum Connectivity: Towards a New Paradigm

Modular curricula and outcomes approaches may be seen as a radical critique of the existing curriculum. However, they do not of themselves, provide an alternative framework. Like the so-called scientific management that FW Taylor applied in analyzing industrial production, breaking up the curriculum into modules is only, at best, half the answer to questions of curriculum organization. It fails to address either the criteria for 'breaking up' or the basis on which the parts (modules) should be combined. What is needed is a new form of systems approach that links modules and outcomes explicitly to overall purposes. In order to do this the last section links the ideas of *connective modularization* and *connective outcomes* that were developed earlier in the chapter with the idea of a *Curriculum of the Future* (Young and Spours, 1992).

Modularizing the curriculum and defining modules in terms of outcomes are the first steps towards the design of a curriculum that could be truly said to involve learners. It is that which makes them at least potentially *connective*. However, neither outcomes nor modules (and here there is similarity to proposals for vouchers or training credits) are a system or a curriculum. Alone they treat learning as if it was like shopping in a supermarket. Whereas no system or relationship with sellers is required to shop in a supermarket except at the cash till, learning *is* a relationship or rather a set of relationships. The concept of connectivity refers to the need to link the purposes of learners, the activities of teachers with how they are connected to developments in the wider society. For example, teachers might design particular modules in technology and social studies which would have some purposes that would be intrinsic to the experiences of the students and their teachers. However decisions to develop such modules would largely need to be through an industrial policy that encouraged the development and marketing of new construction materials, and a welfare policy that was committed to developing new community care.

Connectivity, therefore, does not refer to a particular curriculum model but to how the purposes of a school or college are expressed in all its activities and how these activities work together to articulate and support the purposes of individual learners[2]. In other words, in emphasizing the idea of the curriculum as a whole system, it stresses the interdependence of the whole and the parts. It is useful to see connectivity as having three components:

- *Purposes*

  These refer explicitly to criteria for defining the choice and content of modules and how they can be combined in relation to different routes and pathways. The idea of *connective purposes* is closely linked to the concept *connective modularization* referred to earlier in the chapter.

- *Relationships*

  These refer to criteria for defining relationships between teachers and learners within and between organizations. The emphasis here is on *connective* pedagogies. However a broader notion of pedagogy is implied than just the relations between teachers and students; it would include relationships between schools and colleges and with employers and how these relate to the school or college.

- *Processes*

  These refer to criteria which define how learners will be supported through diagnostic assessment, advice, guidance etc. They are closely linked to the idea of *connective outcomes*, and how outcomes are realized in practice.

A variety of existing developments can be seen as initial and partial attempts to develop the different aspects of connectivity. Those listed below are only intended to be illustrative. Readers will be able to think of many other examples. The groupings are relatively arbitrary and suggest the extent to which they might be seen as emphasizing one or other aspect of connectivity outlined above. All attempt to break out of the division between localism and nationalism. For example:

Developments which emphasize connective purposes

- curriculum frameworks which make explicit a concept of coherence across the post 16 curriculum — for example, the International Baccalaureate and the Technological Baccalaureate.

Developments which emphasize connective relationships

- credit frameworks which facilitate transfer within a modular system-for example, the FEU's National CAT Network, London Together;
- the Northumberland/Surrey learning resources network;
- the Youth Award scheme for accrediting the 'supplementary' curriculum;
- consortia, compacts and federations of schools and colleges;
- the module design group as part of the Hamlyn Unified Curriculum Project.

Developments which emphasize connective processes

- examples of integrated guidance systems (the BP/Tower Hamlets Project).

Concluding Comments

In this chapter I have argued that on their own modularization and outcomes approaches have limitations as curricular strategies that are exposed by considering the context in which they have been developed. In relation to raising achievement levels, they are at best tools rather than a strategy. To suggest what such a strategy might involve, I use the concept of connectivity which extends, to the curriculum, ideas of holographic and neural systems that Morgan (1988) applies to the analysis of organizations. It is a way of expressing the idea that a curriculum of the future needs to be a system, albeit a new kind of *open* system. Two features distinguish *connective* from *traditional* models of system. Firstly, they are open because their concept of purpose involves the future and therefore cannot be fixed or certain. Secondly, they emphasize feedback. A connective curriculum not only shapes learner purposes, it has to be shaped by them.

Within the framework of a connective curriculum modularization offers the possibility of student choice and new combinations of study that can relate student purposes to the options a society has for the future. Likewise outcomes become not just a method of defining module content and providing evidence on which students can make decisions but are linked to the ways that those outcomes may be realized.

Connectivity is a vision of a curriculum of the future, but not only a vision. It can point to specific strategies for teachers whether they are designing modules, recording achievement of their students or assessing their work. It can also make explicit how such everyday practices are linked to the ways that schools and colleges are themselves part of a connective system and the kind of future a society envisages for itself. In so far as connectivity becomes a feature of our educational arrangements, we stand a better chance of converting the current rhetoric of the need for high achievement into a reality.

Acknowledgments

I am most grateful to Andy Green, Annette Hayton, Andrew Morris, Ken Spours and Richard Winter for comments on an earlier draft of this chapter.

Notes

1 Post-16 participation rates have of course increased markedly in the three years since the publication of the IPPR report A British Baccalaureate (Finegold *et al*, 1990) in 1990. However, given that these increases have not been followed either by a substantial increase in staying on at 17+, or by evidence of a significant increase in levels of achievement (HMSO, 1993; Spours, 1993), there is every reason to suppose that the analysis in the report still applies.
2 These suggestions take further an earlier attempt to develop the idea of connectivity through a concept of *A Curriculum of the Future* (Young and Spours, 1992). In that discussion paper we emphasized connectivity at three levels- content and structure (i.e. rules of combinations of modules) process (i.e. guidance, formative assessment, action planning recording achievement and tutorial support) and organization (the lines of communication within colleges and between them and other institutions).

References

CONFEDERATION OF BRITISH INDUSTRY (1993) *Routes for Success*, CBI, London.
FINEGOLD, D. and SOSKICE, D. (1988) '*The failure of training*', *Oxford Review of Economic Policy*.

FINEGOLD, D. *et al* (1990) *A British Baccalaureate: Ending the Division between Education and Training*, London, IPPR.

HMSO (1988) Advancing A-Levels: Report of the Committee chaired by Professor Higginson, London, HMSO.

OFSTED/AUDIT COMMISSION (1993) *Unfinished Business*, London, OFSTED.

JESSUP, G. (1991) *Outcomes: NVQs and the Emerging Model of Education and Training*, London, Falmer Press.

MORGAN, G. (1988) *Images of Organization*, London, Sage Publications.

PROSPECT CENTRE (1991) *Growing an Innovative Workforce*, Kingston.

RAFFE, D. (1984) 'Education and training policy initiatives (14–18) content and context' in WATTS, A.G. (Ed) (1985) *Education and Training; Policy and Practice*, London, CRAC.

SHACKLETON, J. (1989) 'An achievement-led college' in BURKE, J. (Ed) *Competency Based Education and Training*, London, Falmer Press.

SHACKLETON, J. (1990) 'NVQs; a whole college approach' in BEES, M. and SWORDS, M. (1990) (Eds) *National Vocational Qualifications and Further Education*, London, Kogan Page in association with the Open University.

MILLINGTON, J. (1990) 'Engineering training and further education: a changing relationship', in BEES, M. and SWORDS, M. (1990) (Eds) *National Vocational Qualifications and Further Education*, London, Kogan Page in association with the NCVQ.

PETTIT, A. CROOK, G. and SILVER, R. (1990) 'NVQs and the role of guidance in competence-led curricular', in BEES, M. and SWORDS, M. (1990) (Eds) *National Vocational Qualifications and Further Education*, London, Kogan Page in association with the NCVQ.

RAFFE, D. (1992a) *Modular Strategies for Overcoming Academic/Vocational Divisions*, Institute for Educational Research, University of Jyvaskyla, Finland.

RAFFE, D. (1992b) *The New Flexibility in Vocational Education*, University of Twente, Netherlands.

RAFFE, D. *et al* (1992) *Modularization in Initial Vocational Training: Recent Developments in Six European Countries*, Centre for Educational Sociology, University of Edinburgh.

REICH, R. (1991) *The Work of Nations*, New York, Simon Schuster.

SEAC/SCAA (1993) *SEAC sets the standard for modular 'A' levels,* press notice.

SPOURS, K. (1989) *Modularization and Progression (14–19)* Post 16 Education Centre Working Paper No 6.

SPOURS, K. and YOUNG, M. (1988) 'Beyond vocationalism: A new perspective on the relationship between education and work', *British Journal of Education and Work*, January.

TAIT, T. (Ed) (1993) *Discussing Credit*, London, Further Education Unit.

WILMOTT, J. (1983) *The Post 16 CAT framework and modular developments post 14* in *Discussing Credit*, FEU Occasional Paper.

YOUNG, M. (1993a) 'A curriculum for the 21st Century: Towards a new basis for overcoming academic/vocational divisions', *British Journal of Educational Studies*.

YOUNG, M. (1993b) *Recording and Recognising Achievement in a Unified System*, Post 16 Education Centre Working Paper No 13.

YOUNG, M. and WATSON, J. (1992) *Beyond the White Paper: The Case for a Unified System at 16+*, Centre Report No 8.

YOUNG, M. and SPOURS, K. (1992) *A Curriculum of the Future*, Post 16 Education Centre Discussion Paper.

Chapter 11

From Design to Delivery: The Implementation of the NCVQ Core Skills Units

Tim Oates and Joe Harkin

Introduction

This chapter will not deal with the following issues:

- the relationship between style or method of learning and enhanced capacity to transfer skills (see Oates, 1992; and Jessup with Burke, Wolf and Oates, 1990);
- the enduring problem of developing robust differentiated levels of attainment (Oates, 1991);
- the interaction of core skills and context (a challenge to 'common sense' concepts of skill transfer) (Oates, 1992);
- the problems of consistent interpretation of the units by different assessors (Oates, 1991; OFSTED, 1993; ED, 1993).

These issues are fundamental to core skills, and have been treated in some detail in other places. While they demand further, continuing attention, in this chapter we will focus on two areas: the location of the NCVQ's core skills units within the education and training system, and the issue of integrated delivery of core skills.

Background to the 1989 Core Skills Initiative

In his 1989 speech to ACFHE (the Association of Colleges of Further and Higher Education) (Baker, 1989), Kenneth Baker, then Secretary of State for Education, set in train an initiative on core skills for post-16 education and training, the agenda emphasizing the key role which core skills could assume in:

— broadening the content of A/AS programmes;
— enhancing the vocational relevance of A/AS programmes;
— erecting a bridging mechanism between academic and vocational routes;
— broadening the scope of NVQs, in line with the broad concept of 'occupational competence'.

At the heart of this lies the idea of transfer; that using core skills in curriculum development and certification processes will enhance learners' adaptability and flexibility.

The concept of core skills as an essential part of all post-16 provision was also strongly promoted in the November 1989 CBI (Confederation of British Industry) strategic document *Towards a Skills Revolution* and endorsed in reports by the TUC (Trades Union Congress): *Skills 2000*; and HMI (Her Majesty's Inspectorate): *Post-16 Education and Training: Core Skills*.

In this climate of growing interest, Kenneth Baker's successor, John Mac-Gregor, invited the NCC (National Curriculum Council), SEAC (Schools Assessment and Examinations Council), NCVQ (National Council for Vocational Qualifications) and FEU (Further Education Unit) to provide initial reports and subsequent definitions of core skills in: *communication, problem-solving, personal skills, numeracy, information technology* and *modern foreign language*. These were to be stated at four levels of achievement — a problematic requirement, which I will address in a moment. The researchers charged with the work expressed anxiety about the six categories, particularly the very different nature of *information technology* and *modern foreign language*, arguing that these differed from the first four categories and from each other. They drew particular attention to the problem of defining these latter two without substantial overlap with the initial four, with all the subsequent problems of coherent assessment. Notwithstanding these technical objections, policy guidance was given that the work should proceed with the full listing of six.

The initial development work on the definitions was undertaken in a very short timescale (approximately five months); thus allowing no time for an empirically-generated listing. Instead, the four-person Task Group proceeded by:

— scrutinizing existing core skill frameworks (nineteen in total — see Oates, 1990);
— scrutinizing research on each of the six core skills;
— consulting technical experts on each of the six core skills;
— auditing 'A' level and 'AS' syllabuses to identify commonly occurring skills;
— examining National Curriculum standing orders to identify commonly occurring skills.

NCVQ used the general definitions of core skills produced by this initial work to develop Core Skill Units (Oates, 1991) in:

— communication;
— problem-solving;
— improving own learning and performance;
— working with others;
— application of number;
— information technology.

These were developed at four levels of attainment, and used the model devised for NVQ units (Jessup, 1991) to yield detailed specifications amenable to criterion-referenced and performance-based assessment processes (units in modern foreign language were developed through a different project and assumed a slightly different form (Oates, 1991). Later policy development on GNVQs (General National Vocational Qualifications) demanded the generation of five levels of attainment. This resulted in five units in each area above, thus totalling thirty detailed units.

While the core skill units provide a set of specifications for assessment and certification, that they should enhance transfer was an explicit policy objective. To this end, the developers devoted constant effort to identifying general, and generalizable skills which relate to performance in a wide range of settings.

The NCVQ initiated policy discussions on the incorporation of the core skills units into the NVQ framework — leading to a decision to incorporate core skills units into all levels of the NVQ framework and make them widely available across the system. This was endorsed by the Secretary of State for Employment. Meanwhile, SEAC started development work with GCE Board researchers in six GCE examining boards on inclusion of core skills in GCE. In contrast to the NCVQ position on the NVQ framework, this work led to the rejection of formal inclusion of assessment of core skills within 'A' levels. Essentially, assessment of broad-based definitions of communication, personal skills, problem solving etc. could proceed only by substantial use of coursework. Three pressures precluded this. Firstly, the small amount of coursework allowed in GCEs (typically 20 per cent), which was considered inadequate for assessing the full range of core skills Secondly, with the coursework which *was* allowed under the assessment regime, GCE board officers expressed a strong preference for using it for assessing subject-specific knowledge and skills. Thirdly, it was felt that forced inclusion of the core skills would act as a 'distortion' of the nature of the specific subjects. It should also be noted that SEAC was at this time under pressure to produce other innovations in GCE: the 'A' level principles and the 'A' level subject cores. The introduction of core skills was not considered as high a priority as these other aspects of change. The upshot of all these factors was rejection of formal assessment of core skills within 'A/AS' qualifications.

The position of core skills in the education and training system was fundamentally altered by the introduction of General National Vocational Qualifications (GNVQs). In 1991, when the Core Skills Units were first drafted, GNVQs were a twinkle in the policy-makers' eyes. As stated above, Kenneth Baker's 1989 speech (Baker, 1989) — the kickstart behind the current core skills initiative — intended core skills as a remedy to perceived problems in both NVQs and 'A/AS' qualifications. The core skills specifications were seen as having an important role in broadening both vocational and academic qualifications.

On the part of 'A/AS', it was emphasized that too many programmes (combinations of 'A/AS' qualifications) were narrow in scope, failing to equip young people with a broad range of skills in communication, personal skills, etc., which are required for adult and working life — and, some HE commentators emphasized — for effective performance in HE. Whilst the Government did not want to undertake any fundamental revision of the shape of A/AS and their assessment arrangements, Baker perceived that there might be scope for inclusion of assessment of core skills within the assessment schemes for these awards — as outlined, above, an option rejected by SEAC.

On the part of NVQs, there was concern expressed that since these awards were based on analysis of occupational competence[1] they might be equipping people with skills which were too rooted in work *as it is*, as opposed to equipping people with skills which enable them to deal with changing skill requirements. This position underrates one key aspect of these qualifications: NVQs are intended to provide descriptions of competence in an *occupation* and are therefore broader than descriptions of competence as it occurs in a single job function. In addition, the NVQ system allows people to add to their awards by acquiring additional units as the nature of work in an occupational sector changes. However, this still leaves space for the core skills units within the NVQ system, since the units are designed to directly stimulate development of and certificate the achievement of general skills which are instrumental in skill transfer. For example, the units in *improving own learning and performance* are intended to foster more effective approaches to learning — not least through target-settings and reviewing. The units in *problem-solving* are intended to help people adopt more conscious problem-solving strategies — with a direct effect on their capacity to deal with new challenges in unfamiliar settings. The core skills units would thus satisfy a unique place in the NVQ system — that of directly fostering the development of transferable skills.

As the late 1980s passed, the pressure to include core skills as a broadening component in NVQs was increased as the education and training system began to converge on a two-track model. That is, an academic route (GCSEs-'A/AS'-HE) and a vocational route (NVQs). The powerful focus on NVQs was emerging as a dominant feature of Government targets and of the flow of funding available from Training and Enterprise Councils (TECs). Whilst this had the beneficial effect of forcing increased takeup of NVQs, there were some deficits. With funding being driven down the NVQ route, qualifications which had a general education purpose but with a vocational focus — such as BTEC First and National awards — were also under ineluctable pressure to become recognized as NVQs.

Under these conditions, the NVQ model was beginning to be stretched beyond its original design parameters. With this two-track system, schools and colleges wishing to incorporate a vocational component in their post-16 provision were being forced to consider NVQs as the dominant provision. NVQs were not, and are not, designed for delivery in full-time educational settings. Put simply, it was all too easy for a school or college to run into one or both of the following problems:

(i) providing valid evidence for NVQs by using activities in the school/college setting is difficult. This is unsurprising, since NVQs describe occupational competence; it is therefore anticipated that evidence will be derived from work activities. In consequence, it was clear that schools and colleges were often having severe difficulties in generating valid evidence, and in many cases were distorting the standards in the units by the use of invalid evidence;

(ii) the focus on occupational competence in NVQs made them seem extremely narrow in educational settings. Thus, to deliver NVQs with any degree of effectiveness, teachers were having to construct very focused, narrow learning activities at odds with the broad curriculum aims of institutions.

These tensions became all too obvious when BTEC undertook 'conversion' of its General Award in Business in order to meet the requirements of NVQ Business Administration.

It was from these concerns — the dangers of distorting NVQs and/or distorting school/college programmes — that General National Vocational Qualifications (GNVQs) were born. Their function was to rationalize existing post-16 general education with a vocational focus by introducing a standardized model for all subject areas and levels. In doing this, the model included[2]:

(i) units which were designed to be nominally the same 'size' as modules in six-module 'A' levels (such as those from the University of Cambridge Local Examinations Syndicate);

(ii) units which were capable of delivery in full-time educational settings, without a requirement for evidence to be derived from work experience;

(iii) a requirement for all students to complete core skills units in communication, application of number, information technology (note that the units in problem solving, improving own learning and performance and working with others were *not* included — many GNVQ centres are, however, including these in students' programmes).

It was always recognized that the implementation of core skills in NVQs would have to proceed by a delicate process of combined, carefully balanced consensus and compulsion. It was anticipated that take-up in NVQs would proceed at different rates and unevenly across different occupational sectors. However, including the core skills units as a mandatory requirement in all GNVQs quickly became the key mechanism for establishing the core skills within the qualifications system. With the rapid escalation of participants in GNVQs rising from around 10,000 students in the first pilot year to 82,000 in the second (open participation) year, the core skills units quickly became established currency.

But it is wrong to assume that take-up of the core skills units was a reluctant response by teachers and institutions to compulsion. Support for the concept of the core skills was evidenced by the rapid growth — beyond NVQs and GNVQs — of programmes which include the units. Teachers in school, FE and HE settings saw a key curriculum role for the units. RSA initiated in 1993 a project which provides certification of all six core skills in GCSE and 'A/AS' programmes. While the project was restricted to 100 centres in the academic year 93–94, 1000 centres were expressing interest in participation. This indicates a high level of demand for the core skills units as a broadening component of academic awards. By using the core skills units, institutions are meeting the original function of the core skills initiative — while not included in the formal assessment schemes for 'A/AS', the units allow certification of a broad range of skills developed in the learning programmes. Some schools feel that the arrangement where the core skills units have to be certificated by one of the three GNVQ awarding bodies (RSA, C&G or BTEC) and the GCEs remain certificated by GCE Boards involves additional costs and the burden of meeting the requirements of different bodies. However, it is intended that GCE boards will be enabled to deliver GNVQs (projected award starts in 1997) and the certification for a GCE and the core skills units will then be available from single bodies.

But by the beginning of 1994 the takeup of the units ran far beyond this development work. In 1991–92 the Open University (OU) developed a personal development course using the core skills as a key component — an initial print run of 10,000 was undertaken. In addition, the OU undertook a development project to include the core skills units in its foundation courses in science, maths and technology — the year cohort for these courses numbers over **N**. Finally, the national ASDAN programme (Award Scheme) running out of the University of the West of England has incorporated the core skills units as the basis for its certification. This includes well over 50,000 school students, both pre- and post-16.

This takeup of the core skills units has not proceeded either by compulsion or hard selling. The units are considered by practitioners to be a way of enhancing and securing the curriculum intentions of these various programmes in respect of promotion of broad-based, transferable skills.

In all settings, NCVQ encourages integrated delivery of the core skills units. However, integration is not associated with a single mode of delivery. Integration is seen as a *quality of the learning experience*. The following operational definition is used by the core skills development team:

> Successful integration of core skills units: occurs where the core skills are acquired through settings which contextualise the core skills in ways meaningful to students. Students should not see core skills as something abstract and isolated. They should understand how the skills might be applied in future settings. On the one hand, the fact that the skills are applied in real settings should make the learning of the skills more effective. On the other, the acquisition of core skills should actively enhance the learning of vocationally-specific or subject-specific components of programmes.

The outcome of integrated delivery of the core skills — and this points to how it can be detected in programmes — is that the students should be able to mobilize the core skills in a wide variety of settings in order to enhance their performance. They should therefore not see application of number as isolated lessons in maths, nor communication isolated from the work they do in preparing written materials, making presentations in the vocational areas they are working in.

Different models can be adopted to achieve this, and evaluation studies around the core skills units show that workshop-based delivery in one institution (of information technology, for example) can be highly integrated, while workshop-based delivery can lack integration in another. The case studies below highlight the key variables which appear to determine effective integration.

By theorizing integration as a feature of (i) students' perception of links between different components of learning programmes; and (ii) students' capacity to mobilize core skills in a variety of settings, this does not mean that 'it should all be left to students' to make those links and see the opportunities to use core skills. From the case studies below, it can immediately be seen that aspects of institutional organization, teacher behaviour, programme organization can enhance or detract from integration.

- Case study 1: The pendulum swing centre
  One centre originally divided up responsibility for particular core skills to different members of staff. One took responsibility for IT sessions; another for communication sessions, etc. After a while, the IT tutor realized that their sessions were also generating evidence for application of number and communication. The same thing was happening to the communication tutors. So they got together and agreed that they would all assess all of the core skills. After a while, they realized that there was massive duplication going on, with students confused as to why they were being assessed over and over again on the same thing, but in different sessions. Certain gaps were present where everyone thought someone must be covering a particular core skill, but in fact no-one was. The pendulum swing was from particular people assessing specific skills to everybody doing everything and back and fro again.

Remedies discussed with the centre focused on (i) clearly allocated duties; (ii) better planning and anticipation of assessment opportunities; (iii) more effective recording systems including portfolio management and review and formative assessment processes.

- Case study 2: The core skills consultants
  The health and social care team in a GNVQ pilot centre were very concerned about how they would deliver the core skills in application of number. They were struggling. They could see how the communication core skills were relevant and some of the IT skills, but they were perplexed about application of number. The response of the management was that the application of number core skills should be delivered in maths GCSE lessons. But the maths specialists disagreed. They joined the health and social care team meetings where they were designing the year's programme, and helped them to identify meaningful applications of number in health and social care settings. For example, the tutors had no idea of how to build work on probability into the programme. The maths specialist said to the team 'what's the chance of the next person coming through the door being female? . . . What's the chance of them being female and under 30 . . . what's the chance of them being female, under 30 and HIV positive?'. With a few seconds' thought, the maths specialist had contextualized probability in a very meaningful way; relevant to genetics, demography and epidemiology — all key components of the health and social care programme. The number skills would enrich the vocational content, the number skills would be made relevant and not dry as dust, and the retention of the number skills over time by the student is likely to be enhanced.

  But the health and social care team still felt very insecure about teaching probability — they could now see how it could be made relevant, but didn't understand it sufficiently to teach it confidently. The maths teachers took a decision: to jointly teach with the vocational tutors in agreed timetable slots. They did not want to teach the maths in isolation in stand alone maths sessions because *they* weren't confident that they could make it relevant to the vocational content of students' programmes. The maths teachers became 'consultants' to the vocational team — they didn't close down the maths department, but it sometimes seemed like it, with all the maths teachers out doing joint teaching with the vocational tutors.

This was a programme which displayed effective integration; only possible because of the support of senior management and the capacity of staff to collaborate effectively.

- Case study 3: Leaving it until the last moment
  When we visited GNVQ pilot centres in the third term, a number had still done nothing particularly tangible about the core skills. In these centres, everyone had to rush around at the last minute to gather evidence to put into students' portfolios. In the case of communication — where evidence on communicating with different audiences was essential — it was very difficult to find and produce evidence within the timescale. Teachers asked students to remember and write up notes of occasions on which they had presented information to unfamiliar audiences etc.

This is a severe problem, and such centres have to undertake fundamental review of (i) programme management and evaluation; (ii) allocation of staff responsibilities; and (iii) the overall assessment system within the institution.

- Case study 4: So integrated they vanish without trace
  The teachers deliver the GNVQ through assignment-based work. The assignments are very substantial, with two per term being completed. The written projects and presentations to other students are used as the main evidence of achievement. Individual teachers prepare the assignment outlines (up to three pages) and provide supporting reference documents. The assignment has a covering sheet which lists the core skills which will be covered in the assignment. When the assignment is completed, it is marked by the teacher, who infers that the core skills have been covered if they consider that the assignment has been completed well. If a learner has particular difficulty with a core skill — for example, in application of number — then they have the option of asking to attend drop-in workshops to enhance their skills.
  Students frequently covered more core skills than were listed on the front of the project. It all depended on the precise activities which an individual carried out. They could decide to do much more work using IT; they could elect to work collaboratively with fellow students; they could use sophisticated communication skills in gathering information for the assignment. In other cases, students were able to avoid skills which the teacher felt were in the assignment — for example, in number — by adopting other ways of completing the activities.
  The development of the core skills was not focused in any deliberate way — since the teacher had decided that the activity must contain the core skills they had listed on the front, no-one — neither the students nor the teacher — paid any specific attention to them.

Whilst there are some advantages in 'pre-analyzing' learning materials in this way, there are obvious dangers. As with case studies 1 and 3, more sensitive formative assessment processes with greater student involvement are a crucial remedy.

- Case study 5: The drop-in IT centre
  One college in the GNVQ pilot phase delivered the information technology core skills through an IT drop-in centre. The college was better able to serve the increasing demand for IT provision through the centre, and had briefed the drop-in centre staff on the types of demands GNVQ students would be making. One of the things which was stressed was the importance of integration. In was emphasized in general terms that the learning support should be focused on IT which would be 'relevant to the students' work in business, health and care etc'. So far so good; but then consider the following incident. A student from health and social care had done a local survey on the distribution of care services and wanted to analyze the statistics she had collected. She didn't know whether to use a database or a spreadsheet; she arrived at the IT drop-in centre with armfuls of fairly well-organized data and wanted advice on how to analyze it. Both she and her health and social care tutor had identified that this was an opportunity for her to meet some of the requirements of the IT core skills. The IT tutor at the drop-in centre welcomed her on her arrival and asked her what she wanted to do. 'Learn to use a spreadsheet or database by analyzing this data', said the student. The IT tutor took a look at the data and said that it would be much more straightforward to learn how to use a spreadsheet using data (on car sales) which he 'normally used' to teach students spreadsheets. And so that's how they proceeded, and that's how integration vanished in a puff of smoke. She found the work on the spreadsheet using the IT tutor's data uninteresting, and her time schedule for analysing her project data was severely shortened. In the end, she was left to struggle with how to turn her data into something which could be analyzed using a spreadsheet. The tutor had focused on the IT provision without an eye on real integration.

  If only the IT tutor had helped the student deal with the data from her project — data which *meant something* to the student — this approach would have linked the IT tightly into the health and social programme whilst giving the student credit towards the core skills units.

The teaching staff in the college thought the programme was highly integrated — it was suggested by the researchers that a more sensitive form of internal evaluation and monitoring system was required to detect such problems, associated with staff development on programme management.

As emphasized above, these case studies do not point to one model being substantially superior to another, although the approach in case study 2 was clearly ahead of the other programme strategies. Each approach in the more defective settings could be moved far further towards an integrated provision by adopting the remedies outlined beneath each case study. The following generic themes emerged from the work:

Table 11.1

delivery pattern	key integration issues
delivering core skills through programme sessions devoted to the vocational units	care has to be taken to ensure that the core skills are not trivialised or marginalized
	teachers/tutors have to possess adequate skills and be confident in teaching number, IT and communication and how to apply them
	team teaching — combining specialists in maths etc. with vocational teachers — can be very effective in securing integration
delivering core skills through drop-in centres	can help with problems of shortages in equipment and specialist teachers
	great care has to be taken to sustain coherent links between the core skills and vocational components of the programme
programme sessions devoted exclusively to the core skills	can help when students are having difficulties with particular parts of the core skills
	great care has to be taken to sustain coherent links between the core skills and vocational components of the programme

The problems of integrated delivery which these bring to the fore are not new. They were an enduring and intransigent feature of the national development project which Michael Marland reported in *Language Across the Curriculum* (Marland, 1977) in the early 1970s. The problems of delivery of cross-curriculum components have not gone away. It is important to note that the bold aspirations of the National Curriculum *cross-curriculum themes* as an integrating component between the discrete subjects was never realized, falling into political disfavour as unrealistic and undeliverable shortly after their introduction.

But the issue is not that integration is not possible, since experience in the GNVQ innovation (see case study 2 in particular) show that integrated delivery is both feasible and desirable. The issues focus on how the following features of the curriculum, staff, students and institutions combine to either enhance or detract from integration of the core skills.

- the views and teaching/learning strategies adopted/preferred by individual teachers;
- curriculum planning teams;
- teaching teams/co-teaching;
- students' approach to specific subject areas and their capacity to make linkages between programme components;
- the support of management for flexible, integrated delivery patterns;
- recording systems;
- teaching materials;
- staff development.

Integrating Core Skills: Building New Professional Knowledge

In 1991, following the development of outline core skills specifications by the Task Group, four teams of teachers began work to refine the language of the proposed units, and to trial them with learners. The teams were from engineering, hairdressing, business administration, and health care, and were all implementing NVQs relatively successfully. Thanks are due to all teachers and learners who contributed to the development of the core skills. What follows is an abbreviated account of some of the insights that were gained from this early work.

The core skills are already being developed, to some extent, in all learning programmes so the pilot sought to identify existing provision, and to enhance it, as well as to add something new and valuable to curricula. It soon became clear that the implementation of core skills is as much about the process of learning as about the content. It is about how learning takes place, as well as what is covered. The quality of teaching and learning are at the heart of the core skills initiative.

The Legitimacy of the Core Skills

Previous attempts to implement a form of core skills, by the BTEC for example, had been seriously hampered by the issue of *legitimacy*. Learners in post-compulsory education are motivated mainly by extrinsic rather than intrinsic goals. Typically, they want their learning to be related to their vocational ambitions to gain qualifications and improve employment prospects. When aspects of programmes are perceived, rightly or wrongly, to be disassociated from those extrinsic goals, learners very often reject them.

For core skills to be accepted as legitimate by most learners in post-compulsory education they should be rooted in their vocational goals. Which means that they cannot be added on as extra 'subjects' but should arise as a natural and fully contextualized aspect of vocational learning. As the case studies show, it is fine to provide learners with workshops or other means of enhancing the core skills, but the primary responsibility for the development and assessment of the skills rests with teams of vocational teachers, with the help of specialist colleagues if necessary, so long as they are full members of the team.

It was anticipated that, in a natural human desire to minimise the impact of change, some colleges and teams of teachers might take the relatively easy option of either timetabling 'subject' slots for the core skills, or setting up workshops for learners who need *remedial* help, while offering nothing in the way of systematic core skills development for other learners.

The take-up of voluntary workshops is often poor and sometimes dominated by learners preparing for entry to higher education, rather than by those who may have more fundamental needs. The adverse labelling attached to learners who use workshops perceived to be remedial is also a problem. The core skills are intended to improve the learning and performance of *all* learners, using contexts that are important to them. They are intended to enrich learning and performance in whatever field the learners are committed to. Thus the context for the skills should be the learners' main programme of study.

Thus legitimacy can be enhanced by contextualizing the core skills in the subjects that engage learners; by committing all staff to their implementation, and by using a *progression* model to benefit all learners, rather than a *deficit* model intended to benefit only those perceived to be 'remedial'.

Effective Teaching and Learning

The 'infallible expert' model of the teacher (Elliot, 1991) may hamper teachers from accepting their own needs as learners. It may be ineffective in promoting learning and in gathering evidence of performance because it places too much emphasis on the role of the teacher. A model more akin to that of the 'reflective practitioner' (Schon, 1983) as expounded by the FEU in documents such as *Learning by Doing* (1988) and *Supporting Learning* (1992a) may be more suited to meeting the needs of individual learners, and of teachers themselves.

Studies in the United States and in Australia (Kastendiek, 1985; Batten, 1989) have shown that learners regard those teachers as most effective who treat them as adults by creating frameworks for learning in which responsibilities can be shared. It is desirable to strike a balance between teachers taking a directive role based on learner interests and experience, and learners directing their own learning.

The mapping of learner perceptions in a number of countries (Wubbels *et al*, 1987; Wubbels and Levy, 1993) came to the view that, 'Best teachers . . . provide students with a little more responsibility and freedom'. Two types of ideal teacher emerged, a *dominant ideal* where 'there is a lot of cooperative behaviour and a fair amount of leadership and strictness', and a *student-oriented ideal* which 'reflects the teacher's orientation toward student responsibility and freedom'. In post-compulsory education the *student-oriented ideal* may be most appropriate because, unsurprisingly, it was found that, 'older students want more autonomy'. These findings remind us of what has been known for a long time but too often ignored. Classic work on classroom interaction by Flanders (1970) showed that:

> Techniques for analyzing current, average classroom interaction reveal a high degree of teacher domination in setting learning tasks and in thinking through problems so that pupils' ideas and initiative are under-developed. As a result, teachers and pupils rarely experience thoughtful, shared inquiry. In classrooms that are above average in positive pupil attitudes and content achievement, the teacher-pupil interaction exhibits a somewhat greater orientation toward pupil ideas and pupil initiative.

Faced with the language of the core skill units some teachers may feel an understandable degree of uncertainty, especially if they doubt their own competence in the skills. However, if they do not regard themselves as infallible experts but as designers and managers of learning processes, they may share understandings with learners to mutual benefit. After all, some learners may be more familiar with the language of the core skills than their teachers. However, for some teachers the move from 'infallible' subject expert to manager of learning will be very challenging and will need the active help of senior managers in creating an ethos of professional change and opportunities for suitable staff development. In his contribution to this book, Tom Jackson corroborates this from another pilot by remarking that:

. . . despite the availability of considerable staff experience and expertise, there was a significant need for staff development especially of a collaborative, sharing nature.

The process of teachers and learners sharing understandings of units, and sharing responsibilities for learning and assessment, that may be foregrounded by the core skills initiative, may have a profoundly beneficial affect on all aspects of teaching and learning.

Teachers Sharing Responsibilities with Learners

The four teams of teachers in the pilot came to the conclusion that learners, if given supportive frameworks, can share responsibilities with teachers for the setting of learning goals, monitoring of performance, and the gathering of evidence.

Learners can be given the skills and opportunity to take more responsibility for their own learning. Learners can join with teachers to formulate goals and monitor their efforts to attain them. In this way *deep* as distinct from *surface* learning is more likely to occur (MacFarlane, 1992). Deep learning develops knowledge that can be put to use and transferred to new situations; surface learning is retained for a short while and then forgotten.

The practical and ethical desirability of actively encouraging learners to become more autonomous is a theme that runs through many of the contributions to this book. Outcome-based approaches to education carry with them a need for learners to be given explicit information about what is expected of them. Once they have this knowledge they can make claims for existing attainment, can negotiate parts of the learning programme, can share understandings with teachers, and can gather evidence of attainment to present for assessment. If these sorts of responsibilities are not shared with learners, teachers are left to offer relatively rigid learning programmes intended to satisfy the needs of all participants but which will almost inevitably fall short of the needs of some.

Especially with large groups of learners, it is very difficult for teachers to take sole responsibility for assessment. Teachers perceive themselves to be under considerable pressure of work. Especially in the initial stages of implementing new units, there are bound to be some mismatches between what teachers record as having been achieved, and what has actually been achieved. If a particular sequence of work should have led to particular attainments being achieved these are sometimes 'ticked off' in an element-happy way on insufficient evidence. Conversely, attainments that were not foreseen are sometimes missed or ignored. If learners are active in matching what they do to unit specifications the validity of assessment is enhanced. As learners on an NVQ 3 programme in engineering put it:

When you [teachers] give us an assignment, as long as you give us the unit numbers, we can look through them and understand what is expected.

In a debriefing we could look through so that we can get a sense in their (unit) language of what we've actually done, because we know in layman's terms.

During the pilot, a number of initiatives were taken by teaching teams to help learners take responsibility for their own learning and progress. It was found that learners benefit from greater involvement because they become more familiar with the terminology and concepts of the skills they are expected to learn; they have a clearer understanding of how they will be assessed; they feel valued as individuals and their motivation to learn increases.

If learners are to be active in the process of learning and assessment they need a framework which assists them. Induction programmes can be used to:

- give learners full information about what is expected of them;
- give them insight into their own learning styles;
- provide opportunities to share understandings of units with teachers and to claim credit for existing attainment if appropriate.

During learning programmes learners need simple, practical ways of monitoring their own progress and recording achievement. Simple recording instruments, such as *A Core Skills Attainment Profile* and a *Year Planner*, may be devised to help teachers and learners to see at a glance what has been covered and what remains to be done. These can be supplemented by evidence in the form of products or records or processes in, for example, log books.

The processes of learning and recording achievement can be aided by systems of individual action planning, linked to learning contracts and the keeping of personal portfolios and records of achievement. A personal tutoring scheme can also greatly assist the process of learners sharing responsibility for their own learning and performance. Much valuable work has been carried out, particularly by the FEU, in showing how educationalists can help learners in these ways.

It is inevitable that some learners and teachers will have to go through a period of familiarization before they feel comfortable with the core skills specifications. This is already the case for learners embarking on the study of any unfamiliar area of knowledge. If teachers and learners share understandings then the core skills can become an integral part of learning and assessment and may be a means of encouraging a climate of greater cooperation between teachers and learners.

The Challenge to Teachers

Tacit professional knowledge (Argyris and Schon, 1974; Eraut, 1985) equips teachers to 'cut corners' without seriously undermining standards. All professionals acquire 'gut feelings' or 'theories in action' about their work that enable them to make accurate judgments about people and situations. If doctors, lawyers, engineers, teachers or anyone with specialist skills always had to begin with first principles and think through every case they could not cope. As Eraut says elsewhere in this book:

Records and memories of cases and personal theories play an important role in much professional work.

In an engineering workshop, for example, an experienced teacher will know if a trainee has grasped how to use a particular machine or carry out a particular process. The teacher will judge by finished products but will also be alert to many other signs that an outsider might not register — comments that the trainee makes, a way of standing at the machine, the way that a log entry has been completed, the answer to a question that demonstrates underpinning knowledge.

The same engineering teacher may have no similar tacit professional knowledge when it comes to assessing a core skill. Feeling uncertain some teachers will struggle with the language of the unit, will assess more painstakingly than is usually necessary and will eventually become more comfortable and able to assess with ease. Other teachers, especially if they feel under pressure for other reasons, may be inclined to ignore or pay lip service to the core skill; or give all the responsibility to a specialist brought in to teach and assess it who may know little about the vocational context; or suggest that special assignments, divorced from the rest of the learning programme, be devised to assess the skill. These reactions, while understandable, lead to the skills becoming marginal to the learning programme. Learners soon understand, openly or tacitly, that the core skill is not important to the programme, even if it is important to their own learning and development.

In the past it has sometimes happened that teachers and learners collude, sometimes with the tacit approval of external moderators, to sidetrack aspects of the curriculum that present a challenge to current practice. Assessment can be fudged. The NCVQ outcomes-based approach may set in place a more rigorous system of verification but there will always be scope for teachers to duck the full implementation of the core skills.

In the short term, therefore, it is important that when implementing the core skills teachers should share the language of the units with one another and with learners; should plan learning programmes that integrate the core skills; and should be given support in this from their managers. In this way they will soon build tacit professional knowledge of the core skills that will enable them to assess learners accurately and efficiently.

The implementation of core skills is better perceived not as an *addition* to tasks but as a challenge to deliver the whole curriculum in ways that enable learners to be more active in learning and gathering evidence of attainment. In these ways learners can free teacher time for the management of learning programmes, guidance and support to individual learners and the carrying out of summative assessments.

The Integration of Core Skills

The integration of core skills into learning programmes, whether practice or theory-orientated, work or college-based, can be greatly assisted by an audit of the curriculum to see where it is best to develop and assess particular skills. At the same time, it is desirable for there to be some room for amendment of learning programmes in response to negotiation with learners to meet their needs. If learners are to be encouraged to share responsibilities for learning with teachers it follows that they should be able to contribute ideas for assignments and assessment.

Assessment can be a formative element in the learning programme, giving learners useful feedback about their performance that helps them to become competent.

It is desirable that as well as planning for assessment there should be time set aside to review learning so that evidence of attainment gathered by learners and teachers can be assessed. Some learning takes place in 'hot' situations that can only be assessed by reflection after the event. For example, work in settings such as health care and catering sometimes does not permit recording of attainment during the process. Only subsequently can time be set aside for reflection, review and assessment and recording of attainment.

Given time and experience, all teachers can develop expertise in the core skills so that the units become an integral part of the learning and assessment programme.

In practical environments, such as kitchens, salons and engineering workshops, in addition to having regard for health and safety requirements, teachers teach, monitor the performance of many individual learners, and assess them when appropriate. This is a demanding set of duties and it may be desirable sometimes to double staff to give teachers enough time to assess while still monitoring health, safety and performance. This may require creative timetabling.

I will give brief examples of the effective implementation of core skills in two practice-based environments, the first an example of *planned* delivery, the second of the assessment of core skills by *reviewing* performance.

In an engineering workshop five learners sat at a table to work collaboratively in analyzing a design problem. The teacher remained inconspicuously on the periphery to monitor their performance. Meanwhile, another teacher worked with the rest of the learners who were using machines. After half-an-hour there was a review discussion in which the teacher drew from the learners what they had learned, first of all about the engineering design problem, and secondly about the process of working together and communicating their ideas. The teacher then recorded formative assessments of both engineering and communication units.

The second example is from health care. On a ward for the elderly the ward sister sat with an assistant to review her work. The assistant had dealt, as the first person on the spot, with a femoral artery bleed. The review brought out features of the situation that covered a number of core skills, as well as health care skills.

In teaching and learning situations which are more theory and classroom-based the most commonly employed method of learning and assessment is the assignment or project. To be worthwhile in promoting learning these should be designed with care to extend as well as to reinforce learning. They should be challenging but achievable. Most assignments can, sometimes with amendments, cover aspects of the core skills.

The integration of core skills into assignments in effective and efficient ways can be greatly enhanced if teachers collaborate in assignment design so that interesting cross-curriculum challenges can be given to learners, and unnecessary duplication of effort avoided.

Two brief examples of affective assignment design are drawn from hairdressing and health care. Hairdressers were asked to survey the shampoos used in their salons. They talked with clients, colleagues and managers, and produced written reports, some of which made a statistical presentation of findings. As well as enhancing their knowledge of shampoos, a number of core skills were covered.

A ward assistant taking NVQ2 had never had to cope with bereavement on the ward. She suggested to the ward sister, who was also her NVQ supervisor, that she should research what to do if bereavement occurred. The ward sister agreed and the assistant talked to the bereavement officer, read about the needs of relatives after bereavement, and found out what her own responsibilities would be. She presented her findings to the ward sister in a short report. In this way she prepared herself to perform professionally and, in the process, covered a number of core skills.

These examples show that the implementation of the core skills can be the means of enhancing learning in the vocational area. Conversely, the vocational area provides a real context for the development and assessment of the core skills.

The Support of Senior Managers

Teachers need the active support of their senior managers if they are to implement core skills successfully. If teams are to meet regularly enough to audit and plan learning programmes; if learners are to be provided with adequate induction programmes; if teachers are to be given appropriate staff development, then the most senior staff need to create a suitable climate and provide the resources for this to happen. Already much valuable work has been carried out in many schools and colleges.

Two levels of change may be identified, the first possible without major adjustments of current practice in many institutions, the second more profound and challenging.

The following learner entitlements may be provided without major changes to organization or to teacher skills:

- at the beginning of their programmes learners can be given full unit specifications, programme details, assessment details, opportunities to discuss all these with teachers and to share understandings;
- once they have this information, with teacher support, they may monitor for themselves when and where they have covered the core and other skills and record evidence of achievement;
- regular review or debriefing sessions can be provided to assess the evidence and determine attainment. Further learning may then be planned by teachers and learners.

A second level of entitlement, requiring more profound changes to the organization of learning in some institutions, includes the following:

- individual tutorial guidance and support;
- the accreditation of existing attainment;
- the agreeing of individual action plans and learning contracts.

Some of the features of this more flexible approach to teaching and learning may be found in FEU publications, such as *Flexible Colleges* (1992). In such a learning culture there may be a move towards modularity of curriculum provision, and of greater autonomy on the part of learners to contribute to the design and pacing of learning programmes.

Some staff development may be needed by all teachers involved in developing and assessing the core skills. Where teachers are not used to working collaboratively in teams, except occasionally in the sharing of assignments, time and training may be needed to build team work skills. Where teachers are used mainly to assess products, whether machined parts or assignment reports, rather than processes, time for the development of process skills may be necessary. However, in all cases the best method of learning the skills involved is to experience their use, with time out for reflection and the creation of new professional knowledge.

Notes

1 See Technical Advisory Groups Notes on Functional Analysis (Employment Department first printed in and subsequently reprinted), a technique for identifying and describing the components of occupational competence in the form of outcomes. It emphasizes generic descriptions of functions which people perform in occupational areas, rather than detailed, context-specific sequential descriptions of the activities they undertake to discharge those functions.
2 The full set of criteria governing the shape and content of GNVQs is given in the *GNVQ Criteria and Guide*, available from NCVQ; further technical detail on the content is given in the *Rules for editing GNVQs*, available from GNVQ R&D at NCVQ.

References

ARGYRIS, C. and SCHON, D. (1974) *Theory in Practice: Increasing Professional Effectiveness*, San Francisco, CA, Jossey-Bass.

BAKER, K. RT HON, 1989 (Secretary of State for Education and Science) *Speech to the Association of Colleges of Further and Higher Education*, London, HMSO.

BATTEN, M. (1989) 'Effects of traditional and alternative courses on students in Post-compulsory education', *British Educational Research Journal*, 15, 3.

BOUD, D. (Ed) (1988) *Developing Student Autonomy in Learning*, London, Kogan Page.

CNAA (1992) *Case Studies in Student-centred Learning*, London, CNAA.

ED (Employment Department) (1993) *A Year in GNVQs*, Sheffield, Employment Department.

ELLIOT, J. (1991) 'A model of professionalism and its implications for teacher education', *British Educational Research Journal*, 17, 4.

ERAUT, M. (1985) 'Knowledge creation and knowledge use in professional contexts', *Studies in Higher Education*, 10, 2.

FEU (1988) *Learning by Doing: A guide to Learning and Teaching Methods*, London, FEU.

FEU (1992a) *Supporting Learning*, London, FEU.

FEU (1992b) *Flexible Colleges*, London, FEU.

FEU (1993) *Core Skills Action Pack*, London, FEU.

FLANDERS, N. (1970) *Analysing Teaching Behaviour*, Reading, MA, Addison-Wesley.

HAMMOND, M. and COLLINS, R. (1992) *Self-directed Learning*, London, Kogan Page.

JESSUP, G. with BURKE, J., WOLF, A. and OATES, T. (1990) *Common Learning Outcomes: Core Skills in A/AS levels and NVQs NCVQ R&D report #6*, London, NCVQ.

JESSUP, G. (1991) *Outcomes: NVQs and the Emerging Model of Education and Training*, London, Falmer Press.

KASTENDIEK, S. *et al* (1985) 'The balancing act: Competencies of effective teachers and mentors', *Innovation Abstracts*, 5, 4.

MACFARLANE, A.G. (1992) *Teaching and Learning in an Expanding Higher Education System*, Edinburgh, SCFC.

MARLAND, M. (1977) *Language Across the Curriculum*, London, Heinemann.

OATES, T. (1990a) *Common Skills: Part one, Review of Development Issues*, Sheffield, Training Agency.

OATES, T. (1990) *Common Skills: Part two, Review of Core Competences Frameworks*, Sheffield, Training Agency.

OATES, T. (1991) *Developing and Piloting the NCVQ Core Skill Units NCVQ R&D report #16*, London, NCVQ.

OATES, T. (1992) *Core Skills and Transfer: Aiming High in Educational and Training Technology International*, 29, 3, Kogan Page.

OFSTED (1993) *GNVQs in Schools*, London, HMSO.

SCHON, D. (1983) *The Reflective Practitioner -How Professionals Think in Action*, London, Temple Smith.

WUBBELS, T., BREKELMANS, M. and HERMANS, J. (1987) 'Teacher behaviour an important aspect of the learning environment' in FRASER, B. (Ed) *The Study of Learning Environments* (Vol 3), Perth, Curtin University.

WUBBELS, T. and LEVY, J. (Eds.) (1993) *Do You Know How You Look? Interpersonal Relationships in Education*, London, Falmer Press.

Chapter 12

The Assessment of Outcomes

Stephen Steadman

A Brief and Biased History of the Assessment of Outcomes

There have long been worries that the bias towards academic values which has characterized the school-based education system in England and Wales until the recent past has affected even the vocational sector. It is suspected that too much assessment efficiently tests whether candidates know what to do, but not how to do it. However, history has not been kind to previous attempts to introduce systems of learning and training which have emphasized the assessment of outcomes. A trail of pejorative labels runs from the time of *payment by results* in the last century, via Taylor and Bobbit in the 1920s, through to the revival of behaviourism in the 1940s and 50s which fed into programmed learning and teacher proof curriculum packages. But the approach has been persistently followed, even if along different tracks.

The push by the Royal Society for the Arts for Education for Capability promoted wRoughting as the fourth 'R' after Reading, wRiting and aRithmetic, and the work of the Assessment of Performance Unit put a new emphasis on performance by pioneering new methods of assessing practical skills and outcomes in science, mathematics and modern languages. In the USA movements for competency-based educational testing and programmes of minimum competency testing have almost run their course. While in this country there has been a growing emphasis — given forceful impetus by Sir Keith Joseph during his time as Secretary of State for Education and Science — on criterion-referencing in the school examination system. Today the movement continues in two standard-bearing forms: the National Curriculum with its use of Standard Assessment Tasks, and the system of National Vocational Qualifications which is centred upon the specification and assessment of outcomes.

The pejorative labels include: narrow, behaviourist, psychometric (a relatively new term of abuse in educational circles), and anti-intellectual. Critics of assessment driven systems have coined well known, arresting slogans and sayings, for example. 'You don't fatten pigs by weighing them.' or 'If you can measure it, it isn't IT'. Add to these the famous bumper sticker, 'Help stamp out behavioural objectives.' Then there is also the vivid pictorial analogy of a drunk looking for coins under a lamppost, unable to see the bulk of the wealth which lies outside the lamppost's circle of assessment 'light'. The rejoinders are: 'If you can't measure it, you won't improve it. If you won't measure it, you probably don't care.' Finally there is the rather two-edged saying, 'You get what you measure.'

Both the National Curriculum and NVQs have strong Government backing from moods within the Employment Department and Department for Education which eschew the words teaching and education in favour of delivering and training. And the NVQ model claims to break new ground in the way it identifies required outcomes and makes their assessment the bedrock of a valid system of employment relevant qualifications. So what makes NVQ different in its approach to the assessment of outcomes?

Other chapters in this book restate the many ways in which NVQs can claim to be different from previous attempts to design an assessment led system and I do not wish to repeat them here. But one quotation is necessary:

> For accurate communication of the outcomes of competence and attainment, a precision in the language of such statements will need to be established, approaching that of a science. The overall model stands or falls on how effectively we can state competence and attainment. But if we cannot it raises fundamental issues for education and training, irrespective of the model used. If you cannot say what you require, how can you develop it and how do you know when you have achieved it? (Jessup, 1991, p. 134)

This strong declaration carries a clear implication about the nature of training, and perhaps education, in a system designed to work towards achieving pre-specifiable (economic) outcomes. At the same time it leaves little room for those whose main emphasis would be upon education as a process which promotes personal growth through exploration and research which may lead to the unexpected. And it is with this difference of purpose that we start, in order to see why and how NVQs are different.

Purposes of Assessment and Assessment Systems

The purposes of the traditional, largely academic and paper-based assessment processes can be summarized thus:

- selection for further progress through the system;
- monitoring of standards of achievement across groups;
- screening individuals for attention and groups for resource allocation;
- aiding progression;
- record keeping (when the information is often not used);
- prediction of future performance;
- formative/diagnosis;
- summative/certification;
- accountability.

Looking at this list, is it fanciful to see the purposes towards the end as more to do with NVQs, which are not as concerned with detecting differences between individual students, or providing formative information to aid diagnosis of need and progression, as the traditional approaches have been? In theory NVQs focus firmly on the summative business of qualification and certification. What precedes the assessment point is up to the candidate and what s/he can obtain by way of preparatory training. Accountability is signalled in the system of associated arrangements for funding training. These arrangements tie funding to success in gaining NVQ qualifications, but it is early days for the consequences of this type of accountability to appear.

Yet one must add a rider. There is a tendency for an assessment process to start off pure of purpose but become sullied by the accretion of unreasonable expectations of others. So NVQs may be sold now on their primary aim of being no more nor less than a Statement of Occupational Competence, but already there are negotiations with HE to accept NVQs as passes into degree courses, and will employers — faced with a new recruit clutching an NVQ — want to take the award as proof of potential for further progress?

The real differences emerge at the level of the purposes of different systems. In further education there is a history of well-defined courses leading to the assessment of process knowledge as well as performance outcomes. But few would now disagree that too many of the traditionally academic assessment systems in Britain have concentrated on measuring differences between individuals in order to filter out the — always small — proportion of those who 'pass' and may be allowed to continue to higher education or train as a doctor, etc.

The purposes of the new system of NVQs are to:

- increase the economic competitiveness of the country by raising skill levels across all facets of economic activity; and
- define standards of competent occupational performance so that training can be more effectively directed to their achievement, (by whatever routes may be deemed desirable and efficient).

There are three additional co-existing purposes to:

- increase the flexibility of the work force — breaking old linkages to career paths if necessary, which leads to an interest in core skills because of their perceived importance in enhancing the chances of transferability of competencies and skills between different jobs;
- raise the number of workers with recognized qualifications — a major mechanism for this will be through work-based assessment and other changes in access routes such as the accreditation of prior experience and learning; and
- break the stranglehold of the academic bias in existing patterns of qualification so that more emphasis can be given to practical and technical achievements.

The reason for spelling out the purposes of the NVQ system is to understand what is required in the processes and procedures which are used to assess the outcomes that are specified to provide proof of competent performance. This we will proceed to do, but first we need to consider the nature of the outcomes which are to be assessed.

What are Outcomes?

In order to avoid a narrow focus on tasks and procedures, with echoes of behaviourism, competence is defined in a process of functional analysis which focuses on the purposes and outcomes of work activities within an occupational area. Meaningful *units of competence* are delineated which reflect facets of the job and these units are further defined in terms of (say four or so) *elements of competence* which can still be quite broad. In order to demonstrate an element of competence a candidate must satisfy associated *performance criteria*. These criteria often describe a number of activities which the candidate should be able to perform in order to demonstrate competence in the element to the satisfaction of the assessor. Thus the criteria have two facets: as objectives for the candidate; and decision-making aids for the assessor. Finally, because what is sought is something more than mere minimum competency, performance in the element against the performance criteria has to be demonstrated across a stated range (*range statements*) of circumstances which reflect common variations in working patterns. The end result is that many elements of competence are couched in terms which anyone who has tried to specify behavioural objectives will immediately recognise: active verb, object, circumstance. Accreditation is on a unit basis and a candidate merits an NVQ statement of competence in a unit when s/he successfully completes the requisite elements.

In so far as one is dealing with any type of practical activity, the immediate implications which strike a potential assessor are: how close the assessor and candidate need to be if these activities are to be observed; how many potential decision points there are — n = *units x elements x criteria x range*; how these decision points might be sampled to provide sufficient evidence of performance; how much inference will still — inevitably — be necessary; and the need for contact with the candidate over an extended period of time to get all this done.

To draw up such a system is to tread a fine line between too little specification, which would leave too much inference to the assessor and probably damage the validity of the assessment, and too much specification which becomes bureaucratic, increases the cost of assessment and would probably lead to assessors taking short-cuts with other dangers to validity.

A key issue here is the natural size of the assessment bite: whatever the theoretical breakdown of performance into units, elements and criteria, assessors will tend to make judgments in holistic terms which they themselves apply to the working situation. Thus the actual assessment may be based on an assessor's natural grouping of criteria, rather than that specified. We have well attested examples of this kind of thing from other realms. Teachers of young children regularly distinguished those who 'bark at print' from those who read with meaning, although both could complete a reading test which required the performance of reading aloud. At secondary school in modern language classes there is a similar concern with the gap between apparent learning, as measured on practical speaking and comprehension tests build into modular curriculum units, and real learning which is judged on the basis of an amalgam of other evidence available to the teacher. Associated with this question is the one of what levels of inference are necessary to judge a performance as competent. As NVQs have developed, the need for guidance has been recognized and exemplar portfolios, etc. are being gathered to help assessors develop a community of shared understandings.

Without such help the way people work from insufficient evidence has been documented (Mitchell and Cuthbert, 1989), but questions remain over how much evidence is sufficient to form a settled opinion. How many times should the candidate demonstrate the performance before the assessor can be sure? Many of us know how quickly, and silently, skills fade away when left unpractised. What is the shelf-life of a particular skill shown as one of the criteria in an element's specification? An assessor might be advised to concentrate on having clear cut evidence and to check up on the meaning of negative evidence before tackling the problems of inference and adequate sampling. We cannot offer much other help until a great deal more direct observation has taken place of exactly how NVQ assessors interpret their roles and tasks.

But, returning to the question of levels of inference, the experience within the APU in its practical testing of science was that skilful questioning was required to assess the knowledge and understanding which accompanied practical performance. The process of inference is not easy and it is potentially costly and time consuming because of the need to operate in one-to-one or one-to-few groupings. Wood uses one of Ryle's examples to point out:

> . . . judging whether a student knows the difference between a concept and a principle is not at all the same thing as judging whether a man knows how to shoot. This is true even if one uses the most direct means of ascertaining knowledge, which is presumably oral interrogation coupled with requests to demonstrate; . . . (Wood, 1990, p. 53)

This thought brings us to the question of what is an outcome, from another direction because, although the emphasis in NVQs is firmly upon competence and competent performance, the concept of competence has appeared to stretch a little over time. Apparently it subsumes knowledge, understanding and skills which can mostly be assumed if the performance is fully competent. (But this smacks a little of tautology and I am reminded of the University of Manchester technician who taught me the rudiments of black and white darkroom photography on a pre-PGCE course a long time ago. He cheerfully admitted that he knew what worked — and had a set of very useful practical routines — but did not know why they worked). Other terms have come onto the stage. One is *capability* which Eraut sees as knowledge in use and might also be seen as the potential for future performance in circumstances which are not fully foreseeable. This concept might be more applicable to higher level NVQs. On the other hand Bartram (1992), coming from a psychologist's perspective, has referred to *utility* and *usability*. From the practical standpoint, however, NCVQ does now recognize the need to assess knowledge and understanding directly, and accepts that not all skills are practical, only demonstrable by doing.

What in Fact Occurs in the Assessment of Outcomes under NVQs?

The overall answer to this question is that we do not have a collated clear picture obtainable from published sources, but we do have many indicators. The works which are regularly referred to are *Boning, Blanching and Backtacking: Assessing*

Performance in the Workplace, (Wood *et al*, 1989), the Caterbase project (Mitchell and Cuthbert, 1989) and *Credit Through Workplace Assessment* (SCOTVEC, 1990). In the latter 146 of 213 respondents reported no or minor problems in arranging work-based assessments and 199 and 217 assessors said they had little or no difficulty deciding whether the candidate satisfied the requirements of the award. But all of these reports could do with updating.

Harney and Ward (1991) used the NCVQ database to look at the position as at October 1990. Entries were based on forms filled in by awarding body personnel about a mixture of actual practices and new scheme design intentions. They found that assessment was being based on a mixture of approaches which combined performance with other evidence. Performance evidence was used on its own in less than 5 per cent of instances.

The supplementary evidence used most commonly took the form of an externally set written test or examination. This was true in almost a quarter of unit assessments. As evidence was accumulated to award NVQs just over two-thirds were assessed by a mixture of performance and supplementary evidence: less than half were assessed by internal methods alone.

The range of assessment methods included: work place observation; externally and internally set competence/skills tests; externally and internally set assignments and projects; coursework; internally and externally set written tests and examinations; and internally and externally set oral tests and examinations.

Practicalities or the Difficulty with Implementation

Such is the design of the NVQ system that its natural habitat is easily assumed to be the work place. However, although there were early fears that NVQs would wipe away college-based provision as employers found they no longer needed colleges to accredit their employees, this has not happened. Some of the reasons are structural, for example, concerning the financial rules surrounding Employment Training and other forms of training. I do not deal with those factors here, but some of the reasons link directly to the NVQ assessment requirements.

The first is the feeling in many businesses that their supervisors lack the necessary skills to combine the roles of manager, mentor and assessor. According to evidence becoming available through the Vocational Education and Training Research Programme at the University of Sussex, this is not a feeling confined to small firms, although in at least one area of the country it has proved difficult to locate any small firms involved in NVQs in the office practices sector. Second, we have evidence from one large multinational firm that it puts its employees to work in very restricted settings. This means there is little opportunity for an employee to collect the range of experiences necessary to build towards NVQ statements of competence. The range requirement also affects the ability of small firms to provide enough experience for candidates to build satisfactorily towards qualifications. In this respect college-based simulated work settings can be superior in that they can rotate jobs and risk them not being performed very well in a way that a small firm dare not.

Even in a workplace which can avoid range difficulties the tasks facing an assessor will vary according to the natural flow of the work. In some settings there will be an abundance of paper-based records of things done and supervisors will be in regular contact with trainees and, therefore, able to build a picture of their competence. In others this will not be the case. Evidence will need additional efforts to document, and staff movements will disrupt the relationship between mentor/assessor and trainee.

Evidence from the construction industry comes in a report of the Site Supervisor/Site Manager Assessment Project (J. Trill Assocs, 1992). This report was concerned with the development of site supervisory and management standards and subsequent assessment trials. It is a fascinating study which brings out issues of whether the workplace or college is the best location for training; where size of site and employer make a difference to what is possible; and the difficulties occasioned by the non-literary culture of building site work where many supervisors are, 'encumbered by low abilities in writing'.

Due to the oral workplace culture, getting documentary evidence was difficult. Allied to this were problems in compiling portfolios which were regarded as information overkill. Some candidates reported a lack of company support which meant that candidates were not given appropriate roles or workplace support to enable them to be properly assessed. There were problems over college-workplace liaison and these did not all stem from the employers' side. One particular problem was that of candidates who wanted to become qualified but were effectively shut out, either because they were workers who could not obtain the appropriate roles within the workplace, or because they were unemployed. For some mature, experienced supervisors there were difficulties in becoming accredited because they did not have the skills to be able to support their claims of competence in written statements. Other supervisors found it impossible to impose standards on candidates and companies when they perceived their own standards as quite inadequate (see also Callender, 1992).

The intention in this section has been to set the reality against the aims of the NVQ system of assessment and to see where the joins show, with an eye to the gaps being adjusted or sealed. What also has to be remembered is that in many occupations these are still relatively early days.

Many of these problems will ameliorate as awareness spreads and as more and more assessors are trained and gain experience to pass on to colleagues. This will not be an overnight process. It takes time to form a community of agreement about acceptable performance and one-day courses are likely to be only the start of this process. What assessors and verifiers will need is practical and experientially based guidance, with examples of recorded performances on either side of acceptability. They will also need advice and guidance on the sampling of evidence, ways to use evidence so that inferences may be secure rather than guess work, and advice on how to exploit natural opportunities for observation and evidence gathering.

The principles behind the NVQ model are now being tested in a number of new circumstances. In one direction there are GNVQs, in another there is a concern to embed ethical dimensions in occupational standards and secure their assessment. Inevitably these moves mean a reconsideration of appropriate forms of assessment. For example, the following assessment methods are either in use or under active consideration for assessing performance in relation to ethical matters: mentor observation; witness of colleagues; assessment of the correct following of procedures by workplace assessors; oral questioning, interviews and vivas; reflective accounts; projective techniques; work-based projects; simulations and role play; skills rehearsal; case studies and assignments; evidence of prior achievement; and written examinations or tests.

There are many research implications. We need much more detailed observational evidence of what happens at the point of assessment. What is the optimal balance between detailed specification and the application of experienced judgment to infer competent performance from samples of evidence? It is also important to be able to guide assessors in their in-service training from an accurate knowledge of difficulties and successful and unsuccessful practices. It is somewhat ironic that a system which sets such store by demonstration of performance can produce relatively little direct evidence of its own performance at the point of assessment itself.

The Technical Properties of the NVQ Assessment System

The desirable properties of an assessment system are that it should have the confidence of the population, be demonstrably efficient (inexpensive), fair to all candidates, relevant, reliable and valid. I intend to deal with these in reverse order. On validity and reliability the NCVQ position is almost provocative.

> What I am proposing is that we should just forget reliability altogether and concentrate on validity, which is ultimately all that matters. (Jessup, 1991, p. 191 in a note in an Appendix intended 'to make you think!') and . . . if we may assume these standards are indeed valid, the essential question of validity centres on comparing the judgments made on the evidence of competence collected against the performance criteria associated with each element, and not between different assessors or assessments. In these circumstances, reliability is not an issue. (Burke and Jessup, 1990)

The basis for these declarations is threefold. First, that validity can only be judged against how well the published standards accurately reflect the occupational situation whose functions have been analyzed. Second, that reliability is a concept only applicable to norm-referenced measurement systems concerned to differentiate between individuals. Third, that if you look after validity, reliability will look after itself.

As for the first assertion, that validity resides in the standards, I go along with the judgment of PRD (Johnson and Blinkhorn, 1992) in accepting the assertion in so far as it covers the intention to use functional analysis to build in content and construct validity — and therefore, face validity. But there is another form of validity in terms of the system's consequences. If some important consequences of introducing NVQs are unintended and undesirable, then the system will not be a valid system. The jury is still out in many of these system level respects.

With regard to the second assertion I am more wary. Prais (1991) has attacked the overemphasis on validity and the reliability of practical testing in NVQs. However, when Prais writes of reliability he does not always stick to a precise use of the term. At one point in his criticisms of the positions taken by those he sees as having 'modern' views, he writes:

> Any lower reliability of such procedures resulting from the supervisor knowing his own trainee or for any other reason, it has sometimes incautiously been suggested, is of no consequence.

This is a telling comment, but not altogether in the sense intended. The obviously curious point is that Prais implies it is some kind of defect for supervisors to know their own trainees. But underneath this there is a more important point: a basic lack of trust in a situation where the trainer is also the assessor. The same view has been in evidence, without open articulation, in successive attempts to deny school teachers any significant role in assessing their own pupils: witness the recent history of ministerial intervention against teachers assessing course work in GCSE and insisting on externally set 'pencil-and-paper' tests for the standard assessment task (SAT) testing at ages 7, 11 and 14. It is important to recognize this line of thought behind these arguments.

Eraut has proposed the following relationship:

Degree of trust in the assessor X Cost of assessment = A constant

Arguments against mentor assessment are almost always advanced on grounds of cost, but the hidden agenda is a lack of trust. Once this is recognized as a true concern, one can set about building arrangements into an assessment system for quality assurance and to provide safeguards at points where assessors may be fallible, either for reasons of underdeveloped assessment skills or because of possible interpersonal bias.

How does this refer to Jessup's position? It means that while, in principle, a perfect validity ought to produce reliability, this statement rests on two crucial assumptions. The first assumption is that it is possible to state competence and attainment through functional analysis (or any other means) in standards which completely, unarguably and faithfully represent performance of an occupation. I leave this assumption for the reader's contemplation. The second assumption is that there can be perfectly reliable interpretations of the perfectly valid statements of competence with all their attendant units, elements, etc. Alison Wolf (1993) has pointed out that there are inherently intractable problems for both norm and criterion-referenced systems in attempting this. The unavoidable tension between overspecification and too high a degree of inference on the part of assessors is the root of these difficulties.

There is also a legitimate question in the public mind about whether an NVQ gained at employer X is fully comparable with the same NVQ gained at employer Y. After all, to be thoroughly mischievous, in a competitive business environment doesn't one employer have a vested interest in misleading another? Or employer X may be known to be spending less on training than employer Y. Is s/he more efficient, or cutting corners? This is exactly the same concept as intermarker reliability in any other situation, and to say that everything will be fine as long as everyone interprets the standards perfectly is not really to dismiss the problem.

There are answers as I have noted above. There need to be procedures in place to ensure quality control. Part of this is the use of internal and external verifiers who are already employed by NVQ awarding bodies directly to ensure consistency of interpretation. The best mix of moderating assessment decisions and moderating assessment procedures is still being worked out. Another procedure could lie in the ideas advanced by Nuttall and Thomas (1993) which build on existing methods of statistical quality assurance to propose a bundle of measures which include cross-verification studies and statistical monitoring using some common written papers for assessment at unit level.

The relevance of the NVQ system is built into the process of derivation of standards and the fairness of the system can be assured using the same methods as are described above for ensuring consistency from assessor to assessor. Which brings us to the question of efficiency or cost.

The unhappy message of the equation above which relates cost of assessment to the degree of trust accorded to the assessors (by the public, or more importantly, politicians) is that a new system cannot afford to be cheap if it is to gain trust. Cost is extremely important. In evaluating an assessment system, one has to examine not only its overt costs but also its hidden costs. The direct fees paid for assessment may represent only a small proportion of the total cost, depending on the amount of time expended by employees of a company or college. This has been a major concern about new patterns of assessment, both NVQs and SATs. The defence has been that most of this time is not extra time: the assessment can become either part of the normal ongoing supervision process or an integral part of the training.

One might expect considerable variation in this respect, not only between different qualifications, but also between different employers and/or providers and between different occupational sectors because the context in which assessments have to be managed can affect costs heavily. It will affect how easily the training and assessment can be built into existing routines and supervisory relationships. There has been, and still is, a tendency to count costs as if they were a total bolt on to existing systems. This was perhaps unintentionally encouraged in early trials for example, in some building society settings, by operating NVQ requirements in addition to, and separate from, existing systems of training instead of NVQs being integrated into ongoing quality assurance processes.

Empirical research is needed to establish a proper basis for costing such assessments and I understand that the National Council for Vocational Qualifications has already commissioned studies in this area. However, I would not be surprised if the cost of NVQ assessments turned out to be greater than that of the system being replaced. These costs will presumably have to be justified by the savings arising from more efficient training (less irrelevant material) and more effective training, resulting in improvements in the quality of job performance.

Will NVQs Succeed in Their Aims?

The first part of the answer to this question depends on whether and why NVQs are taken up. Evidence of take-up is accumulating. A recent national survey of 2000 employers by the Institute of Management Studies (Callender *et al*, 1994) reported that almost half of large employers (>500) are currently using NVQs and a further 30 per cent are planning to do so, but only 6 per cent of small companies are using them. Half the users reported difficulties in the implementation of NVQs, the most common difficulty being with assessment. Smaller studies have been undertaken by IMS in the construction and retail sectors (Callender, 1992; Toye, 1994). Toye (1994) concluded:

The overall impact of competence based systems within the UK will be immense. While many larger employers may continue to use and develop their own systems, the outcome-led national system of NVQs and GNVQs will be the main influence on design of training and on assessment. (p. 18)

But the question of success really depends on whether the NVQ Model can fulfil the aspirations which have been put upon it. One worry is that the mechanisms by which efficient training methods, once discovered, will be disseminated through the system remain undescribed. Indeed, moves to introduce competition between schools and colleges, as there is between businesses, militate against the dissemination of profitable innovation. Thus effects on the workplace are likely to emerge slowly over time and probably have three manifestations.

- a gradual adjustment of work practices to take account of the greater availability of well qualified workers;
- workers will start to appear with a different range of skills which can be deployed to advantage in the organization;
- and from work-based training a greater awareness will develop of ways in which the central goals of the organization may be attained.

The assumption behind this scenario is that the enticement to 'Teach to the test' will result in higher skill levels. This ultimately depends on candidates and providers finding and inventing more effective routes to the qualifications. The one realistic expectation is that success will be partial and, as ever, it will be exceedingly difficult to demonstrate convincingly. Goldstein (1983) has described the technical reasons why it is almost impossible to prove, beyond a reasonable doubt, real changes in educational standards over time. But far more serious is the attitude of key opinion formers. One has only to look at the experience over recent times with reactions to rises in GCSE pass rates. However, in one important respect NVQs have already succeeded. They have begun to seep across the academic/vocational divide in the shape of GNVQs and the Enterprise Initiative in HE (cf Burke, 1991). And for a small select band of assessment freaks it will be a success if it continues to broaden and deepen our knowledge, understanding, skills and competence in the future work on assessment.

Acknowledgments

My thanks for comments on this chapter go to Michael Eraut, Ann Hill, David Stuart and Harry Torrance, and to Paul Mitchell for permission to draw upon his research data. During the period of preparation of this chapter I was sponsored by NCVQ to investigate the area of work-based assessment.

References

BARTRAM, D. (1992) *Defining Sufficiency of Evidence for the Assessment of NVQs*, Sheffield, Employment Department.

BURKE, J. (1990) *Competency Based Education and Training*, London, Falmer Press.

BURKE, J. (1991) 'Competence and higher education: Implications for institutions and professional bodies' in RAGGATT, P. and UNWIN, L. (Eds) *Change and Intervention: Vocational Education and Training*, London, Falmer Press.

BURKE, J. and JESSUP, G. (1990) 'Assessment in NVQs: Disentangling validity from reliability in the assessment of NVQs' in HORTON, T. (Ed) *Assessment Debates*, London, Hodder & Stoughton for the Open University.

CALLENDER, C. (1992) *Will NVQs Work? Evidence from the Construction Industry*, Falmer, Institute of Manpower Studies.

CALLENDER, C. *et al* (1994) *National and Scottish Vocational Qualifications: Early Indications of Employer's Take-up and Use*, Falmer, Institute of Manpower Studies.

GOLDSTEIN, H. (1983) 'Measuring changes in educational attainment over time: Problems and possibilities', *Journal of Educational Measurement, 20*, 4, pp. 369–77.

HARNEY, A. and WARD, C. (1991) *Assessment and Verification in NVQs — Emerging Patterns*, Internal Report for NCVQ.

JESSUP, G. (1991) *Out comes: NVQs and the Emerging Model of Education and Training*, London, Falmer Press.

JOHNSON, C. and BLINKHORN, S. (1992) *Validating NVQ Assessment*, R&D Series Report No 7, Sheffield, Employment Department.

MITCHELL, L. and CUTHBERT, T. (1989a) *The Caterbase Project: Workplace Assessment and Accreditation for the Hotel and Catering Industry*, R&D Series Report No 2, Sheffield, Employment Department.

MITCHELL, L. and CUTHBERT, T. (1989b) *Insufficient Evidence? Report of the Competency Testing Project Based at Scotvec*, Briefing Series Report No 2, Sheffield, Employment Department.

NUTTALL, D. and THOMAS, S. (1993) *Monitoring Procedures Based on Centre Performance Variables*, R&D Series Report No 11, Sheffield, Employment Department.

PRAIS, S.J. (1991) 'Vocational qualifications in Britain and Europe: Theory and practice', *National Institute Economic Review*, May, pp. 86–92.

SCOTVEC (1990) *Credit Through Workplace Assessment*, Edinburgh, SCOTVEC.

TOYE, J. (1994) *The Use in Employment of NVQs and Other Competence Based Systems*, Employment Brief No 27, Falmer, Institute of Manpower Studies.

J. TRILL ASSOCS. (1992) *The Site Supervisor/Site Manager Assessment Project*, Sheffield, Employment Department.

WOLF, A. (1993) *Assessment Issues and Problems in a Criterion-Based System*, London, Further Education Unit.

WOOD, R. (1990) 'The agenda for educational measurement' in HORTON, T. (Ed) *Assessment Debates*, London, Hodder and Stoughton for the Open University.

WOOD, R., BLINKHORN, S., JOHNSON, C. and ANDERSON, S. (1989) *Boning, Blanching and Backtacking: Assessing Performance in the Workplace*, Briefing Series Report No 1, Sheffield, Employment Department.

Chapter 13

Outcomes and Autonomy

Stephen McNair

Introduction

This chapter explores the relationship between the idea of individual autonomy and an outcomes led approach to learning. It begins from a belief that an undue concentration on educational processes has led us in the past to neglect achievement, and the result has been an education and training system which lacked accountability, was inaccessible and inefficient, and where 'quality' and 'standards' formed a powerful, but fragile, organizing myth.

The development of a knowledge-based economy, and mass lifelong learning requires that as a community we find better ways of understanding, developing and accrediting achievement — of the outcomes of all learning, whether it be institutional, workbased, or voluntary; formal or informal; further, higher or adult; vocational, general or academic. However, this does not imply that existing models of outcomes are satisfactory. Rather, I believe that a better 'language of outcomes', and better ways of using that language, could support the creation of a society where individuals were more autonomous, and that this will benefit both individual and society.

The issue of individual autonomy in a post-industrial society is a complex one, and this chapter does not claim to be authoritative in all the academic fields which it touches on. Rather I approach this issue as someone who has worked for more than twenty years with adult learners, ten of them at the interface between education and public policy. I believe that a more open, democratic learning society would be more economically productive and more rewarding for its members, and that this can only be achieved through more open debate and exploration of ideas and practice where none of us have clear answers. This chapter therefore seeks to raise some new questions, and contribute to that ongoing debate. It is an invitation to dialogue, not a summary of conclusions.

Why Autonomy Matters

The principal driving force for change in British education and training in the last fifteen years has been the concern to match our competitor nations in terms of the skills base of the economy. This has dominated thinking about educational change, and has been graphically highlighted by Sir Christopher Ball's work for the RSA (Ball, 1990a and 1990b), which has attempted to define a common ground between those whose objectives are purely instrumental, and those concerned with personal growth and fulfilment for more altruistic reasons. The argument is that we have inherited a culture built on selection and exclusion, and one which sets low expectations of most individuals, to which they respond with low achievement. The resultant loss of human potential is a waste both for the individuals, whose lives could be richer and more satisfying, and for society, which fails to make maximum economic use of its principal resource — the human talent of the population. To overcome this we must find ways of increasing individual motivation, and developing each individual's unique potential.

At the same time we have seen widespread disillusion with collectivist social policies, not only in terms of the role of the state, but of large employers. The dominant ideology of Britain in the 1980s sought to transfer responsibility from the state and employer back to the individual. Increasing economic instability and volatility in the labour market coincided with a growing view that the increasing pace of technological change implies multiple careers and less dependence of individuals on single employers. This was reflected in the CBI's launch of the notion of 'careership' (CBI, 1989) which stressed the need to encourage individuals to think of their careers as something which they owned, planned and managed themselves as they moved in an out of employment and learning throughout their lives. At the same time, the growth of educational and vocational guidance, and employee development schemes in their different ways reflected the fact that individual empowerment had become a matter of urgent public policy.

This economic trend has brought those with instrumental economic objectives close to a much older tradition of interest in autonomy, represented in the long standing concern of educators, and especially perhaps adult educators, with personal growth. Maslow and Rogers, for example, emphasize developing the potential of individuals in order to enable them to live the most satisfying lives possible (Rogers and Stevens, 1987). They stress individual self-actualization and the creation of personal meaning as the only true goal of learning (not, note, 'education'), and explicitly reject instrumental approaches: as Jourard (1972) argues, 'learning is not a problem or a task, it is a way to be in the world'. For adults, Maslow (1968) argues, delight and boredom are the fundamental criteria which determine what and how adults choose to learn.

A further argument for autonomy concerns the functioning of a mature democracy. The roots of this tradition go back at least to Forster's argument in introducing the 1880 Education Act that 'we must educate our masters'. In adult education these ideas blossomed in the aftermath of the two World Wars, perhaps especially in the 1919 Ministry of Reconstruction report. The central idea is of lifelong learning as the foundation of a democracy, where individuals are empowered through education to act autonomously, both individually and collectively, for the good of society and themselves.

Underlying the most recent developments is a fundamental shift in attitudes to the relationship between individuals and the state, and between employers and employees. Viewed positively, it assumes that the individual should become a more active partner in economic and social processes, and that if the requirements of particular kinds of employment, and the skills which individuals have, are made more explicit, a more equal and creative relationship is possible. Viewed negatively, on the other hand, the autonomous individual can be isolated, politically and economically weaker, at least in the short term, than the dependent one. It is not therefore surprising that attempts to encourage individual autonomy among employees, through employee development schemes, for example, have sometimes been perceived as attempts by employers to evade responsibility for proper pay or job security.

What Do We Mean by Autonomy?

Whatever the rationale, the promotion of individual autonomy has become an issue worth exploring, and while this chapter is not the place to present a philosophical dissertation on the nature of autonomy, a working definition is needed if we are to explore the relationship between autonomy and outcomes. The following characteristics would probably command fairly widespread agreement. I take it that autonomy is:

- a positive quality — we would regard someone who did not seek to become more autonomous as abnormal;
- an internal quality — related to the individuals' sense of themselves, rather than to their environment;
- related to personal power — autonomy enables the individual to make decisions and act to change her world, however large or small that may be;
- independent of particular circumstances — a wider range of choices does not make one more autonomous, although it does provide more opportunity to exercise autonomy;
- demonstrated in a context — we recognize autonomy through what people do or think in the real world. Thus it may be more evident in the personal, educational or vocational sphere, but there is no such thing as 'vocational autonomy' per se;
- a matter of degree — one is not either autonomous or not autonomous, one is more or less autonomous;
- a quality which can develop, and be developed;
- not necessarily individualistic — the autonomous individual can choose whether to act with, against or independently of others;
- distinct from isolation — an autonomous person may choose to live as a hermit, but living alone is not the same as being autonomous.

Since autonomy relates to the will to act, not the range of actions possible, we will not succeed in creating autonomous people by changing the environment alone. Our primary concern must be to find ways of changing their psychological state. If an outcome-led approach to education and training is to maximize autonomy, it must address how people feel about themselves.

Autonomy and Adult Learning

This issue has been one of the principal strands of thinking about the education of adults for several decades. It is therefore perhaps useful to examine briefly the insights which come from this theoretical perspective. This is not to imply that autonomy is not an issue in initial education, or that no important and relevant work has been done there. It does reflect, however, that educators working outside the constraints of compulsory initial education see learning in a rather different way, and that these insights may be particularly relevant to the present argument.

In talking about adult learning we are not primarily concerned with something which happens in formal institutions under the direction of professional teachers. Most adult learning happens outside the formal education system, in the workplace and the home, and most of it without the benefit of formal teaching of any kind. The typical adult learner gathers ideas and knowledge eclectically, drawing on resources, academic disciplines and the assistance of friends, colleagues and supervisors as they seem relevant to the issue in hand. Such learning is often exploratory, driven by ill-defined aims or by simple curiosity. There is no doubt that the outcome matters, but it is often not clearly specified in advance, and even where the intended outcomes were carefully planned, unintended ones sometimes prove more useful or interesting.

Perhaps the most helpful model of adult learning for our purposes is that of 'andragogy'. Malcolm Knowles (1990) has distinguished andragogy from 'pedagogy' precisely because, unlike pedagogy (which he argues is characteristic of traditional models of initial education for young people), andragogy assumes that the learner is in some degree autonomous, and seeks to increase that autonomy through learning. He summarizes the theory of andragogy in six principles of adult learning:

Need to know	Adults need to know why they need to learn something before undertaking it.
Self-concept	Adults need to be recognized as capable of self-direction, and they resist teachers imposing their wills. If they meet resistance of this kind, the result is either surface learning or none at all.
Role of experience	Experience provides simultaneously a resource, a starting point and a source of blocks to learning. Adults also define themselves in terms of their experience, and resist its devaluation.
Readiness to learn	Adults seek learning in response to felt needs.
Orientation to learning	Adults learn better within frames set by their own problems, rather than other people's knowledge structures.
Motivation	Adults are most powerfully motivated by internal pressures like job satisfaction, self-esteem or quality of life, rather than simply promotion or higher salaries.

The common link between these elements is the focus on the individual's unique qualities, and sense of self: the key questions are 'who am I?', 'who do I want to be?' (rather than what) and 'how will this learning help me to become this?' This is true not only of those learning tasks which are clearly directed to personal fulfilment, but also to learning with more practical and instrumental purposes, and this is widely recognized in the practice of trainers working with adults. Thus the learning processes needed to achieve instrumental ends often reflect a 'liberal' educational philosophy.

It is not a coincidence that much work on adult learning focuses on the notion of 'self-confidence', which is often the term used to describe how adults change in the course of learning. Jones and Charnley (1978), for example, drew attention to how much more highly this was rated by adult literacy students than measurable performance in reading. It was clear that for learners and teachers there was an inner quality, about how people felt about themselves, which was of central importance to them.

Autonomy is at the centre of Knowles' vision of andragogy, and it is certainly possible to argue that the development of autonomy underpins most of our notions of level and progression in education and training. The NVQ levels of supervision (NCVQ, 1991), the Dreyfus and Dreyfus 'novice-expert' model (Dreyfus and Dreyfus, 1992), the SOLO taxonomy (Biggs and Collis, 1982), and academic progression from secondary to higher education, all reflect a notion of progression founded, at least in part, on growing individual autonomy.

What, then, can andragogy teach us about the development of autonomy? Firstly, and perhaps most importantly, that, however narrow and specific the learning objectives may be, learning will increase autonomy most if it recognizes and builds on the individual's sense of self. In the strict sense, adult learning is about the 'recreation' of the individual. In Eraut's (1992) terms it begins with 'personal knowledge', which starts with impressions, and uses reflection and synthesis to build this into a 'scheme of experience'—an internal map of the self and its relationship to the world. Unless it begins with personal knowledge (knowledge why) it will never arrive at process knowledge (knowledge how), let alone propositional knowledge (knowledge that).

If this is so, then the key to developing autonomy must lie in enabling individuals to relate their learning to their sense of self, which points to a familiar agenda of strategies based on deep, rather than surface learning, positive uses of assessment, the development of critical and reflective skills. It also suggests that personal ownership of what is being learned and achieved will be critical. If an outcome-led approach is to increase autonomy it must increase each individual's sense of owning her achievement.

A Language of Outcomes

The central notion of an outcome-led approach to education and training is simple. It is that the purpose of all serious learning is to change the learner, and that its effectiveness can only logically be measured in terms of those changes. Outcome descriptions are therefore explicit statements of achievement: what someone can do, know or understand as a result of a piece of formal or informal learning — something possible now that was not possible before. In using the term like this I am also assuming that any new human achievement is the result of learning, that for practical purposes 'outcomes' and 'learning outcomes' are therefore the same thing, and that many kinds of human achievement, including occupational competence, can be described in outcome terms.

The development of an outcome-led approach to education and training is, in a sense, the creation of a new language, to support new kinds of communication about human achievement. It is therefore worth reflecting on the characteristics of language itself, and what light this sheds on the development of this particular example. This is particularly relevant to this chapter, since language defines a culture, reflecting and shaping its values and priorities, embodying a set of ways of seeing the world, and its vocabulary defines what objects and ideas can be discussed and recognized, and how they will be valued. It is within this framework that we define our identity, which is intimately linked to our individual autonomy.

Language permits communication where it was not previously possible, enabling people to collaborate to achieve more than they could individually. When writing is added to the spoken language it becomes possible to communicate more widely and to collaborate at a distance, but as the circle expands we have to formalize the linguistic conventions, since we are now communicating with people who share less with us in common experience and ongoing dialogue. The development of a new language of outcomes is part of a process of expanding the community in which human achievement is understood and discussed, and making new kinds of collaboration possible. It is about crossing traditional boundaries, and opening the 'secret gardens' of crafts, professions and academia.

Language defines community — who is, and is not, a member of the group — and it can range from the intensely personal to the highly formalized. At the personal end lies the language I use with those closest to me, full of personal references, private jokes and overtones which mean something only to those who know me well. We change this language continuously in dialogue and in the light of our evolving shared experiences, reinforcing our shared values, and refreshing our sense of our own identity by excluding others from our private dialogue. Beyond the circle of personal language lie versions of language which are common to a profession, class, region or nation. These too are subtle, complex and changing, each community collectively evolving their own ways of thinking, and value systems, while at the outermost range of the language lie highly formalized versions, like the English of the air traffic controller, or restaurateur's French, which enable people who have no other knowledge of the language, to communicate with each other in very specific, and very critical contexts. To do this they use a highly controlled vocabulary and grammar, designed to maximize precision by minimizing ambiguity, flexibility and individual ownership.

A language also has a vocabulary, which defines what concepts and objects can be recognized. Things which are not valued do not have names, and if a word does not exist, it is difficult for us to discuss the concept. At one level this is simple — an Inuit has a larger vocabulary for kinds of snow, and a smaller one for kinds of camel than an Arabic speaker — but at another, superficially similar words carry fundamentally different overtones, buried in their linguistic roots and associations, created through ongoing dialogue and tradition. This points to a crucial distinction between a language which one can manipulate superficially, and one which one 'speaks' in the full sense. Armed with a phrase book I can communicate at a superficial level with a native Russian speaker but, in what I read out, he will hear layers of subtlety which I cannot detect, and may not have meant. The phrase book does not enable me to identify these overtones, nor to extrapolate the underlying rules of the language which would enable me to increase my understanding. Unless I talk to him in a common language, or through a bilingual interpreter, I must continue to think in English, and translate crudely, and the messages I convey will not be genuinely my own. In considering a language of outcomes, we may wish to reflect on how far we are creating phrasebooks, rather than languages.

Language enables change to take place. Living languages are in constant evolution, under internal and external pressures, and changes in vocabulary and syntax make it possible to recognize new concepts, lose old ones and develop new ways of communicating. Most of the time this is done through dialogue — direct or in writing, and though some societies (like the French) have tried to formalize the recognition of new forms and words, most languages evolve through the vast body of conversation. This is not merely a question of acquiring new vocabulary (as English has acquired new words, from 'ship' to 'samosa'), it is also a question of evolving concepts and values. As we lose, through repeated usage, the distinction between 'disinterested' and 'uninterested', we lose the way to simply distinguish the concepts themselves. At a more elaborate level, our ability to use metaphor makes it possible for language itself to generate new ideas. When, for example, we start to talk about 'internal contracting' in the management of organizations, we are using metaphor to create a new concept. In doing so we change the status which we attach to particular kinds of relationship, developing our own value system, as well as our understanding of managerial relationships.

Outcomes: Being Explicit

The first thing which the language of outcomes does is to open conversation about achievement to a wider community. When outcomes are explicit and visible it is easier to see what is possible, in learning or employment, and what routes must be followed to achieve it. An outcome-led approach thus gives individuals more opportunity to make informed choices, and to match their interests, needs and talents to the requirements of the real world. This is undoubtedly a step forward from the traditional 'trust the expert' model, where many of the criteria, standards and judgments were based on hidden, and sometimes questionable, beliefs and assumptions in the heads of those within a closed academic or employment culture.

However, proponents of an outcome-led approach have sometimes seemed to claim that absolute explicitness and objectivity in outcome descriptions is possible, and should be pursued at any cost. However, such explicitness in the written description of human achievement is bound to fail, unless it limits itself to the entirely trivial, and to pursue the quest too far is to lose sight of the real world behind a mountain of paper. The NVQ experience demonstrates this. A relatively simple structure has, over time, become increasingly elaborated: we have added to the key purposes, units and elements, a burgeoning structure of performance criteria, range statements, guidance on assessment and on underpinning knowledge and understanding. Each stage represents an increase in precision, and yet increasing elaboration makes the whole increasingly difficult to comprehend. Thus the development of standards involves a constant tension between technical completeness, which pulls towards greater detail and complexity, and intelligibility, which presses for simplicity and elegance. Paradoxically, the attempt to make things intelligible may ultimately make them too complex for their users to grasp: if the manual is too long and intimidating to read, I may decide not to look at it at all, whatever other people may tell me to do.

Outcomes: Talking to Each Other

Explicitness makes choice easier, but if my autonomy is to be increased outcomes must also help me change the way I feel about those choices, and increase my sense of my power over my life and the world. To do this I must feel that it is, at least in some sense, my language, describing those things closest to my own identity, and enabling me to grow and develop. If the language of outcomes is to increase individual autonomy we must therefore address at least three questions — whose values and culture does the language support? can it recognize the personal and collective achievements which are closest to autonomy? and can it accommodate and support continuing change, in the individual and the world around?

Whose Values and Culture?

Whether our motives are economic or ideological, in most fields our society no longer accepts the right of small elites to define standards, unchallenged by the consumer. We also believe that we need far more people to learn more, faster, than traditional mechanisms allow. It follows that we need processes to make explicit and public what was previously private: and outcomes provide us with a language to do this. However if this new language is to increase autonomy, we need to consider carefully how far the structures, vocabulary and processes of development of the language include or exclude those whom we wish to empower.

The problem was vividly demonstrated in the UDACE project on Learning Outcomes in Higher Education (Otter, 1992), which explored how the outcomes of HE were understood and described by employers, academics and students. Not only did the three groups describe different things as the outcomes of the same process, they also used different language to do so. If my achievement is expressed in language which I perceive as alien, or imposing a set of values which I don't recognize, I must either reject the language or reject my sense of my self. However, since my existing language defines and reinforces existing cultural and professional structures, if this is to change I must learn the new language, and to feel a sense of ownership of it.

The dilemma of ownership is demonstrated vividly in the case of NVQ occupational standards. Here, the Government's intention is for the structure of the language to be defined by NCVQ and the Employment Department, while the vocabulary is defined by employment interests. The intermediaries between these forces are the lead bodies, and the professional standards consultants. Despite the intention to give ownership to the employer, the strategy tends, inevitably perhaps, to militate against this. The need to formalize the language, to make it explicit to the wider community, creates a key role for specialist consultants as custodians of the grammar, and this in turn creates a barrier between the employers and the language, as has become evident in some recent criticism (Everard, 1993). This problem applies even more to those who practise the competence described, and this perhaps explains why the process of accrediting prior learning (APL) in NVQs has proved more elaborate and time consuming than many hoped. While APL bypasses the formal course, it still requires that the individual learns a new language in which to describe and present their achievement.

Can the Language Recognize Autonomy?

One of the commonest criticisms of an outcome-led approach to learning is that some, and perhaps the most important, outcomes can be developed, but cannot be defined and assessed. If this is the case, the approach is bound to divert attention away from what matters to what is measurable. At the core of this debate are personal skills, 'process outcomes' and collective achievement.

Personal skills are important to individuals and to the economy. They are also centrally related to individual autonomy, but they are difficult to measure, as is autonomy itself. Nevertheless, any language to describe human achievement which did not recognize them would have failed.

It is difficult to conceive of an autonomous individual who was not good, at things which have often been defined as personal transferable skills, and research has repeatedly shown that qualities like planning, taking initiative, making decisions, problem solving, learning independently, and communicating with others are highly prized by employers, teachers and individuals. However, because such outcomes are less easy to describe and assess than many more mechanical activities, it has often been assumed that the only cost effective way of measuring them is by proxy — on the basis that those who have been through a particular kind of process can be assumed to have arrived at the outcome. It is believed, for example, that there are some outcomes of traditional British higher education, fundamental to our notion of what a degree is, which are produced by three years residence in a specific place. These are rarely defined and almost never assessed, and yet despite this, in some universities, only those who have been through the process can get the qualification.

While there may be disagreement about the degree to which some achievements can be measured, it is self evident, as Jessup (1991) has pointed out, that if an achievement can be described it must be, possible to assess it. The existence of the word in our vocabulary implies that a number of people could agree about whether it was, or was not, present in a given situation, and within some limits they are likely to be able to agree about how well it was achieved. If the language of outcomes cannot articulate these qualities, it has failed, and those who are designing the language need then to review how it works, not relegate such important issues to the realm of mystery from which we have been emerging. Fortunately, there is evidence that such qualities can be assessed with a reasonable degree of accuracy. Examples include recent work by the Employment Department on Personal Competencies, and earlier UDACE work on student potential (Otter, 1989) and the competencies of entrants to higher education (Otter, 1991). However, the issue remains unresolved of how they can be best integrated into structures of formal qualification.

Collective outcomes present a different issue. There are a wide range of educational or development processes whose principal outcomes are collective rather than individual. However, although the principal strategy for defining occupational standards in outcome terms in Britain is functional analysis, which begins with collective purposes rather than individual activity, the end result is a very individualist one.

Collective outcomes are very varied. At the community development end of adult education, groups come together to learn how to challenge a road scheme, produce a local history or address a social problem, but collective outcomes are also evident where a quality circle learns to improve the quality of a product, or a professional group meet to refine their own practice. In all cases there can be individual achievements, but it would be perverse to suggest that they are always the most significant. Collective outcomes present us with two problems. Most importantly, individual autonomy is often substantially enhanced by the experience of being a member of a 'winning team' even if the individual's measurable outcomes are very limited. Group processes, well-managed, can be very powerful sources of support and motivation to individual self confidence which is central to individual autonomy. The second problem is that the development of a language of outcomes to define individual achievement more clearly, may end up diverting attention from important collective ones.

Integration, Change and Development

The final question is how far the language of outcomes can support the continuing growth of the individual, and a changing world around. The arguments touched on earlier suggest that individuals, in approaching their own learning, seek to build new achievement into a pattern which they perceive as a whole. I am likely to reject, and not learn (at any deep level) ideas and knowledge which challenge my sense of self too radically, or which I cannot relate to who I think I am, or want to be. In so far as a language of outcomes helps me to add new dimensions to my evolving self they will support my autonomy, but if they encourage me to think of myself as a bundle of dissociated skills or knowledge they will reduce my power over myself and my world. It follows that, if outcomes are to be useful to me, I need tools for integrating them, as well as analyzing them, to counteract the dangers of reductionism inherent in many approaches to outcome definition.

There is a particular problem here that effective lifelong learners are continually reflecting on previous learning and experience, reconfiguring it into new 'schemes of experience'. There will thus be outcomes which do not manifest themselves, or whose significance does not become apparent, for months or years, and there is a danger that such learning will be devalued if the performance of education and training services comes to be evaluated against its ability to deliver outcomes in too short a timescale. If premature judgments are made about the relevance or impact of particular learning, valuable outcomes may be devalued or lost.

Traditional education, training and professional development processes allow individuals to talk to each other about change, and to evolve new individual and collective responses within the closed community. We cannot replicate the closed dialogue of the traditional professional group across the whole of society, but neither can we commit everything to paper. We need a new solution to the problem of what, in a much wider and more complex community, will replace the internal dialogue of the profession. There may be some clue to this in the experience of some of those who use functional analysis for the development of occupational standards, but have found the process itself a powerful tool for professional development, helping the organization and its members to understand what they do, and why, more clearly. Without the tool of functional analysis and the language of outcomes this process would be less productive: but without the dialogue it would be less empowering for the participants.

Conclusion

There are many reasons to believe in the development of individual autonomy. They include a view about the importance of individual growth and fulfilment; a commitment to a more active and democratic society; a belief about the economic need to tap the full potential of the population. They may also include equally powerful arguments about dependence and independence. In the circumstances of the 1990s, both the state and employers may be more fearful of the potential burden of looking after us, than they are of our freedom. Autonomous individuals look after themselves: dependent ones have to be provided for. Whatever the motivation, those who do believe in individual autonomy would do well to capitalize on the expressed interest, and consider carefully how the development of an outcome-led education and training system might contribute.

Firstly, explicitness matters. There is no doubt that exposing hidden criteria and standards and developing explicit descriptions of individual achievement provides individuals with greater choice, and more opportunity to exercise their autonomy. The critical issues here are to ensure that the vocabulary and structures of the language can recognize all the qualities which are valued, and do not, by accident or design, exclude important achievements. We need to ensure that the descriptions are usable, steering the course between unmanageable elaboration and oversimplification, and ensuring that the language is not formulated or policed in ways which exclude particular individuals or groups. If we wish to develop the potential of all individuals, and autonomy is an essential part of this, then we must have a language of outcomes which can embrace a multiplicity of cultures, value systems and schemes of experience.

However, explicitness alone is not enough to develop autonomy, which is concerned with how people see themselves, and their motivation. For this people need both choice and a means to relate themselves to the changing world around. This requires that we address rather different questions, for which we need a language, rather than a catalogue. A language can enable us to talk together, to develop and refine understanding and construct personal patterns of meaning, and to reshape the world. Outcome descriptions can provide a basis for such a language, but if they are to do so we need to develop not only the form in which we describe them, but the way they are used. We need a language which is intelligible to a wider range of stakeholders, and which invites more people into ongoing dialogue. It is the active engagement which goes with contributing to definition, reflecting on practice and debating the assessment of achievement which will make us autonomous.

This will call for a wide and diverse dialogue, embracing those who describe outcomes, those who demonstrate them and those who use them. The central purpose of this language must be not to ask 'has my achievement satisfied you?' but 'do we agree that this is right?' and 'what makes it right?'. This is the dialogue of professional education in its traditional, perhaps idealized, form, where new recruits are initially dependent on dialogue with senior members to help them to understand what achievement is. As they develop and increase their competence, they internalize those definitions, criteria and values, and come to be confident in the ability to understand them, to enter into a debate in which the whole profession, reflects on, challenges and evolves its understanding of achievement, and passes those findings on to new members and each other.

The challenge is to take this professional model, which is itself an empowering and developmental one, and extend it to a much larger community and a much larger range of activity. We want to find ways of ensuring that all individuals feel ownership of their own achievement, and are contributors to the constant evolution of the notion of achievement itself, in the same way that some professions have done, on a smaller scale, in the past.

There are many ways in which this can, and is being done. Quality circles and total quality management are examples in the world of work, functional analysis in staff and organizational development are others. In the educational context processes of recording achievement, action planning and collaborative approaches to accreditation through Open College Networks, are all examples of attempts, using an outcome-based language, to create the ongoing dialogue across traditional cultural barriers.

At the core of all this debate is the notion of a community of interest, in which a wide range and diversity of qualities are valued and recognised, and a language is available in which individuals can debate and develop their own understanding of their competence and opportunities. A language of outcomes might do this, and there are encouraging signs, but there are also dangers, of over-formalizing and overdependence on written language to handle things which can only be understood through discussion. More fundamentally, we cannot avoid the crucial political question of who is to be allowed into this dialogue. If we really wish to develop all the human resources of our community we need a language which is as inclusive as possible, and where dialogue is actively encouraged. If we construct the language of outcomes in a way which excludes many people, or which prevents change or dialogue we may increase choice, but we will not fully empower. It would be a sad end to an important enterprise.

References

BALL, C. (1990a) *Learning Pays*, London, RSA.

BALL, C. (1990b) *More Means Different*, London, RSA.

BIGGS, J.B. and COLLIS, K.F. (1982) 'Enhancing the quality of learning: The SOLO taxonomy' quoted by Gibbs in BARNETT, R. (Ed) *Learning to Effect*, London, SRHE/Open University.

CBI (1989) *Towards a Skills Revolution*, London, CBI.

DREYFUS, H.L. and DREYFUS, S.E. (1992) quoted in BARNETT, R. (Ed) *Learning to Effect*, London, SRHE/Open University.

ERAUT, M. (1992) 'Developing the knowledge base', in BARNETT, R. (Ed) *Learning to Effect*, London, SRHE/Open University.

EVERARD, B. (1993) in 'Transition'. BACIE, London, April.

JESSUP, G. (1991) *Outcomes: NVQs and the Emerging Model of Education and Training*, London, Falmer Press.

JONES, A. and CHARNLEY, A. (1978) *Adult Literacy: A Study of its Impact*, Paris, NIACE.

JOURARD, S.M. (1977) 'The psychology of open teaching and learning' quoted in KNOWLES, M. (Ed) (1990) *The Adult Learner*, Houston, TX, Gulf.

KNOWLES, M. (Ed) (1990) *The Adult Learner: a Neglected Species*, Houston, Gulf.

MASLOW, A.H. (1968) *Towards a Psychology of Being*, New York, Van Nostrand

NCVQ (1991) Guide to National Vocational Qualifications, London, NCVQ.

OTTER, S. (1989) *Student Potential in Britain*, Leicester, UDACE/NIACE.

OTTER, S. (1991) Admission to Science and Engineering Degree Courses: A Handbook for Admissions Tutors, BP/UDACE, 1991.

OTTER, S. (1992) *Learning Outcomes in Higher Education*, Leicester, UDACE/NIACE.

ROGERS, C. and STEVENS, B. (1987) *The Problem of Being Human*, London, Souvenir Press.

Chapter 14

Work-based Learning and Outcomes

Margaret Levy

Introduction

This chapter is concerned with a specific model of work-based learning, *Work-Based Learning: A Good Practice Model* (Levy, 1991). This model was described at its initiation as outcomes-oriented, and could be perceived as having contributed to the genesis of the Jessup outcomes model. Readers may find that the work-based learning (WBL) model illuminates some of the issues associated with the Jessup model. The WBL model was explicit in its overall aims, values and purposes: to develop the skills base of the UK workforce to support UK economic needs.

The chapter is divided into three parts: the first deals with the R&D approaches to developing the 'good practice model' and the tools and strategies for its implementation; the second deals with the model itself; and the third looks at outcomes and learning issues.

Developing the Good Practice Model and Tools and Strategies for its Implementation

Background

The author joined an MSC policy branch in September 1981 and shortly afterwards introduced the phrase '*work-based learning*' to the training and development community and presented a proposal for research and development (R&D) on a work-based learning (WBL) model for the delivery of vocational education and training (VET). This became one of the Manpower Services Commission's (MSC) major projects and was funded from 1982 to 1985 by the European Social Fund and funding was continued from 1986 to 1990 by the MSC and Training Agency. The work was led by the author first from within MSC and, following her resignation from MSC in 1984, from the Staff College.

September 1981 was a positive time for developers in MSC:

- The New Training Initiative (NTI) consultations had resulted in the publication of a Government White Paper on training, *A Programme for Action*, in December, followed within a few days by the MSC document *NTI — An Agenda for Action*.

- The aims and issues associated with the system had been clearly spelled out and apparently a consensus had been reached.
- There was considerable hope and determination in the MSC that at last the country was going to have a first class (if not world class) vocational education and training (VET) system.
- There was apparently no shortage of money to support the development of a new system.

There were nevertheless many lobby bodies wanting to ensure their views were heard and taken account of in development work, particularly in the high profile but incipient youth training scheme. For a full exposition of the political background around this period see Keep (1986). One of the advantages of obtaining European Social Fund money for a three-and-a-half-year R&D project was that there was less interference with the R&D aims, unlike some MSC research projects which were subject to requests for change of remit en route — sometimes as much as one year into a two-year project. There is a problem for developers/researchers when lobby bodies persuade ministers and their advisors to intervene and support only that part of development work/research which seems to them to be politically user-friendly at that time. It makes long-term development work extremely difficult to manage.

Curriculum Influences on the Work-based Learning R&D Work

One difficulty curriculum developers face in working in a highly political environment is that it is not always expedient to be totally explicit about curriculum aims/values and their implementation, if funding and support of employers and Government is required. For example, if the intention is to develop a VET model which under Government policy is to be funded mainly by employers, it may not be politically feasible to emphasize that improved general education and personal development for 16–18s is one of the aims of the model. Key contributors to VET policy development also have to ensure they are aware of the value systems among interested parties since these can affect implementation strategies and the outcomes of those strategies. The author has expressed concern (Levy, 1992a) that any new UK VET model, could fail in its intentions if account were not taken of how institutions and individuals might distort its intended practice and procedures to serve their own values and purposes. The paper explores this in relation to *recognizing achievement*, and lists twelve ways in which the outcomes of achievement (NVQs) might be used outside the intention of the developers.

Two excellent curriculum documents from FEU influenced the development of the work-based learning model. The first, *Experience, Reflection, Learning* (FEU, 1978), provided considerable insight into curricular approaches to melding work activity with learning opportunities, utilized an adult learning model and emphasized that 'training and education are related aspects of a single process of learning designed both to prepare for employment and to lead to a broader personal development'. The second, *Developing Social and Life Skills* (FEU, 1980), provided important insights into values and perceptions held by tutors, teachers, trainers and the way this affected the learning approaches, content and opportunities *they* thought should be offered to learners (fieldwork evidence from WBL R&D during 1983 to 1985 confirmed and added to this information, see Oates, 1987).

Also influential was the *Model of the Curriculum in Action* (Eraut *et al*, 1975). This emphasized the need to recognize, whether covertly or explicitly, that all curriculum models have underlying aims or values (declared or assumed justification for the curriculum activities) and these in turn lead to the identification of four curriculum components: (i) declared objectives/outcomes (which can include aspirations and expectations), (ii) learning approaches, (iii) learning content and (iv) evaluation/assessment unified through aims. Eraut highlighted the interaction and interdependence of all four components and pointed out the need to ensure their consistency in relation to the overall aims. This is exceptionally important particularly in a model which has specific economic aims, and has major implications when trying to transfer a curriculum model across to other arenas (for example, the transfer of the NVQ model to GNVQs).

In setting up the national fieldwork to develop a new curriculum model and curriculum tools for its implementation a major difficulty was the lack of understanding among implementers, policy makers and employers of what was meant by curriculum. Many thought curriculum was another word for syllabus. The author introduced the following overhead transparency to audiences in 1981 to raise awareness of curriculum issues.

Figure 14.1: Questions to be asked in regard to developing VET learning opportunities

The curriculum or training programme is:
any activity *planned* to promote learning

How is the activity derived?

1 who are the recipients of the learning?
2 What is intended to be learned?
3 What is the purpose of the learning?
4 Why is it being learned the way it is?
5 How is the success of the activity measured?

What values, attitudes and assumptions are associated with the learning activity?

What criteria are used in making the decisions?

In running workshops in 1993 on WBL and/or the delivery of National Vocational Qualifications (NVQs) and General National Vocational Qualifications (GNVQs) this set of questions is still useful and encourages implementers to think about the *kinds* of learning and the *processes* of learning required for occupational competence. (For a good, practical discussion regarding the nature of an FE curriculum to support work-based learning see Boffy, 1990.)

Developing the Good Practice Model of Work-based Learning

The stated intention of the 1982–1985 R&D project was two-fold: first, to investigate the dimensions of work-based learning in the context of NTI, and second, to provide a range of tools/policy instruments to assist policy makers, providers and administrators achieve the innovation and change in VET sought by Government. The following conceptual framework was used to assist with the substantial interrogation and analysis undertaken of MSC and Government publications and rhetoric in order to establish strategies for innovation and change (see Levy, 1992b, Section 4).

Figure 14.2: Framework for the generation of prototype developmental strategies

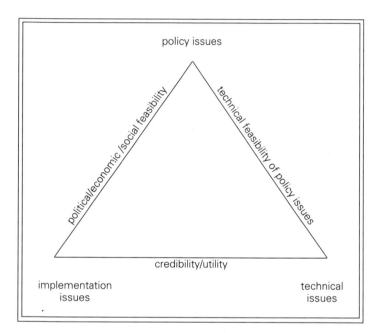

Policy issues or intentions were separately interrogated to consider the implications of the implementation of each in a defined system or systems (for example the 16–18 cohort, employers, workers, FE colleges, private training agencies, industry sector bodies, parents, MSC field staff, examining validating bodies, local labour market). Each of the implementation issues raised in this way was then examined, first, for economic, political and social feasibility in the light of existing know-how and background information, and second, for technical feasibility in the light of existing technical know-how and support available or what might be developed in an acceptable timescale. The result of the technical feasibility interrogations on the implementation issues was then taken back to the original policy intentions/issues. Thus there was an iterative or spiral process of analysis and argument which ultimately led to an interpretation of each policy intention in terms of action to be taken to further that intention.

The policy intentions included in the analysis were:

* an employer-led programme;
* new standards relating to knowledge and skills actually required in the performance of a job or range of jobs, and performance-based criteria;

- a mobile workforce with flexibility, adaptability, transferability;
- a technically competent workforce;
- identification of new kinds of skills for the workforce of the future;
- access to learning across all abilities/all ages/all occupations;
- a work-based learning programme;
- introduction of participative learning approaches and encouragement of autonomy in learning.

It was emphasized that even when all the parameters of policy, technical and implementation issues are known, bringing them together successfully in action, requires that the *feasibility* of these must also be associated *with credibility and utility for intended users*.

The technical/curricular functions of the tools/policy instruments were identified and included:

- providing a language of skill which can bridge existing occupational and educational languages; and so address transition and access issues, integration issues, and reviewing/guidance processes across a wide range of users of VET programmes;
- investigating the accreditation of work-based learning, issues of credit transfer, 'progression', and formative assessment;
- assisting with design of VET programmes which deliver occupational competence in a way which develops transferable skills and which encourages the development of a technically competent workforce;
- helping to provide a broader base of information for employer selection purposes and a common language for the recognition of competence;
- providing a framework for autonomous, effective learning in the workplace;
- developing learner awareness of transferable skills and the ability to use these in tackling new tasks;
- workplace analysis to help employers identify more clearly what kinds of competence they want in their workforce together with strategies for developing these;
- diagnosis of training needs by the employer/supervisor, by FE, or by the learner.

Identification of the Major Aims and Aspirations of the Good Practice Model of Work-based Learning

Following the analyses set out above, three major aims and aspirations of the proposed new model for VET within the framework of NTI were consolidated:

Aim 1 — to encourage access to learning for all, using an occupational base and real work.
Aim 2 — to deliver new standards, new certification, progression and skill transfer.
Aim 3 — to establish a technically competent, versatile, adaptable workforce.

The target group for the new model was 20 million workers and it was to offer the possibility of continuous lifelong learning, the prime purpose being to stimulate learning for occupational competence. The following figure provides a summary of the intended outcomes of the new model.

Figure 14.3: *An overview of the intended outcomes of the work-based learning model for VET*

Work-based learning: A new model for vocational education and training

The new model:

1 is work driven: its aims and objectives derive from the future needs of the work-place, the worker and the labour market;
2 involves new approaches to learning design: it is not an education/training model with fixed syllabuses but is outcomes oriented. The approaches are relevant to all occupational sectors and to all kinds and sizes of the workplace;
3 encourages training to be embedded in the structure of work;
4 provides a strategy for encouraging employer commitment and worker motivation to skill development;
5 offers new kinds of partnership between employers, workers, FHE, training providers and examining/validating bodies;
6 offers new ways of structuring learning to develop new kinds of workplace skills:
    * learning to manage change
    * learning to learn new skills
    * learning to recognize and develop skills used in the workplace
    * learning to 'unpack' workplace activities
    * learning to synthesize existing skills and new skill into new workplace activities
    * skill transfer

Activities to Develop the Tools and Strategies to Implement the Good Practice Model of Work-based Learning

Extensive field work to develop tools and strategies began in January 1983. The report (Levy, 1992b) details the project systems and outcomes of 1982–85 and includes activities under eight themes (work-based learning design and delivery, learning for skill transfer, accreditation of work-based learning, new standards, certification, progression, integration, staff development). Initial activities concentrated on developing one of the major curriculum tools, now known as the WBL core skills (see Levy, 1993), and work-based learning materials (known as work-based projects). Publications and papers from field work are available from the Staff College Librarian *WBLP Papers and Publications* (1992).

Technical issues regarding accreditation of WBL, new standards and assessment and certification processes were logged throughout 1983 to 1985. Initially very little technical expertise was available regarding assessment in the workplace and the role of workplace supervisors in assessment. In late spring 1983 representations were made to the senior civil servant heading the MSC regarding the lack of recognition by policy makers of the highly technical nature of new standards, assessment and certification and the amount of specialist work needed in the field. Support was requested from the Chief Psychologist's Branch and in July 1983 Gilbert Jessup was seconded to the R&D project and worked within the WBL/ NTI framework. A few months later he was formally in overall charge of assessment in YTS. At the end of 1983 negotiations were successful in getting another assessment specialist, David Mathews, seconded to the R&D project from EITB.

Having no national framework or system for qualifications and no national standards was a considerable barrier to progress in fieldwork activity on assessment and certification. One approach was through a regional examination board that had control of examinations and certificates in its own region. Bob Mansfield (one of the original core skills researchers) in conjunction with Yorkshire and Humberside Association for Further and Higher Education, one of the R&D field work centres, developed learning and assessment models (see YHAFHE/MSC, 1986). These kept close to the WBL design model and attempted to deal with assessment and certification of core skills, ability to transfer and occupational competence. They could almost be said to be the forerunners of NVQ elements and units of competence in the way they were written.

This period of R&D work contributed considerably to practical and theoretical awareness of assessment and certification issues and resulted in a number of papers on assessment, occupational competence and standards being published during 1985–87 (in particular Mathews, 1985a, 1985b, 1986a, 1986b and 1986c; Mathews and Mansfield, 1985). Also as a result of R&D activity, a model of job competence was introduced (Mansfield and Mathews, 1985). This has since been further developed and now forms the basis for functional analysis, one of the major tools used in developing National Vocational Qualification standards, which reflect functions undertaken within a work role.

In 1985 the Government began to take the development of national standards and qualifications seriously, including the provision of associated resources, and, following the Review of Vocational Qualifications Working Group, set up the National Council for Vocational Qualifications (NCVQ) in 1986. It was fortunate in terms of innovation and change strategy that Gilbert Jessup was placed in charge of R&D in the new organization. This meant that the knowledge of WBL R&D already undertaken was available in the new body. This knowledge included the operational definition of work-based learning and the extensive work on curriculum tools to support the implementation of work-based learning.

Concomitant with the establishment of NCVQ, continued research into issues of learning and the management and delivery of work-based learning was funded by the Training Agency from 1986 to 1990 through the Staff College Work-based Learning Project. This freed the NCVQ to concentrate on developing national systems for standards and a framework for the delivery of standards across all occupational sectors. In other words, major aim 2 (see above) '*to deliver new standards, new certification, progression and skill transfer*', which required a massive national undertaking, was at last being taken seriously by the Government and appropriately resourced. Simultaneously, other issues of curriculum development within the new outcomes model continued to be researched and developed by the Work-based Learning Project, close collaboration being maintained between the Work-based Learning Project and NCVQ researchers and consultants throughout 1986–1990. Thus the Jessup outcomes model was able to utilize fully the work-based learning R&D undertaken from 1982–1990.

The Good Practice Model of Work-based Learning

The Operational Definition of the Good Practice Model of Work-based Learning

Learning is at the heart of the WBL good practice model. In terms of the four Eraut curriculum components, the model would be described as follows:

(i)   a work driven model rather than an education/training driven model for the derivation of objectives, values, attitudes, assumptions;

(ii)   new learning approaches to develop the new kinds of skills needed in the future workforce;

(iii)   new content which is vocationally, occupationally and personally relevant to the needs of young workers and adults;

(iv)   new methods of assessment and recording aimed at competence, performance, self-learning, new standards, new skills.

The major characteristic of the good practice model is *linking learning to the work role*. This focuses the learning on the worker doing a job and ensures that the learning is seen as relevant both to employer and worker needs. The *purpose* of linking learning to the work role is to motivate workers to improve their performance and development at work, and to motivate employers to support learning for this purpose. Both parties experience long-term gain: by *linking learning to the work role* the employing company will be more effective in coping with change by having a responsive and highly skilled workforce, trained for company current and future needs; individual workers will have their company-related skills and know-how updated on a regular basis, with possible increase in bonus or share of productivity, and have more opportunity to develop themselves both personally and in career terms and so enjoy greater job satisfaction.

In addition to *linking learning to the work role*, the good practice model has three interrelated components, each of which provides an essential contribution to the learning:

(i)   structuring learning opportunities in the workplace (*allocated work activities which are productive and at the same time provide an opportunity for learning*);

(ii)   providing appropriate on-job training/learning opportunities (*sustained learning/instruction in specific aspects of the job which is carried out in the workplace but does not make a net contribution to productivity*);

(iii)   identifying and providing relevant off-the-job learning opportunities (*opportunities for learning away from where the worker-learner normally works and outside normal productive work activities*).

For further explication and discussion on the three components and their use see Mathews, Oates and Levy, 1992. In the extracted example provided below, the intended outcomes, which are not written in competence terms, are related to the specific, perceived needs of the organization the learner is in and to his/her career development needs within the organization. The purposes/learning outcomes of the three components could be related to NVQs if required.

Figure 14.4: Example of linking learning to the work role and using the three components of work-based learning

---

Example: For a systems analyst/programmer working in the information technology division of a large finance house

Learning in the workplace

- Moving from working in a group involved in reviewing and improving existing software in use in the company, to a recently formed team developing software and implementing a new system to run on newly-purchased hardware. Intended outcome: to gain experience of what it is like to implement *new* systems, etc., rather than improve existing ones.
- After a suitable period, and in preparation for possible promotion, being given responsibility for training of junior programming staff. Intended outcome: gaining first experience of supervisory responsibility within company.

On-the-job training/learning

- Being allocated a set period of two/three hours each week to learn a new high-level computer language using manuals, and having the support of an experienced colleague if problems or queries arise. Intended outcome: competence in using the new computer language in various company projects.

Off-the-job learning

- Attending seminars run by external training organization with expertise in financial management systems. This provides an opportunity to discuss, with outside experts, pressing implementation issues and problems associated with a current project. Intended outcome: identifying alternative options for completion of project.

The Good Practice Model Requires Partnership in Learning

The work-based learning good practice model has learning as its prime aim, its target group being 20 million or more employed workers. It is a partnership model, the partners being production professionals (employers/managers/supervisors), worker-learners (employed workers) and learning professionals (teachers/trainers/tutors). Guidance professionals (careers officers/personnel officers) have a support role.

Work-based learning is essentially contractual in nature since it is work driven and funded by employers. The nature of the contract is that both employers and workers have to contribute resources to the learning process. Employers contribute resources in the form of finance, workplace facilities and training support; workers contribute effort and energy in learning, in applying new skills and in coping with change. During training, employers may temporarily lose some production/profit, while workers may lose bonus payments and also expose themselves to risk in offering to learn new skills — for example, loss of status from being an experienced worker to being a learner.

There is an essential role for skilled learning professionals in any outcomes model of VET. This is the group that specializes in learning methods, designing learning materials and approaches, overcoming learning difficulties, helping to maximize the use of learning resources. The prime function of production professionals is to ensure that workers are effectively and efficiently carrying out functions required by the enterprise. They also have an important role in providing day-to-day feedback to workers on their performance, and helping them reflect on how they are undertaking a particular activity, but this, although it supports learning, is not regarded as training (see *Training in Britain — The Main Report*, HMSO, 1989). Production professionals, who know their experienced workers and workplaces, can, in *partnership* with learning professionals, plan how these workplace resources can best be used for learning purposes. Worker-learners, if they are to be motivated to learn, and to develop some autonomy in learning must also have a stake in their own learning. They therefore have a major part to play in partnership with learning professionals and production professionals. The fundamental need in a new UK VET model is to develop skilled learners and this requires a partnership approach if the new VET model is to change the training culture of the UK and be embedded in the structure of work. The role of the various partners was investigated during the R&D work 1982–90 and tools and strategies developed which could be used in partnership (see below).

Outcomes and Learning Issues

The Meaning of Outcomes in the WBL Model

Outcome here is used in the sense that it represents the *intended effects of all the curriculum activities*, i.e. *all* the changes brought about in learners participating in a particular curriculum model with particular curriculum processes. Intended outcomes might be short-term, long-term, hard (explicit and quantifiable), soft/developmental (for example, strategies, processes, know-how). There can be collective outcomes (for example, improved employer participation in VET) and individual outcomes (for example, achievement of a particular NVQ/an interest in making a career move). Outcomes might well be described as objectives for learning, or as guidance for learners *and* those who control and manage learning.

'Outcome' in current literature appears to have a variety of meanings, as for example, in achievement outcomes, outcome statement, performance outcome, learning outcome, occupational standards, etc., and there may be an incorrect assumption of a community of judgment which in fact covers up quite important differences.

The way in which outcomes are specified are fundamental to any curriculum model and the theoretical basis for that specification should reflect the totality of the model. One of the disadvantages of the NVQ outcomes model is that only explicit and quantifiable outcomes expressed in terms of national occupational standards are assessed and recognized. This means that outcomes which cannot be described in terms of such standards, even though they may be important to the individual learner, the employer or the economy, are currently unlikely to be recorded and accorded public recognition. On the other hand, because occupational standards describe the expectation of any individual performing a particular work role, the considerable detail involved in their description could be liberating to an individual learner since it exposes what performance comprises, the range of contexts and the kinds of evidence that s/he might present.

In the WBL model the development of new kinds of workplace skills was specified (figure 14.3 outcome 6) in order to develop a workforce able and willing to respond to rapidly changing demands including new organizational structures, whether these arise because of new technology, new products and working methods, new markets etc. However, *occupational competence in the work role* was also to be a major outcome for the individual. This is not to specify that every learner has to take the same route to learning in regard to occupational competence and managing change — learners will each have different starting points depending on their earlier experience, and can be helped to find the best or alternative *ways* to learning particular kinds of things (Kolb, 1984; Honey and Mumford, 1986). Account also needs to be taken of the fact that the *way* learners learn affects their ability to use that learning in different contexts (Sternberg and Wagner, 1986; Wolf, 1989) and this is important to skill transfer, an essential outcome in the WBL model.

If the aim of a new UK VET model is to develop skilled learners, the learning *process* as opposed to content cannot be ignored in the drive for qualifications. A fully *qualified* workforce is not necessarily a *skilled* workforce in terms of today's and future workforce needs, although a well planned and up-to-date qualifications framework can help guide the skills of the workforce in the most appropriate directions for economic success.

Jessup (1991) argues that 'if education and training is defined by its outcomes it opens access to learning and assessment in ways which are not possible in traditional syllabus or programme based systems'. An issue that needs to be considered here is whether it opens up access to learning *process* as well as to the implied learning content set out by the performance criteria and evidence specification as in NVQs. How do learners learn to achieve the specified outcomes? Can we assume they are skilled learners and know where and how best and most effectively to learn for particular outcomes? We certainly can't guarantee that they even have access to the necessary content as set out in the specifications for particular occupational standards. These are implementation issues which require further investigation.

Work-based Learning Strategies and Tools and Their Intended Outcomes

In designing WBL as a new curriculum model for the delivery of VET, the overall system in which UK VET would operate was taken into account. Many people, agencies and institutions in that system had to learn about new approaches to VET and be enabled to participate in them without too much difficulty if the VET system was to be changed. Curriculum tools and processes developed therefore had to be as accessible and widely understandable as possible and have credibility and utility for *all* users. They had to promote motivation among *all* those in the system toward greater participation in training. Evidence (reported in *Training in Britain — The Main Report*, HMSO, 1989) confirmed that many UK employers still do not provide training and also that a large proportion of the workforce are themselves still not interested in taking part in training). It was also essential to recognize the structural factors mitigating against a training culture/strategy and to allow for them. For a good review of these see Finegold and Soskice (1988).

The WBL model and its tools and strategies also had to take account of structural changes occurring in industry and commerce, for example from hier-archical to flat structures and networking; changes in working practices because of new technologies, new materials, changing markets, etc.; and industrial relations and human resource issues. The model and tools therefore had to encompass considerable flexibility to deal with different occupational sectors, all levels in the work force, and large and small enterprises.

In the partnership model, each of the three prime partners (production pro-fessionals, worker-learners, learning professionals) has a responsibility to assist with the management and development of learning, and the process of assessment and collection of evidence, and strategies and tools developed during 1982–90 support this. They must assist with analysis of workplace activities, and be usable (with minimum training) by *all* the partners in learning including those at shop floor level, and not confined to specialists or consultants for example, as is the case with functional analysis.

Thus the intention in WBL was to achieve a range of outcomes for organ-izations (see above) and for individual learners particular learning outcomes, for example, new kinds of workplace skills (not all of which could be assessed to standards). However, since outcomes are the result of an activity but do not specify how that activity is to be undertaken, the tools and strategies were in-tended to be used with flexibility. During 1986–1990 considerable field work was undertaken on nearly all the tools listed below and manuals with illuminative examples from field work are now available (WBL, 1992).

1   The operational definition of work-based learning: helps partners in learn-ing to consider the availability, appropriateness and financial implications of various learning environments.
2   Eighteen strategies for structuring learning opportunities in the workplace: helps partners consider in more detail the uses of the workplace resources to satisfy particular learning needs.
3   Work-based learning core skills: the 103 'skills' are defined as 'those skills which are common in a wide range of tasks and which are essential for competence in those tasks' and help partners in a number of different ways, to implement work-based learning. In particular they provide a framework for analysing workplace activities which is not confined to specialists (core analysis). They provide a new language of skill for de-scribing aspects of occupational competence, assist with design and ac-creditation of work-based learning; develop learners' awareness of transferable core skills and their own ability to use them to tackle new tasks; provide approaches which encourage autonomy of learning and develop personal effectiveness; assist with selection by providing a broader base of information for selectors in employment and further and higher education; assist with the diagnosis of individual worker's learning needs.
4   The job competence model: provides partners with a second analytical framework for analysing workplace activities to identify the kinds of skills needed to become occupationally competent. These are in terms of task skills, task management skills, contingency management skills and job/role environment skills.
5   The individual development plan: provides partners with a format and pro-cesses for action planning which enable them to collaborate in specifying

and reviewing a programme of learning for an individual learner. It provides opportunities for formative and summative assessment and for the informed collection of evidence by learners.

6   The assessment matrix: provides a simple format for partners to encourage logging of a range of learning environments and so help learners with collection of evidence.

7   Work-based projects: these are learning materials which utilize the three components of work-based learning, link learning to the work role, and are written in such a way to help learners participate actively in their own learning.

8   The Guide to Work-based Learning Terms: this defines and comments on ninety-six terms currently used in work-based learning. It aids communication in organizations by offering them a common language for discourse.

Note that the work-based learning model is designed specifically for employed worker-learners. However, the above tools are of use in any learning programme containing work experience, practical assignments/experience as a feature: for example, sandwich courses, social work, caring, nurse training; teacher training, articled teacher training, developmental teacher appraisal; employee induction, training, retraining; accreditation of prior learning; work experience in schools, FE, TVEI; project work, assignment work in general. The tools have been trialled in a number of these fields and have been well received by reviewers.

The NVQ Emerging Outcomes Model and Issues Requiring Clarification

Are the six intended outcomes set out in the new WBL model for VET (figure 14.3) appropriate and relevant for the work force of the future?

Can the NVQ/SVQ (Scottish Vocational Qualification) qualifications framework and current approaches satisfy/deliver all the characteristics needed by the work force of the future, in particular, long term outcomes such as 'new kinds of workplace skills', which are almost impossible to quantify, but are essential especially for young people, for example, those undertaking NVQs/SVQs and GNVQs/GSVQs at levels 2 and 3?

Consider the following extract from the *Guide to National Vocational Qualifications* (NCVQ, 1991). The NVQ *statement of competence* should be derived from an analysis of functions within the area of competence to which it relates. It must reflect:

*   competence relating to task management, health and safety and the ability to deal with organizational environments, relationships with other people and unexpected events;
*   the ability to transfer the competence from place to place and context to context;
*   the ability to respond positively to foreseeable changes in technology, working methods, markets and employment patterns and practices;
*   the underpinning skill, knowledge and understanding which is required for effective performance in employment.

However, although the NVQ/SVQ qualification title, together with the detail in the units of competence, elements of competence, performance criteria and range statements are jointly known as 'a statement of competence', i.e. the NVQ/SVQ makes a statement about the *competence* of any individual who possesses the qualification; an *inference* model is being used, namely that the various *performances* (in the contexts the range statements cover and on which evidence has been collected) constitute *competence* within the occupational/functional area. Competence is a hypothetical construct (as are work-based learning core skills), and occupational standards provide the means by which competence is described (although in partial terms to retain manageability) but competence has to be inferred from a succession or variety of single performances.

There should be no problem in accepting the inference model since it is commonly used whatever form certification takes, for example, 'A' level, degree level, NVQ/SVQ. It is possible to get good grades in an academic examination, in which only a percentage of knowledge has been examined, but the inference is likely to be that the candidate had covered all the knowledge set out in the syllabus. The advantage of the NVQ/SVQ approach over some others is that it provides a more detailed structure which assists the inference process, but we must nevertheless always remember we are using an inference model in specifying competence possessed by an individual.

However, a different issue concerns the ability to achieve the 'same' outcomes by totally different routes, an important selling point with regard to NVQs/SVQs. If different routes are taken in different companies, with different working practices, different organizational structures, and different uses and provision of technology, the underpinning skill, knowledge and understanding is likely to be very different. There is thus no guarantee that while NVQs/SVQs may provide a basis for *credit* transfer, that we have a similar basis for *skill* transfer (skill here being used in its widest sense).

This again should not cause too much concern since the inference model used for competence is similarly true of the ability to transfer, the ability to respond to change in technology, etc., and of the underpinning skill, knowledge and understanding.

The author's proposition is that by introducing appropriate learning strategies, which would include core analysis (using work-based learning core skills which provide a generalized language of 'skill') and analysis using the job competence model, it would be possible to improve the validity of the inferences currently being made in respect of the second and third components of the statement of competence.

References

BEES, M. and SWORD, M. (1990) (Eds) *National Vocational Qualifications and Further Education*, London, Kogan Page in association with the National Council for Vocational Qualifications.

BOFFY, R. (1990) '*Occupational competence and work-based learning: The future for further education in National Vocational Qualifications and Further Education*, BEES, M. and SWORDS, M. (Eds).

ERAUT, M. *et al* (1975) '*Model of the curriculum in action*' in *Analysis of Curriculum Materials*, University of Sussex Occasional Paper No 2.

FEU (1978) *Experience, Reflection, Learning*, FEU, London.

FEU (1980) *Developing Social and Life Skills*, FEU, London.

FINEGOLD, D. and SOSKICE, D. (1988) 'The failure of training in Britain: Analysis and prescription', *Oxford Review of Economic Policy*, 4, 3.

HMSO (1989) *Training in Britain — The Main Report*, London, HMSO.

HONEY, P. and MUMFORD, A. (1986) *The Manual of Learning Styles*, Berkshire, Honey.

HUNT, M. (1991) *Using Individual Development Plans: The Work-based Learning Approach to Action Planning*, Blagdon, The Staff College.

JESSUP, G. (1991) *Outcomes: NVQs and the Emerging Model of Education and Training* London, Falmer Press.

KEEP, E. (1986) *Designing the Stable Door: A Study of How the Youth Training Scheme Was Planned*, Warwick Papers in Industrial Relations No 8 Industrial Relations Research Unit, School of Industrial and Business Studies, University of Warwick, Coventry.

KOLB, D.A. (1984) *Experiential learning — Experience as the Source of Learning and Development*, London, Prentice Hall.

LEVY, M. (1987) *The Core Skills Project and Work Based Learning — An Overview of the Development of a New Model for the Design, Delivery and Accreditation of Work-based Learning*, Blagdon, The Staff College.

LEVY, M. (1989) *A Guide to Work Based Learning Terms*, Blagdon, The Staff College.

LEVY, M. (1991) *Work Based Learning — A Good Practice Model*, Blagdon, The Staff College.

LEVY, M. (1992a) *Developing VET Policy: Political, Social and Technical Feasibility*, Blagdon, The Staff College.

LEVY, M. (1992b) *The Core Skills Project Research Report: Work-based Learning — Tools for Transition*, Blagdon, The Staff College.

LEVY, M. (1993) *An Introduction to Work-based Learning Core Skills* (in draft).

LEVY, M. and MATHEWS, D. (1988) *MSC Core Skills*, Blagdon, The Staff College.

MANSFIELD, B. and MATHEWS, D. (1985) *Job Competence — A Description for Use in Vocational Education and Training*, Blagdon, The Staff College.

MATHEWS, D. (1985a) *Issues of Accreditation of Work Based Learning*, Blagdon, The Staff College.

MATHEWS, D. (1985b) 'The formation of occupational standards', Annexe 13 in LEVY, M. (Ed) (1992b) *The Core Skills Project Research Report: Work-based Learning Tools for Transition*, Blagdon, The Staff College.

MATHEWS, D. (1986a) *Assessment in the Workplace — News from the Faraway Land of which we know little*, Blagdon, The Staff College.

MATHEWS, D. (1986b) *YTS Core Skills and the Accreditation of Work Based Learning* (written for a national seminar of the Association for Sandwich Education regarding students on placement) Blagdon, The Staff College.

MATHEWS, D. (1986c) *The Accreditation of 'Ability to Transfer Skills and Knowledge to New Situations'*, Blagdon, The Staff College.

MATHEWS, D. and MANSFIELD, B. (1985) *Occupational Standards — Job Competence and the Measurement of Achievement*, Blagdon, The Staff College.

MATHEWS, D., OATES, T. and LEVY, M. (1992) *Strategies for Structuring Learning Opportunities in the Workplace and Implementing Work-based Learning*, Blagdon, The Staff College.

MSC (1981a) *NTI-An Agenda for Action*, Sheffield, MSC.

MSC (1981b) *NTI A Programme for Action*, Sheffield, MSC.

OATES, T. (Ed) (1987) *Supervisor Snapshots — Descriptions of Workplace Supervisors and their Roles in Work-based Learning*, Blagdon, The Staff College

STERNBERG, R.J. and WAGNER, R.K. (Eds) (1986) *Practical Intelligence: Nature and Origins of Competence in the Everyday World*, Cambridge, Cambridge University Press.

The Work Based Learning Project: Publications and Papers (1992) Blagdon, The Staff College.

The Work Based Learning Project: Publications (1993) Blagdon, The Staff College.

WOLF, A. (1989) *Learning in Context — Patterns of Skill Transfer and Their Learning Implications*, University of London Institute of Education, Department of Mathematics, Statistics and Computing.

YORKSHIRE and HUMBERSIDE Association FOR FURTHER AND HIGHER EDUCATION (1986) *Learning and Assessment Models for Office, Clerical and Administrative Occupations*, Leeds YHAFHE/MSC.

Chapter 15

Outcomes in Management

David Mathews

Before Outcomes

Analysis of outcomes provides a novel way of thinking about managers and management. There are a number of understandings of management which account for the style and rationale of the management curriculum in education, training and employment generally. They refer to:

(i) a concern with the organization;
(ii) varying degrees of belief that management is learnable or even teachable;
(iii) the qualities of individual managers or prospective managers.

The conviction that the organization *per se* is perfectible[1] has its origins in the USA. It contrasts with other perceptions of business as being about trading, making deals, designing or marketing. Psychologists and sociologists have a fascination with the organization, a concept which might have been created simply for its amenability to investigation.

There has developed a similar faith in the teachability of management. It entails good management being seen as having a specifiable philosophy, and being able to be practised through sets of techniques or even formulae of the kind propounded by leading management thinkers[2].

Managers are often seen as possessing particular qualities which are associated with successful management. In some cases this is simply a popular understanding; in others the result of empirical investigation. The qualities involve high orders of generalization about individual personality or behaviours, often denoted as *competencies*[3]: leadership, motivation, decisiveness, innovativeness, vision, flexibility. In the UK it is common for these attributes to be termed *personal competences*. At the extreme managers can be seen as *types*, and even as a class or *cadre*, identified as such by the qualities of those who enter the class rather than their achievements within it.

It is also recognized that effective management rests on a body of knowledge. This knowledge includes a range of learnable techniques for such 'hard' processes as planning, analysis and monitoring and for the 'softer' ones: negotiation, discussion, counselling, guidance. Knowledge also extends to understanding of how organizations, markets, people work. Knowledge is seen as combining with personal competences to bring about effective action, results and achievement for the organization.

Qualifications and Management Development

This adds up to a belief in the efficacy of management education and development, apparent in the extent of provision of management programmes. In employing organizations, in university and other management schools and colleges and in the growth of assessment centres and development centres these programmes are designed to identify and realize potential. Almost universally they focus on personal competences and knowledge, including understanding the contexts in which management takes place. The style with which these constructs are tackled varies; from ad hoc, on-the-job learning to dedicated, off-the-job programmes of education.

Qualifications in management include HNDs and first degrees in business administration, mixtures of management and technical specialisms and, importantly, post-experience qualifications: notably Certificates and Diplomas in Management Studies and the MBA, Master of Business Administration. In addition managers may obtain various ranks of membership in a range of management institutions, some linked to the above qualifications.

Within employing organizations, human resource management and human resource development include the development of managers among that of other workers or learners. Among managers themselves models of knowledge and personal competence mix with a variety of beliefs and nostrums in development and in the day-to-day practice of management.

There is competition between the provision of management training and organizational development. While the disinterested observer might equally identify the need for management development or for organizational development, management developers are more likely to opt for the former and organizational developers the latter. Ultimately, of course, there may be no universal condition to be diagnosed, and no universal remedy.

Earlier Measures of Competence

Management education and development has operated at several removes from the ultimate measure of effectiveness. Personal competences and knowledge, however much they *contribute to* effective performance, do not directly represent that performance.

There again, management performance itself bears only a partial relationship to the effectiveness or success of an organization. Managers are there to run the business. They have to contend, more than most other workers perhaps, with factors beyond their control which may confound their best efforts. Measures of profit, profitability, productivity, sales, customer satisfaction, corporate image are certainly indicators of success, but are none too easy to attribute to the performance or competence of the individual manager. Even the more immediate results such as volume, quality, costs, service levels are highly circumstantial. Organizations feel able to reward individuals on the basis of such measures as an incentive to try harder or in an effort to distribute profit fairly, but the ethos of education and development requires generalization beyond specific circumstances to infer competence or capability rather than simply success.

One could despair, on this analysis, of being able to measure management performance. It is said, however, that if you can't measure it you can't manage it. What has been lacking all these years is a measure of management performance which is directly expressive of the effect which managers have on the performance of their organizations. We need this to evaluate programmes and other interventions and to validate the use of personal competences and knowledge as indirect measures of competence. Individual organizations have had their own ways of measuring — in appraisal, for example. But these lack the universality of application which can spread more effective management practice throughout the economy and society.

Outcomes provide a tool which has the required immediacy to the management role. Outcomes provide criteria of effective performance and assessment of competence which reflects the real difference which management makes to the success of an organization.

Outcomes

'Outcomes' denotes an organizing principle for the management curriculum — for the practice of management and management education, training and development. It has three main expressions:

(i)   A focus on the results of education, training and development in terms of effective management performance in organizations.
(ii) A focus on the effects of management action — outcomes in management practice.
(iii) A link, in identifying the effectiveness of management action, to the ultimate consequences in terms of the organization and its stakeholders.

Outcomes of Education, Training and Development

For a long time an issue in management training (as in other training and development) was *transfer of training* — the value gained in terms of performance and effectiveness from this or that training input. Study after study struggled to identify factors in the training model which would maximize the transfer. Gradually the futility of simply addressing the individual without reference to their context or without adjustment within their organization became apparent, and links to the needs of the individual in context have helped to create models of learning which are more *work-based* in character: project-based, problem-centred learning, negotiated with the employer and drawing on the demands of current and anticipated work, supported by tutoring, mentoring inside as well as outside the workplace — all features growing in significance in both initial education and in-work provision. This is a move towards what Eraut in his chapter applies to all professionals: namely, an extrinsic orientation of the learning process.

Outcomes in Management Practice

A managed organization may be expected to differ from a disciplined organization (an army, for example) in that those who are managed are expected to be involved in decisions as to how to act. They have a degree of autonomy which is denied in a disciplined force. The outcomes concept applied to management practice suggests that what a manager does should be judged not so much by whether he/she is following the correct procedure, but by whether the results of action are desirable in the context and circumstances in which the manager is operating. This is a principle which is not exclusive to management as a formal position, but applies to any worker's management of his/her own job: work should be judged by its effects.

Linking to the Big Picture

The effectiveness of management action can be of various orders. A narrow, somewhat person-centred view may be that it is simply to do with immediate survival — getting through the problem with minimal damage. We all take this view at times, often with good excuse. An 'outcomes' view of management, however, would take account of a greater range of factors involved and focuses on management's contribution to the performance of the organization. Even then the perspective can be a limited one, encouraging stable, conservative routines and operations. Here a manager may be seen as a follower of procedures or formulae, granted seniority/authority but not the autonomy to take a view of the future. A more ambitious, upwards and onwards approach to outcomes takes in the *Big Picture*: the ultimate consequences of management action seen in the positioning and future direction of the organization. The main problem with this approach is that of attributing the success or failure of an organization to the acts of individual managers, or even management as a whole.

Standards

The device which unites these expressions of outcomes as an operating principle is *standards* — occupational standards in the form created for National Vocational Qualifications and Scottish Vocational Qualifications (NVQs and SVQs).

Standards are a specification of performance across a defined domain of activity. The basis for the specification is the separation of activity into *functions*. To each function is attached a set of criteria which define the limits of acceptable performance.

Function

A function is a transformation of inputs into outputs as part of a system — in the case of standards, a human activity system. In standards a *function* is expressed by means of its *outcome* — its effects, its consequences — rather than by the means by which the transformation is effected and the outcome achieved. Outcomes are broader concepts than the common understanding of outputs, as they include the unwanted effects as well as the intended effects of activity. For functions to be useful in specifying performance, they need to be sufficiently broad in scope to allow a manageable number to cover an occupation or role. A function therefore groups together activities by generalizing their outcomes. For example:

David Mathews

Define future personnel requirements

Assess and select candidates against team and organizational requirements

Monitor and control activities against budgets

The generalization covers a range of contexts in which activities may take place. The degree to which a function transcends context is as much part of its definition as the outcome itself.

Performance Criteria

The performance criteria applied to each function allow a performer or a commentator to differentiate acceptable performance from unacceptable, and, by a process of inference across the domain, competence in that function. For example, in the case of *Monitor and control activities against budgets*, the performance criteria (MCI, 1991) include:

Expenditure is within agreed limits, does not compromise future spending requirements and conforms to the organization's policy and procedures

Any modification to agreed budgets during the accounting period are consistent with agreed guidelines and correctly authorised

Comparison with Other Measures

Human performance can be described in ways which may focus on the performer or on that which they are required to perform. Five important ways of doing this are[4].

(i) Behaviour description — in which overt behaviours are described, rather than what the operator is required to do.

(ii) Behaviour requirements — behaviours which *should* be demonstrated or are *assumed* to be required.

(iii) Ability requirements — abilities or other personal characteristics required if performance in tasks is to be maximized.

(iv) Task characteristics — performance is characterised by the conditions *external to the performer* which elicit performance.

(v) Performance outcomes — the effects, including side effects, of performance; sometimes characterised as the *functional* approach.

The first four categories are those which have been of concern to management educators, developers and researchers, generalized into models of personal competence. Standards are based on the last and share the fourth, provided one takes a sufficiently broad view of task characteristics to cover context.

The Anatomy of Standards

Standards are organized in a number of components. An individual standard is based around a distinct function, known as an element. Each element includes:

(i)   A title for the element — the function which it represents.
(ii) Performance criteria — the indicators which characterise successful performance of any instance of activity within the range (see below).
(iii) Range — defining the boundaries of context and circumstance forming the domain for the element.

These three components specify competence — the ability to perform to standard across the domain. By way of further assistance, particularly to those who have to assess performers or develop learning programmes, two further components are commonly presented:

(i)   Knowledge and understanding — underpinning performance and able to be used in planning of learning and for corroborative and complementary assessment.
(ii) Assessment guidelines — showing the sources and forms of evidence on which a candidate and assessor can draw.

The element from the Supervisory Management standards shown on page 250 contains the components found in all the management standards.

Knowledge and Understanding

In assessment, questioning of a candidate may be used to elicit knowledge for several purposes:

• To corroborate performance.
• To judge whether performance demonstrated in one context would be likely to be repeated in another.
• To explore likely performance under conditions or contingencies not yet encountered.

Assessment Guidelines

The standards are designed to specify performance which, occurring across the range for an element, amounts to a picture of competence. Assessment of candidates against each element involves inferring the achievement of competence from evidence, first and foremost, of performance of management activities falling within the range. Further evidence can take the form of responses to questioning, for example, or performance in simulations or assignments. Any evidence which is capable of corroboration is allowable.

Assessors are expected to be confident that the candidate can perform the function (element) across the specified range. Assessment against standards has a

Unit 6 **Create, Maintain and Enhance
Productive Working Relationships**

Element 6.1 **Create and Enhance Productive Working
Relationships With Colleagues and Those for
Whom One has Supervisory Responsibility**

PERFORMANCE CRITERIA:

(a) Efforts are made to establish
and maintain productive
working relationships

(b) Opportunities to discuss work-
related matters are readily
provided

(c) Advice is offered in a helpful
manner and where necessary
individuals are referred to
specialists

(d) Differences are dealt with in
ways that maintain productive
working relationships

(e) Undertakings to others are
met

(f) People are sufficiently
informed about changes in
policy and working practices
which may affect them

(g) Where there is concern over
the quality of work, the
matter is directly raised and
discussed with the people
concerned

(h) Individuals are encouraged to
offer ideas and views and due
recognition of these is given

(i) Where ideas are not taken up,
the reasons are clearly given

(j) Opportunities for individuals to
discuss personal problems are
readily available

EVIDENCE SPECIFICATIONS:

Sources of Evidence:

Performance at work over a period
of time to cover all categories of
range.

Where the candidate does not
have the opportunity to cover all
categories of range within the
work place, evidence may be
supplemented by oral questioning
for principles and methods for
dealing with disagreements,
conflicts and handling confidential
information.

Forms of Evidence:

Personal report, witness testimony,
outputs and products of
performance e.g. documentation,
records.

RANGE STATEMENTS:

People:
- *those for whom one
  has responsibility*
- *line managers*
- *staff representatives*
- *colleagues*
- *customers*
- *suppliers*

Information:
- *formal*
- *informal*
- *oral*
- *written form*

KNOWLEDGE AND UNDERSTANDING

1) Purpose and context is an important
category of knowledge and
understanding, and the content of this
category is detailed in the accompanying
guidance notes.

2) Principles and methods relating to:
- *establishing constructive relationships
  with others*
- *informing and consulting staff about
  proposals and encouraging them to
  offer ideas and views*
- *providing praise and constructive
  criticism to encourage staff and
  improve future performance*
- *supporting team members in relations
  with others outside the team*
- *seeking and exchanging information,
  advice and support*
- *handling disagreements and conflict*
- *handling confidential information*
- *forming and managing work groups
  and teams*
- *motivating staff to reach work
  objectives, through encouraging
  participation in setting them and using
  different styles of direction and
  supervision*

3) Data relating to:
- *views of others on current and
  proposed activities*
- *interests, priorities, needs and
  concerns of others*
- *promises, undertakings and
  agreements with others*
- *areas of mutual interest and potential
  conflict*
- *resources and information which
  might be exchanged*

subjective quality, like all assessment. It is a supportable estimate rather than a logical deduction of some objective truth, completely independent of context and circumstances.

National Standards in Management

The outcomes approach in management is represented in the work of MCI, the Management Charter Initiative. Through Government-funded developments they have produced standards and awards which are now in use in employment, education and training. The awards are defined at three levels:

(i) *Supervisory Management*, intended for a large group of people with managerial responsibility often described as 'supervisors'. The qualifications based on these standards are at Level 3 of the NVQ and SVQ frameworks.[5]

(ii) *First Line Managers* — the MI standards. The Certificate Level qualification based on these standards is at NVQ/SVQ Level 4.

(iii) *Middle Managers* — the MII standards, intended for managers who had responsibilities including the managing of other (first line) managers, while being responsible to more senior managers in the organization. The Diploma Level qualification based on these standards is at NVQ/ SVQ Level 5.

What is the Extent of 'Management'?

The MCI developments were aimed at general management up to and including middle management. They thereby excluded the most senior managers and did not claim to specify all the standards appropriate to people with technical as well as managerial responsibility. The titles of the standards — Supervisory, First Line and Middle — derive from traditional hierarchical models. Individual managers, in small, flat, cooperative organizations and others which do not conform to this convention find that they can identify the standards which apply to them more by their content than their title.

Management, as a generic title for a variety of roles, encompasses company direction, strategic management and operational management of various orders. It includes specialist roles, generally taken as managerial in quality, where people may contribute their specialist competence to management teams or boards of directors. These include some personnel and training and development roles. Standards for training and development (through the Training and Development Lead Body) and for quality management have been developed, and standards are being developed for personnel management.

The Status of Standards

Since the publication of the First Line and Middle Manager standards in 1990, MCI management standards have become the default for specifying management performance in occupational standards for NVQs and SVQs. Bodies developing qualifications for sectors of the economy are required to use the MCI model when specifying management functions at Levels 3 and 4. This applies to sectors as varied as agriculture, retail, construction, environmental conservation, health and social care and engineering.

Employing organizations have started to make use of the standards for a variety of purposes. Many schools and colleges of management have remained aloof from standards which they see as dry and reductionist losing sight of the 'whole' person[6]. Others together with a variety of management centres around the country are offering the Certificates and Diplomas in Management Studies. These are being achieved by managers who are relatively new to their competences and by those who have been competent for some time but who, until now, have had no way of attesting to their competence.

Just as significantly, many people have come to hear, see, criticize and get excited about management standards and the new agenda they create for developing managers and, indeed, management itself in a wide variety of organizations.

A Perfect Model?

As is implied in the view of schools and colleges of management, the management standards — and even the very concept of standards — have their critics. And the management standards are indeed far from perfect.

For example, the analysis commissioned for developing the management standards was deliberately attenuated. Senior management was excluded from the brief and with it *strategic* management. As a result, the model of middle management in particular is lodged to some degree in a concept of management which is less proactive, for example, than current views on good practice would suggest.

The current standards have, perhaps, too little of the Big Picture apparent in the performance criteria used to specify effective performance. In any situation, effective performance requires the selection of the right option among the actions one can perform, complemented by carrying out that action to produce the desired result. For standards to reflect the needs of management (and thereby inform management education and development) the criteria of effective performance must capture these desired results. They must reflect as much of the Big Picture of success as can be attributed fairly to the individual.

The standards fail to take the opportunity to promote the benefits of diversity. While they specify adherence to equal opportunities legislation, they do not positively embrace the exploration of the benefits of employing or catering for groups which are more diverse than traditional target populations.

When it comes to assessment, the management standards are intended to cover a wide range of contexts. Uncertainty about transfer from one context or activity to another raises questions about the security of assessment. Just because we can find words through which to generalize about outcomes and contexts, it does not follow that we can infer transfer across our verbal generalizations. Nor does it follow that competence in management in one sector of the economy is the same as that in another, for all that the competence is described in the same way and may be equally meritorious.

Having said that, qualifications and assessment prior to the standards model are of no less uncertainty and lack the great virtue of standards which is to make available to the assessor a largely unambiguous specification of both performance and the domain against which to make an informed judgment. The limitations of a pioneering model should not obscure their revolutionary nature and innovative potential.

A Common Management Curriculum?

The management standards are a major component of a common management curriculum. Their promotion by MCI and by the accreditation bodies for vocational qualifications (NCVQ and SCOTVEC) is in effect a statement of national policy on the qualities and processes to be encouraged in UK management in all sectors — in public administration, voluntary and private organizations. Management, however, is an area of activity noted for its pluralism. Organizations are free to practise management more or less as they wish, with relatively few legal constraints and relatively little input from the social partners and other stakeholders in the organization. (This pluralism, represented in the variations among organizations, is not too often reflected *within* organizations. There conformity to organizational style and ethos is expected, and diversity is not too much encouraged.)

How does a common framework of competence sit with this partially pluralist tradition?

Curriculum and Standards

Curriculum may be defined by:

- Objectives
- Content areas, themes and emphases
- Learning approaches
- Assessment
- Evaluation

An outcomes approach to management links four of these components through standards. Standards, complemented by knowledge and personal competences, provide the objectives, the content and the framework against which summative assessment can take place. They do not, however, determine particular learning strategies. Instead, through their focus on the outcomes of learning, they open up wide possibilities for innovative strategies to be developed.

The objectives, content, learning and assessment components of the management curriculum are not the only uses to which standards can be put. Other uses of the standards within and outside qualifications have been recognized. For example:

- Providing goals for learners
- Evaluating management development programmes
- Enabling managers to be aware of their level of achievement in respect of employer/employment expectations

- Appraisal of managers and directors
- Providing a template of good practice

These uses suggest that the management curriculum is concerned, not just with the formal development of managers, but with the practice of management itself. Any tension, therefore, between commonality and plurality cannot be set aside as a nicety of learning provision, but exists at the heart of working practice. Pluralism in management is part of pluralism in society in that it determines how we encourage or allow each other to work, earn, collaborate and compete with each other and determine and further social priorities. The tensions need to be a matter of debate, and a balance found between plurality and commonality to which that society can subscribe.

> For a pluralist society to flourish, or even to survive, at least two crucial conditions must be satisfied: (1) there has to be a sufficiently broad range of commonly held ideals, values and procedures; (2) all the constituent groups must have regard for the common good in the pursuit of their own objectives.[7] (Crittenden, 1982)

Expected Functions

The qualifications so far developed from the standards express the expectation that managers should be able to deal with the broad functions of managing:

- Operations
- Finance
- People
- Information

The functions under these headings (for example, the units and elements of the Level 5 management qualification — shown on page 255) constitute the dimensions on which the standards are based: that is, of which activities count as management. By requiring candidates to succeed in all functional areas to achieve a qualification, the MCI framework lays down a challenge for assessment to be broadly-based. Competent managers should be able to deal with finance as well as operations, people as well as information. They should not need to refer every suggestion of a specialist function to a specialist functionary.

One of the beliefs underlying the development of management standards is that managers tend to take too narrow a view of their responsibilities. They tend too readily to pass on to others matters from outside what they see as their specialism. Personnel and financial administration, typically, suffer in this way. Perhaps nothing suffers more than the training/development of subordinates in the workplace.

Further, the integration of these functions is at a premium. Pettigrew *et al*[8] (1991) suggest that organizational effectiveness:

> . . . depends on the ability to integrate a variety of activities that have frequently been compartmentalized; to get people to address a number of

OCCUPATIONAL STANDARDS FOR MANAGERS

KEY PURPOSE:
TO ACHIEVE THE ORGANIZATION'S OBJECTIVES AND CONTINUOUSLY IMPROVE ITS PERFORMANCE

UNITS OF COMPETENCE AND ASSOCIATED ELEMENTS OF COMPETENCE

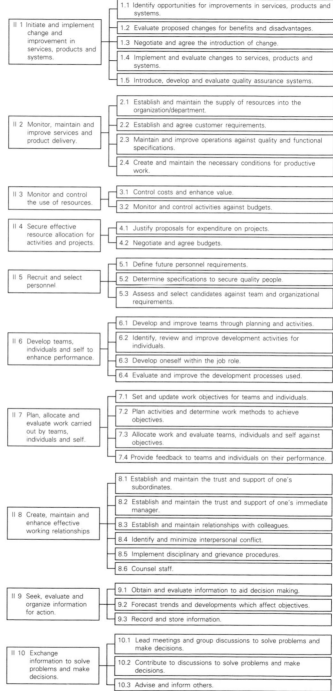

UNITS	ELEMENTS
II 1 Initiate and implement change and improvement in services, products and systems.	1.1 Identify opportunities for improvements in services, products and systems.
	1.2 Evaluate proposed changes for benefits and disadvantages.
	1.3 Negotiate and agree the introduction of change.
	1.4 Implement and evaluate changes to services, products and systems.
	1.5 Introduce, develop and evaluate quality assurance systems.
II 2 Monitor, maintain and improve services and product delivery.	2.1 Establish and maintain the supply of resources into the organization/department.
	2.2 Establish and agree customer requirements.
	2.3 Maintain and improve operations against quality and functional specifications.
	2.4 Create and maintain the necessary conditions for productive work.
II 3 Monitor and control the use of resources.	3.1 Control costs and enhance value.
	3.2 Monitor and control activities against budgets.
II 4 Secure effective resource allocation for activities and projects.	4.1 Justify proposals for expenditure on projects.
	4.2 Negotiate and agree budgets.
II 5 Recruit and select personnel.	5.1 Define future personnel requirements.
	5.2 Determine specifications to secure quality people.
	5.3 Assess and select candidates against team and organizational requirements.
II 6 Develop teams, individuals and self to enhance performance.	6.1 Develop and improve teams through planning and activities.
	6.2 Identify, review and improve development activities for individuals.
	6.3 Develop oneself within the job role.
	6.4 Evaluate and improve the development processes used.
II 7 Plan, allocate and evaluate work carried out by teams, individuals and self.	7.1 Set and update work objectives for teams and individuals.
	7.2 Plan activities and determine work methods to achieve objectives.
	7.3 Allocate work and evaluate teams, individuals and self against objectives.
	7.4 Provide feedback to teams and individuals on their performance.
II 8 Create, maintain and enhance effective working relationships	8.1 Establish and maintain the trust and support of one's subordinates.
	8.2 Establish and maintain the trust and support of one's immediate manager.
	8.3 Establish and maintain relationships with colleagues.
	8.4 Identify and minimize interpersonal conflict.
	8.5 Implement disciplinary and grievance procedures.
	8.6 Counsel staff.
II 9 Seek, evaluate and organize information for action.	9.1 Obtain and evaluate information to aid decision making.
	9.2 Forecast trends and developments which affect objectives.
	9.3 Record and store information.
II 10 Exchange information to solve problems and make decisions.	10.1 Lead meetings and group discussions to solve problems and make decisions.
	10.2 Contribute to discussions to solve problems and make decisions.
	10.3 Advise and inform others.

key performance criteria simultaneously (viz. quality, reliability, cost efficiency, delivery). Strategic management is about having a grasp of the whole.

Almost by definition, strategic management starts to happen when an organization's managers are forced into addressing increased complexity in their external and internal work environment; when they start to encourage employees generally to perceive the connection between activities in the different parts of the firm; and when they organise the work process accordingly.

It is a matter of some debate as to whether the standards as presently constructed go as far as Pettigrew suggests is necessary. Generally the issue is whether the prescription of common functions of management is too ambitious or not ambitious enough and rightly or wrongly oriented.

Criteria for Performance

The tension between commonality and plurality, however, extends beyond the issue of which functions are included in the standards. The curriculum is further defined through the detail of the standards attached to the individual functions.

Performance criteria identify what is held to be successful performance, and the range for each element specifies the contexts and circumstances across which a competent manager is able to perform successfully. If a management curriculum should also reflect the challenges which management faces in terms of change, for example, turbulence, managing internal and external environments, promoting quality and equality, then it would also be in these components of standards that they would be seen. Personal competences, knowledge of the standards themselves should also exhibit the creativity, analysis or proactivity needed to handle these challenges. The MCI work certainly addresses these areas, though new developments will no doubt improve on what has been achieved so far.

However much agreement is obtained on these aspects of objectives, content or assessment, plurality in management is likely to be required in the style of response to these common issues and challenges. In this regard, the management standards should not constrain performance where such constraint does not affect the outcome. The method by which things are done is less important than what is achieved, and it is in the method that the scope for plurality lies.

Values

This is not to say that the standards are neutral. As was suggested above, pluralism requires common values, ideals and procedures, and these are not to be found in the management standards beyond the setting out of the bare functions. For example, an element on the selection of candidates expresses compliance with equal opportunities legislation, the need for confidentiality and the need to keep candidates informed about what is happening. Nowadays these are not contentious matters, though they are honoured a good deal in the breach as well as the observance, but the opportunity was taken to make them explicit in the standards.

By contrast, the standards have little to say about diversity, which is more than compliance with equal opportunities legislation. Perhaps the advantage to be gained from increased diversity in selection and promotion, for example, is not only a matter of values, but it is the kind of issue which would form part of a debate on the common content of standards as opposed to an optional, local interpretation.

There will remain, even with a high order of commonality, values which are distinctive to a particular organization. Even these can be treated within standards, though indirectly. Draft standards for boards of directors include the formation of a set of values for the organization, their translation into policies to inform action and their monitoring and evaluation. This is the tantalizing boundary between commonality and pluralism, where competence requires values to be dealt with but does not lay down what those values should be.

Different Perspectives

Experience of the management standards in use[9] (Janes and Burgen, 1992) suggests that the management standards are quite robust, but that individual organizations can benefit from clarifying and increasing the specification the standards contain for their own context and purposes. It has also been found that a variety of strategies for developing managers can make use of the standards.

For a common framework to be successful, and not simply acceptable, it has to embrace aspects of competence which, applied commonly, will bring about better performance than a free-for-all approach. 'Performance' incorporates a variety of economic, personal and social dimensions, addressing between them a whole range of stakeholders. Benefits from the commonality of standards *per se* include gains to individuals, employers and the economy through the smoothness of managers' transition from one organization to another and through the process of credit accumulation and transfer which allows individuals to continue on a nearly seamless progress to certification. The art of such a common specification clearly is to introduce constraint sufficient for such benefits while allowing enough local interpretation to encourage the innovation and allow the recognition of the standards as local and sensitive to the needs of the manager, the context and the interests of stakeholders.

There are a number of perspectives from which one can estimate benefits. They include:

- National economy
- Regional and local economy and labour market
- Industrial sector
- Organization
- Stakeholder — including the manager, other employees, shareholders, customers, clients, community

A Curriculum for the Future?

Most of the influences on standards involve a degree of uncertainty. Designing standards which will be useful in five years' time rather than right for yesterday involves making a judgment about management and the nature of its contribution. The very best anticipation of trends, whether based on formal analysis or on the ideas of participating practitioners, might turn out to be false.

Experience in respect of boards of directors provides a cautionary tale. In the 1970s it was anticipated that boards would be subject to increasing regulation and that their businesses would be operating in a stable economy with low inflation. Then came increases in oil prices and a tendency to deregulate. Expectations of what would be required of directors were quite wrong.

This suggests that standards need to be expressed at a level of inclusiveness which transcends different scenarios or contexts. It is arguable whether the present standards satisfy this requirement. Trying to capture such breadth will never be easy if one is to retain sufficient purchase on individual instances of performance to be able to make a reasonably unequivocal judgment. The lesson for the development of standards is that the experience of assessment must be drawn more into the process of forming the standards.

I have not attempted here to adjudicate on commonality verus plurality. Rather I have indicated some of the aspects of standards which become part of the debate, in the hope of suggesting that standards development — one expression of outcomes — can become more mature and more able to incorporate a variety of political and implementation issues as well as technical ones.

Looking Ahead

Outcomes in management are most strongly represented in the management standards so far developed. They are imperfect, but powerful and influential.

While, for example, they retain the conventional separation of financial from human resources, they do require managers who wish to attain the standards to be competent across the full breadth of management responsibilities. Indeed it is that very definition of the responsibilities which is the most dramatic intervention into the management curriculum.

The standards have been, in their early days, more associated with assessment than with learning. This is not surprising in the context of the development of NVQs and SVQs where there is a commitment to standards against which people can be assessed, regardless of the route by which they have achieved their competence.

The standards form a specification which is concerned with effective work performance in a way which is more direct than traditional measures in the UK. Yet they perform the difficult balancing act of defining competence in terms of effectiveness without it being tied exclusively to business success beyond the influence of the individual manager.

Whatever the virtues of the existing management standards, there are many more steps needed to bring the full benefits of standards and outcomes more generally to the management curriculum. This is not surprising given the scope and ambition of a programme which seeks to influence UK management at all levels and in all sectors of the economy.

What has perhaps not been fully exploited in the development and application of the management standards to date is the recognition that functions, the generalizations of activity on which standards are based, must be as much a matter of context as outcome. A function is about changing the state of some small part of the world. It is defined not just by the end state, but by the relationship between the end state and the pre-existing state. Crucially, however, such a concept remains at a distance from other concepts based on descriptions of process and personal qualities.

Development of standards has so far taken the form of research and development projects rather than public debate. This may well be necessary to ensure a product rather than simply an analysis, but the implications of what is derived are considerable for the management curriculum. This is something in which we are all stakeholders and all liable to have a view. Ways will need to be developed for incorporating debate into the regular revision of standards.

Standards are being developed for senior managers and for boards of directors. In both cases the standards are seen as being part of a model which includes knowledge, personal competences and context, albeit directed towards the outcomes which are as close as we can come to ultimate measures of achievement and performance. The greater integration of the various constructs involved in these developments will have lessons for management standards as a whole, and will perhaps answer some of the critics who are concerned (largely unnecessarily) about standards' not being connected in a holistic model of performance and competence. The two developments between them tackle areas of management excluded from the MCI work, in particular strategic management, including setting company or organizational direction, the formation of policy and strategies, the structuring of organizations.

Notes

1 See for example Lawrence, P. (1992) Management development in Europe: a study in cultural contrast. Human Resource Management Journal, 3 (1), 11–23.
2 For an introduction, see, for example, Kennedy, C. (1991) *Guide to the management gurus*. London, Century Business.
3 See for example Buchanan, D. and Boddy, D. (1992) The expertise of the change agent: public performance and backstage activity; Boyatsis RE (1982) The competent manager: a model for effective performance. New York, Wiley.
4 Developed from Fleishman and Quaintance (1984) Taxonomies of human performance. Orlando, Florida, Academic Press Inc.
5 The NVQ/SVQ Levels and framework are described in Jessup's chapter.
6 A concern expressed in Barham, Fraser and Heath, Management for the future, Ashridge Management College and Foundation for Management.
7 Crittenden, B. (1982) Cultural pluralism and common curriculum. Melbourne, University Press.
8 Pettigrew, Hendry and Sparrow (1991) Corporate Strategy and Human Resource Management University of Warwick, Department of Employment.
9 Janes, J. and Burgess, B. (1992) Applying the management standards within organisations. Research and Development Series Report No 8. Employment Department's Methods Strategy Unit.

Chapter 16

Outcomes and Professional Knowledge

Michael Eraut

For every incompetent professional, there are probably several who are competently doing the wrong thing. The apparent contradiction stems from the application of two different sets of criteria: one relatively narrow set of criteria judges competence according to the task rather than the occupational role, the broader set judges right and wrong according to the most beneficial outcomes for the client. Sometimes, however, it is possible to argue that the criteria being used to judge competence are those which prevail, or at least are commonly found, within the profession; while a client-centred perspective still judges 'competent' behaviour as wrong. In these circumstances, preparing the professionals of the future is highly problematic. Research on professional socialization (Lacey, 1988) suggests that they are more likely to follow what they see than what they are taught.

The aim of this chapter is to argue that in all professional education priority should be given to the outcomes of professional action; and to discuss some of the consequences of implementing this principle. Not only does such a focus on outcomes broaden the range of relevant knowledge, but it also presents a continuing challenge to the validity of that knowledge. Professional knowledge does not often rest on foundations as secure as those claimed for scientific knowledge. It is periodically revised and updated. Moreover, it is rarely sufficiently specific to prescribe detailed courses of action for individual cases and situations; it has to be interpreted by professionals in accordance with specific, and often rapidly changing, circumstances. Thus, in considering the outcomes of professional action, we shall also be directly addressing the question of what constitutes professional knowledge and how it is validated. Only then will we be in a position to discuss what should be the outcomes of professional training.

To translate this argument into the terms currently used by the Employment Department, SCOTVEC and NCVQ, occupational standards for the professions and most of the service sector should not be based on current practice alone. Their validity depends on the outcomes for clients and other stakeholders. Whereas, most of this book is properly concerned with the outcomes of education and training, I am arguing that we have to take equal cognizance of the outcomes which result from the actions of those who have been trained, *i.e. the outcomes beyond the outcomes of training.*

The Outcomes of Professional Action

The principal purpose of this section is to highlight the problems of outcomes-based evaluations of professional work; and in so doing to draw attention to the wide range of professional knowledge that might be necessary for a professional to be truly accountable to his/her clients. Four types of problem are readily identified:

- the relative significance of short-term and long-term outcomes;
- considering indirect (or secondary) outcomes as well as direct outcomes;
- ambiguities in the causal connection between professional action and subsequent outcomes;
- whether professional actions are the prime responsibility of an individual, a team or a whole organization.

The extent of these problems will become clearer if we discuss some examples; and I have selected these to cover several different types of professional action: designs, procedures, reports, consultations, decisions and ongoing processes.

The Design of a Building

When an architect designs a building there are several types of outcome. First the design itself emerges, and is clearly considered sufficient evidence for the cognoscenti to judge, as for example in architectural competitions. Less sophisticated people will want to withhold even their aesthetic judgment until the building has been constructed, finding it difficult to judge the scale, texture, and relationship to the environment from drawings or even from models. At this stage, however, issues such as quality of construction, choice of materials and interior decoration will affect perception of the original design. Unless the building is small, it will have been designed by a whole team of architects and other professional groups will also have contributed — quantity surveyors, building service engineers, building technologists, etc. Their necessary mutual adjustment will render problematic the attribution of responsibility for a significant number of decisions. Another surprising aspect is likely to be the level of uncertainty about the life-expectancy of the building, especially if new materials or construction methods have been used.

It is possible, even common, to consider the building as a product without paying attention to its function, thus ignoring the third type of outcome which concerns usability. Who will live and/or work in the building, and how will they find the experience? Will there be any systematic assessment of user experience and will it be relayed back to the architect? I very much doubt it. There is probably some relevant research on user responses to buildings, but how far has it been disseminated or given widespread attention? Again, there will be problems of attributing responsibility for any dissatisfaction with the final outcomes. Was it the architect's original brief that was wrong, the prototype design to which the clients agreed, the plans drawn up for furnishing and using the space, or the traditional work-habits of the unprepared occupants? People often complain of insufficient or ineffective consultation; but does this result from the architects' neglect or lack of consultation skills, from the hierarchical nature of the client organization or from collusion between them to do a rush job and keep the price down?

Procedures in Medicine

Most routine procedures are properly delegated to sub-professional workers whenever the organization of work so permits. However, professional expertise is required when procedures have to be modified according to circumstances which cannot be wholly predicted. In surgery, for example, the surgeon has to recognize and adjust to the internal anatomy of patients and to new evidence of their condition. Such procedural skill is likely to be evaluated by observation rather than outcomes, whereas the original decision to use the procedure can be evaluated only by outcomes, either directly or by getting a range of 'second opinions'. The onset of medical audit now makes it possible to compare one surgeon's success rate with that of others, but does not distinguish whether deviations from the norm derive from the choice of procedure or the manner of its implementation.

The main argument for not delegating the administration of routine procedures is when the task provides an important opportunity for additional communication with the client, for offering advice or gaining further understanding of the client's needs, preferences and circumstances. (Boylan, 1974) It may also improve the quality of monitoring, as regular client contact allows slight changes in behaviour to be detected which might otherwise pass unnoticed, a phenomenon that has been well documented in the case of nurses (Benner, 1984).

Reports

Reports will usually involve some form of investigation or collection of evidence, possibly followed by an analysis of the implications or the respective merits of different interpretations or courses of action: they may conclude with recommendations or points for discussion. But to what level of thoroughness is the investigation pursued? How are decisions made about what tests or techniques to use, when cost is a major consideration? Are there clues which affect the probability of further inquiry being worthwhile? Some assessment of risk or pay-off is likely to be involved, but this may be highly intuitive. Will there be outcomes data to confirm or disconfirm that decision? Probably not, if the professional ethos is one of concealing one's doubts from one's clients and communicating an air of certainty.

Both the analysis and the presentation of a report may be judged either for
their intrinsic content (presumably by fellow-professionals using criteria of accuracy and inclusion of vital information) or for their impact on various audiences. Have readers understood and noted the issues and the information which needed to be drawn to their attention? If they have not, can the report be said to have been adequately prepared? Or, to ask an ever more difficult question, have the intended recipients taken appropriate subsequent action? One could argue that this last type of outcome is beyond the responsibility of the report writer. But evidence from the evaluation literature suggests that reporting needs to be viewed as a process rather than a product in situations where cognitive or attitudinal change is envisaged: it takes time for people to digest and accommodate to new ideas or new

information. Presumably an outcomes-focused evaluation of professional work would be concerned about whether professionals knew how to influence their audiences.

This process aspect of report writing is well recognized by town planners and social workers, for whom the process of consulting a range of interested parties is crucial for credibility and will usually have a major effort on the acceptability of their recommendations. Some would argue that it is the responses to a report which are the real outcomes, even when they depend on many factors beyond the reporter's control.

Consultations

In some aspects, consultations resemble the reporting process without the report. Although they ensure a period of direct interaction between a professional and a client, the circumstances may not always be propitious for achieving the most beneficial outcome. Typical handicaps include:

- time pressures which curtail conversation;
- limited opportunities for either party to reflect, think or consult;
- little, if any, prior acquaintance between the people involved;
- tensions which impede both communication and the client's ability to remember what advice was given.

Elsewhere I have analyzed in some detail how these and other factors, such as hidden agendas, impinge on teacher-parent consultations about children's progress at school; and suggested that the way consultations are organized can be as important as how they are conducted when they eventually occur (Eraut, 1988).

Ideally, the sequence of outcomes will be as follows:

(i)   the professional makes an accurate assessment of the client's needs and preferences;
(ii)   good advice is given, because the professional is aware of all the relevant options and can assess their relative benefits for the client;
(iii) the client understands and remembers the advice;
(iv)   the client acts on the advice;
(v)   the final outcomes are as predicted.

Again, it could be argued that the fourth outcome is the sole responsibility of the client; but there could also be circumstances in which the failure to anticipate and discuss barriers to a client following good advice could be partly the responsibility of the professional.

Decisions

While most of the actions described above have involved decisions of some kind, I have not given much attention to the decisions themselves. Making a good decision will depend on:

(i)   the right analysis of the problem or situation;

(ii)   considering the full range of options for action and assessing their risks and benefits;

(iii) finding the best fit between the situations and one of the decision options (which could of course include a decision to wait until further information became available).

It should be noted that assessing the options may require as much information about the client's preferences and circumstances as did the original analysis of the problem. Consider, for example, the management of chronic illness.

In order to make good decisions, a professional needs to be a good investigator, knowledgeable about options, able to reason critically and able to learn from experience. Learning from experience involves reflecting on particular issues in the light of their eventual outcomes; and knowledge about options should incorporate evidence from outcomes, reported in the literature or by colleagues. Such evidence does not on its own guarantee the right conclusion, because many factors affect outcomes; but critical thinking which comprises and contrasts evidence from several cases is likely to improve the quality of decision-making. However, even this may depend on whether the original analysis of the problem was appropriate.

The introduction of computerized information systems will help with the collection and analysis of outcomes data, provided that people feel that the effort involved in accurately entering data is worth the effort entailed and problems of confidentiality or commercial secrecy can be overcome. Information about the frequency of occurrence of diseases and the success probabilities of different treatments is beginning to become available in several branches of medicine; but there is also evidence that some doctors have considerable difficulty in making use of this kind of data (Dowie and Elstein, 1988).

Ongoing Processes

Prolonged periods of contact characterize work in some helping professions, for example teaching and psychiatric nursing. Professional intervention is then seen more as an ongoing process than a small number of distinct decisions. This can be a disadvantage, when tradition and custom prevail, and there is little deliberative decision-making involving the genuine exploration of alternative policies and practices. Moreover, evaluation tends to be in terms of instant client response rather than medium or long-term outcomes. Outcome priorities which tend to go against the grain include (a) developing client independence of professional support; and (b) changing client attitudes in order to affect long-term behaviour.

Another feature of prolonged periods of contact is that they often take place in organizational settings, where the influences of management style, policy and climate transcend those of individual professionals. It is surely no accident that research on school effectiveness appears to be more conclusive than that on teacher effectiveness. This suggests that an important component of professional knowledge is how to contribute to the quality of the organization in which one works, above and beyond the quality of one's own personal work.

Both for individuals and for organizations, the problems of outcomes-based evaluation are considerable. When there is prolonged interaction it is difficult to determine what caused what; so research which tries to disentangle the effects of different variables has rarely been a useful source of advice for practitioners.

Whose Outcomes?

Implications for the Professional–Client Relationship

One conclusion to be drawn from the foregoing analysis is that the evaluation of professional work needs to take into account longer term outcomes and a wider range of outcomes than is normal in most professions. This problem has arisen for a number of reasons. Where the professional is paid for a specific service, his or her interest ceases (at least in the pecuniary sense) as soon as that service has been completed. Further pursuit of outcomes evidence may be regarded as too intrusive, too expensive or something to be left to researchers. It is likely to take time and effort which might otherwise be devoted to other clients. A more cynical explanation might be that a professional's interest in self-evaluation is limited to the *outcomes for the professional* — the construction of a building, the production of a report, the completion of treatment, the end of a consultation, the conclusion of a process, etc. — and takes little notice, beyond polite expressions of concern, of the *outcomes for the client.*

This brings us back to the ideology of professionalism, and the informal concordat by which it was believed that expert knowledge was protected from abuse by being entrusted to self-governing professions dedicated to the service of their clients. However, the Victorian concept of service preceded universal suffrage and was essentially profession-centred. Except when clients were exceptionally powerful it was the professional alone who decided what their needs were: the client's contribution was relatively small. Restoring the client's role from that of object to that of subject in accord with the expectations of the twenty-first century entails giving primacy of attention to the *outcomes for the client.*

This concern for outcomes may affect not only the evaluation of professional work, but also its very nature. Outcomes become part of the content of professional discourse: the professional seeks to ascertain client preferences and priorities with respect to outcomes, the client seeks advice on the probable outcomes of the range of alternative courses of action about which the professional is able to provide information. Clarity of communication is vital for the success of these kinds of consultations, but is inhibited by understandable differences of perspective. The professional has to estimate probabilities and may not be too confident about the figures: the client is looking for certainties.

Implications for the Teacher–Student Relationship

In professional education, the question 'whose outcomes' is even more complex, because there are two sets of clients: the immediate clients are learners, who may have student status or qualified status; the ultimate clients are those who receive, or will in the future receive, services from those learners. To the natural variation we have been discussing in the relationship between professional action and outcomes for the client, we have to add that variation which arises during the learning process itself. We can anticipate variation in the learning outcomes achieved by different students, even when the programme is organized to ensure that all of them acquire the competence needed to practise; and we can anticipate differences in the priorities which different students accord to these outcomes. If we are to give professional learners the same rights as other clients, we need to discuss these matters with them from the outset.

Client-centred discussion of outcomes matches recent theories of adult education and pedagogic theories of the type advocated by TVEI and proponents of flexible learning (see chapters 13 and 9). Their purpose is to develop confident, independent learners; priority is given to learning contracts, action planning and formative evaluation of progress; the role of the teacher is to negotiate flexible learning goals and advise and support the learner in achieving them. Intermediate objectives are likely to be discussed and modified on a number of occasions, as learning progresses and interests and opportunities unfold; so the model differs markedly from the classical tradition of objectives-based curriculum planning which entailed detailed specification with little or no learner participation.

There are good reasons, however, why the outcomes of initial professional education are not wholly determined by student-clients. The interests of the ultimate clients of those students take precedence; that is why we have standards and qualifications. Moreover, students willingly enrol on professional courses, knowing that most of the curriculum is already decided. Where students perceive course objectives as authentic, i.e. as genuinely serving the interests of their future clients, they readily take ownership of them; so that externally specified objectives become personal goals as well. Then there is no distinction between the intended outcomes of the professional educator and those of the student client. However, where students (and often many practitioners as well) perceive course objectives as inauthentic they tend to resent them, possibly starting a process of alienation from professional education which will affect their future professional development. Thus external determination of objectives neither precludes nor guarantees ownership by the students. Given the psychological importance of such ownership, it behoves professional educators:

(i) to be able to justify their curriculum in terms of the needs of future clients of their profession; and

(ii) to ensure that students perceive, understand and agree with this justification.

The Outcomes of Professional Training

Other contributors, notably Otter (Chapter 17) have addressed the question of general, transferable skills in higher education. Her conclusion is that programmes address such skills to varying degrees: although some general skills figure prominently amongst the outcomes of such programmes, there is considerable scope for broadening the range of such skills and increasing the priority given to them in curriculum development, teaching and learning. All the skills discussed by Otter are extremely important in professional work; and this has several implications. First, the skills which student professionals bring to their training should play an important part in the admission process, both on entry to higher education and, for graduate entrants, on acceptance for professional training. Second, such skills should be further developed during professional training. Third, they need greater recognition as having value for other occupations — professional training may not be as specialized as is often implied. Fourth, they also need to feature in continuing professional development: although it is often recognized that senior managers may need to enhance their communication skills, IT skills and even numeracy skills, the same requirement is rarely extended to senior professionals.

Nevertheless, it would be a mistake to consider general, transferable skills in isolation. For much professional work they have to be used in very specific ways to tackle particular cases and problems; and this requires further professional training. Similarly, professional workers may draw upon knowledge acquired from discipline-based study in general higher education but still need to learn how to build that knowledge into their professional practice. However, my purpose in this particular chapter is not to analyse the interface, overlap or distinction between professional training and general higher education. My focus is on the outcomes of professional training, which are necessary for future professionals to be able to meet their future clients' needs and expectations. What kind of professional knowledge and expertise is needed when validity is determined by outcomes for the client? And what are the implications for programmes of professional education?

How Should We Define Professional Knowledge?

Writers on professional education frequently get entangled in the different meanings accorded to the term 'knowledge' in our society. While accepting the logic of Ryle's (1949) argument that knowledge incorporates 'knowing how' as well as 'knowing that' and accepting Polanyi's (1966) arguments for the importance of 'tacit' knowledge, they nevertheless regress to the everyday usage of the term 'knowledge' to mean propositional knowledge alone; or, worse still, to cover only facts. This regression is evident in the official guidelines on occupational standards, when they distinguish between competence and underpinning knowledge with the clear implication that being 'competent' is more than being 'knowledgeable' (the term 'knowledgeable' carries this same limiting connotation). They also reify knowledge by using the term 'knowledge and understanding', which appears to imply that knowledge resides outside people while understanding resides within them. Their clearly stated intention is to de-academicize professional training; but in so doing they reinforce what I consider to be the false distinction between academic knowledge and practical knowledge which lies at the heart of our educational system.

In order to make my point I shall begin on the academic side. If one asks the question 'what constitutes historical knowledge?', the answer will probably include these three criteria:

- the knowledge must be recorded, usually in the form of print;
- it must be accepted as authentic and valid by a significant number of professional historians;
- it must qualify as history, rather than psychology or mathematics.

There will be many cases where the interpretation of these criteria is disputed, but more often there will be a consensus. The main issues concern validity and classification.

If, however, one asks the question 'what is the knowledge requirement for a professional historian?', the answer will be rather different.

- It will refer to knowledge in a particular field, thus covering only a fraction of the domain of historical knowledge.
- It may contain knowledge not classified as historical knowledge including both historical information not yet published and knowledge from other disciplines, for example, economics, which is used in historical research.
- It will include knowledge of how to study and research in history, and how to write history; process knowledge as well as propositional knowledge.

While 'historical knowledge' is confined to publicly available propositional knowledge located in a particular section of the library, the 'knowledge of the professional historian' is both narrower (focused on a specialist field) and broader because it includes aspects of other disciplines, unpublished material and the process know-how required for historical research. Moreover, its boundaries are defined not by the content of the knowledge but by the use to which it is put. Any knowledge which can be used for constructing or evaluating history is potentially part of the professional historian's repertoire. Validity is still an issue; but so also are relevance to purpose and the historian's professional capability or competence. Throughout this chapter, I shall be using the term professional knowledge to refer not to the contents of a professional library but to *the knowledge possessed by professionals which enables them to perform professional work with quality.* This leads me to four conclusions.

(i) Professional knowledge includes both process and propositional knowledge, knowing how as well as knowing that.
(ii) The propositional knowledge of a professional is not exclusively derived from public sources. Confidential records, memories of cases and personal theories also play an important part in professional work.
(iii) The purpose and quality of professional work must ultimately depend on the outcomes for the client.
(iv) The boundaries of professional knowledge should be determined by the purposes of professional action rather than any prespecified categories of content.

(i) and (ii) have been discussed in detail elsewhere (Eraut, 1985, 1988 and 1992), while (iii) provided the focus for the early part of this chapter. But (iv) needs further elucidation before we proceed to discuss the implications of these conclusions for developing professional programmes. From a student perspective we have to recognize that, although knowledge may be included in the curriculum because somebody else has deemed it relevant to professional practice, it does not become part of professional knowledge unless and until it has been used for a professional purpose. Thus a piece of biological knowledge does not become professional knowledge for a nurse until he or she has used it as part of a nursing process.

The Curricular Implications of a Knowledge Use Perspective

The above argument leads me to formulate three radical but important principles for programmes of initial professional education:

(i) if knowledge is not used for a professional purpose within the programme itself, it should not be included; and

(ii) if the time-gap between the introduction of such knowledge and its first use is too large, it is being introduced at the wrong point in the sequence.

(iii) the objectives for the theoretical aspects of professional education programmes should be defined, not in terms of knowledge use *per se*, but in terms of knowledge use in professional contexts.

These principles are not just my personal preference. They are founded on (a) the value assumption that in an overcrowded curriculum the main selection principle should be the needs of the student professionals' future clients; and (b) empirical evidence from several professions that knowledge not perceived as professionally relevant is accorded low status by students, memorized if needed for examinations but rapidly forgotten thereafter. Indeed, some knowledge sanctioned by custom and tradition has been rendered wholly irrelevant by technological progress or changing patterns of work.

Taken together, these principles provide a strong argument against the common practice of front-loading discipline-based knowledge in professional education programmes. However, for reasons discussed below, knowledge use should be interpreted broadly so as to include professionally relevant project work as well as practical situations. The response to breaches of the second principle can be either (a) to insert practical work closer to the point where the topic is introduced or (b) to postpone the introduction of the topic until a relevant context for using it has become available. In some cases, it might be better introduced after completion of the initial qualification.

The third principle also raises the important issue of how people learn to use propositional knowledge in a professional context. Too many curricula are based on the assumption that all that is necessary is the provision of appropriate learning opportunities. More careful examination suggests that such an assumption is rarely justified in professional learning. Eraut's analysis of modes of knowledge use (1985) suggests that simple replication of knowledge plays only a small part in professional work. Application of established knowledge requires further knowledge about when and how to use it, derived from experience of situational analysis (see below). Equally common, and in some professional work predominant, is the interpretative use of propositional knowledge. Concepts, theories and principles have to be interpreted in order to be used; and this involves not only situational analysis but working out the appropriate form/meaning/version of the concept, theory or principle to use. Thus using propositional knowledge in practical situations requires considerable intellectual effort, and learning how to use concepts and ideas is usually a more difficult cognitive task than simply comprehending them and reproducing them. In curriculum terms, this implies that as much time and effort should be allocated to enabling and supporting the use of propositional knowledge as is currently devoted to its acquisition. The time required to learn how to use propositional knowledge in professional contexts is considerable; so there is a potential conflict between time allocated to the acquisition of such knowledge and the time required to learn how to use it.

The Nature of Process Knowledge

Let us now transfer our attention to process knowledge, for people need more than propositional knowledge in order to engage in professional work. They also need the appropriate skills and attitudes and the ability to combine their knowledge and know-how into an integrated approach in selecting, planning, implementing and evaluating those professional activities which are best matched to the clients, situations and problems they encounter.

A useful typology of such processes is depicted in the diagram below: one dimension concerns the rapidity of the process, the other distinguishes between analysis, decision and action.

SPEED

ANALYSIS	Instant Recognition	Rapid Interpretation	Deliberative Analysis
DECISION	Instant Response	Rapid Decisions	Deliberative Decisions
ACTION	Routinized Unreflective Action	Action Monitored by Reflection	Action following a period of Deliberation

Instant recognition hardly merits the description of analysis, because it is a wholly intuitive process. However, it is based on prior experience some of which may have involved more conscious analysis of the information input (consider, for example, learning to recognize a new species of bird). The boundary between instant recognition and rapid interpretation is certainly not clearcut. Rapid interpretation is characteristic of human communication: there is some conscious thinking about what people are saying to one, but the expectation of a rapid response precludes any deliberation at the time. People have to analyse the situation, which is itself changing as new information is received, and make the most appropriate response very quickly. Though there is some chance to think about it briefly, the probability is that the response will be fairly similar to those one has given on previous occasions; because frequently used responses are the most available for action and therefore the most likely to be used in a hurry. Under conditions of rapid interpretation some kinds of information are more likely to be noticed than others, with priority being accorded to the most recent, the most salient and that which most conforms with prior expectations. Thus not only can mistakes easily happen, they can become self-confirming as well. Even contrary opinions can be explained away by those unwilling to change their minds.

The pace of professional work means that rapid analysis of situations is often the norm. So how can professional persons limit their susceptibility to making mistakes. Four possibilities are:

- getting second opinions fairly regularly, and following up significant differences;
- becoming more aware of one's tendency to misinterpret situations;
- gathering additional information in a more systematic way;
- engaging in periods of deliberative analysis from time to time to bring one's behaviour under more critical control.

In general, situational analysis is unlikely to take into account outcomes of previous actions unless there has been some deliberation. The connection between professional action and medium or long-term outcomes can only be established by deliberation: otherwise the complexity of the context will make reaching the wrong conclusion quite a common occurrence. Sustaining a high quality professional performance depends both on conducting occasional deliberative reviews to maintain critical control over rapid interpretations and on knowing when a particular situation is so difficult as to merit an additional period of deliberative analysis. This might involve not only thinking, but consultation and further inquiry as well. Whether such deliberations occur will depend on professionals having both the thinking skills to put them to good use and the disposition to allocate the necessary time.

The three type of decision-making present a similar contrast. Rapid decisions are necessary to cope with many types of professional work, but need to be regularly reviewed in order to prevent bad habits from developing. Difficult decisions require further investigation and deliberation, perhaps consultation with others; though this will not happen unless they are recognized as difficult and the professional is prepared to allocate much more time. Deliberative decision-making is likely to involve consideration of outcomes in the manner described in earlier sections. But once a pattern is established these kinds of decision will get made much more rapidly, probably becoming subject to error over time unless they are regularly reviewed. New research or changing circumstances will create new decision options or affect the relative merits of old ones. But they also threaten established routines and may be disregarded by those whose determination to keep up-to-date is weakening.

What are the implications for professional education? Priority needs to be given to developing the quality of professional thinking, the disposition to create time for deliberation and the willingness to keep up-to-date. The habits of over-routinization and losing sight of the ultimate outcomes for the client are easily acquired during years of practice. So strong resistance to them has to be built into professional education. The importance of learning from experience and linking theory with practice means that it may take some years for full proficiency to develop; and much of this time will involve learning on-the-job. However, there is also evidence from research on professional socialization that prolonged exposure to prevailing professional norms in many practice settings is prone to discourage the development of professional thinking and the allocation of time to deliberation and keeping up-to-date.

Conclusion

I began this chapter by arguing that the evaluation of professional work needs to take into account longer term outcomes and a wider range of outcomes.

Achieving this goal requires:

(i)   a wider conception of the role of professionals in society and their duties towards their clients;
(ii) appropriate attitudes towards self-evaluation and accountability;
(iii) a wider range of professional knowledge and patterns of thinking;
(iv) a willingness to commit time and resources to improving the quality of professional work.

These are more likely to become outcomes of professional education if

(a)   the teachers concerned come (i) closer to practice, according it greater priority and focusing more of their attention on knowledge use; and (ii) closer to clients, reviewing cases and conducting research into outcomes for clients
(b)   practitioners engage in more deliberation, more evaluation and more continuing education.

They are less likely to become outcomes if either party drifts in the opposite direction, or becomes dominant over the other.

References

BENNER, P. (1984) *From Novice to Expert: Excellence and Power in Clinical Nursing Practice*, Menlo Park, CA, Addison-Wesley.

BOYLAN, A. (1974) 'Clinical communication', *Nursing Times*, 28 November, pp. 1858–9.

DOWIE, J.A. and ELSTEIN, A.S. (Eds) (1988) *Professional Judgement: A Reader in Professional Decision Making*, Cambridge, Cambridge University Press.

ERAUT, M. (1985) 'Knowledge creation and knowledge use in professional contexts', *Studies in Higher Education*, 10, 2, pp. 117–33.

ERAUT, M. (1988) 'Learning about management: The role of the management course' in DAY, C. and POSTER, C. (Eds) *Education Management: Purposes and Practices*. London, Routledge.

ERAUT, M. (1992) 'Developing the knowledge base: A process perspective on professional education' in BARNETT, R. (Ed) *Learning to Effect*, Society for Research into Higher Education and Open University Press.

ERAUT, M. and COLE, G. (1993) *Assessing Competence in the Professions*, Report No 14, Research and Development Series, Sheffield, Methods Strategy Unit, Employment Department.

LACEY, C. (1977) *The Socialization of Teachers*, London, Methuen.

POLANYI, M. (1966) *The Tacit Dimension*, London, Doubleday.

RYLE, G. (1949) *The Concept of Mind*, London, Hutchinson.

Chapter 17

Learning Outcomes in Higher Education

Sue Otter

The process of exposing the objectives of higher education and the debate which surrounds it will be most illuminating. So much is currently hidden behind woolly concepts . . . that it is difficult to discuss its role and function, and consequently the extent to which they are achieved. (Jessup, 1991).

Introduction — Why Learning Outcomes?

The UDACE project, 'Learning Outcomes and Credits in Higher Education' (1991) provided a fresh impetus for thinking about the outcomes of learning in higher education. The findings of that project and the developments in several universities which have followed have gone some way both towards 'exposing the objectives', and to examining the extent to which current assessment practices in higher education measure their achievement.

The early UDACE work on outcomes began from the premise that outcomes were an important means of helping adult learners. They provided descriptions of what was to be achieved by following a particular course of learning, and thereby made adult access, through processes like APEL, and the accreditation of work-based learning, simpler. Outcomes reflected the fundamental principle of credit in HE.

> Learning, wherever it is acquired, and provided that it can be assessed, can be given credit towards awards in higher education.

Outcomes had potential benefits too in helping all learners to make better informed choices about their intended course of study. It was evident then, as now, that many University students choose courses on relatively flimsy evidence and advice, and that making an inappropriate choice affected both retention and motivation. The recent Audit Office report *Unfinished Business* (1993) has highlighted the wasted resources arising from misguided choices in further education. The growth of modular courses, where students have potentially much greater freedom to choose subject combinations, requires provision of better information on which students can make choices at the start of and during their study.

The UDACE project showed that the existing language of course documentation was largely input based. It described the body of knowledge of the subject and the processes by which this knowledge would be imparted (lectures, tutorials, etc.). Many course documents made no reference to either the intellectual, or the personal skills of graduates. Yet it was evident that these were a crucially important part of what many academic staff expected students to achieve, and what employers sought in recruiting graduates. There was often a tacit assumption that these skills would be developed as part of the process of higher education, but many of them were never clearly described to students, nor specifically assessed.

It was evident too that there was a considerable range of views among academic staff on the meaning and relative importance of skills and competences in higher education, and that there were widely different expectations within course teams, as well as different standards applied to their recognition. The project showed that the tacit understanding of broader intellectual and personal skills in many courses was clarified by descriptions of outcomes, and this was advantageous to both staff and students.

Student numbers in higher education were increasing rapidly in many universities, and there was a growing realization that increased staff/student ratios required greater student autonomy and more emphasis on independent learning and motivation. The virtual disappearance of the personal tutorial system in many universities, and of many of the small group teaching structures which were traditional in HE, was also removing an important mechanism by which the expectations of staff were communicated to students. Clear written descriptions of outcomes were very helpful to students, and the UDACE project provided evidence of better student motivation, where outcomes were used to define the staff expectations of seminar programmes. It was evident too that many course documents were written primarily for the purposes of validation and review, and that some students never had access to the detailed aims and objectives of the courses they were undertaking. For some institutions describing their learning outcomes provided an important means of communication between staff and students.

Writing Learning Outcome Statements

The starting premise for the UDACE Learning Outcomes project was that outcomes in higher education needed to reflect the views of three groups of people, academic staff teaching courses in universities, students undertaking those courses, and graduate employers. The project brought these groups of people together in various ways to discuss what the outcomes should include and to draft agreed outcome statements. The three groups had widely different views as to what the outcomes should include. Students and graduate employers focused mainly on personal skills, and placed much less emphasis on the understanding of a body of subject specific knowledge than did the academic staff. While there was some measure of agreement between the three, the exercise of consultation helped to clarify two things:

— that graduate employers valued a broad set of personal transferable skills, and would welcome evidence of the achievement of these in new graduates;

— that many students had clear vocational aspirations and understood the nature and need for developing personal transferable skills in the graduate labour market.

The academic staff participating in the project were left to wrestle with the problem of including these broad skills and competences in their outcome statements, while retaining a subject specific content to the degree. Some simple technical questions emerged from the exercise of getting down to writing outcome statements.

Where to Begin?

It was quickly apparent that there was a range of views on how to begin. Some of the academic staff groups believed that it was quite sufficient to rewrite the aims and objectives of their existing courses and modules in a passive sense. Such outcomes tended to focus on 'understanding' a body of knowledge.

For example: 'understand appropriate technological principles' (design group) and 'understand and come to terms with own emotional uncertainties' (English group).

This approach tended to leave out outcomes which related to personal skills and competences, and resulted in statements which were very general and proved difficult to assess subsequently. Others favoured completely rethinking the nature and purpose of the degree in terms of outcome, and then grouping modules around these. The project sought to find ways of doing the latter, and examined some possible structures based on defining a central core of outcomes common to all graduates with subject specific skills and knowledge related to these. Several possible models emerged, and some of these have been refined in subsequent work in universities involved in the original work.

A series of workshops on the functional analysis methodology provided a possible alternative route for the more vocational subjects, but not for English and social sciences. The difficulty here was in defining a key purpose, since there were widely differing views within the groups. Eventually some of the groups developed overarching key statements, as distinct from key purposes; however these appeared to be course aims in all but name.

For example 'Engineering involves the acquisition and use of scientific and other pertinent knowledge and skills to create, operate and maintain optimal systems and processes of practical value' (engineering group).

These statements served some purpose in bringing together the views and concerns of the group members, but they were not key purposes in the sense that the outcomes flowed from them, or described 'what has to be done for the key purpose to be achieved', as they do in a functional analysis. It appeared that a key purpose was for many courses a complex mixture of achieving personal development and growth for the student, accompanied by the acquisition of certain basic skills, and the experience of a particular sort of process designed to achieve a level of scholarship, or immersion in a subject, for the subject's sake.

More recent development work has tended to follow the route of writing outcome statements for each existing module. This has been done partly in an attempt to make the assessment of prior learning simpler (if the module describes what students are expected to achieve then it is simpler to match students' prior learning), and partly as a means of developing a more strategic approach to assessment and to teaching and learning.

Where this has been undertaken with modular programmes, it has become evident that there may be considerable variation between the programmes for different students, and questions of coherence and standards have been raised. There have been suggestions that there should be a set of core outcomes which all students should achieve, despite their choice of modules. Systems of personal profiling, portfolios and records of achievement have been proposed as a means of ensuring that all students achieve certain outcomes despite the subject, or the range of modules included in their degree programme.

It may be that an outcome approach in higher education is best used in examining existing courses and modules, and leads logically to the consideration of the outcomes of the overall programme.

Different Types of Outcome

Other approaches to writing outcome statements have used three categories of outcome; knowledge, skills, and personal competence. One university adopting this approach suggests that the knowledge outcomes are 'cognitive gains in the broadest sense', and include knowledge of substantive material, understanding of theoretical perspectives and issues, and ability to apply knowledge and solve problems. Skill-based outcomes include specific skills like data analysis, word processing, vocationally specific skills, (mainly field and laboratory-based), and skills related to the process of learning and to the development of learning autonomy. Personal outcomes include interpersonal skills, and personal motivation and organizational skills of various kinds. The guideline document states that there is inevitably a degree of overlap between the three types, but that the categorization aids breadth, and ensures that personal competences are included in all modules.

One group (engineering) in the original UDACE project used a taxonomy of objectives (Carter, 1985) as a checklist to ensure that a full range of outcomes was included. This approach has been favoured by other departments, and continues to prove a popular approach in engineering departments.

How Do Outcomes Differ From Existing Course Objectives?

The requirement to assess learning outcomes places a particular discipline on the writing of an outcome statement. In essence the questions asked are:

- what do I want the student to achieve? and
- how will I know that s/he has achieved that?

The requirement to be able to assess questions the use of words like 'understand', which are common in the language of course objectives and important for the academic validation of courses. Such words do not, however, describe what a student will have to do to demonstrate understanding, and do not help a student to grapple with the range of expectations of 'understanding' from different staff members. Some academic staff argue that this is a perfectly acceptable level of dissonance, and is important to the whole concept of higher education. Others argue that it is a means of hiding woolly thinking and that better descriptions of what is required will benefit students and encourage greater achievement.

A typical example is:

Objective: to achieve an understanding of post-structuralism
Outcomes: to analyse arguments logically;
to present clear and coherent arguments;
to identify presuppositions and question them.

Other objectives describe what the module or course will provide, for example

Objective: acquire a range of core biochemical practical skills.

The outcomes may describe more precisely how a student will be deemed to have achieved the objective.

Outcomes: measure the rate of an enzyme catalyzed reaction;
assay protein and glucose concentrations;
construct and use calibration curves;
distinguish between good and bad analytical practice.

Assessment Strategy

The most far-reaching findings of the UDACE project were in relation to assessment. A major element of the project was concerned with producing outcome statements, which then formed the basis of looking at the existing assessment strategy of the participating course teams. A number of problems were immediately evident.

In some cases there was no existing assessment strategy, there was simply an unseen examination (answer four questions from ten, with a 40 per cent pass mark), sometimes accompanied by assessed coursework. The relationship between existing course objectives and assessment strategy was sometimes far from clear. The requirement that outcomes stated what the student had to achieve, and how that would be recognized, suggested that many existing approaches to assessment would not allow a student to demonstrate many outcomes. This led to considerable concern about an increase in the amount of assessed work a student had to complete, as well as in the amount of marking which staff had to undertake.

Assessment was a serious problem for some staff as the rise in student numbers had produced a huge increase in the amount of marking of traditional forms of written work. These placed intolerable burdens on staff, and led to poor feedback to students. It was increasingly impossible to provide realistic individual feedback to students, and marked work was often returned many weeks after completion, further adding to loss of feedback.

Describing outcomes offered several helpful solutions. Some groups of staff in the original project used outcomes as a basis for describing detailed criteria for completion of written work. This made student self-assessment simpler, and provided better student feedback.

Using outcomes also proved to be valuable in developing greater student responsibility for learning. The principle that assessment is about judgment of sufficient evidence was particularly useful. Recent work in some universities suggests that some course teams have adopted the principle that students are provided with the outcomes for their course/module/unit and are offered several modes of assessment through which they can provide evidence of the achievement of the outcomes. Increased responsibility is placed on students actively to demonstrate that they have achieved the outcomes, rather than on staff actively to seek to find such evidence. Further work on the assessment of outcomes showed that describing outcomes allowed students to self-assess their progress more effectively, and allowed greater use of peer assessment and of formative feedback to students.

The descriptions of outcomes raised an interesting question about the existing assessment strategy. If outcomes described what the student was required to achieve, was it feasible for the student to avoid being tested on some of them, or fail to achieve some of them? Did they all need to be assessed? Current assessment practice was based on overall performance, and the principle of compensation is common practice in many universities. Here good performance in one area of the course could compensate for poor, and sometimes inadequate, performance in others. There was a general expectation that students might not achieve all the outcomes, but a growing question as to whether this was appropriate. Current assessment strategies were designed to separate the 'best and brightest' from the rest, and many assessment practices were designed to feed ultimately into the classification of the degree. While outcomes did not necessarily suggest a wholesale move to criterion-referenced forms of assessment, and hence to an unclassified degree, they did propose that there was a very clear and broad standard which all students might be expected to achieve.

Learning outcomes posed difficult questions. Overall they provided a better definition of satisfactory and not satisfactory performance, and demonstrated that assessing the breadth of achievement of a student might in some cases be preferable to using assessment to rank student achievement. The description of outcomes offered a means of rethinking the assessment strategy. For some courses this meant identifying outcomes which had to be achieved by all students for the purposes of progression or satisfactory completion, and of other outcomes which could be graded and provide information on ranking and classification.

Outcomes and Process — Could Everything Be Described in Terms of Outcomes?

The early work on learning outcomes in higher education was criticized for its emphasis on the outcome, rather than on the value of the process of higher education. Outcomes in vocational education are explicitly intended to separate the definition of standards from the process of learning (see Jessup in this volume). The deliberate separation of the teaching and learning process from the definition of what it is intended to achieve has provided the means of using lead bodies (employers) to define standards, and has served to widen access by offering routes to qualifications which do not involve classroom study and formal courses. Such a separation is more problematic in higher education, since the process of the degree course is generally understood to be an integral part of the concept of a degree.

The work on assessment strategy was useful since it made clear that everything did not need to be assessed. It identified that there were some aspects of courses which were concerned with providing students with experience of a particular learning process, and that what students achieved as a result of that process was not usefully assessable. It was evident too that much of the defence of the process in higher education was a screen for some relatively woolly thinking, and that in some cases the value of the process perceived by the staff was not shared by the students. Nevertheless there was evidence that there were some process outcomes where it was more important to ensure that students had the experience, rather than that they had achieved something specific as a result of it. For example, higher education provided an environment in which students were encouraged to speculate and experiment — making mistakes was an important part of the learning process, but not a part which would be assessed.

How Can Detailed Knowledge Be Included in Outcome Statements?

Some universities have developed outcome statements for modules, but have sought ways in which to include a syllabus which describes the detailed knowledge which a student is expected to cover separately. In some cases there are qualifying statements for each outcome, describing the activities which students will have to undertake in order to demonstrate the achievements. In some cases these are described as assessment criteria, and in some as range statements.

For example, (taken from a year one module in information technology where the module is based on a major case study):

Learning Outcome — Information flows and data stores are analyzed.
Range Statement   — Must include data flow diagrams, logical data structures and data dictionaries.
Learning Outcome — Clerical procedures are documented.
Range Statement   — Must include process descriptions, structured English, decision tables, narrative description.

What About Levels?

The relationship between outcomes in HE and level is complex. The question of levels was avoided by the groups in the UDACE project, since they chose to develop their learning outcome statements without reference to levels. This was largely because the structure of courses in the same subject area showed that material which was included in the first year of some courses occurred in the second and final year of others. This reflected the very different ethos of some courses and different approaches to course design, for example:

the first year of some courses was devoted to coverage of a series of fundamental principles or areas of the subject. These were built on in the second year, and the third year covered applications of this information in different settings.

Other courses began with a broad consideration of applications and what one member called 'real world problems', and then developed specific knowledge relating to these in the remaining years of the course.

The fact that the groups in the project reached a broad measure of agreement in the description of learning outcomes, without starting from levels, suggested that levels could be regarded as stages in a course, rather than levels of attainment. This follows the original CNAA approach to level, which simply proposed a relationship between the year or stage of a course and the 'standard' of work. Some of the universities currently developing outcomes have used the Bloom (1956) taxonomy to describe levels as:

Level 1   comprehension of basic principles
Level 2   application of theory
Level 3   evaluation of theory, and analysis and synthesis of own ideas

Others have defined levels based on the increasing autonomy of the learner. This approach suggests that the early stages of a course are defined and largely delivered by the staff, i.e. information is presented to the student. At higher levels students are expected to retrieve information for themselves and to develop a wider range of learning and problem solving skills. At the final level, the student was expected to think and learn independently, develop self-motivation, and develop intellectual curiosity in developing new ideas and solutions.

These approaches are complicated by an increasing awareness of the need to link academic credits with credits achieved through National Vocational Qualifications. Here the system of levels is more complex and includes further quite different concepts like the nature of the work role, routineness, predictability, and unpredictability, and the degree of autonomy and responsibility for others.

Both approaches to levels assume a hierarchical logical system of development, which is contradicted by the evidence of the development of individual learners. Students in the first year of degree courses are often able to provide evidence of analysis and independence of thought, albeit often from a relatively narrower information base, as well as their counterparts in the final year. One of the potential problems posed by the development of learning outcomes may be to show that students at initial stages of a course can provide evidence of achievement at higher level. This may present a serious challenge to the more traditional approaches to course design.

If levels are not clearly definable as stages of attainment, but are simply a device for ensuring and monitoring progression within a course, then it is not necessary to define learning outcomes at each level. The UDACE project suggested some answers and some difficulties with this approach. Some groups felt that some of their learning outcomes were clearly related to specific stages of a course, and that a student might be required to demonstrate them before progressing from one stage to the next. Both the social science and the design groups produced models which did this. Other groups suggested that some learning outcome statements could be described in three levels, usually achieved by making the criteria for assessment more demanding at each level. It was suggested that the criteria in fact determined the increasing autonomy of the student.

Overall there were two views. One was that learning outcomes should be described at the graduate level. Some learning outcomes, might, depending on the construction of the course, be demonstrated at earlier stages than others. Some learning outcomes might therefore act as progression requirements at different stages.

An alternative was that learning outcomes might be described at the graduate level and have incremental assessment criteria which reflected the increasing autonomy of the student. In practice it appeared that the construction of most courses meant that some learning activities, particularly project work, were only offered at later stages, and that some learning outcomes could not actually be demonstrated until the student had completed that part of the course. The construction of the course effectively determined when the learning opportunities were provided, and therefore when some learning outcomes could be demonstrated.

It seems that the question of level may not hamper the development of learning outcome statements for existing courses, and that it is the relationship between the outcome and the learning opportunity offered the student which is crucial. The question of levels is, however, fundamental to the development of credit transfer, and to the relationship between outcomes for vocational programmes like NVQs and academic programmes. The credit framework proposed by the FEU (1992) is based on an alignment of the academic and vocational system of levels. Its translation into a national system for credit transfer will require a more careful conceptualization of levels if it is to realize the aim of widening participation.

Unplanned Outcomes

One of the major expectations of higher education is that students will create their own unplanned outcomes, and that staff do not wish to define these in advance. The ability of students to create their own agenda for development is an important feature of some courses, and the description of the outcomes which must be achieved should not preclude or discourage the recognition of other achievements.

This suggests that the role of outcomes in higher education may be better applied to describing, and ensuring a specified range of achievement for all graduates, than in seeking to provide exact and exhaustive descriptions of all achievement. This may have relevance to quality assurance mechanisms, since there is considerable evidence of excellence in higher education, but also evidence that many students do not substantially improve their level of achievement as a result of the experience of higher education.

Outcomes and National Standards

While outcomes may have some utility in HE, it is evident too that there are subtle differences between outcomes as standards for the vocational framework of NVQs and the outcomes of degree courses. Vocational standards, as applied in NVQs, are nationally defined, and directly related to work practice in occupational areas. They are intended to provide a clear definition of the line between acceptable performance in a work role, and non-acceptable performance. Such standards clearly play an important role where the qualification is in some way either a preparation for, or a licence to practise in the occupational area. Outcomes in higher education derive from a different philosophy. Higher education argu-ably has a less instrumental role, its objectives are both vocational (professional), and the intellectual pursuit and development of the disciplines; the growth of knowledge. Vocational degrees of the same name awarded by different institu-tions may share some common outcomes, but are likely also to include widely different outcomes derived from different approaches to teaching and learning.

A degree, regardless of subject and institution, is, however, widely thought to provide evidence of certain sorts of achievement and potential. Hence its role in the labour market. There is a widely held, if sometimes impenetrable, academic view as to what these achievements are, and to how they are related across dif-ferent subjects and institutions. The degree classification system serves in some mysterious way to provide a comparison of the level of achievement in different subjects.

While the notion of standards may be inappropriate in higher education, outcomes may be highly relevant, in making clear to employers, what the achieve-ment of graduates in different subjects can be, and in helping students to choose wisely those courses which will best provide for their needs.

Conclusions

The debate on outcomes in higher education has yielded more than simply a better understanding of the existing higher education curriculum. The process of de-scribing outcomes almost inevitably questions their purpose, ownership and util-ity. There are four important arguments currently used by universities in developing an outcome based approach.

The Content and Purposes of the HE Curriculum

Discussion of outcomes raises questions about the purpose of higher education, and the extent to which the curriculum designed for the 'best and brightest' of the 18-year-old age group will meet the needs of the one-third of the age group, shortly projected to participate in higher education. At the same time the market for graduates has become more uncertain. Traditional graduate traineeships now represent a shrinking share of the available opportunities. However, the concept of a 'graduate job', retains a dominant influence, increasingly out of line with the actual choices available to graduates. Young graduates are expected to assume greater responsibility than was the case ten years ago. Ways of working are shift-ing towards teams and projects requiring temporary groups, which can be reor-ganized and restructured to meet changing needs.

Economic recovery is not likely to bring about a massive increase in the traditional graduate jobs, and the uncertain trend is likely to continue. The devel-opment of a more effective job market in an uncertain climate will require better information for both recruiter and graduate. This will mean more information about the broader skills and competences of graduates as well as about their aca-demic attainments. New ways of working will call for greater team work and communication, improved personal responsibility and initiative, greater emphasis generally on the achievement and demonstration of personal competence.

The Relationship Between Outcomes, and Assessment and Teaching and Learning Methods

The description of the outcomes of higher education, permits a closer analysis of the extent to which existing assessment methods provide evidence that students achieve what is expected of them, as well as of the extent to which current teaching and learning methods provide opportunities for their development. The increase in student numbers has placed considerable pressure on the traditional forms of assessment in higher education, and for many staff the major advantage of outcomes may be to offer a means of managing assessment effectively.

In some universities the move to outcomes has been driven by a need to review teaching and learning methods in the light of increasing student numbers and declining resources. The description of outcomes provides a means of relating teaching and learning resources to student achievement, and may be an important management tool in the future.

Outcomes and Quality

The measurement of quality in higher education has traditionally been difficult to separate from the processes of course delivery and the tacit internal values shared by academic staff, and it has been hard for those who are not members of the culture to gain access to, or understand the criteria by which quality is judged. Outcomes provide a means of exploring and describing these criteria and relating them to assessment and to the credit framework. This may help to establish criteria through which the quality of the teaching and learning processes in higher education could be measured.

The HE Charter

The HE Charter, shortly to emerge from the Department for Education, will place greater emphasis on the student as customer of the higher education system, rather than beneficiary. This suggests that greater transparency, in course content, assessment and teaching and learning support will be an important feature of higher education in the future. Learning outcomes could provide the means of describing what students and employers seek from higher education, at the same time enabling greater student choice, through the provision of better information at the point of entry, and during the process of higher education.

The Role of NVQs in Higher Education

The development of NVQs at higher levels will have a significant effect on courses which lead to a professional qualification, but will also have an impact on the content of non-vocational degree courses, and the extent to which they provide outcomes which are relevant to subsequent graduate employment. Graduate employability appears on the current *Times Higher* league tables (1993) and is likely to be a significant performance indicator in the future. An outcome based curriculum in higher education may provide a better means of integrating NVQ units, and of indicating the achievement of the competences desired by graduate employers.

References

BLOOM, B. (Ed) (1956) *Taxonomy of Educational Objectives, Book 1, Cognitive Domain*, London, Longman.

CARTER, R. (1985) 'A taxonomy of objectives for professional education', *Studies in Higher Education*, 10, 1.

CNAA (1991) *Handbook*, London, CNAA.

FEU (1992) *A Basis for Credit?*, a paper for discussion, London, FEU.

JESSUP, G. (1991) *Outcomes: NVQs and the Emerging Model of Education and Training*, London, Falmer Press.

OTTER, S. (1992) *Learning Outcomes in Higher Education* London, UDACE. *The Times Higher Education Supplement*, 14 May 1993.

Part Five

Issues in Progression

Chapter 18

Aspiration, Achievement and Progression in Post-secondary and Higher Education

David Robertson

Introduction

Considerations of post-compulsory education usually reflect an unease with the inefficiencies and inequities of learning opportunities for prospective students beyond school. Proposals for reform, advanced over recent years, have often done little other than rearrange prevailing inadequacies; until recently the pivotal role of post-secondary and higher education in sustaining personal and national advantage has gone unrecognized.

In large measure, this can be explained by an absence of strategic direction. During a period of post-imperial drift, insufficient attention has been paid to the wider macro-policy environment of post-secondary and higher education: tensions between elite provision and democratic participation have gone unresolved; the interactions of education, training and individual life-career requirements have been overlooked; and post-secondary education has only incidentally connected with the aspirations of most individuals. Consequently Britain has lived with a disjointed and unrewarding jumble of post-compulsory educational provision, barely connected to personal or national economic prosperity.

The most pressing feature of this macro-policy environment is the extent to which policy towards post-secondary and higher education in Britain has failed in its principal purpose: the successful development of socially productive, technologically inventive and economically competitive contributors to national prosperity. The tendency to protect particular elite privileges (via selective university entrance) and the suppression of learning aspirations amongst the majority of the population (via an inadequate supply of places in colleges and universities) has reduced the capacity of the national economy to compete in the global market. The national skills base, reflected in the density of qualifications held throughout the population, has been lowered below that of our historic competitors in many areas of scientific and technological provision. Consequently, Britain now faces a strategic crisis in determining its placement in the global market of the next century.

David Robertson

The Crisis of Achievement

It is not surprising therefore that an emphasis on the outcomes of post-secondary and higher education has assumed an unparalleled significance in the affairs of all modern industrial societies, including Britain. Opinion has shifted over the past few years from the treatment of education principally as a personal or general good to the assessment of education specifically as an asset in national competitive strategy.

This shift in attitude represents more than a change from liberal to utilitarian orientations towards education; it represents a recognition of the fundamental importance of investment in a well-educated and well-qualified labour force for international economic competitiveness. The globalization of markets has made advanced industrial nations attend to their infrastructures for securing competitive advantage with a new-found diligence.

For Britain this has become an acutely visible problem. Ambiguously placed in the global market, without the benefits once bestowed by Empire and with an aging and substantially infirm industrial infrastructure, the British economy has been beset by aspirations and attitudes defined by a glorious past and realities shaped by a precarious future.

Those modifications to economic policy pursued throughout the 1980s appear not to have altered significantly the downward momentum of economic performance (see, for example, Healey, 1993). Economic indicators on growth in national industrial production since 1950 reveal the relative under-performance of the British economy. Industrial output in Britain increased by 250 per cent over the period whereas our major competitors were able to increase performance much more impressively: USA and France (450 per cent), Germany and Italy (600 per cent) and Japan (3319 per cent)[1].

The reduction of labour costs, the encouragement of inward investment and the generation of new productive initiatives may have established the landmarks of an 'enterprise culture' during the mid-1980s, but as instruments of economic policy they have failed in themselves to provide an adequate platform for national success. More recently attention has turned to the need to provide sustained investment in the skills development of the labour force. An assessment of the conditions of the global market by the turn of the century suggests that the national economy will not be able to compete in the low-skill, low wage, low added value end of that market. The emerging economies of the Chinese Economic Area (China, Korea, Taiwan, Vietnam) together with those of Eastern Europe are likely to dominate competition in this market. The principal chance for the British economy therefore appears to lie at the opposite end of the global economy, competing on product and quality.

To achieve any sustained success in the high-wage, high skill and high added value global market, an improvement in education and training achievement is essential. As a recent Government initiative comments:

> Those countries which have experienced the sharpest rise in relative competitiveness have also developed strong approaches to encouraging the foundation skills of young people and to learning throughout life for all . . . Britain cannot match the skills of major competitors in Northern Europe, North America and Japan; and competitors in the Pacific basin

and Southern Europe are advancing fast . . . British companies are forced to compete on lower quality, with lower value-added, because they lack technical skills. (National Training Task Force, 1992)

This has been reinforced by the National Institute for Economic and Social Research which reveals that in 1987, at the post-secondary level, Britain awarded 30,000 engineering qualifications compared with 98,000 in France and 134,000 in West Germany (Green and Steedman, 1993). Calling for the establishment of national training targets as a means of reversing this endemic skills deficit, the National Training Task Force has reemphasized that which has become evident from a number of sources-British education does not provide an adequate platform from which to meet competitive economic challenge.

Making Up Lost Ground

The problem is compounded by the realization that other nations are not waiting for Britain to catch up. In the USA, public debate has responded to the challenge posed by Japanese economic ascendancy by focusing on the role and purpose of education and training to support a galvanization of the American economy (Unwin, 1991). France during the 1980s has sought to emulate German infrastructural performance as part of the strategy to tie itself into a trans-European economic bloc. Efforts have been made to reposition national priorities towards workforce skills development using the qualifications structure of the colleges and universities. France has now overtaken Britain in the density of qualified skilled employees in the workforce (Steedman, 1991).

Both Japan and Germany remain outstanding in their ability to articulate national economic priorities with an infrastructure of education and training; accordingly both nations remain the most competitive and productive in the global economy (Green and Steedman, 1993). Australia and New Zealand have recently overhauled their post-secondary sectors. In the case of New Zealand, this has led to the establishment of a nationally comprehensive qualifications structure under the auspices of the New Zealand Qualifications Authority (NZQA, 1992; Robertson, 1993a).

From available evidence, countries which achieve high standards in education and training:

> . . . would appear to have one thing in common: as nations they place great emphasis upon educational achievement, engendering high aspirations amongst individual learners. They tend to have a 'learning culture' in which parents and teachers have high expectations of their children's educational achievements, where the education systems are designed to provide opportunities and motivation for learners of all abilities, and where the labour market and society in general reward those who do well in education. (Green and Steedman, 1993, p. 14)

Encouragingly, in Britain policy appears finally to concur with the view that improved educational aspiration, manifested in progression from post-secondary to higher education, is essential and that this should be coupled with improved levels of achievement and qualification. The successive White Papers (DES, 1987, 1991a and 1991b), together with the parallel establishment of the National Council for Vocational Qualifications, lock in place the constituent elements in this strategy (see Robertson, 1993b). Successive reports from the Confederation of British Industry have lent weight to the argument (CBI, 1989, 1991 and 1993). Britain is finally joining other major industrial nations in the democratization of participation in post-secondary and higher education and in the clarification of its strategy for a rational qualifications system.

The reform process is long overdue. The pattern of aspiration, achievement and progression throughout British post-secondary and higher education have largely been taken for granted. A minority of socially-privileged, educationally-selected students have been carefully nurtured through secondary school and the 'A' level tradition to take their place in higher education; the majority have been discharged ill-prepared into the labour market, neither properly trained for survival nor seeking a return to educational opportunities.

The further education sector has been unable to find the resources or the policy commitment to fulfil an adequate role. Colleges have neither effectively bridged the gap between school and the labour market, nor have they been able to achieve their potential in fuelling demand for higher education. For years, colleges have been deployed as poorly focused institutions, caught between competing government employment initiatives and constantly nervous about stable sources of funding. They have been beset by difficult conditions in local government, by a morass of courses and qualifications and by uncertainties over their general purpose. Instead of playing a pivotal role in defining learning for vast numbers of students in post-compulsory eduction, further education colleges have been forced into short-term responses to fluctuating government policies.

The crisis of the further education sector has been a symptom of the crisis of national education priorities. Since further education (FE) colleges have generally defined their purpose as vocationally-focused, 'second chance' institutions, they have not enjoyed the status bestowed upon academically-focused sixth forms or universities. They have come to symbolize the rift between academic and vocational learning, between education and training, that has defined British post-secondary education. This rift has, in turn, retarded our national ability to reform our provision for the benefit of the majority of citizens.

Moreover, universities (and their former polytechnic analogues) have been distinguished from the post-secondary and further education colleges by their attendance upon the needs of a selective academic elite. The demand from universities for the preparation of a particular type of student — academic and other-worldly — has had an unusually distorting influence both upon the curriculum of schools and colleges and upon the chances of gaining access to this 'secret garden' of scholarship. These distortions have militated against the development of a diversity in the qualities and capabilities that would fit prospective students for higher learning.

To a limited extent, the former polytechnics proved themselves more amenable to the absorption of a broader range of aptitudes, including vocationally-relevant skills; students from a wider range of social backgrounds, ages and learning experiences have been able to enter higher education via these 'new' universities. However, the general character of higher education remains firmly orientated to the academic reproduction of the next generation of scholars, a disposition which may be further sustained if, following their change of status, the 'new' universities seek to emulate the character and style of the established universities.

Habituated to a selective intake of able 18-year-olds, universities have rarely needed to concern themselves with the achievement of students or their labour market destination. Until 1987 only 11 per cent of the 18-year-old age group participated in higher education. They generally succeeded in large measure to achieve their purpose — the award of a degree. Few questions were asked about the character of that qualification, its purpose or utility in the labour market. 'Good' graduates would naturally progress to postgraduate programmes; the rest could progress into employment. Since graduates were relatively scarce in the labour market, 'graduate jobs' remained in good supply and graduates could, after a period of perseverance and patience perhaps, anticipate premium labour market placement.

The curriculum in higher education has conventionally been inward-facing and self-defining. It has generally reflected the aspirations and values of the scholarly community, largely predisposed towards research, the reproduction of the next generation of academics and occasionally nodding in the direction of kindred professions. Students entering universities have generally been expected to suspend most questions concerning the appropriateness of their learning programmes for future labour market aspirations, deferring to the view that the 'experience' of higher education was an end in itself.

The specific objectives of the curriculum have rarely been presented for public inspection; the criteria for excellence have generally been imputed rather than demonstrated; and the quality and standards of higher education have tended to be internally-asserted, self-verified and largely unavailable for public scrutiny. This has been a reflection of two powerful converging forces: the influence of academic professionalism as a device for controlling and shaping the character of scholarly purpose; and the use of the principle of academic freedom as a buttress against any challenge to institutional (and individual) autonomy.

We are invited to support the view that higher education is at once removed from the utilitarian concerns of the marketplace, concentrating instead upon the development of the higher powers of the mind, the liberation of individuals from habituated patterns of thought, and the pursuit of knowledge in its purest form through research and scholarly enquiry. Above all, we are invited to believe that universities provide people with space to think, and by this means we generate the excellent outcomes which define the contribution of the British university to the national and international professional and scientific community.

Indeed, universities would fairly claim that they have always engaged in direct work with industry and commerce; their research outcomes are frequently cashed in terms of productive gain; they contribute directly to regional economic activity and they educate and inform generations of successful citizens. It might be added that, since 1987, they have absorbed 50 per cent more students at lower unit costs; they have encouraged wider participation through access courses, franchising arrangements with local further education colleges and other joint partnership arrangements; they have also begun to modify their curriculum structures, embracing modularization, credit systems, learning outcome statements, new assessment arrangements and a more diversified definition of higher learning which begins to include work-based and experientially-based learning.

Moreover, universities often feel that they are being asked to address too broad a range of objectives. They are expected to maintain a strong research base but also to teach twice and three times the numbers of students; they are proficient at developing capabilities of general application but are urged to educate students with specific employment skills; they are expected to provide strength in national and international scholarship, yet also to respond imaginatively to local and regional problems. Above all, they are expected to maintain quality and excellence under conditions of diminishing resources and policy fluctuations.

Notwithstanding this evenhandedness, it can still be asserted that universities sustain, in a manner modified elsewhere in education and other public services, a suspicion and hostility towards public accountability and critique of purpose. To ask questions — what can graduates do? what is higher education for? has been to invite highly defensive reaction. This disposition of the universities has resulted in a series of discontinuities between higher education and further education, between academic and vocational learning, between national institutions and practice in other countries, and between the mission of many universities and the requirements of national prosperity.

Access and Accountability

The challenge to the universities and colleges is therefore very clear; it may be expressed as problems of access and problems of accountability. Access problems concern how to manage educational *progression* from post-secondary and further education into higher education and thereafter through higher education into employment. Of this, there is a second dimension: the organization of student mobility between academic and vocational learning at any level of attainment. Accountability problems concern the extent to which the *outcomes* of post-secondary and higher education are to be made available to key stakeholders and consumers. These outcomes may go beyond the analysis of performance indicators and address the central purpose of post-secondary and higher education: the production of well-qualified graduates capable of using their full potential in gainful employment.

Some important elements stand out:

- as post-secondary and higher education are expected to contribute directly to national prosperity, they will need to describe how access to learning opportunities can be granted more readily to a broader range of prospective students;
- as institutions admit twice and three times the number of students, they will need to consider how appropriate it is to offer courses and qualifications designed with much smaller numbers in mind;
- however universities and colleges choose to arrange learning opportunities for mass participation, they will need to determine the responsibilities they bear towards the labour market opportunities of increased numbers of graduates and qualified leavers.

Answers to these matters may be provided by a treatment of the publicly-definable outcomes of education and training. Whatever intrinsic individual benefit derives from participation in post-secondary and higher education, students are inevitably exercised by the extrinsic advantages the opportunity claims to bestow. It has been argued earlier that restricted participation allowed the benefits of higher education to be cast largely in intrinsic terms: subsequent advantageous labour market placement could be guaranteed. With mass participation (and therefore mass graduation), future generations of qualified leavers will need much greater exposure to the impact of their academic programmes upon employment opportunities.

This has been given prominence in a report from the Association of Graduate Recruiters which comments:

> The restrictive view of 'appropriate' jobs for graduates is considerably out of line with the actual choices open to them, both at the outset and throughout their careers. Obsolete beliefs are limiting the constructive growth of a wide range of good choices . . . (We) strongly encourage the growth of 'employment-friendly' cultures in higher education: better integration, more cooperation and mutual understanding. (AGR, 1993, p. ii)

It is clear then that the general repositioning of post-secondary and higher education towards greater accessibility cannot be separated from the *consequences* of increased participation. Enhanced involvement in post-compulsory learning requires that learners make some connection early in their learning careers with employment prospects. This need not imply a crude vocationalism, nor an inappropriate utilitarianism. Instead, students may be offered learning experiences which are accountable in terms of future labour market opportunities, permitting learners the choice of how to take control of their individual learning careers.

Towards a Qualified Society

Many of these matters will arise as post-secondary and higher education adjust to the consequences of an engagement with the National Council for Vocational Qualifications (NCVQ). The curriculum model proposed by the NCVQ presents a fundamental challenge to the prevailing orthodoxies particularly of higher education (see Jessup, 1991; NCVQ, 1991). Based on the celebration of explicit and demonstrable learning achievements defined by performance standards, the NCVQ approach to the curriculum explicitly emphasizes the outcomes of learning.

As a vocational qualifications body, the NCVQ begins with a radically different approach to the purpose of learning; such learning is the means by which vocationally-relevant achievement may be demonstrated, thus leading to an appropriate qualification approved according to national occupational standards. This is fundamentally different from the cultural and intellectual traditions of universities where the *process* of learning is celebrated in its own right.

As Marks (1991) points out in a report to the former Committee of Directors of Polytechnics, this approach cuts across much that higher education has stood for. The cultural and professional values of academic life may be directly challenged by the need to accommodate the prescriptions required by the NCVQ:

- universities have generally maintained a distance from the award of purely vocational qualifications; however occupationally-referenced many degree and diploma qualifications may be, universities have rarely claimed for them the characteristics of vocational awards;

- institutional autonomy and diversity have produced circumstances in which there has never been much agreement about what constitutes an under-graduate degree. All degrees are held notionally to be of the same standard but there is little shared agreement about how to define that standard. Moreover, it has currently proved beyond the capacity of higher education to answer the question: what can graduates do? (Otter, 1992). The former Council for National Academic Awards (CNAA) attempted un-successfully to provide some notion of national standard, but its successor body, the Higher Education Quality Council (HEQC), lacking the statutory authority, is unlikely to be any more successful. This may pose problems for an accommodation with the NCVQ whose qualifications are defined by a common standard of achievement;
- higher education has generally been concerned with the process of learning; achievement has been seen as the corollary of effective process. Far greater attention has therefore been paid to matters attendant on the inputs to learning than upon the outcomes of learning. Recently, some universities have begun to address the outcomes-led curriculum but these efforts remain shallowly-rooted and in the minority;
- the close association between many universities and professional bodies tend to limit the scope for modifications to the undergraduate curriculum. Since they bestow accredited status upon higher education courses and receive graduates into professional membership, universities are often constrained to remain in good standing with professional bodies. In turn professional bodies are generally concerned with the maintenance of discrete professional standards; flexibility and mobility in the curriculum or labour market are of less direct concern to them.

Higher education provides more of a direct test of the impact of employment-related curriculum orientations than further education. In the latter colleges, they are not only more used to managing a vocationally-focused curriculum, they are also subject to a wide diversity of qualifications and external awarding bodies. Under such heterogenous conditions, the development of common performance standards, unifying a range of qualifications, may certainly be welcomed.

Moreover, the attainment levels of many students in further education may be more easily described in terms of competence and formal performance criteria. The range of learning capabilities may be narrower; the balance of operational performance to conceptual knowledge may facilitate more objective measures of achievement; and the variety of assessment strategies may be greater. This is not to say that higher education cannot legitimately be subject to a similar exercise in curriculum accountability; rather, that the issues are more complex and the outcome of the exercise more difficult to predict (cf Otter, 1992, p. ii).

The Impact of the NCVQ on Higher Education

For the purposes of the argument, it is important to select one instrument in the strategy to produce a *qualified society* and test the consequences for achievement and progression. In this case, the recent development of General National Vocational Qualifications (GNVQs) offers an ideal 'laboratory' within which to explore the possibilities and difficulties of an introduction of a different type of curriculum focus into higher education.

From the earlier discussion it will be apparent that, if higher education is to address the needs of the democratic mass of students, rather than a selective elite, it will need to adopt a more sophisticated and responsive approach to student labour market opportunities. This may be assisted if universities embrace NCVQ-derived curriculum strategies and accept significant modifications to current curriculum practice.

Higher education may need to accept the legitimacy of claims that its curriculum objectives must be rendered more publicly accountable and visible; students may expect to know what it is they are expected to achieve as a consequence of their experience in higher education (cf Burke, 1991, p. 34). Future labour market conditions will require that students-as-learners be equipped both with the generalizable attributes of learning but also with the specific skills relevant to the exploitation of labour market opportunities.

To date, universities have maintained a sceptical position with respect to the applicability of occupationally-specific National Vocational Qualifications (NVQs) either to admission or progression in higher education. Their intellectual focus has been held to be too narrow, and their knowledge base too shallow, for immediate absorption into the fabric of higher education programmes. Universities have not yet been seriously tested by the development of lower level NVQs, which have not aspired to claim admission and progression from further to higher education.

Work currently in progress to develop higher level NVQs, at levels 4 and 5, will sharpen attention in universities, particularly if professional bodies are persuaded of the relevance and importance of NCVQ accreditation. Nevertheless, this is unlikely to solve the principal dilemma: universities believe that NVQs apply a different definition of achievement from that which has traditionally obtained in higher education.

The area of greatest interest in the future is likely to lie in the extent to which a higher level NVQ, or units drawn therefrom, can enable a student to claim academic credit towards a university qualification. Given that the performance criteria and assessment outcomes will be publicly available, universities will not be able to claim lack of information upon which to judge the quality of the student achievement. It remains an open question therefore to determine how universities will react to claim for academic credit from students bearing higher level NVQs.

GNVQs and the Problem of Access

In the meantime, the commitment of higher education to access and accountability is likely to be tested more seriously with the arrival of General National Vocational Qualifications (GNVQs). GNVQs will test higher education at the level of entry qualifications (GNVQ Level 3) and within the main academic programmes, where GNVQs Level 4 are to be benchmarked against the first two years of an undergraduate degree (see figure 18.1).

At the point of entry, a GNVQ Level 3 is to be established as equivalent to two 'A' levels — a basic university entry qualification. In principle, universities will accept this qualification alongside other entry criteria; in practice, admissions tutors may still work with a familiar hierarchy topped out by 'A' levels.

Figure 18.1: National qualification framework

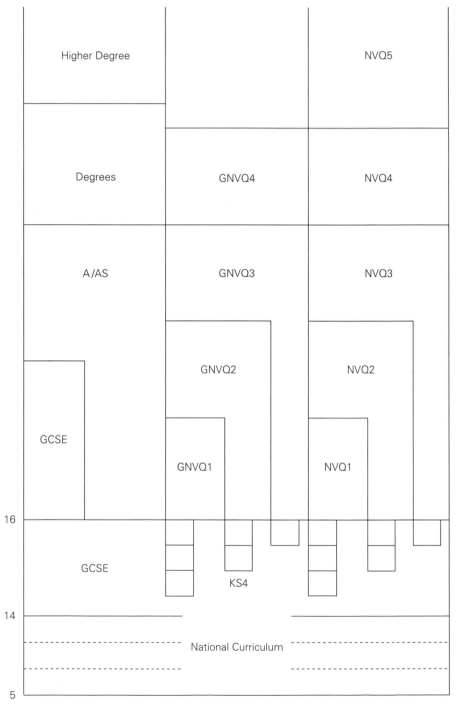

The problems facing the widespread adoption of GNVQs as an entry vehicle go to the heart of the general problem of the university curriculum. In their conventional and unmodified forms, academic programmes are heavily defined by disciplinary specialisms which rely upon dedicated subject knowledge. This subject knowledge has been supplied more or less adequately by 'A' levels; all other entry criteria tend to be compared with this benchmark. It has not affected the predisposition of admissions tutors towards 'A' levels that they correlate poorly with subsequent performance; their preferences merely reflect the cultural habituations of their institutions, regarding input characteristics as more influential than outcome performance.

To gain genuine parity of esteem for GNVQs at the point of entry, either of two conditions will have to obtain:

- *either* GNVQs will have to provide an adequate subject knowledge base to support students successfully on otherwise unmodified higher education programmes;
- *or* higher education programmes will need to be modified in ways consonant with the objectives of GNVQs if students are to gain success in universities.

If the former condition obtains, there will be the danger that GNVQ-bearing students come to be treated as 'second class' entrants, questionably prepared for unmodified programmes in higher education. Students may therefore fail disproportionately, seriously prejudicing the credibility of GNVQs as an access vehicle amongst admissions tutors. Moreover, if schools and colleges come to treat the GNVQ route as appropriate only for a non-'A' level cohort, similar and irrevocable damage will occur. Some of these concerns would be diminished if the NVQ attached to familiar qualifications — BTEC awards for example — and pragmatic considerations of recruitment numbers will also conspire to lessen the problem. On the other hand, the fall-out could be that the integrity of universities in promoting wider access would be questioned, whilst universities would respond by claiming a defence on the grounds of academic quality.

Therefore, it seems to follow that the second condition must obtain if there is to be an uncontested acceptance of GNVQs: universities may need to modify at least their first cycle of higher education to allow GNVQ-bearing students to give expression to their potential. This will probably involve the exploitation of modular credit-based programmes to construct a more broadly-based initial programme in higher education reflecting the subject knowledge and core skills components of GNVQs. It is not yet clear how far some universities are prepared to take their modular developments in this direction.

GNVQs and the Problem of Progression

The development of higher level GNVQs at Level 4 raises further fundamental questions about the character and structure of academic programmes in higher education. It raises important questions about the extent to which learning derived from NCVQ-defined awards can count legitimately alongside learning achievement in higher education. How can the different learning experiences be articulated within a unified qualifications framework?

These matters raise concerns about the extent to which the structure of the higher education curriculum is yet sufficiently flexible to accommodate the diverse learning activities sponsored by the NCVQ. Further questions surround the extent to which the standards represented by GNVQs can be universally accepted throughout the award-bearing programmes of diverse and autonomous universities. Moreover, what roles and responsibilities do the professional bodies have in facilitating (or hindering) the accommodation of higher education and the NCVQ?

NCVQ-derived achievements are legitimately acceptable to higher education but their incorporation into the academic programme structure would be facilitated principally through the widespread and systematic adoption of a modular and credit-based system of flexible learning. The interaction between academic and vocational elements of an academic programme and lifelong labour market opportunities needs to be considered in the context of a series of staged awards, flexible entry into and from higher education, a greater role for sequential learning and for diverse definitions of accreditable learning achievement, and radical modifications to assessment strategies, guidance and information systems and the professional role of the lecturer.

On the other hand, universities may retain a scepticism towards an unreconstructed NCVQ model, arguing that it is unlikely to be sufficiently intellectually potent or professionally convincing to most academics if changes are not made. A number of concerns can be identified:

- the apparent emphasis given to learning outcomes at the expense of the learning process;
- the perceived imbalance between skill and knowledge;
- the weakness of the competence model in terms of linguistic inflexibility;
- the over-emphasis of employer interests to the detriment of other scholar interests;
- an apparent failure to engage with learning as a totality of experiences;
- a perceived lack of clarity over how GNVQs can be articulated with awards and practices within higher education.

Many of these issues can be addressed by a more sophisticated dialogue between universities and the NCVQ. Such discussions are likely to occur as a consequence of proposals to move towards a definition of higher level NVQs and GNVQs.

In many ways, progress on these matters is most timely. Universities and colleges have moved substantially over the past few years to adopt curriculum structures which facilitate the accommodation of more flexible and diverse learning programmes. Although individual cultural values and institutional traditions often lag behind recent initiatives, there are signs that institutions at the senior level are now committed to managing flexible participation in post-secondary and higher education in a manner consonant with improved personal development and national economic success.

Towards a National Framework for Achievement and Progression

Considerable attention continues to be directed to the development of a national framework within which learners might move freely amongst learning opportunities, guided by reliable information, constructing individual learning programmes, and leading to recognized qualifications.

A national framework for *vocational* qualifications is currently being developed by the NCVQ and it has been described by Jessup (1992); the development of a national *credit* framework goes beyond this. In a national *credit* framework, 'credit' is the system of currency enabling students to trade and negotiate their individual learning needs with providers. It offers the prospect of a genuine framework of progression, facilitating mobility between vocational and academic programmes and between different sectors and institutions of learning.

It is now commonly agreed that a national framework will need to facilitate:

- improved mobility for students between post-secondary and higher education;
- an erosion of boundaries between academic and vocational learning, and between education and training;
- a legitimation of learning, both within institutions and 'off-campus', in the workplace and learning derived from experience;
- a coherent framework of qualifications, interim awards, access points and achievement standards;
- a coherent and accountable representation of learning achievement, employing an outcomes-led curriculum supported by individual transcripts of achievement;
- an environment providing learner support, information and guidance;
- the means by which the individual learner is provided with the resources, including personal financial entitlement, to negotiate and obtain individually-relevant learning opportunities.

These features have been elaborated on other occasions (Robertson, 1992a and 1993b) and they represent a fundamental repositioning of how achievement and progression might be organized in the future. Further influential proposals have emerged from the Further Education Unit (FEU, 1992 and 1993) which offer the basic elements of a comprehensive post-secondary and higher education credit framework. Recently, the NCVQ has published a discussion document (NCVQ, 1993) which describes some difficulties with existing arrangements, but points the way forward towards an accommodation of different systems.

The key features of the FEU proposals, essential to any authentic credit framework and generally supported by the NCVQ, are:

- the specification of *modules* as units of learning delivery;
- the use of *learning outcome statements* to define the learning achievement of any module;
- the use of a defined unit of *credit*, attached as a tariff to any module, to define the relative value of diverse learning experiences.

The 'Golden Triangle' of modules, outcomes and credits lies at the heart of a national credit framework. From this platform it may be possible to construct the comprehensive network of learning opportunities and qualifications that give meaning to the principles of individual flexibly-negotiated learning.

An Entitlement Model of Post-Secondary and Higher Education

An 'entitlement' model of post-secondary and higher education and training is the natural corollary of the development of a national credit framework. Whereas the framework offers the means to enable achievement to be recorded towards qualifications, and progression through education into work thereafter, an individual education and training entitlement strikes at the heart of the 'British problem'.

Most of the deficiencies of British post-secondary and higher education can be reduced to problems of accessibility. This problem can be disaggregated further:

- the problem: the need to generate an adequate supply of education and training places commensurate with individual potential;
- defined by: a culture of atrophied aspiration, limiting demand for suitable places from motivated and adequately qualified individuals;
- compounded by: a false dichotomy between (academic) education and (vocational) training, producing a status hierarchy which proscribes flexible access to appropriate learning opportunities for many potential students;
- sustained by: a failure amongst employers to stimulate aspirations towards education and training because of 'short-termism', complacency, low quality thresholds and a lack of strategic vision;
- formalized by: the inertia of successive governments: either because they could not resolve the tensions between elite privileges and popular participation (the political Right); or because they believed the problems of disadvantage lay elsewhere, for example in secondary education (the political Left).

A resolution of this historic logjam may be achieved through an acceptance that access to education and training is indeed a lifelong entitlement. That entitlement may be most effectively exercised when individuals have the means to purchase directly their desired learning opportunities; this would imply the direct personal financial empowerment of eligible individuals through a voucher or quasi-voucher scheme. Such schemes have been prefigured by the Training Credits arrangements, variants of which may reappear as aspects of a future Graduate Contribution Scheme for higher education. Political solutions to these matters may take some time to appear. In the meantime, attention may need to turn to some fresh thinking about how we conceptualize post-secondary and higher education.

A recent report by the Institute for Public Policy Research argued for the reshaping of higher education into a series of cycles within a general *stage* of post-secondary learning (Robertson, 1992b). Although the terms of the various cycles could be modified, and their notional boundaries negotiated, the principle holds good for a system of comprehensive access:

- Foundation cycle: encompassing (modified and modular) 'A' level, access courses, franchising arrangements between FE and HE institutions, preparatory and 'bridging' courses, NVQ/GNVQ3, Open College Federation Level 4, *together with* the Level 1 (first year) of the undergraduate programme and initial components of a GNVQ4. The *foundation cycle* would be broadly-based, mixing academic and vocational components, but could be route- and qualification-directed in terms of subsequent progression.

Much of this cycle could be delivered in further education and community colleges.

- Graduation cycle: encompassing Levels 2 and 3 (years 2 and 3) of the undergraduate programme, leading towards the honours degree award and increased specialization, as desired perhaps by individual students, professional bodies and employers. During the graduation cycle, students might also receive a GNVQ4. This cycle would usually be delivered within the higher education institution, or under its direct supervision in 'off-campus' environments.

- Employment cycle: encompassing postgraduate programmes, post-experience and qualifying training for profession careers, career updating, and leading to postgraduate awards, professional qualifications, NVQs Level 5. This cycle could be delivered within the conventional postgraduate environment of universities, within graduate schools, professional training schools, or within a work-based or company-based setting under direct supervision.

As the Institute for Public Policy Research commented:

> The advantages of organizing learning in cycles of activity is that students can enter and leave at various points, accumulating credit for achievement at their own pace. We can begin to abandon notions of the appropriate time of life by which a learner must have completed each part of the cycle, or even the sequence in which they may be undertaken. Moreover, it allows us to recast our understanding of the *site* of learning in a way which places the process *around* rather than merely *within* the education institution. The cycles in the stage of post-compulsory education could provide the linking arrangements between post-16 and postgraduate learning and would facilitate access to a programme of comprehensive post-secondary lifelong learning (*ibid*)

We may now be on the threshhold of a yet more fundamental breakthrough in the development of individual learning careers. As the framework for the operation of a national credit system begins to take shape — uniting further and higher education, academic and vocational learning, and on-campus and off-campus achievement — it is possible to conceive of the means by which this might be held in place.

If individual learners are able to claim the personal financial entitlements to enable them to purchase their particular learning programmes and to trade between different learning opportunities, then learning 'suppliers' — the universities and colleges — will learn to respond quickly and directly to their new needs. Conventional products, in the form of familiar qualifications, will retain their attraction for only as long as they offer improved chances of success in the competitive labour market of the future.

As individual learners begin to understand and accept that learning in a post-school environment is not something to be completed by a certain age, but may be negotiated throughout a career, then they will begin perhaps to draw upon their education and training 'entitlement' at different stages of their lives.

Moving in and out of the cycles of post-secondary and higher education, mixing conceptual and practical skills, drawing upon various means of demonstrating learning achievement, progressively earning credit towards recognized qualifications, mobile and resourceful learners will contribute to a fundamental reshaping of the ways in which learning is defined and provided. For the sake of personal comfort and national prosperity, this modernization of the learning relationship cannot be long resisted.

Note

1 'Economic and financial indicators: Industrial production', *The Economist*, 20 March 1993. Considerable analytical complexity underpins explanations of this data but it confirms the historical slide in national economic performance.

References

ASSOCIATION OF GRADUATE RECRUITERS (1993) *Roles for Graduates in the Twenty-First Century*, Cambridge: AGR.

BURKE, J. (Ed) (1989) *Competency Based Education and Training*, London, Falmer Press.

BURKE, J. (1991) 'Competence in Higher Education: Implication for institutions and professional bodies', in RAGGATT, P. and UNWIN, L. *Change and Intervention*, London, Falmer Press.

CONFEDERATION OF BRITISH INDUSTRY (1989) *Towards a Skills Revolution*, London, CBI.

CONFEDERATION OF BRITISH INDUSTRY (1991) *World Class Targets*, London, CBI.

CONFEDERATION OF BRITISH INDUSTRY (1993) *Routes for Success*, London, CBI.

DES (1987) *Higher Education: Meeting the Challenge*, Cmnd 114, London, HMSO.

DES (1991a) *Education and Training for the 21st. Century, Vol. I & II*, Cmnd 1536, London, HMSO.

DES (1991b) *Higher Education: A New Framework*, Cmnd 1541, London, HMSO.

FINEGOLD, D. (1992) 'Breaking out of the low-skill equilibrium', Paper No 5, National Commission on Education in *Education Economics*, 1, 1.

FURTHER EDUCATION UNIT (1992) *A Basis for Credit?*, London, FEU.

FURTHER EDUCATION UNIT (1993) *Discussing Credit*, London, FEU.

GREEN, A. and STEEDMAN, H. (1993) *Educational Provision, Educational Attainment and the Needs of Industry: A Review of Research for Germany, France, Japan and Britain*, London, National Institute for Economic and Social Research.

HEALEY, N. (Ed) (1993) *Britain's Economic Miracle: Myth or Reality?*, London, Routledge.

INSTITUTE FOR PUBLIC POLICY RESEARCH (1992) *Higher Education: Expansion and Reform*, London, IPPR.

JESSUP, G. (1991) *Outcomes: NVQs and the Emerging Model of Education and Training*, London, Falmer Press.

JESSUP, G. (1992) 'Developing a coherent national framework of qualifications', *Education and Training Technology International*, 29, 3.

MARKS, R. (1991) 'Implications of National Vocational Qualifications for the polytechnic sector', *Project Report for the Committee of Directors of Polytechnics*, December.

NATIONAL TRAINING TASK FORCE (1992) *National Targets for Education and Training*, London, NTTF.

NCVQ (1991) *Guide to National Vocational Qualifications*, London, NCVQ.

NCVQ (1993) *Towards A National System of Credit Accumulation*, A Discussion Paper, May.

NEW ZEALAND QUALIFICATIONS AUTHORITY (1992) *A Qualifications Framework for New Zealand: An Introduction to the Framework*, Wellington, NZQA.

OTTER, S. (1992) *Learning Outcomes and Higher Education*, Leicester, UDACE.

RAGGATT, P. and UNWIN, L. (Eds) (1991) *Change and Intervention*, London, Falmer Press.

ROBERTSON, D. (1992a) 'The National CATS Task Force: An agenda for action', *Adults Learning*, 4, 2.

ROBERTSON, D. (1992b) 'Courses, qualifications and the empowerment of learners', in IPPR (1992) *Higher Education: Expansion and Reform*, London, IPPR.

ROBERTSON, D. (1993a) 'Credit systems: An international comparison' in Further Education Unit (1993) *Discussing Credit*, London, FEU.

ROBERTSON, D. (1993b) 'Flexibility and mobility in further and higher education: Policy continuity and progress', *Journal of Further and Higher Education*, 17, 1, spring.

STEEDMAN, H. (1991) 'Improvement in workforce qualifications: Britain and France 1979–88' in RAGGATT, P. and UNWIN, L. (Eds) *Change and Intervention*, London, Falmer Press.

UNWIN, L. (1991) 'Meeting the needs of a "Global Society": Vocational education and training in the United States of America', in RAGGATT, P. and UNWIN, L. (Eds) *Change and Intervention*, London, Falmer Press.

Part Six

International Comparison

Chapter 19

Competencies, Attributes and Curriculum: The Australian Agenda

Peter Raggatt

Previous chapters in this book have discussed the development of an outcomes approach and have explored its implications for the curriculum and for learning from a British perspective. In this final chapter we return selectively to a number of the themes and issues confronted in earlier chapters and examine how they are being tackled in Australia. Necessarily the discussion of any one theme will be more fleeting than was the case in earlier chapters but the comparisons and contrasts drawn may serve to raise questions that would not otherwise arise from a solely English debate on the relationships between outcomes, the curriculum and learning.

The central argument in this chapter is that though many of the changes reflect, indeed they follow, changes made in England there are important differences. These differences arise from the form which the original analysis took, the broader agenda for reform which encompassed post-compulsory education and training and the parallel standards development programme which included industry, schools, colleges and the professions. The comparison is not exact. Australia is at an earlier stage in the development of an outcomes-based system and there are few deeds to assess though there are important statements of intent.

As with most educational reform it is important to appreciate the concerns to which it was a response. We begin, therefore, with a brief discussion of the origins of the outcomes approach in Australia. This will be followed by an outline of the changes being introduced before focusing on particular issues.

The Origins of Change

The 1980s were a difficult time for Australia. As a resource rich nation its infrastructure and industry base had developed around a low value-added commodity/resource export strategy (COSTAC, 1990). It was highly vulnerable to fluctuations in world prices in the commodity and resource markets and its economy was badly affected by the sharp decline in those markets in the early 1980s. The situation was further exacerbated by the uncompetitive nature of traditional industries, most clearly revealed by the metals industry, which was pushed close to the point of total collapse by the tariff cuts in the 1970s and 1980s.

The extent of the problem was graphically described by the Treasurer who declared that the country was well on the way to becoming a 'banana republic' and had to control its surging national debt and begin paying its way in the world[1]. Australia was enjoined to become a 'clever country', one in which a highly educated and well trained workforce would use advanced technologies to produce high quality, high tech goods and services yielding high value added returns.

For several reasons — some shared and some different — employers, unions and the Labour administration, which had been elected in 1983, were able to find common cause with this sentiment[2]. But if international comparisons demonstrated that Australia was in relative economic decline they also showed that other countries were doing better. Not surprisingly there was interest in the ways in which skilled workers were trained by Australia's competitors. This led to a tripartite working party visiting Europe in 1987.

Industry and Training

The group was much impressed by the German approach to skills formation in which the Federal *Bundesinstitut fur Berufsbildungforschung* played a leading role in articulating standards and developing a curriculum around the standards. This was supported by the strong commitment to a social partnership between employers and trade unions in the delivery of training and the quality assurance procedures used, an approach which fitted the style of industrial relations in Australia where a Labour administration had been elected in 1983. The continuation of general education alongside vocational training was also viewed as important. Germany, then, provided the conceptual model for the definition of standards and the process of skills formation through partnership in delivery and quality assurance, but the idea of a national framework came from England[3].

While the groundwork was laid by this first report the major impetus to training reform was given by the next report *Australia Reconstructed* (ACTU/TDC, 1987), which was chaired by Laurie Carmichael, an officer from the metal workers' union[4]. This was again the product of a Government-sponsored tripartite mission. This group was strongly influenced by the emphasis given to working in teams in parts of European industry, the absence of restrictive practices and the extent of multi-skilling. It also became more aware of deficiencies in work organization in Australian industry[5]. The group was particularly impressed by the commitment to training: 'The most striking aspect of active labour market policies is the emphasis placed on skill formation, skill enhancement, skill flexibility and overall training' (p. 107); and the importance of continuing education for personal and skills development: 'Vocational education and training is not seen as a one-off exercise but as a process of lifetime learning, contributing to both personal and career development' (p. 109).

The importance of lifelong learning was reaffirmed by the Department of Employment, Education and Training (DEET) sometime later in a review of case studies:

> The new technologies will require a broadening of skills, a greater emphasis on conceptual rather than manipulative skills, ability to work with a team and the need for frequent retraining or skill upgrading during an individual's working life. (Krbavic and Stretton, 1988, p. 6)

There was a broad affirmation of support from the social partners for the analysis and for the prescription offered by the Carmichael Report. What is particularly interesting is the persistent emphasis on the importance of personal and conceptual skills as well as technical skills that appears through the various reports dealing with the preparation of skilled workers.

The essence of the reforms for skills formation and recognition as proposed in the Carmichael Report was that the new system should be based on the skills (or competencies) required for employment, that more learning effort should focus on the workplace, that it should be open as to time, place and methods. The competencies would be defined by industry bodies. With minor modifications this is the system that is being put in place by the National Training Board[6].

The Australian Standards Framework

National standards are the keystone for the new VET system. They comprise the competencies required for effective performance in employment. They are defined by industry parties and are endorsed by the National Training Board (NTB). The Australian Standards Framework complements this and provides a link between the competencies required for work and the outcomes of the vocational education and training system. It also provides the basis for the recognition of prior learning and for recognizing competencies acquired abroad.

The ASF has eight levels. The main differentiating factors between levels relate to the increasing amount of discretion and autonomy in the work role, the range of contexts and the complexity of work involved, the level of responsibility undertaken, the increase in the complexity and the depth of knowledge required. Reflecting this, Level 7 is regarded as entry-level for the professions.

The units of competence are defined by Competency Standards Bodies (Lead Bodies), which are drawn from national, State and Territory Industry Training Advisory Bodies and/or from bodies recognized under industrial awards. The unit is the minimum level for certification of competence. Combinations of units representing groups of jobs or areas of work are defined by Competency Standards Bodies (CSBs) and, when endorsed by the NTB, constitute the industry standard at an ASF level. When seeking endorsement CSBs must indicate to the NTB the variation permissible in the combinations of units of competency for competency to be recognized at an ASF level. Individual units may be part of the group at more than one level — individual units are not aligned with ASFs, only the group of units is aligned.

Units may be packaged into acceptable groups in a number of ways: as a single set of competencies which achieve an ASF level; by defining a core or essential group of units plus a number of optional units; a core plus specialist option units; or by defining a minimum number of units from an approved list of units.

The flexibility available through this procedure provides enterprises with a considerable degree of freedom to select from an array of units of competence and package them into a group relevant to the jobs and work organization of the enterprise and still meet the requirements for an ASF level. They have a further degree of freedom in that they can develop units relevant to their specific needs. If the enterprise chooses to do so it can submit these units to the CSB as being equivalent to units in the endorsed standard and, if accepted, these will be accorded the same status as industry units, with portability of credit and so on. If the units are substantially different from existing units the CSB may seek endorsement from the NTB and their entry in the National Register of Competency Standards, after which they can be used by any enterprise. This facility enables leading edge companies to develop units which reflect new working practices and production methods and it provides, through recognition in the ASF, a way of regenerating or updating units of competence which can be more widely used. It does, however, also dilute the principle of national standards and can create problems for the portability of qualifications.

The format of unit specification is similar to that in England. It comprises: elements of competence, performance criteria, a range of variables statement and an evidence guide. At several points in the guidelines on standards development there are reminders that standards should take account of the requirements of workplace reform and the emerging needs of industry: 'Capturing the ability to apply skills in new situations and changing work organization, rather than simply reflecting the tasks currently performed, is . . . critical' (NTB, 1992, p. 29). It also notes the importance of knowledge and understanding and of attitudes and values in competent performance.

Progress in defining and endorsing the standards has been slower than expected. This appears to be due, at least in part, to the realization by some employers (including some Australian State governments) that standards are likely to impact on wage rates for jobs which have historically been underpaid. This has encouraged them to slow the rate at which standards are being developed and endorsed — all the players in standards development have the power of limited veto[7].

Schools and Colleges

Schools, too, have been moving towards an outcomes model. The work, which has been directed by the Australian Education Council (AEC), involved a curriculum mapping exercise which evolved into the development of National Subject Statements and Subject Profiles. Subject profiles are agreed descriptions of student outcomes and are establishing levels of achievement for all learning areas in the schools sector. The first profiles in English and mathematics specify six levels of achievement and cover the compulsory years of schooling.

A concurrent examination of the relationships between schools and colleges was also launched by the AEC. This reported to ministers in June 1990 with a proposal for a national review of the future development of post-compulsory education and training in Australia.

The subsequent review body was chaired by Brian Finn (IBM) and included Laurie Carmichael. It was instructed to advise on a new national target for participation in post-compulsory education and training; on appropriate national curriculum principles designed to enable all young people to develop key competencies, together with the associated implications for curriculum development; and on the means by which links could be drawn between different education and training pathways and sectors to expand the options available to young people. The use of the term 'key competencies' in the terms of reference for a review of all post-compulsory education and training is perhaps indicative of the way in which the agenda was set by economic concerns.

The opening sentences of the Report, *Young People's Participation in Post-compulsory Education and Training*, effectively captures the tone of the report and the main proposition, arguing that the reform agenda for education and training is a common one:

> Both individual and industry needs are leading to a convergence of general and vocational education. There is an increasing realization internationally that the most successful forms of work organization are those which encourage people to be multi-skilled, creative and adaptable. . . .
>
> There is . . . a related process of convergence between the concepts of work and education. Increasingly, as regular updating of skills and knowledge becomes essential to maintaining and enhancing productivity in the workplace the concepts of working and learning will converge.
>
> This implies that in order to serve their clients' needs both schools and TAFE (Technical and Further Education) will need to change: schools to become more concerned with issues of employability and the provision of broad vocational education; TAFE to recognize that initial vocational education courses must increasingly be concerned with competencies that are more general than those which, for example, characterize the traditional craft-based apprenticeships. (Finn, 1991, p. ix)

A key section of the text, which was substantially lifted to provide the opening paragraphs in the Executive Summary, stresses the review group's perception of the growing union between 'education' and 'training', between 'theoretical' and 'practical' and 'general' and 'vocational' education. It argues that multi-skilled, creative and adaptable people are:

> ultimately more productive because they know and understand their work, their product or their service. They are encouraged to work in teams, to become involved in problem solving, planning and decision making . . .
> They are also better equipped to participate actively in the range of roles outside employment which are required as members of a complex society. (*ibid*, p. 6)

This is the agenda for core skills (see Oates and Harkin in this volume, chapter 10).

A central recommendation of the Committee was that the curriculum for school and TAFE should incorporate 'employment-related key competencies'. It argued that 'the interconnection of increasing participation and increasing achievement — the explicit purpose of participation in post-compulsory education and training . . . was the acquisition of a set of competencies, a standard of performance' (Ruby, 1992) and that 'curriculum outcomes be explicitly structured into standards frameworks which are compatible across school and TAFE/training sectors to allow for consistent and credible assessment and reporting on student achievement in key competencies' (Finn, 1991, p. xvii).

The Committee did not set out a framework or content for the key competencies, choosing to recommend that this work be carried out by a further committee which would include other groups which had evident interests in the definition of key competencies, notably the Schools and the National Training Board. This Committee was duly established with Eric Mayer as Chair.

The work of the Finn Committee had stressed the equivalence of the two sectors. This was underlined by the Mayer Committee's view that the key competencies have immediate relevance for entry to employment from school or entry level training and for young people going on to further study. This proposition is currently being tested through industry exercises and through a higher education reference group.

An important feature of this preliminary work was that Finn brought key competencies, or core skills, to prominence before occupational competencies had been defined by industry bodies and endorsed by the NTB, i.e. it influenced ideas about standards and their content at a formative stage in the development of policy. Mayer maintained the pressure.

Professional Bodies

The third strand in the reform process which has informed the development of the Australian Standards Framework (ASF) is the work on competency standards being conducted by the professional bodies. The driving force behind this is the National Office of Overseas Skills Recognition (NOOSR). NOOSR was created in 1989 as part of the Australian Commonwealth Government's multicultural agenda. NOOSR's task was to find a fairer way of assessing overseas professionals who were settling in Australia and the competency-based approach was an attractive option. A national standards-based approach also opened the way to the mutual recognition of professional qualifications across the individual states and territories — a policy which fitted closely with the administration's strategy to improve labour mobility between states and was a feature of employers' support for a national standards framework.

The formation of NOOSR coincided with reforms which the professional bodies were undertaking. The motives of these bodies varied but all saw benefits in working with NOOSR and using the competency approach[8]. This work, which has used a variety of methodologies and has proceeded in parallel with the development of NTB standards of occupational competence, has been characterized by an approach which seeks to integrate the analysis of professional practice, i.e. performance in the workplace, with an analysis of the 'attributes' such as knowledge, abilities, skills and attitudes which underlie professional competence.

The importance of this contribution, together with that of the key competencies issue highlighted by the Finn and Mayer reports, is that it has helped to keep the debate on the nature of competence open. It has made the content of standards problematic, open to discussion about the significance of, for example, the scope of the knowledge content underpinning competence, the relevance of values, attitudes and ethics, core skills, the emotional dimension of work and performance, metacompetence or 'tacit knowledge'. That said the NTB, which is the major player in this area, although noting the influence of values and attitudes on the achievement and exercise of competency, goes on to suggest that it may not be appropriate or possible to reflect them in industry standards. The Board has encouraged the use of key competencies in standards but has stopped short of mandating their inclusion: 'The Board will keep the question of the inclusion of key competencies in standards under review in light of Government decisions' (NTB, 1992, p. 44).

This debate is only now emerging in England — with the competency model and many of the standards firmly in place at 'lower' levels — as part of the discussion of GNVQs (see Jessup, Harrop and Oates and Harkin in this volume), higher level competencies and professional work (see Mitchell and Eraut in this volume), and as the significance of the outcomes approach is explored in the context of higher education (see Otter in this volume). Mitchell is surely right when she argues that any issues and developments arising at higher levels which lead to changes in methodology and philosophy must apply across the whole framework. As she notes, values and ethics are not the sole domain of professionals. Equally one can argue that the truly competent worker through reflection on experience will develop a 'theory in action', to use Schon's expressive phrase; they will have substantial propositional knowledge as well as process knowledge (see Eraut and McNair in this volume).

Core Skills

In England the issue of core skills was placed on the agenda by the CBI (1989) and the TUC (1989) and was supported by Kenneth Baker, then Secretary of State for Education. The development work has been largely carried out by the NCVQ (Jessup, 1990) (see Oates and Harkin in this volume). Six core skills have been identified and are expressed at five levels loosely related to the NVQ framework and aligned with the National Curriculum, 'A' levels and NVQs as far as this is possible (Jessup, 1990). They are a mandatory component in GNVQs where they are integrated into subject areas (rather than bolted-on additions) but are explicitly assessed. As Oates and Harkin have shown they have the potential to bridge the academic-vocational divide which so debilitates the English education and training system and to facilitate new learning strategies with an emphasis on learner autonomy. Core skills are not, however, a mandatory requirement for NVQs although 'Lead Bodies will be *invited* to examine where the (core skills) units might be incorporated into their standards' (Oates, 1992, p. 8, my emphasis).

In Australia the importance of core skills emerged from a comprehensive review of the purpose of post-compulsory education and training. They have been associated with the ability to respond to changes in the nature and organization of work but are also viewed as necessary personal and social skills for *all* citizens:

> Key competencies are competencies essential for the effective participation in the emerging patterns of work and work organization. They focus on the capacity to apply knowledge and skills in an integrated way in work situations. Key competencies are generic in that they apply to work generally rather than being specific to work in particular occupations or industries. This characteristic means that key competencies are not only essential for effective participation in work but are also essential for effective participation in further education and in adult life more generally. (Mayer, 1992, p. 1)

Figure 19.1:   Key competencies, core skills and workplace know-how[1]

Key Competencies	UK Core Skills	US Workplace Know-How
• Collecting, analysing and organizing information	• Communication	• Information • Foundation skills: Basic skills
• Communicating ideas	• Communication • Personal skills: Improving own learning and performance	• Information • Foundation skills: Basic skills
• Planning and organizing activities	• Personal skills: Improving own learning and performance	• Resources • Foundation skills: Personal qualities
• Working with others and in teams	• Personal skills: working with others	• Interpersonal skills
• Using mathematical ideas and techniques	• Numeracy: Application of number	• Foundation skills: Basic skills
• Solving problems	• Problem solving	• Foundation skills: Thinking skills
• Using technology	• IT	• Technology • Systems

Source: Mayer (1992).

N.B. Where 'core skills' and 'know-how' appear in more than one key competency they have been repeated.

The competencies identified by the Finn Committee were in the areas of: language and communication; mathematics; scientific and technological understanding; cultural understanding; problem solving; and personal and interpersonal characteristics. These were redefined by Mayer as:

- Collecting, analysing and organizing information
- Communicating ideas and information
- Planning and organizing activities
- Working with others in teams
- Using mathematical ideas
- Solving problems
- Using technology

There are strong similarities with the core skills identified by NCVQ and by the Secretary of the Department of Labour's Commission on Achieving Necessary Skills (SCANS) in the United States, as may be seen from figure 19.1.

The importance of key competencies has been acknowledged by the NTB:

> Inter-personal, analytical and communication skills are significant aspects of [the] emerging requirement for broader skills so that general competencies are assuming greater importance in this context. These trends have implications for the (National Training) Board's approach to standards development.
>
> *. . . Standards must also reflect not only industry's current but future needs.* Standards *must* (my emphasis) therefore include problem solving, team work, communications and the underlying skill and knowledge to enable competence to be demonstrated in new and unexpected situations. (NTB, 1992, p. 8)

But, as we have seen, it has stopped short of mandating their inclusion in standards, choosing instead to wait for a lead from the Government. A comparable situation exists in England where the Employment Department has consistently avoided pressing lead bodies to include core skills in NVQs.

In England core skills have been defined at five levels loosely related to the NVQ framework; the Mayer Committee, however, rejected the idea of using levels from the ASF as reference points for performance in key competencies. The Committee concluded that industry competency standards and key competencies differed in three important respects: industry standards focus on the requirements of the job rather than what the individual can do in a range of employment-related settings including voluntary and other unpaid work; they tend to be specific to the needs of the industry rather than generic; and they are primarily concerned with the here and now of work and the skills needed rather than oriented to the future as is the intention with the key competencies.

The Committee judged that a range of levels was needed to reflect different levels of achievement. Moreover, the differences between levels should be sufficient to enable clear descriptions of performance to be made at each level and thus facilitate implementation across a wide range of educational and training settings. In developing this position the Committee was strongly influenced by field studies across a variety of work settings which included unpaid, community and voluntary work where it was clear that responsibility, initiative, planning and organization as well as knowledge were important features. At higher levels the ability to evaluate and reflect on actions to improve practice and to transfer skills to new areas was regarded as important and the greater knowledge base enabled broader principles to be applied to activities.

These factors, together with the ASF and an assessment of the achievements and contexts of young people in school and higher education, led the Committee to a three-level framework:

Performance Level 1 describes the competencies needed to undertake activities efficiently and with sufficient self-management to meet the explicit requirements of the activity and make judgments about the quality of outcome against established criteria.

Performance Level 2 describes the competencies needed to manage activities requiring the selection, application and integration of a number of elements, and to select from established criteria to judge quality of process and outcome.

Performance Level 3 describes the competencies needed to evaluate and reshape processes, to establish and use principles in order to determine appropriate ways of approaching activities, and to establish criteria for judging quality of process and outcome. (Mayer, 1992)

Applying this prescription to the key competency 'Working with others and in teams' at Performance Level 1 the emphasis is on interactions that follow established patterns of procedure and with established roles; Performance Level 2 is concerned with collaborative planning and achieving agreed outcomes. This may well include negotiation around the roles and tasks undertaken by members of the work group. Performance Level 3 focuses on defining and redefining interactions, processes and objectives, as is illustrated in the example below.

Performance Level 3

At this level a person:

- defines purposes and objectives to be achieved by working with others;
- establishes roles, procedures and timeframes taking into account different perspectives; and
- negotiates them with others to define objectives and where necessary to monitor and redefine them.

Applications at this level could include:

- directing a play;
- working in a sales team;
- leading a team on a building site;
- representing a point of view in a debate.

Key Competencies and the Curriculum

There is a strong commitment to the integration of key competencies into the learning programmes across schools and colleges. All subjects will be involved in implementing and assessing key competencies and no subject is expected to carry the whole responsibility for a key competency. In many instances aspects of the key competencies are already present in the curriculum but it will be necessary for schools and colleges to make these explicit and to expand their range. More particularly the curriculum will need to provide a stronger applied focus to learning through which young people will be able to develop and demonstrate the 'employment-related' key competencies. This has implications for the way in which the curriculum is designed, the learning opportunities which are created — for example, more use might be made of work placements, community and voluntary work etc. — and for the organizational arrangements provided which may include, for example, induction programmes explaining the nature of assessment, the criteria which are used, student responsibilities, opportunities for personal reviews and action planning and so on.

For many teachers and tutors these are substantial changes. Cross-school teams will be needed to plan how the key competencies will be integrated in the curriculum, to ensure that all elements are adequately covered without unhelpful duplication, and that the same criteria and standards are used for assessment in different subjects and by different tutors. Tutors who are accustomed to teaching and assessing subject knowledge will need to create learning and assessment opportunities according to new criteria and will need to work with others in designing assessment. As Oates and Harkin point out, in an outcomes-based system it is essential for tutors to cooperate in the design of assessment if key competencies are to be effectively integrated. But for many teachers whose cultural and professional identities were forged and focus around subjects and disciplines or specific jobs — 'I am a biologist, a historian, a plumber, etc.' — this is a very major change. Their claims to be 'an authority' are based on subject/job expertise not on key competencies and pedagogy.

The key competencies give significantly greater responsibilities to learners for negotiating goals, planning and organizing activities, working as part of a team, solving problems and so on. New forms of assessment will be required to enable learners to demonstrate competency in problem solving and other competencies. Portfolios providing evidence referenced against specified key competencies, examples of work products, simulated practice, possibly tape and video recordings will all need to be considered. Some tutors will have difficulty in shifting from a teacher-centred to a learner-centred style with negotiated assessments. They will require time and support to adjust to the new language and the broader range of learning and assessment strategies. The danger is that some will not be committed to the inclusion of key competencies and may try to marginalize them by separating them from the 'serious' subject work — and signalling lower status to the students.

Pathways and Progression

During the next few years the proportion of young people involved in post-compulsory education and training is expected to rise substantially such that by the end of the decade almost all young people will have received twelve years of education and training. The range of students will be wider than in the past, particularly in schools which are expected to take the bulk of the expansion. In order to serve the 'new' school population effectively, schools will need to provide a richer variety of flexible programmes including, for example, part-time school and part-time work, joint ventures between schools and colleges, more vocational courses and more opportunities for work experience. There will be an associated demand for credit transfer arrangements between schools and TAFE and between learning programmes provided by educational organizations and industry. As schools, TAFE and industry increasingly adopt outcomes or competency specifications for at least some of their activities this should become easier. As Geoff Stanton points out, the outcomes approach enables progression to be planned on a more rational basis.

In the previous discussion so far two broad types of competency have been identified:

- Key competencies required by all young people (and adults)
- Specific competencies required for effective performance in an occupational role

So far as the specific competencies are concerned there is a clear articulation between vocational courses and the industry standards. Vocational courses provide opportunities to develop the competencies required by industry. The outcomes of such programmes can be related to those offered elsewhere — by schools, TAFE, private training providers and to industry's requirements. Moreover, learners should be able to transfer credit for units achieved to new settings.

The three-level framework for key competencies has a similar potential. It enables credit to be transferred between schools and colleges. The missing link is industry. It would, however, be possible for an industry through its CSB to define its entry-level requirements in terms of occupational competencies *and* key competencies, i.e. to establish competency profiles for entry. Competency profiles for entry-level training would probably be different in different industries, for example a higher level of performance on using mathematical techniques would be required for entry to accountancy than to journalism, but in all cases learners would know exactly what standards had to be achieved. The linkages, pathways and progression routes between education, training and the world of work would be clearer and this would benefit learners and would help tutors and trainers who are responsible for the design of vocational courses. A considerable investment in staff development would be required to assist tutors and trainers in providing support for learners engaged in developing key competencies and to provide valid assessment — as would be the case if the policy were introduced for NVQs.

Key competencies are relevant to all learners in post-compulsory education and training and will be integrated into subjects across the curriculum. Beyond that learners will have opportunities to follow a primarily academic pathway, a primarily vocational one or a mixture. Moreover, if they change courses (or pathways) they should be able to carry some credit with them for proven achievements.

The issue of credit for occupational competencies is not quite as clear as implied above because it has not yet been resolved what outcomes can be legitimately be the responsibility of formal education and training and which must be left to the workplace. The central issue is whether or not industry competencies can be assessed in schools and colleges. In England this has been resolved in different ways depending on the specifications of lead bodies and the capacity of schools and colleges to undertake assessment under realistic working conditions. For example, in hairdressing and catering assessment can be conducted in college salons, kitchens and restaurants that operate realistic working environments, but in some other occupational areas competence may be assessed only in the workplace.

It is probable that a similar resolution will emerge in Australia. In some areas schools and colleges will be able to offer learning opportunities and assessment for competency-based occupational qualifications; in other instances the role of schools and colleges will be restricted to providing the underpinning knowledge and facilitating the development of relevant skills through college-based practice and work placement. Unless they had a collaborative arrangement with industry to assess learners/candidates while on placements' assessment would be deferred until the candidate was in employment. Once in work, however, the candidate should quickly achieve the relevant occupational qualification.

Professional and Higher Level Competencies

The definition of higher level (professional) competencies in England is giving rise to an interesting and fruitful debate (see Mitchell, Eraut and Otter in this volume). The same may be said of the discussions in Australia where Gonzi, Hager and colleagues at the University of Technology, Sydney have argued strongly for an integrated approach to conceptualizing professional competence and have reviewed a wide range of methods for identifying the core components of professional work. In the integrated approach key tasks or elements that are central to professional practice are identified and are then analyzed in terms of the attributes (knowledge, abilities, skills and attitudes) that are required for competent performance of those key tasks (Gonzi *et al*, 1990).

The development of the integrated approach has been guided by the need to strike a manageable balance between a comprehensive and exhaustive analysis of discrete observable tasks involved in professional work and an analysis of competent behaviour based on attributes but isolated from practice. The latter approach used on its own suffers from obvious disadvantages and all too easily produces an inflated curriculum, parts of which are unrelated to occupational practice. The particular dangers of the first approach are that the extensive checklist of specific competencies that it generates distracts attention from the (acceptable) variations in ways of completing tasks, from the higher order competencies involved in professional work, from longer term considerations of client care which affect professional behaviour and judgments and from the holistic nature of professional competence. Discussing this last point Gonzi, Hager and Athanasou (1992) claim the 'Experience has shown that when both of these (approaches) are integrated to produce competency standards, the results do capture the holistic richness of professional practice in a way which neither of the two approaches could' (p. 16).

The integrated approach is compatible with the NTB's commitment to a 'broad concept of competency' and has been widely used by professional bodies sponsored by NOOSR. Most professions have chosen to use a combination of techniques to cover the analysis of task/role and attributes. These have included interviews, competencies interviews, critical incidents technique, general surveys, DELPHI, nominal group technique, DACUM, functional analysis, and observation.

Implications for the Curriculum

The analysis of professional tasks and roles has a number of effects on curriculum content. Its primary effect is to establish criteria for inclusion (and exclusion) in the curriculum. The knowledge, skills, abilities and attitudes identified through this process have a *prima facie* case for inclusion in the professional curriculum. Equally if there is no evidence from this analysis that attributes conventionally included in professional programmes are used in professional practice there is a *prima facie* case for their exclusion. Equally important for curriculum design is the identification of the practical contexts and situations in which knowledge is applied. These are, if you wish, the range indicators. For our purposes they enable the curriculum designer and tutor to bring theory and practice together in planning learning activities (hands-on and simulated practice, case study analysis and so on) in which knowledge, skills, attitudes and abilities are applied in realistic professional situations. The same principle applies to assessment activities where a variety of methods are needed to ensure validity.

The style of analysis used in the integrated approach also reveals the ways in which competent professionals use a range of interpersonal, problem solving and other core skills in combination with attitudes, knowledge and previous experience to develop hypotheses and to make judgments. These are process skills (Eraut in this volume) and provide further information for the curriculum designer. At one level they emphasize the core skills at another they draw attention to the importance of using learning strategies which stimulate their development (Oates and Harkin in this volume) and facilitate the transferability of these skills to new situations.

Summary

Developments in Australia have a number of features in common with England. Both countries have moved towards an outcomes approach. In Australia this is apparent across the whole of the post-compulsory sector of vocational education and training. It is also clearly evident in the development of competency-based standards in the professions and will, as a consequence, selectively affect those areas of higher education concerned with professional development.

The two major reviews of post-compulsory education and training argued strongly that there is a convergence between the concepts of work and education and between working and learning. At the heart of this convergence is the concept of key competencies which are seen to be as essential for effective participation in work as they are for effective participation in education and in adult life. The further proposals are logical and consistent: the key competencies should be integrated into all school and college learning programmes *and* into occupational standards. In the latter case the NTB has encouraged CSBs to incorporate key competencies into occupational standards but has stopped short of requiring it. A similar situation prevails in England.

Institutionally the notion of convergence between 'education' and 'training', 'general' and 'vocational' education is manifested in the development of various initiatives in which schools and colleges, schools and industry, and colleges and industry are working collaboratively and in joint ventures. It is also apparent in the emphasis on more flexible pathways and progression routes between schools, colleges and industry. In the longer term more young people will stay on longer at school. They will require learning programmes combining general and vocational education and, perhaps, periods in work. Individual combinations will vary. Some learners will have a strong 'academic' focus, others will have a vocational focus. Many more will be uncertain and will seek broadly-based learning programmes. The emergence of a system facilitating such flexibility and individual choice will be made easier by the clear specification of outcomes of learning programmes and the development of credit transfer arrangements.

All of this will call for imaginative approaches to curriculum design and delivery and new strategies for learning which integrate key competencies in subjects and vocational programmes and provide greater autonomy for learners. It will require a substantial staff development programme to help teachers, tutors and trainers develop the new skills which they will need.

Notes

1 Elaborating on this point one well placed civil servant commented 'Labour took over in 1983. The balance of payments was going through the floor. The public never realized how close we were to becoming a banana republic'. Interview data, December 1992.
2 Ashenden (1992); Raggatt (1993); TCRC (1990); provide fuller accounts of the coalition of interests supporting the 'skills agenda' in Australia including comment on the particularly distinctive relationship between the skills agenda and industrial restructuring — a process through which skill levels are related to pay rates — and makes training a key agenda item in future negotiations between unions and employers.
3 Based on an oral report from a participant in this group.
4 Carmichael was a research officer in the Metal Workers Union and has since become a major figure in the reform of the Australian vocational education and training system. Often called 'the boss' by John Dawkins, the Federal Treasurer, Carmichael is regarded by many as the architect and power behind the reforms — though closer scrutiny suggests that the earlier report laid much of the groundwork.
5 Interview data, Member of the Committee.
6 There are very strong echoes with the reform agenda in England. There, too, there was an emphasis on skills training based on standards of competence relevant to employment (rather than time serving), on recognition for the workplace as a site for learning and to increasing the opportunities for adults to acquire, increase or update their skills and knowledge throughout their working life.
7 I am indebted to Clive Chappell, University of Technology, Sydney for this point and for comments on an early draft of this chapter.
8 The nursing profession was 'no longer hospital based and this led to a review of what were the core features in the work of a nurse. The search to define the profession ended up in competencies — it was not a discipline and didn't have an intrinsic structure'. With accountancy there was 'conflict was between what education wanted to teach or thought they should teach and what employers wanted — accountants were prepared (academically) but weren't ready for the job'; in the case of architects they wanted to move to a national registration scheme, and this led them to say 'let's define the job; and dieticians were a threatened profession and set out to define the core purpose of their occupation'. Interview data, 1992.

References

ASHENDEN, D. (1992) 'The Australian skills agenda: Productivity versus credentialism', *Competence and Assessment*, 19.
AUSTRALIAN COUNCIL OF TRADE UNIONS/TRADE DEVELOPMENT COUNCIL (1987) *Australia Reconstructed: A Report by Mission Members* (The Carmichael Report), Canberra, AGPS.

AUSTRALIAN EDUCATION COUNCIL AND MINISTERS FOR VOCATIONAL EDUCATION, EM-
PLOYMENT AND TRAINING (The Mayer Report) (1992) *Key Competencies* (Draft).

AUSTRALIAN EDUCATION COUNCIL REVIEW COMMITTEE (The Finn Report) (1991) *Young
People's Participation in Post-Compulsory Education and Training,* Canberra, AGPS.

COSTAC (1990) *A Strategic Framework for the Implementation of a Competency-based
Training System,* Canberra, AGPS.

CONFEDERATION OF BRITISH INDUSTRY (CBI) (1989) *Towards a Skills Revolution- A Youth
Charter,* Interim Report of the Vocational Education and Training Task Force,
London, CBI.

DEPARTMENT OF EMPLOYMENT, EDUCATION AND TRAINING (DEET) (1991) *Australia's
Workforce in the Year 2001,* Canberra, AGPS.

GONZI, A., HAGER, P. and ATHANASOU, J. (1992) *A Guide to the Development of
Competency-based Assessment for the Professions,* (Draft Paper), NOOSR, Canberra,
AGPS.

GONZI, A., HAGER, P. and OLIVER, L. (1990) *Establishing Competency-based Standards in
the Professions,* NOOSR Research Paper No 1, Canberra, AGPS.

JESSUP, G. (1990) *Common Learning Outcomes: Core Skills in A/As Levels and NVQs*
with Contributions from John Burke, Alison Wolf and Tim Oates Report No 6,
London NCVQ.

KRBAVIC, L. and STRETTON, A. (1988) 'Skill formation and structural adjustment: the
responsiveness of industry training', *DEET Discussion Paper No 3,* Canberra, AGPS.

MAYER, E. (1992) Key Competencies (draft document).

NATIONAL TRAINING BOARD (NTB) (1992) *National Competency Standards: Policy and
Guidelines* (2nd edn), Canberra, AGPS.

OATES, T. (1993) *Developing and Piloting the NCVQ Core Skills Units,* Research and
Development Report No 16, London, NCVQ.

RAGGATT, P. (1993) 'Contrasting routes to competence', *Occasional Paper,* CYAS, Open
University.

RUBY, A. (1992) 'If Freeman Butts calls tell him we might be changing course: A
perspective on the notion of competency and Australia's schools', a paper presented at the conference on Higher Education and the Competency Movement,
Australian National University.

TRADES UNION CONGRESS (TUC) (1990) *Skills 2000,* London, TUC.

TRAINING COSTS REVIEW COMMITTEE (TCRC) (1990) *Training Costs of Award Restructuring: Report of the Training Costs Review Committee,* Vol 1 The Report, Canberra,
AGPS.

Notes on Contributors

Dr John Burke is a Senior Lecturer in Education at the University of Sussex. He has directed a number of research projects for the NCVQ since its inception in 1986 and has held an NCVQ Research Fellowship over the past five years. He was a member of the small conceptual design team convened by Gilbert Jessup to devise the prototype GNVQ framework, and had a major rôle in devising and setting up the national VET research programme (with a focus on NVQs and GNVQs) at the University of Sussex. He currently supervises a number of VET research students, and is involved in various research projects. He has published widely, and is currently editing *NVQs and GNVQs: The Cutting Edge*, a series of research papers from the VET programme (*forthcoming*, Falmer Press). With Gilbert Jessup, he co-authored *Core Skills and the Needs of Employment* which is about to be published by the Institute of Continuing and Professional Education, University of Sussex.

Institute of Continuing and Professional Education, EDB, University of Sussex, Falmer, Brighton, BN1 9RG.

Paul Ellis has been involved in the education, training and qualifications system for over twenty years. He is a qualified psychologist and a member of Council of the Association for Educational and Training Technology.

Having worked in higher education, further education and national bodies he has researched and implemented learning and assessment arrangements from a range of perspectives and has also worked on large scale manpower planning exercises.

In 1985 he was appointed national manager of one of the first projects developing standards and assessment arrangements in the style that was to lead the way for NVQs. He is currently Head of NVQ Research and Development at the National Council for Vocational Qualifications.

Michael Eraut is Professor of Education in the Institute of Continuing and Professional Education at the University of Sussex. He directs the Sussex Research Programme in Vocational Education and Training which is studying the introduction of NVQs and GNVQs, and is a member of the newly-launched Centre for Research and Development for the Professions. His recently completed research projects include the Assessment of Competence in the Professions, Ethics in Occupational Standards and S/NVQs, Groupwork with Computers and Management of Flexible Learning in Schools. He has published widely in the fields of Curriculum, Evaluation and Professional Development; and his recent book *Developing Professional Knowledge and Competence* has just been published by Falmer Press.

Institute of Continuing and Professional Education, EDB, University of Sussex, Falmer, Brighton, BN1 9RG.

Dr Joe Harkin is a Senior Lecturer in Post-compulsory Education at Oxford Brookes University. His main interests are in curriculum and staff development, and especially in the enhancement of communication skills for teachers and learners. He carried out pilot projects on the core skills on behalf of the NCVQ. He is developing materials on communication skills (to be published by Collins Educational, 1994) and is currently researching the effects of outcome-based learning on the communication styles of teachers and learners.

The School of Education, Oxford Brookes University, Wheatley, Oxford, OX9 1HX; telephone 0865 485883.

Jane Harrop is Head of GNVQ Implementation at NCVQ where she is working closely with the piloting and further implementation of GNVQs in colleges and schools. She has a professional background in music both as a performer and teacher, and has worked as a music coach in the UK and USA. In her teaching career she has taught all age groups working for several local education authorities and as a senior staff member and administrator at Benenden School, Kent.

She subsequently worked in educational administration and research for over six years in the US focusing on secondary and higher education. She gained her doctorate at the University of Virginia researching college student development in international education and joined the staff of the university president's office dealing with resources and evaluation of university programmes. She joined NCVQ in 1991 after a brief period at the Department of Education and Science.

Born in Germany to an English father and German mother, **Tom Jackson** was educated in the USA at Groton School, Princeton University and Columbia University. After a short service commission in the US Navy he continued his education at Fitzwilliam College, Cambridge with an MA and PGCE in English. As successively, teacher of English, head of department and head of a large sixth form, he taught in three large 11–18 mixed comprehensive schools; this was followed by three years as Vice Principal of Brighton, Hove & Sussex Sixth Form College. In 1988 he became Principal of Portsmouth College, an open access sixth-form college which has developed an unusually wide curriculum to cater for students drawn from the full range of ability and vocational as well as academic interests. Tom's leisure interest is offshore yacht racing and he writes regularly for the yachting press.

Gilbert Jessup has played a central role in the development and implementation of outcome-based qualifications for over ten years, starting in the Manpower Services Commission in 1983. While in the MSC, he operationalized the concept of 'new kinds of standards' as proposed in the New Training Initiative (1981). This led to his setting up the first projects in specifying occupational standards, initially in the context of the Youth Training Scheme. He also played a central role in designing the curriculum framework for YTS and introducing the first Record of Achievement.

When the NCVQ was set up in 1986, Gilbert Jessup became its first Director of Research and Development, a post he still holds combined with being Deputy

Chief Executive. At NCVQ he developed the NVQ criteria and much of the methodology which underlies the new qualification framework. Since 1991 he has directed the GNVQ development and implementation programme, and has pioneered the concept of a national framework of qualifications.

Earlier in his career, he set up and became the first Director of the Government's Work Research Unit, which had the remit to improve the quality of working life in the UK, and was Chief Psychologist in the Department of Employment.

He is the author of numerous reports and articles and, in particular, the book *Outcomes: NVQs and the Emerging Model of Education and Training*. He was made an honorary Professor of Occupational Psychology at the University of Nottingham in 1976.

Following employment as a research assistant **Margaret Levy** taught maths and science in ILEA FE (1958/78). In 1976 she initiated the first UK 'Return to Study in Science' and the first access course in science. In 1979 she joined FEU as their first Regional Development Officer. In 1981 she was head-hunted by the MSC, was in charge of YTS design and content, and initiated and directed the Core Skills Project funded from 1982–85 by the European Social Fund to develop a new model for VET. During 1981/82 she introduced the phrase work-based learning to the training and development community as an alternative to the European phrase *alternance*. From 1986–90 she directed the TA-funded Work Based Learning Project based with the Staff College and now continues with the development of work-based learning on a consultancy basis and as an associate tutor for the Staff College.

David Mathews has been associated with the field of occupational standards development from its outset. He is the author of guidance on standards development methodology and on the management of development projects. With colleagues in David Mathews Associates he has been responsible for standards development in sectors as diverse as environmental conservation and school management.

Recently he has been involved in the development of occupational standards for senior management (published by the Management Charter Initiative in April 1994) and, separately, for company boards of directors (published by the Institute of Directors in February 1994). His work now includes the implementation of these and other occupational standards, through learning programmes, assessment, appraisal and other processes of individual and organizational development.

Stephen McNair has worked in all parts of the education system, but principally in adult continuing education, notably as Head of the Unit for the Development of Adult Continuing Education. He is now Associate Director (HE) for the National Institute of Adult Continuing Education and an HE Adviser to the Employment Department. In this latter capacity he is now responsible for the coordination of a network of development projects on Guidance and Learner Empowerment in Higher Education, he has been closely involved in the development of occupational standards in guidance and the foundation of the National Advisory Council for Careers Education and Guidance.

Stephen McNair can be contacted at NIACE, 21 De Montfort Street, Leicester, LE1 7GE.

Lindsay Mitchell is a Director of Prime Research and Development Ltd, an independent organization specializing in research and development in vocational education and training. Lindsay has worked on a number of projects mainly with a methodological and technical focus in a wide range of sectors, such as management, accountancy, and health and social care. She has also directed a number of action research projects and authored articles and books, such as: *Guidance on Knowledge and Understanding in NVQs/SVQs* (with David Bartram); *Enhancing the Candidate's Role in Assessment* (with Jackie Sturton); *Assessing Management Competence for the NHS Training Directorate*; a Higher Level Stimulus Paper for the Employment Department. Lindsay's interest remains one of improving the practice of vocational and professional education and training within the UK.

Lindsay can be contacted at:

Prime Research and Development Ltd, 15 East Parade, Harrogate HG1 5LF. Tel-0423 566540.

Colin Nash has worked in education for more than thirty years and for the greater part of that time has been a classroom teacher in London comprehensive schools committed to active learning methods. He has wide experience of school management as practitioner and trainer and as a school governor.

He has been associated with educational research and development at the University of Sussex since 1980. He carried out a policy evaluation of INSET for a large LEA and tutored various courses, particularly in pre-vocational education for schools and further education. In a freelance capacity he has organized courses in professional self-development.

From 1983–93, he was a full-time Research Fellow at Sussex, working on several TVEI funded national projects on the management of Flexible Learning. The handbook *Flexible Learning in Schools* (1991), of which he was principal author, was disseminated to all schools and colleges in the UK. He has conducted workshops, lectured widely and contributed to several publications on flexible learning.

More recently, he has been involved in evaluating the use of CD-Rom in schools and was co-author with Stephen Steadman of a report published by NCET.

Institute of Continuing and Professional Education, EDB, University of Sussex, Falmer, Brighton, BN1 9RG.

Tim Oates is Head of GNVQ Research and Development at the NCVQ. Tim's key areas of interest include evaluation methodology, core/generic skills and assessment. From 1980–82, he undertook curriculum evaluation work for a number of Government agencies, and in 1983 he became a member of the independent evaluation team for the ESF/MSC-funded Work Based Learning Project. In 1987, at the end of this project, he joined the Work Based Learning Project Team based at the Staff College, Coombe Lodge. In 1990, he was invited by the NCVQ to become NCVQ Research Fellow based at the University of London Institute of Education. He was a member of the inter-agency four-person Core Skills Task Group (1990–91), and his recent work has focused on the development of the NCVQ Core Skill units and research intelligence input into the GNVQ policy and development strategy. In October 1993, Tim assumed his present post at the NCVQ.

National Council for Vocational Qualifications, 222 Euston Road, London, NW1 2BZ; telephone: 071 728 1885.

Sue Otter is an Adviser on Further and Higher Education to the Department of Employment, with particular interest in the fields of work-based learning, learning outcomes and the development of core skills within the curriculum. She works with seven Midlands universities on the Enterprise Initiative programme. Sue is also working with the CVCP on an investigation of the development of vocational qualifications in HE, having done extensive work with the universities and colleges on the introduction on G/NVQs.

Sue moved from an academic background in microbiology to work with UDACE on learning outcomes and then to Nottingham Polytechnic (now Nottingham Trent University) where she managed the CATs scheme.

Peter Raggatt is Director of the Centre for Youth and Adult Education at the Open University. He combines academic interests in comparative educative and vocational education and training and has published widely in these fields. He has undertaken a number of studies on quality assurance and the management of assessment for NVQs and contributed to the development of the Awarding Bodies Common Accord. He is currently engaged in several funded studies for the Employment Department, the FEU and NCVQ. These include researching the profile of NVQs candidates and the NVQ curriculum in colleges of further education, and examining the processes and principles used by assessors and verifiers when making decisions about sufficiency of evidence. In a longer term study he is exploring the politics of the outcomes approach. When he can, he goes scuba diving in warm waters. He can be contacted at the School of Education, The Open University, Walton Hall, MK7 6AA (E mail P.RAGGATT @OPEN.AC.UK).

Professor David Robertson is Executive Director for Policy Development at Liverpool John Moores University. Previously as Director of Academic Programmes, he was responsible for the development and management of the Integrated Credit Scheme, a large credit-based modular scheme at the University. He was also the founder and first Director of the Merseyside Open College Federation (a regional Access consortium) which, together with the Integrated Credit Scheme, enables learners to progress through an extensive regional credit framework.

He is author of the Report of the National CATS Development Project, supported by the DFE and the Employment Department, and published by the Higher Education Quality Council.

A member of the Further Education Unit group which produced *A Basis for Credit?*, and joint author of the CNAA Report *Practising CATS* (1991) and the 'think-tank' report (IPPR, 1992), he has contributed to numerous journals, conferences and public lectures, and has published very extensively in this field. His research interests embrace public policy, the management of change, education and socioeconomic development, and wider access.

Executive Director, Liverpool John Moores University, Rodney House, 70 Mount Pleasant, Liverpool, L3 5UX.

Stephen Steadman took his degree in physics into the Meteorology Office and then teaching before taking up a succession of R&D posts. From the University of Manchester he went to the Schools Council where his work included a comparability study of the European Baccalaureate and GCE/'A' levels, and new forms of examining sixth form mathematics. A highlight of this period was leading a course on testing and evaluation with Desmond Nuttall in Singapore for the British Council. At the University of Sussex he co-directed the Schools Council's Impact & Take-up Project. Then at the University of London Institute of Education he worked on the Evaluation of Testing in Schools and Work Based Learning Projects. A Senior Research Fellow, ICAPE, University of Sussex, since 1988 he convenes the Vocational Education & Training research programme.

Institute of Continuing and Professional Education, EDB, University of Sussex, Falmer, Brighton, BN1 9RG.

Dr Michael Young has been Head of Centre since it was established in 1985. Michael Young was one of the authors of the influential report *A British Baccalauéate*, published in 1990 by the Institute for Public policy Research, and in 1991 was Specialist Advisor on 16–19 Education to the House of Commons Select Committee on Education.

He is currently directing three projects, the *Hamlyn Post 16 Unified Curriculum Project*, (with Professor John Woolhouse, University of Warwick) *Learning for the Future* a curriculum project in association with the Banking Information Service and the Royal Society of Arts and a National Development Project funded by the Employment Department on *the Accreditation of Work-based learning of Teachers and Trainers*. His main research interest is in the social, economic and educational basis of curriculum models for overcoming academic/vocational divisions.

Index